READINGS IN CRIMINAL JUSTICE

compiled and edited
by
Jack Donald Foster
Youngstown State University

McCutchan Publishing Corporation
2526 Grove Street
Berkeley, California 94704

Library of Congress Catalog Card No. 77-89637
Standard Book No. 8211-0528-0

TABLE OF CONTENTS

IV. THE TRIAL AND SENTENCING PROCESS

PREFACE

It is important that every citizen have an understanding of how our system of criminal justice actually works. While few of us expect to be accused of a crime, most of us will sometime become victims of crimes and will become involved with the system as complainants. Many of the procedures observed will seem like unnecessary delays and "loop holes" that benefit only the accused. Many people are aware of terms like arrest, search and seizure, preliminary hearing, arraignment, trial, jury, bail and the like, but few people know of the history, legal philosophy or importance of these aspects of criminal procedure. It is hoped that the insightful, scholarly articles that make up this book will help the reader gain a greater appreciation for our system of criminal justice.

This book is neither a polemic against nor a defense of the current system of criminal justice. Indeed, the President's Commission on Law Enforcement and Administration of Justice has adequately documented the immediate need for reform. The intention here is to familiarize the reader with some of the issues involved so that he may evaluate proposed alternatives more intelligently.

This is not a "law book" in the usual sense. Much technical detail is omitted in order to concentrate on certain controversial aspects of criminal justice administration since these are the elements of the system debated at the present time. It is hoped that all students will find it understandable and informative.

Literally hundreds of books and articles have been written about the administration of criminal justice. As any editor realizes, much really fine material has to be omitted or else the book becomes a library. These particular articles were selected for their scholarship, readability by laymen, and objectivity.

I wish to express my appreciation to the authors and publishers who so graciously granted permission to reprint their work. Unfortunately, it was necessary to omit all footnotes in order to keep the book size within reasonable limits. Readers should consult the original sources for these references.

Youngstown, Ohio
June 1969

INTRODUCTION

America's System of Criminal Justice

The system of criminal justice America uses to deal with those crimes it cannot prevent and those criminals it cannot deter is not a monolithic, or even a consistent, system. It was not designed or built in one piece at one time. Its philosophic core is that a person may be punished by the Government if, and only if, it has been proved by an impartial and deliberate process that he has violated a specific law. Around that core layer upon layer of institutions and procedures, some carefully constructed and some improvised, some inspired by principle and some by expediency, have accumulated. Parts of the system—magistrates' courts, trial by jury, bail—are of great antiquity. Other parts—juvenile courts, probation and parole, professional policemen—are relatively new. The entire system represents an adaptation of the English common law to America's peculiar structure of government, which allows each local community to construct institutions that fill its special needs. Every village, town, county, city, and State has its own criminal justice system, and there is a Federal one as well. All of them operate somewhat alike. No two of them operate precisely alike.

Any criminal justice system is an apparatus society uses to enforce the standards of conduct necessary to protect individuals and the community. It operates by apprehending, prosecuting, convicting, and sentencing those members of the community who violate the basic rules of group existence. The action taken against lawbreakers is designed to serve three purposes beyond the immediately punitive one. It removes dangerous people from the community; it deters others from criminal behavior; and it gives society an opportunity to attempt to transform lawbreakers into law-abiding citizens. What most significantly distinguishes the system of one country from that of another is the extent and the form of the protections it offers individuals in the process of determining guilt and imposing punishment. Our system of justice deliberately sacrifices much in efficiency and even in effectiveness in order to preserve local autonomy and to protect the individual. Sometimes it may seem to sacrifice too much. For example, the American system was not designed with Cosa Nostra-type criminal organizations in mind, and it has been notably unsuccessful to date in preventing such organizations from preying on society.

The criminal justice system has three separately organized parts—the police, the courts, and corrections—and each has distinct tasks. However, these parts are by no means independent of each other. What each one does and how it does it has a direct effect on the work of the others. The courts must deal, and can only deal, with those whom the police arrest; the business of corrections is with those delivered to it by the courts. How successfully corrections reforms convicts determines whether they will once again become police business and influences the sentences the judges pass; police activities are subject to court scrutiny and are often determined by court decisions. And so reforming or reorganizing any

From President's Commission on Law Enforcement and Administration of Justice. "America's System of Criminal Justice," *The Challenge of Crime in a Free Society,* 1967, pp. 7–12.

part or procedure of the system changes other parts or procedures. Furthermore, the criminal process, the method by which the system deals with individual cases, is not a hodgepodge of random actions. It is rather a continuum—an orderly progression of events—some of which, like arrest and trial, are highly visible and some of which, though of great importance, occur out of public view. A study of the system must begin by examining it as a whole.

The chart on the following page sets forth in simplified form the process of criminal administration and shows the many decision points along its course. Since felonies, misdemeanors, petty offenses, and juvenile cases generally follow quite different paths, they are shown separately.

The popular, or even the lawbook, theory of everyday criminal process oversimplifies in some respects and overcomplicates in others what usually happens. That theory is that when an infraction of the law occurs, a policeman finds, if he can, the probable offender, arrests him and brings him promptly before a magistrate. If the offense is minor, the magistrate disposes of it forthwith; if it is serious, he holds the defendant for further action and admits him to bail. The case then is turned over to a prosecuting attorney who charges the defendant with a specific statutory crime. This charge is subject to review by a judge at a preliminary hearing of the evidence and in many places if the offense charged is a felony, by a grand jury that can dismiss the charge, or affirm it by delivering it to a judge in the form of an indictment. If the defendant pleads "not guilty" to the charge he comes to trial; the facts of his case are marshaled by prosecuting and defense attorneys and presented, under the supervision of a judge, through witnesses, to a jury. If the jury finds the defendant guilty, he is sentenced by the judge to a term in prison, where a systematic attempt to convert him into a law-abiding citizen is made, or to a term of probation, under which he is permitted to live in the community as long as he behaves himself.

Some cases do proceed much like that, especially those involving offenses that are generally considered "major": serious acts of violence or thefts of large amounts of property. However, not all major cases follow this course, and, in any event, the bulk of the daily business of the criminal justice system consists of offenses that are not major—of breaches of the peace, crimes of vice, petty thefts, assaults arising from domestic or street-corner or barroom disputes. These and most other cases are disposed of in much less formal and much less deliberate ways.

The theory of the juvenile court is that it is a "helping" social agency, designed to prescribe carefully individualized treatment to young people in trouble, and that its procedures are therefore nonadversary. Here again there is, in most places, a considerable difference between theory and practice. Many juvenile proceedings are no more individualized and no more therapeutic than adult ones.

What has evidently happened is that the transformation of America from a relatively relaxed rural society into a tumultuous urban one has presented the criminal justice system in the cities with a volume of cases too large to handle by traditional methods. One result of heavy caseloads is highly visible in city courts, which process many cases with excessive haste and many others with excessive slowness. In the interest both of effectiveness and of fairness to individuals, justice should be swift and certain; too often in city courts today it is, instead, hasty or faltering. Invisibly, the pressure of numbers has effected a series of adventitious changes in the criminal process. Informal shortcuts have been used. The decision making process has often become routinized. Throughout the system the importance of individual judgment and discretion, as distinguished from stated rules and procedures, has increased. In effect, much decision making' is being done on an administrative rather than on a judicial basis. Thus, an examination of how the criminal justice system works and a consideration of the changes needed to make it more effective and fair must focus on the extent to which invisible, administrative procedures depart from visible, traditional ones, and on the desirability of that departure.

The Police

At the very beginning of the process—or, more properly, before the process begins at all—something happens that is scarcely discussed in lawbooks and is seldom recognized by the public: law enforcement policy is made by the policeman. For policemen cannot and do not arrest all the offenders they encounter. It is doubtful that they arrest most of them. A criminal code, in practice, is not a set of specific instructions to policemen, but a more or less rough map of the territory in which policemen work. How an individual policeman moves around that territory depends largely on his personal discretion.

That a policeman's duties compel him to exercise personal discretion many times every day is evident. Crime does not look the same on the street as it does in a legislative chamber. How much noise or profanity makes conduct "disorderly" within the meaning of the law? When must a quarrel be treated as a criminal assault: at the first threat or at the first shove or at the first blow, or after blood is drawn, or when a serious injury is inflicted? How suspicious must conduct be before there is "probable cause," the constitutional basis for an arrest? Every policeman, however complete or sketchy his education, is an interpreter of the law.

Every policeman, too, is an arbiter of social values, for he meets situation after situation in which invoking criminal sanctions is a questionable line of action. It is obvious that a boy throwing rocks at a school's windows is committing the statutory offense of vandalism, but it is often not at all obvious whether a policeman will better serve the interests of the community and of the boy by taking the boy home to his parents or by arresting him. Who are the boy's parents? Can they control him? Is he a frequent offender who has responded badly to leniency? Is vandalism so epidemic in the neighborhood that he should be made a cautionary example? With juveniles especially, the police exercise great discretion.

Finally, the manner in which a policeman works is influenced by practical matters: the legal strength of the available evidence, the willingness of victims to press charges and of witnesses to testify, the temper of the community, the time and information at the policeman's disposal. Much is at stake in how the policeman exercises this discretion. If he judges conduct not suspicious enough to justify intervention, the chance to prevent a robbery, rape, or murder may be lost. If he overestimates the seriousness of a situation or his actions are controlled by panic or prejudice, he may hurt or kill someone unnecessarily. His actions may even touch off a riot.

The Magistrate

In direct contrast to the policeman, the magistrate before whom a suspect is first brought usually exercises less discretion than the law allows him. He is entitled to inquire into the facts of the case, into whether there are grounds for holding the accused. He seldom does. He seldom can. The more promptly an

A general view of The Criminal Justice System

This chart seeks to present a simple yet comprehensive view of the movement of cases through the criminal justice system. Procedures in individual jurisdictions may vary from the pattern shown here. The differing weights of line indicate the relative volumes of cases disposed of at various points in the system, but this is only suggestive since no nationwide data of this sort exists.

xi

1 May continue until trial.

2 Administrative record of arrest. First step at which temporary release on bail may be available.

3 Before magistrate, commissioner, or justice of peace. Formal notice of charge, advice of rights. Bail set. Summary trials for petty offenses usually conducted here without further processing.

4 Preliminary testing of evidence against defendant. Charge may be reduced. No separate preliminary hearing for misdemeanors in some systems.

5 Charge filed by prosecutor on basis of information submitted by police or citizens. Alternative to grand jury indictment; often used in felonies, almost always in misdemeanors.

6 Reviews whether Government evidence sufficient to justify trial. Some States have no grand jury system; others seldom use it.

7 Appearance for plea; defendant elects trial by judge or jury (if available); counsel for indigent usually appointed here in felonies. Often not at all in other cases.

8 Charge may be reduced at any time prior to trial in return for plea of guilty or for other reasons.

9 Challenge on constitutional grounds to legality of detention. May be sought at any point in process.

10 Police often hold informal hearings, dismiss or adjust many cases without further processing.

11 Probation officer decides desirability of further court action.

12 Welfare agency, social services, counselling, medical care, etc., for cases where adjudicatory handling not needed.

arrested suspect is brought into magistrate's court, the less likelihood there is that much information about the arrest other than the arresting officer's statement will be available to the magistrate. Moreover many magistrates, especially in big cities, have such congested calendars that it is almost impossible for them to subject any case but an extraordinary one to prolonged scrutiny.

In practice the most important things, by far, that a magistrate does are to set the amount of a defendant's bail and in some jurisdictions to appoint counsel. Too seldom does either action get the careful attention it deserves. In many cases the magistrate accepts a waiver of counsel without insuring that the suspect knows the significance of legal representation.

Bail is a device to free an untried defendant and at the same time make sure he appears for trial. That is the sole stated legal purpose in America. The Eighth Amendment to the Constitution declares that it must not be "excessive." Appellate courts have declared that not just the seriousness of the charge against the defendant, but the suspect's personal, family, and employment situation as they bear on the likelihood of his appearance, must be weighed before the amount of his bail is fixed. Yet more magistrates than not set bail according to standard rates, so and so many dollars for such and such an offense.

The persistence of money bail can best be explained not by its stated purpose but by the belief of police, prosecutors, and courts that the best way to keep a defendant from committing more crimes before trial is to set bail so high that he cannot obtain his release.

The Prosecutor

The key administrative officer in the processing of cases is the prosecutor. Theoretically the examination of the evidence against a defendant by a judge at a preliminary hearing, and its reexamination by a grand jury, are important parts of the process. Practically they seldom are because a prosecutor seldom has any difficulty in making a prima facie case against a defendant. In fact most defendants waive their rights to preliminary hearings and much more often than not grand juries indict precisely as prosecutors ask them to. The prosecutor wields almost undisputed sway over the pretrial progress of most cases. He decides whether to press a case or drop it. He determines the specific charge against a defendant. When the charge is reduced, as it is in as many as two-thirds of all cases in some cities, the prosecutor is usually the official who reduces it.

In the informal, noncriminal, nonadversary juvenile justice system there are no "magistrates" or "prosecutors" or "charges," or, in most instances, defense counsel. An arrested youth is brought before an intake officer who is likely to be a social worker or, in smaller communities, before a judge. On the basis of an informal inquiry into the facts and circumstances that led to the arrest, and of an interview with the youth himself, the intake officer or the judge decides whether or not a case should be the subject of formal court proceedings. If he decides it should be, he draws up a petition, describing the case. In very few places is bail a part of the juvenile system; a youth whose case is referred to court is either sent home with orders to reappear on a certain date, or remanded to custody. This decision, too, is made by the screening official. Thus, though these officials work in a quite different environment and according to quite different procedures from magistrates and prosecutors, they in fact exercise the same kind of discretionary control over what happens before the facts of a case are adjudicated.

The Plea and the Sentence

When a prosecutor reduces a charge it is ordinarily because there has been xiii

"plea bargaining" between him and a defense attorney. The issue at stake is how much the prosecutor will reduce his original charge or how lenient a sentence he will recommend, in return for a plea of guilty. There is no way of judging how many bargains reflect the prosecutor's belief that a lesser charge or sentence is justified and how many result from the fact that there may be in the system at any one time ten times as many cases as there are prosecutors or judges or courtrooms to handle them, should every one come to trial. In form, a plea bargain can be anything from a series of careful conferences to a hurried consultation in a courthouse corridor. In content it can be anything from a conscientious exploration of the facts and dispositional alternatives available and appropriate to a defendant, to a perfunctory deal. If the interests of a defendant are to be properly protected while his fate is being thus invisibly determined, he obviously needs just as good legal representation as the kind he needs at a public trial. Whether or not plea bargaining is a fair and effective method of disposing of criminal cases depends heavily on whether or not defendants are provided early with competent and conscientious counsel.

Plea bargaining is not only an invisible procedure but, in some jurisdictions, a theoretically unsanctioned one. In order to satisfy the court record, a defendant, his attorney, and the prosecutor will at the time of sentencing often ritually state to a judge that no bargain has been made. Plea bargaining may be a useful procedure, especially in congested urban jurisdictions, but neither the dignity of the law, nor the quality of justice, nor the protection of society from dangerous criminals is enhanced by its being conducted covertly.

In the juvenile system there is, of course, no plea bargaining in the sense described above. However, the entire juvenile process can involve extra-judicial negotiations about disposition. Furthermore, the entire juvenile process is by design invisible. Though intended to be helpful, the authority exercised often is coercive; juveniles, no less than adults, may need representation by counsel.

An enormously consequential kind of decision is the sentencing decision of a judge. The law recognizes the importance of fitting sentences to individual defendants by giving judges, in most instances, considerable latitude. For example the recently adopted New York Penal Code, which will go into effect in autumn of 1967, empowers a judge to impose upon a man convicted of armed robbery any sentence between a 5-year term of probation and a 25-year term in prison. Even when a judge has presided over a trial during which the facts of a case have been carefully set forth and has been given a probation report that carefully discusses a defendant's character, background, and problems, he cannot find it easy to choose a sentence. In perhaps nine-tenths of all cases there is no trial; the defendants are self-confessedly guilty.

In the lower or misdemeanor courts, the courts that process most criminal cases, probation reports are a rarity. Under such circumstances judges have little to go on and many sentences are bound to be based on conjecture or intuition. When a sentence is part of a plea bargain, which an overworked judge ratifies perfunctorily, it may not even be his conjecture or intuition on which the sentence is based, but a prosecutor's or a defense counsel's. But perhaps the greatest lack judges suffer from when they pass sentence is not time or information, but correctional alternatives. Some lower courts do not have any probation officers, and in almost every court the caseloads of probation officers are so heavy that a sentence of probation means, in fact, releasing an offender into the community with almost no supervision. Few States have a sufficient variety of correctional institutions or treatment programs to inspire judges with the confidence that sentences will lead to rehabilitation.

Corrections

The correctional apparatus to which guilty defendants are delivered is in every respect the most isolated part of the criminal justice system. Much of it is physically isolated; its institutions usually have thick walls and locked doors, and often they are situated in rural areas, remote from the courts where the institutions' inmates were tried and from the communities where they lived. The correctional apparatus is isolated in the sense that its officials do not have everyday working relationships with officials from the systems's other branches, like those that commonly exist between policemen and prosecutors, or prosecutors and judges. It is isolated in the sense that what it does with, to, or for the people under its supervision is seldom governed by any but the most broadly written statutes, and is almost never scrutinized by appellate courts. Finally, it is isolated from the public partly by its invisibility and physical remoteness; partly by the inherent lack of drama in most of its activities, but perhaps most importantly by the fact that the correctional apparatus is often used—or misused—by both the criminal justice system and the public as a rug under which disturbing problems and people can be swept.

The most striking fact about the correctional apparatus today is that, although the rehabilitation of criminals is presumably its major purpose, the custody of criminals is actually its major task. On any given day there are well over a million people being "corrected" in America, two-thirds of them on probation or parole and one-third of them in prisons or jails. However, prisons and jails are where four-fifths of correctional money is spent and where nine-tenths of correctional employees work. Furthermore, fewer than one-fifth of the people who work in State prisons and local jails have jobs that are not essentially either custodial or administrative in character. Many jails have nothing but custodial and administrative personnel. Of course many jails are crowded with defendants who have not been able to furnish bail and who are not considered by the law to be appropriate objects of rehabilitation because it has not yet been determined that they are criminals who need it.

What this emphasis on custody means in practice is that the enormous potential of the correctional apparatus for making creative decisions about its treatment of convicts is largely unfulfilled. This is true not only of offenders in custody but of offenders on probation and parole. Most authorities agree that while probationers and parolees need varying degrees and kinds of supervision, an average of no more than 35 cases per officer is necessary for effective attention; 97 percent of all officers handling adults have larger caseloads than that. In the juvenile correctional system the situation is somewhat better. Juvenile institutions, which typically are training schools, have a higher proportion of treatment personnel and juvenile probation and parole officers generally have lighter caseloads. However, these comparatively rich resources are very far from being sufficiently rich.

Except for sentencing, no decision in the criminal process has more impact on the convicted offender than the parole decision, which determines how much of his maximum sentence a prisoner must serve. This again is an invisible administrative decision that is seldom open to attack or subject to review. It is made by parole board members who are often political appointees. Many are skilled and conscientious, but they generally are able to spend no more than a few minutes on a case. Parole decisions that are made in haste and on the basis of insufficient information, in the absence of parole machinery that can provide good supervision, are necessarily imperfect decisions. And since there is virtually no appeal from them, they can be made arbitrarily or discriminatorily. Just as carefully formulated and clearly stated law enforcement policies would help policemen, charge policies would help prosecutors and sentencing policies would help judges, so parole policies would help parole boards perform their delicate and important duties.

In sum, America's system of criminal justice is overcrowded and overworked, undermanned, underfinanced and very often misunderstood. It needs more information and more knowledge. It needs more technical resources. It needs more coordination among its many parts. It needs more public support. It needs the help of community programs and institutions in dealing with offenders and potential offenders. It needs, above all, the willingness to reexamine old ways of doing things, to reform itself, to experiment, to run risks, to dare. It needs vision.

THE AIMS OF THE CRIMINAL LAW

HENRY M. HART, JR.

I
INTRODUCTION

In trying to formulate the aims of the criminal law, it is important to be aware both of the reasons for making the effort and of the nature of the problem it poses.

The statement has been made, as if in complaint, that "there is hardly a penal code that can be said to have a single basic principle running through it." But it needs to be clearly seen that this is simply a fact, and not a misfortune. A penal code that reflected only a single basic principle would be a very bad one. Social purposes can never be single or simple, or held unqualifiedly to the exclusion of all other social purposes; and an effort to make them so can result only in the sacrifice of other values which also are important. Thus, to take only one example, the purpose of preventing any particular kind of crime, or crimes generally, is qualified always by the purposes of avoiding the conviction of the innocent and of enhancing that sense of security throughout the society which is one of the prime functions of the manifold safeguards of American criminal procedure. And the same thing would be true even if the dominant purpose of the criminal law were thought to be the rehabilitation of offenders rather than the prevention of offenses.

Examination of the purposes commonly suggested for the criminal law will show that each of them is complex and that none may be thought of as wholly excluding the others. Suppose, for example, that the deterrence of offenses is taken to be the chief end. It will still be necessary to recognize that the rehabilitation of offenders, the disablement of offenders, the sharpening of the community's sense of right and wrong, and the satisfaction of the community's sense of just retribution may all serve this end by contributing to an ultimate reduction in the number of crimes. Even socialized vengeance may be accorded a marginal role, if it is understood as the provision of an orderly alternative to mob violence.

The problem, accordingly, is one of the priority and relationship of purposes as well as of their legitimacy—of multivalued rather than of single-valued thinking.

There is still another range of complications which are ignored if an effort is made to formulate any single "theory" or set of "principles" of criminal law. The purpose of having principles and theories is to help in organizing thought. In the law, the ultimate purpose of thought is to help in deciding upon a course of action. In the criminal law, as in all law, questions about the action to be taken do not present themselves for decision in an institutional vacuum. They arise rather in the context of some established and specific procedure of decision: in a

Reprinted, with permission, from a symposium on *Sentencing,* appearing in *Law and Contemporary Problems,* Vol. 23, No. 3 (Summer 1958); published by the School of Law, Duke University, Durham, N.C. Copyright © 1958 by Duke University.

constitutional convention; in a legislature; in a prosecuting attorney's office; in a court charged with the determination of guilt or innocence; in a sentencing court; before a parole board; and so on. This means that each agency of decision must take account always of its own place in the institutional system and of what is necessary to maintain the integrity and workability of the system as a whole. A complex of institutional ends must be served, in other words, as well as a complex of substantive social ends.

The principal levels of decision in the criminal law are numerous. The institutional considerations involved at the various levels differ so markedly that it seems worth while to discuss the question of aims separately, from the point of view of each of the major agencies of decision.

II
THE PERSPECTIVE OF CONSTITUTION MAKERS

We can get our broadest view of the aims of the criminal law if we look at them from the point of view of the makers of a constitution—of those who are seeking to establish sound foundations for a tolerable and durable social order. From this point of view, these aims can be most readily seen, as they need to be seen, in their relation to the aims of the good society generally.

In this setting, the basic question emerges: Why should the good society make use of the method of the criminal law at all?

A. What the Method of the Criminal Law Is

The question posed raises preliminarily an even more fundamental inquiry: What do we mean by "crime" and "criminal"? Or, put more accurately, what should we understand to be "the method of the criminal law," the use of which is in question? This latter way of formulating the preliminary inquiry is more accurate, because it pictures the criminal law as a process, a way of doing something, which is what it is. A great deal of intellectual energy has been misspent in an effort to develop a concept of crime as "a natural and social phenomenon" abstracted from the functioning system of institutions which make use of the concept and give it impact and meaning. But the criminal law, like all law, is concerned with the pursuit of human purposes through the forms and modes of social organization, and it needs always to be thought about in that context as a method or process of doing something.

What then are the characteristics of this method?

1. The method operates by means of a series of directions, or commands, formulated in general terms, telling people what they must or must not do. Mostly, the commands of the criminal law are "must-nots," or prohibitions, which can be satisfied by inaction. "Do not murder, rape, or rob." But some of them are "musts," or affirmative requirements, which can be satisfied only by taking a specifically, or relatively specifically, described kind of action. "Support your wife and children," and "File your income tax return."

2. The commands are taken as valid and binding upon all those who fall within their terms when the time comes for complying with them, whether or not they have been formulated in advance in a single authoritative set of words. They speak to members of the community, in other words, in the community's behalf, with all the power and prestige of the community behind them.

3. The commands are subject to one or more sanctions for disobedience which the community is prepared to enforce.

Thus far, it will be noticed, nothing has been said about the criminal law which is not true also of a large part of the noncriminal, or civil, law. The law of torts, the law of contracts, and almost every other branch of private law that can be mentioned operate, too, with general directions prohibiting or requiring described types of conduct, and the community's tribunals enforce these commands. What, then, is distinctive about the method of the criminal law?

Can crimes be distinguished from civil wrongs on the ground that they constitute injuries to society generally which society is interested in preventing? The difficulty is that society is interested also in the due fulfillment of contracts and the avoidance of traffic accidents and most of the other stuff of civil litigation. The civil law is framed and interpreted and enforced with a constant eye to these social interests. Does the distinction lie in the fact that proceedings to enforce the criminal law are instituted by public officials rather than private complainants? The difficulty is that public officers may also bring many kinds of "civil" enforcement actions—for an injunction, for the recovery of a "civil" penalty, or even for the detention of the defendant by public authority. Is the distinction, then, in the peculiar character of what is done to people who are adjudged to be criminals? The difficulty is that, with the possible exception of death, exactly the same kinds of unpleasant consequences, objectively considered, can be and are visited upon unsuccessful defendants in civil proceedings.

If one were to judge from the notions apparently underlying many judicial opinions, and the overt language even of some of them, the solution of the puzzle is simply that a crime is anything which is *called* a crime, and a criminal penalty is simply the penalty provided for doing anything which has been given that name. So vacant a concept is a betrayal of intellectual bankruptcy. Certainly, it poses no intelligible issue for a constitution-maker concerned to decide whether to make use of "the method of the criminal law." Moreover, it is false to popular understanding, and false also to the understanding embodied in existing constitutions. By implicit assumptions that are more impressive than any explicit assertions, these constitutions proclaim that a conviction for crime is a distinctive and serious matter—a something, and not a nothing. What is that something?

4. What distinguishes a criminal from a civil sanction and all that distinguishes it, it is ventured, is the judgment of community condemnation which accompanies and justifies its imposition. As Professor Gardner wrote not long ago, in a distinct but cognate connection:

The essence of punishment for moral delinquency lies in the criminal conviction itself. One may lose more money on the stock market than in a court-room; a prisoner of war camp may well provide a harsher environment than a state prison; death on the field of battle has the same physical characteristics as death by sentence of law. It is the expression of the community's hatred, fear, or contempt for the convict which alone characterizes physical hardship as punishment.

If this is what a "criminal" penalty is, then we can say readily enough what a "crime" is. It is not simply anything which a legislature chooses to call a "crime." It is not simply antisocial conduct which public officers are given a responsibility to suppress. It is not simply any conduct to which a legislature chooses to attach a "criminal" penalty. It is conduct which, if duly shown to have taken place, will incur a formal and solemn pronouncement of the moral condemnation of the community.

5. The method of the criminal law, of course, involves something more than

the threat (and, on due occasion, the expression) of community condemnation of antisocial conduct. It involves, in addition, the threat (and, on due occasion, the imposition) of unpleasant physical consequences, commonly called punishment. But if Professor Gardner is right, these added consequences take their character as punishment from the condemnation which precedes them and serves as the warrant for their infliction. Indeed, the condemnation plus the added consequences may well be considered, compendiously, as constituting the punishment. Otherwise, it would be necessary to think of a convicted criminal as going unpunished if the imposition or execution of his sentence is suspended.

In traditional thought and speech, the ideas of crime and punishment have been inseparable; the consequences of conviction for crime have been described as a matter of course as "punishment." The Constitution of the United States and its amendments, for example, use this word or its verb form in relation to criminal offenses no less than six times. Today, "treatment" has become a fashionable euphemism for the older, ugly word. This bowdlerizing of the Constitution and of conventional speech may serve a useful purpose in discouraging unduly harsh sentences and emphasizing that punishment is not an end in itself. But to the extent that it dissociates the treatment of criminals from the social condemnation of their conduct which is implicit in their conviction, there is danger that it will confuse thought and do a disservice.

At least under existing law, there is a vital difference between the situation of a patient who has been committed to a mental hospital and the situation of an inmate of a state penitentiary. The core of the difference is precisely that the patient has not incurred the moral condemnation of his community, whereas the convict has.

B. The Utility of the Method

We are in a position now to restate the basic question confronting our hypothetical constitution-makers. The question is whether to make use, in the projected social order, of the method of discouraging undesired conduct and encouraging desired conduct by means of the threat—and, when necessary, the fulfillment of the threat—of the community's condemnation of an actor's violation of law and of punishment, or treatment, of the actor as blameworthy for having committed the violation.

The question, like most legal questions, is one of alternatives. Perhaps the leading alternative, to judge from contemporary criticism of the penal law, would be to provide that people who behave badly should simply be treated as sick people to be cured, rather than as bad people to be condemned and punished. A constitutional guarantee to accomplish this could be readily drafted: "No person shall be subjected to condemnation or punishment for violation of law, but only to curative-rehabilitative treatment." Would the establishment of this new constitutional liberty be well-advised?

Paradoxically, this suggested guarantee, put forward here as an abandonment of the method of the criminal law, is not far removed from a point of view that has been widely urged in recent years as a proper rationale of existing law. Professors Hall and Glueck express this point of view in their recent casebook, more moderately than some of its other exponents. They recognize that "no general formula respecting the relative proportions of the various ingredients of the general punitive-corrective aim can be worked out." But they then go on to say:

It is the opinion of many of those who have studied both the causes of crime and the results of its treatment by means of the death penalty and the usual forms of incarceration, that for the vast majority of the general rule of delinquents and criminals, the corrective theory, based upon a conception of multiple causation and curative-rehabilitative treatment, should clearly predominate in legislation and in judicial and administrative practices. No other single theory is as closely related to the actual conditions and mechanisms of crime causation; no other gives as much promise of returning the offender to society not with the negative vacuum of punishment-induced fear but with the affirmative and constructive equipment—physical, mental and moral—for law-abidingness. Thus, in the long run, no other theory and practice gives greater promise of protecting society.

This suggests the possibility of a modified version of the constitutional guarantee in question, directing that "The corrective theory of crime and criminal justice, based upon a conception of multiple causation and curative-rehabilitative treatment, shall predominate in legislation and in judicial and administrative practices." Would such a provision be workable? Would it be wise?

Any theory of criminal justice which emphasizes the criminal rather than the crime encounters an initial and crucial difficulty when it is sought to be applied at the stage of legislative enactment, where the problem in the first instance is to define and grade the crime. How *can* a conception of multiple causation and curative-rehabilitative treatment predominate in the definition and grading of crimes, let alone serve as the sole guide? But even if it were possible to gauge in advance the types of conduct to be forbidden by the expected need for reformation of those who will thereafter engage in them, would it be sensible to try to do so? Can the content of the law's commands be rationally determined with an eye singly or chiefly to the expected deficiencies of character of those who will violate them? Obviously not. The interests of society in having certain things not done or done are also involved.

Precisely because of the difficulties of relating the content of the law's commands to the need for reformation of those who violate them, a curative-rehabilitative theory of criminal justice tends always to depreciate, if not to deny, the significance of these general formulations and to focus attention instead on the individual defendant at the time of his apprehension, trial, and sentence. This has in it always a double danger—to the individual and to society. The danger to the individual is that he will be punished, or treated, for what he is or is believed to be, rather than for what he has done. If his offense is minor but the possibility of his reformation is thought to be slight, the other side of the coin of mercy can become cruelty. The danger to society is that the effectiveness of the general commands of the criminal law as instruments for influencing behavior so as to avoid the necessity for enforcement proceedings will be weakened.

This brings us to the crux of the issue confronting our supposed constitution-makers. The commands of the criminal law are commands which the public interest requires people to comply with. This being so, will the public interest be adequately protected if the legislature is allowed only to say to people, "If you do not comply with any of these commands, you will merely be considered to be sick and subjected to officially-imposed rehabilitative treatment in an effort to cure you"? Can it be adequately protected if the legislature is required to say, "If you do not comply, your own personal need for cure and rehabilitation will be the predominating factor in determining what happens to you"? Or should the legislature be enabled to say, "If you violate any of these laws and the violation is culpable, your conduct will receive the formal and solemn condemnation of the community as morally blame-worthy, and you will be subjected to whatever punishment, or treatment, is appropriate to vindicate the law and to further its various purposes"?

On the sheerly pragmatic ground of the need for equipping the proposed social order with adequate tools to discourage undesired conduct, a responsible constitution-maker assuredly would hesitate long before rejecting the third of these possibilities in favor of either of the first two. To be sure, the efficacy of criminal punishment as a deterrent has often been doubted. But it is to be observed that the doubts are usually expressed by those who are thinking from the retrospective, sanction-imposing point of view. From this point of view, it is natural to be impressed by the undoubted fact that many people do become criminals, and will continue to do so, in spite of all the threats of condemnation and of treatment-in-consequence-of-condemnation that society can offer. But the people who do *not* commit crimes need to be taken into account, too. A constitution-maker, thinking from the prospective point of view of the primary, as distinguished from the remedial, law has especially to think of them, if he is to see his problem whole. So doing, he will be likely to regard the desire of the ordinary man to avoid the moral condemnation of his community, as well as the physical pains and inconveniences of punishment, as a powerful factor in influencing human behavior which can scarcely with safety be dispensed with. Whether he is right or wrong in this conclusion, he will align himself, in reaching it, with the all but universal judgment, past and present, of mankind.

Moreover, there are other and larger considerations to be weighed in the balance. The case against a primarily rehabilitative theory of criminal justice is understated if it is rested solely on the need for the threat of criminal conviction as an instrument of deterrence of antisocial conduct. Deterrence, it is ventured, ought not to be thought of as the overriding and ultimate purpose of the criminal law, important though it is. For deterrence is negative, whereas the purposes of law are positive. And the practical fact must be faced that many crimes, as just recognized, are undeterrable. The grim negativism and the frequent seeming futility of the criminal law when it is considered simply as a means of preventing undesired behavior no doubt help to explain why sensitive people, working at close hand with criminals, tend so often to embrace the more hopeful and positive tenets of a curative-rehabilitative philosophy.

However, a different view is possible if an effort is made to fit the theory of criminal justice into a theory of social justice—to see the purposes of the criminal law in their relation to the purposes of law as a whole. Man is a social animal, and the function of law is to enable him to realize his potentialities as a human being through the forms and modes of social organization. It is important to consider how the criminal law serves this ultimate end.

Human beings, of course, realize their potentialities in part through enjoyment of the various satisfactions of human life, both tangible and intangible, which existing social resources and their own individual capacities make available to them. Yet, the social resources of the moment are always limited, and human capacities for enjoyment are limited also. Social resources for providing the satisfactions of life and human capacities for enjoying them, however, are always susceptible of enlargement, so far as we know, without eventual limit. Man realizes his potentialities most significantly in the very process of developing these resources and capacities—by making himself a functioning and participating member of his community, contributing to it as well as drawing from it.

What is crucial in this process is the enlargement of each individual's capacity for effectual and responsible decision. For it is only through personal, self-reliant participation, by trial and error, in the problems of existence, both personal and social, that the capacity to participate effectively can grow. Man learns wisdom in choosing by being confronted with choices and by being made aware that he must abide the consequences of his choice. In the training of a child in the small circle of the family, this principle is familiar enough. It has the same validity in the training of an adult in the larger circle of the community.

Seen in this light, the criminal law has an obviously significant and, indeed, a fundamental role to play in the effort to create the good society. For it is the criminal law which defines the minimum conditions of man's responsibility to his fellows and holds him to that responsibility. The assertion of social responsibility has value in the treatment even of those who have become criminals. It has far greater value as a stimulus to the great bulk of mankind to abide by the law and to take pride in so abiding.

This, then, is the critical weakness of the two alternative constitutional provisions that have been discussed—more serious by far than losing or damaging a useful, even if imperfect, instrument of deterrence. The provisions would undermine the foundation of a free society's effort to build up each individual's sense of responsibility as a guide and a stimulus to the constructive development of his capacity for effectual and fruitful decision.

If the argument which has been made is accepted and it is concluded that explicit abandonment of the concept of moral condemnation of criminal conduct would be unsound, what then is to be said of the soundness of an interpretation of existing law which tries to achieve a similar result by indirection—treating the purpose of cure and rehabilitation as predominating, while sweeping under the rug the hard facts of the social need and the moral rightness of condemnation and of treatment which does not dilute the fact of condemnation?

C. Constitutional Limitations on the Use of the Method

It is evident that the view which the constitution-maker takes of the function of criminal law will be important in shaping his attitude on inclusion in the document of many of the traditional guarantees of fair procedure in criminal trials. Most of these, such, for example, as indictment by a grand jury or even trial by a petit jury, are largely or wholly irrelevant to the offender's need for, or his susceptibility to, curative-rehabilitative treatment. Indeed, as already suggested, even the basic concept that criminality must rest upon criminal conduct, duly proved to have taken place, would come into question under a purely rehabilitative theory. Present laws for the confinement and care of mentally-ill persons do not insist upon this requirement, and, if criminality were to be equated with sickness of personality generally, its rationale would not be readily apparent. But if what is in issue is the community's solemn condemnation of the accused as a defaulter in his obligations to the community, then the default to be condemned ought plainly to consist of overt conduct, and not simply of a condition of mind; and the fact of default should be proved with scrupulous care. The safeguards which now surround the procedure of proof of criminality or the essentials of them, in other words, will appear to be appropriate.

Should the constitution-makers go further and prescribe not only procedural safeguards, but substantive limitations on the kinds of conduct that can be declared criminal? For the most part, American constitution-makers have not done this. They have relied, instead, primarily on the legislature's sense of justice.

Secondarily, they have relied on the courts to understand what a crime is and, so, by appropriate invocation of the broad constitutional injunction of due process, to prevent an arbitrary application of the criminal sanction when the legislature's sense of justice has failed. Whether they have been wise in so doing is a question which can best be left to the reader's judgment, in the light of the examination which follows of the actual handling of the problems by legislatures and courts.

III
THE PERSPECTIVE OF THE LEGISLATURE

A legislature deals with crimes always in advance of their commission (assuming the existence of constitutional prohibitions or practices excluding ex post facto laws and bills of attainder). It deals with them not by condemnation and punishment, but only by threat of condemnation and punishment, *to be imposed always by other agencies*. It deals with them always by directions formulated in *general terms*. The primary parts of the directions have always to be interpreted and applied by the private persons—the potential offenders—to whom they are initially addressed. In the event of a breach or claim of breach, both the primary and the remedial parts must be interpreted and applied by the various officials—police, prosecuting attorneys, trial judges and jurors, appellate judges, and probation, prison, and parole authorities—responsible for their enforcement. The attitudes, capacities, and practical conditions of work of these officials often put severe limits upon the ability of the legislature to accomplish what it sets out to accomplish.

If the primary parts of a general direction are to work successfully in any particular instance, otherwise than by fortunate accident, four conditions have always to be satisfied: (1) the primary addressee who is supposed to conform his conduct to the direction must know (a) of its existence, and (b) of its content in relevant respects; (2) he must know about the circumstances of fact which make the abstract terms of the direction applicable in the particular instance; (3) he must be able to comply with it; and (4) he must be willing to do so.

The difficulties of satisfying these conditions vitally affect the fairness and often even the feasibility of the effort to control the behavior of large numbers of people by means of general directions, subject only to an after-the-event sanction. This is so even when the sanction is civil, such as a judgment for compensatory damages or restoration of benefits. But the difficulties are especially acute when the sanction is criminal. For then, something more is involved than the simple necessity of getting the direction complied with in a sufficient proportion of instances to keep it in good working order—that is, to maintain respect for it and to avoid arbitrary discrimination in singling out individual violators as subjects of enforcement proceedings. If what was said in part two is correct, it is necessary to be able to say in good conscience in *each* instance in which a criminal sanction is imposed for a violation of law that the violation was blameworthy and, hence, deserving of the moral condemnation of the community.

This raises two closely related questions which lie at the heart of the problems of the criminal law: *First,* what *are* the ingredients of moral blameworthiness which warrant a judgment of community condemnation? *Second,* retracing the ground of part two, can the position be maintained that guilt in the sense of the criminal law is an individual matter and cannot justly be pronounced by the community if the individual's conduct affords no basis for a judgment of moral condemnation?

These questions present themselves in different guises in different types of criminal statutes. They can best be examined separately in relation to the various major types of purposes for which a legislature may seek to employ a criminal sanction.

A. The Statement of the Minimum Obligations of Responsible Citizenship: The Control of Purposeful Conduct

The core of a sound penal code in any view of the function of the criminal law is the statement of those minimum obligations of conduct which the conditions of community life impose upon every participating member if community life is to be maintained and to prosper—that is, of those obligations which result not from a discretionary and disputable judgment of the legislature, but from the objective facts of the interdependencies of the people who are living together in the community and of their awareness of the interdependencies.

In the mind of any legislator who recognizes this central and basic job as a distinct one and who is trying to do it faithfully and intelligently, a variety of aims will coalesce, to the point of becoming virtually indistinguishable. The inculcation of a sense of social responsibility throughout the society will be the dominant aim. But the stated obligations will, at the same time, represent desired standards of conduct and so will necessarily involve the aim of deterrence of undesired conduct. Since violators are to be condemned as defaulters in their duty to the community and treated accordingly, the aim can also be described as punitive. And if the conduct declared to be criminal does, indeed, evince a blameworthy lack of social responsibility, the declaration will also constitute an essential first step in identifying those members of the community whose behavior shows them to be in need of cure and rehabilitation, and this aim will likewise be included. So also, subordinately, will be the aim of temporary or permanent disablement of certain of the more serious offenders.

Returning now to the four conditions earlier stated for the successful operation of a general direction and to the problem of deciding when a failure of compliance due to a failure to satisfy one of the conditions is blameworthy, it will be seen that in this area of the criminal law, the difficulties are minimal, so long at least as the legislature is denouncing purposeful or knowing, as distinguished from reckless or merely negligent, conduct.

If the legislature does a sound job of reflecting community attitudes and needs, actual knowledge of the wrongfulness of the prohibited conduct will usually exist. Thus, almost everyone is aware that murder and forcible rape and the obvious forms of theft are wrong. But in any event, knowledge of wrongfulness can fairly be assumed. For any member of the community who does these things without knowing that they are criminal is blameworthy, as much for his lack of knowledge as for his actual conduct. This seems to be the essential rationale of the maxim, *Ignorantia legis neminem excusat,* which has been so much misunderstood and abused in relation to regulatory crimes, involving conduct which is not intrinsically wrongful.

Similarly, knowledge of the circumstances of fact which make the law's directions applicable will ordinarily exist when harms are inflicted or risks created of the elementary and obvious types sought to be prevented by these intrinsically wrongful crimes. But suppose that knowledge does not exist? The traditional criminal law, concerned almost exclusively with crimes of this kind, has ready to hand a solution in the traditional maxim that ignorance of fact excuses, as well as in cognate doctrines such as that of claim-of-right in the law of theft. If the legislature can depend upon the courts to read these doctrines into its enactments, the requisite of blameworthiness as an element of criminality will be respected.

Obligations of conduct fixed by a fair appraisal of the minimum requirements for the maintenance and fostering of community life will, by hypothesis, be obligations which normal members of the community will be *able* to comply with, given the necessary awareness of the circumstances of fact calling for compliance. But suppose that in a particular case, this ability does not exist? Again, the traditional law provides materials for solution of the problem when inability negatives blameworthiness; and the only question is whether the legislature can count upon the courts to make use of the materials. The materials include doctrines with respect to duress, as well as doctrines providing for the exculpation of those individuals who because of mental disease or defect are to be deemed incapable of acting as responsible, participating members of society.

There remains only the question of willingness to comply. In relation to directions which make a reasonably grounded appeal to the citizen's sense of responsibility as a citizen, this willingness is likely to be at a maximum. Individuals who are able but unwilling to comply with such directions are precisely the ones who ought to be condemned as criminals.

In the sphere of conduct which is intrinsically wrongful, the legislature's task is further simplified by its ability (or the ability which it is entitled to suppose it has) to rely upon the courts for the elaboration of detail and the solution of unanticipated or peripheral problems. Indeed, this was a body of law which was largely built up by English judges without benefit of acts of Parliament and which in this country required the intervention of the legislature, on its primary side, only to satisfy the theoretical and emotional appeal of the maxim, *Nullum crimen sine lege.* Despite the maxim, most American legislatures have been content to make use of familiar words and phrases of the common law, relying upon the courts to fill in their meaning, and even leaving whole areas of doctrine, such as criminal intent and various phases of justification, entirely to the courts. So long as the courts are faithful in their reflection of the community's understanding of what is morally blameworthy, judgments of conviction are not subject to the reproach of being, even in spirit, ex post facto.

B. The Statement of the Minimum Obligations of Responsible Citizenship: The Control of Reckless and Negligent Conduct

Special difficulties are presented when the criminal law undertakes to state an obligation of conduct in a way which requires an addressee, if he is to comply with it, to have a certain kind of general knowledge or experience, or to exercise a certain degree of skill and attention, or to make an appraisal of the probable consequences of what he does or omits to do with a certain degree of accuracy. When can a criminal sanction be properly authorized in cases in which the addressee fails in one or another of these respects and harm results or a risk is created because of his failure?

For example, one who undertakes to practice as a physician does not know that flannels saturated with kerosene will tend to produce severe burns if applied directly to the flesh of a patient. A foreman of a railroad section gang misreads a timetable and orders railroad tracks to be taken up for replacement just before a train is due. The owner of a night club fails to realize that the means of egress would be inadequate if a fire were to break out when the club was crowded.

Upon precisely what kind of showing can a legislature justly provide that such people are to be condemned and punished as criminals? If the legislature requires that an awareness of the risk be brought home to the actor and that the risk be one which, by the general standards of the community, is plainly excessive, a direction for criminal punishment creates no difficulty of principle, however trying may be the problems of application. For judgment about whether a given risk can justifiably be taken to promote a given end depends upon the evaluations implicit in community standards of right and wrong to which each member of the community can justly be expected to conform his conduct. If an individual knowingly takes a risk of a kind which the community condemns as plainly unjustifiable, then he is morally blameworthy and can properly be adjudged a criminal. He is criminally reckless in the traditional sense articulated with precision by the draftsmen of the American Law Institute's Model Penal Code.

This concept of criminal recklessness may well embrace not only situations in which the actor adverts directly to the possibility of the ultimate harm, but those in which he adverts only to his own deficiencies in appraising the possibility of harm or preventing it from coming to pass and to the possible consequences of *those* deficiencies. Thus, the doctor who swathes his patient with kerosene-soaked rags, without even suspecting what is going to happen, may, nevertheless, know that special knowledge and training is generally needed in order to treat patients safely and successfully and that he does not have that knowledge and training. In any such situation, if the actor knows of his deficiency and of the risk which such a deficiency creates, and if *that* risk is one which in community understanding is plainly unjustifiable, there is a basis for legislative condemnation of the conduct as criminally reckless.

Moreover, as considered more fully under the next subheading, if the actor knowingly goes counter to a valid legislative determination that the risk he is taking is excessive, even though he himself does not believe it to be, there is an independent basis for moral condemnation in this deliberate defiance of law.

The question remains whether simple unawareness of risk, without awareness of any deficiency preventing appreciation or avoidance of it and without any element of knowing disregard of a relevant legislative decision, can justly be declared to be culpable. The answer would seem clearly to be no, at least in those situations in which the actor lacks the ability either to refrain from the conduct which creates the risk or to correct the deficiency which makes engaging in the conduct dangerous, for otherwise, the third of the requisites above stated for the successful operation of a general direction is impossible to satisfy. But suppose the actor has this ability? Guilt would, then, seem to depend upon whether he has been put upon notice of his duty to use his ability to a degree which makes his unawareness of the duty, in the understanding of the community, genuinely blameworthy. In exceptional situations of elementary and obvious danger, the circumstances of fact of which the actor is conscious may be sufficient in themselves to give this notice. But this can be true only when the significance of the circumstances of fact would be apparent to one who shares the community's general sense of right and wrong. If this is not so—if appreciation of the significance of the facts depends upon knowledge of what happens to be written in the statute books—then, the problem becomes one of the nature and extent of the moral obligation to know what is so written, which is discussed under the next subheading.

Criminal punishment of merely negligent behavior is commonly justified not on the ground that violators can be said to be individually blameworthy, but on the ground that the threat of such punishment will help to teach people generally to be more careful. This proposes, as legitimate, an aim for the legislature which is drastically different from that of inculcating minimum standards of personal responsibility to society. The issues it raises are examined under the subheading after the next.

C. The Regulation of Conduct Which Is Not Intrinsically Wrongful:
Bases of Blameworthiness

The statute books of the forty-nine states and the United States are filled with enactments carrying a criminal sanction which are obviously motivated by other ends, primarily, than that of training for responsible citizenship. The legislature simply wants certain things done and certain other things not done because it believes that the doing or the not doing of them will secure some ultimate social advantage, and not at all because it thinks the immediate conduct involved is either rightful or wrongful in itself. It employs the threat of criminal condemnation and punishment as an especially forceful way of saying that it really wants to be obeyed, or else simply from lack of enough imagination to think of a more appropriate sanction. Such enactments present problems which neither the courts nor the legislature of this country have yet succeeded in thinking through.

When a legislature undertakes to prohibit or require conduct theretofore untouched by the criminal law, what considerations *ought* to guide it in deciding whether to declare that noncompliance with its direction shall be a crime?

1. If the legislature can, in good conscience, conclude that the new direction embodies standards of behavior which have to be observed, under existing social conditions, if social life is to be maintained, then the use of a criminal sanction raises no difficulty. Obviously, there is room for growth, as conditions and attitudes in society change, in the central body of law earlier discussed which undertakes to state the minimum obligations of responsible citizenship. Obviously also, the legislature is an appropriate agency to settle debatable questions about the appropriate extent of growth, whether or not it is desirable for courts to have a share in the process.

Statutes which make well-considered additions to the list of the citizen's basic obligations are not open to the objection of undue multiplication of crimes. Normal principles of culpability, moreover, can properly apply to such offenses, and should apply. Absent exceptional circumstances, in other words, ignorance of the criminality of the conduct (act or omission) which is forbidden ought not to be a defense. *Per contra,* ignorance of the facts ought to be. And, of course, the usual defenses based on inability to comply should be available.

2. If the legislature cannot, in good conscience, regard conduct which it wishes to forbid as wrongful in itself, then it has always the option of declaring the conduct to be criminal only when the actor knows of its criminality or recklessly disregards the possibility that it is criminal. For knowing or reckless disregard of legal obligation affords an independent basis of blameworthiness justifying the actor's condemnation as a criminal, even when his conduct was not intrinsically antisocial. It is convenient to use the word "wilful" to describe this mode of culpability, although the term is by no means regularly so limited in conventional usage.

The inclusion in a new regulatory crime of the requirement of "wilfulness" avoids any difficulty of principle in the use of the criminal sanction—assuming that the requirement comprehends not only a culpable awareness (knowing or reckless) of the law, but a culpable awareness also of the facts making the law applicable, together with a sufficient ability to comply. The requirement, moreover, mitigates any objection on the score of undue multiplication of regulatory crimes, although it can hardly eliminate it entirely.

3. Under what, if any, circumstances may a legislature properly direct the conviction as a criminal of a person whose conduct is not wrongful in itself and who neither knows nor recklessly disregards the possibility that he is violating the law?

To engage knowingly or recklessly in conduct which is wrongful in itself and which has, in fact, been condemned as a crime is either to fail to comprehend the community's accepted moral values or else squarely to challenge them. The maxim, *Ignorantia legis neminem excusat,* expresses the wholly defensible and, indeed, essential principle that the action, in either event, is blameworthy. If, however, the criminal law adheres to this maxim when it moves from the condemnation of those things which are *mala in se* to the condemnation of those things which are merely *mala prohibita,* it necessarily shifts its ground from a demand that every responsible member of the community understand and respect the community's moral values to a demand that everyone know and understand what is written in the statute books. Such a demand is *toto coelo* different. In no respect is contemporary law subject to greater reproach than for its obtuseness to this fact.

Granting that blame may, in some circumstances, attach to an actor's antecedent failure to determine the legality of his conduct, it is, in any event, blame of a very distinctive kind.

a. The blame in such a case is largely unrelated, in gravity or any other respect, to the external conduct itself, or its consequences, for which the actor is purportedly convicted. Indeed, all such instances of conduct in ignorance of laws enjoining *mala prohibita* might well be thought of as constituting a single type of crime, if they constitute any kind of crime at all—the crime of ignorance of the statutes or of their interpretation. Knowledge of the facts and ability to comply may be formal requisites of criminality, but in the absence of knowledge of the law, they are irrelevant, and willingness to comply remains untested. The whole weight of the law's effort to achieve its purpose has to be carried, in the first instance, by the effort to get people to know and understand its requirements.

b. In such cases, the essential crime, if that is what it is, is always a crime of omission. If the purported crime is itself one of omission, as in the failure to take out a license, then the offense is doubly negative. As Professor Graham Hughes has recently abundantly demonstrated,

. . . *a penal policy of omissions and a criminal jurisprudence of offenses of omission are overdue. . . . [W]here inaction is evidently socially harmful, no good reason appears for shrinking from penal prohibition. Any penal policy, however, must be linked with a consciousness of the need to promulgate and publicize offenses of omission and a recognition by the judiciary that conventional attitudes to mens rea, particularly with respect to ignorance of the law, are not adequate tools to achieve justice for those accused of inaction.*

Even when the nominal crime is one of commission rather than omission, the problem of promulgating and publicizing the offense, which Professor Hughes mentions, is likely to be serious if the nature of the affirmative conduct gives no warning of the possibility of an applicable criminal prohibition. But it is especially likely to be serious when the nominal crime is itself one of omission, for mere inaction often gives no such warning whatever.

c. The gist of a crime of statutory ignorance may lie not in the failure to inform oneself of the existence of an applicable statute, which is always in some sense a do-able thing if the statutes are published and there is a decent index to them, but in the failure to divine their meaning, which may be altogether non-do-able. All statutes are, of necessity, indeterminate in some of their applications. When a criminal enactment proscribes conduct which is *malum in se*, such as murder or manslaughter, however, the moral standards of the community are available always as a guide in the resolution of its indeterminacies, and there is a minimum of unfairness when doubt is resolved against a particular defendant. This guidance is missing when the proscribed conduct is merely *malum prohibitum*. The resolution of doubts must, thus, depend not upon a good human sense of moral values, but upon a sound grasp of technical doctrines and policies of statutory interpretation. Dean Pound has justly observed of American lawyers and judges that "we have no well-developed technique of developing legislative texts." To condemn a layman as blameworthy for a default of technical judgment in a matter which causes trouble even for professional judges is, in many cases, so manifestly beyond reason that courts have developed various makeshift devices to avoid condemnation in particular situations. And the draftsmen of the Model Penal Code have devised for such cases a generalized defense of limited scope. Until the nature and dimensions of the problem have been more fully perceived, however, no genuinely satisfactory solution can be reached.

d. No doubt there are situations in which one who engages in a particular course of conduct assumes an obligation, in general community understanding, to know about the law applicable to that kind of conduct. Sometimes, this may be true in areas of statutory law affecting people generally, such as motor vehicle laws. It is most likely to be true of laws applicable to particular occupations. One cannot say categorically, therefore, that ignorance of a law creating a merely statutory crime never affords a basic for moral condemnation. What can be said, in general terms, is that (1) the criminal law as a device for getting people to know about statutes and interpret them correctly is a device of dubious and largely unproved effectiveness; (2) the indiscriminate use of the device dilutes the force of the threat of community condemnation as a means of influencing conduct in other situations where the basis for moral condemnation is clear; (3) the loss to society from this dilution is always unnecessary, since the legislature has always the alternatives of either permitting a good faith belief in the legality of one's conduct to be pleaded and proved as a defense, or of providing a civil rather than a criminal sanction for nonwilful violations.

e. Under what, if any, circumstances may a legislature properly direct the conviction as a criminal of one who knows about the applicable law but who has been negligent, although not reckless, in ascertaining the facts which make the law applicable to his conduct—where the kind of conduct involved is morally neutral, both from the point of view of the actor and in actuality?

In the usual situation of assertedly criminal negligence earlier discussed, the harm caused or threatened by failure of advertence is one which it would be morally wrongful to cause advertently. The assertion of a duty of attention is, thus, strengthened by the gravity of the risks actually involved. In the situation now under discussion, the facts are morally neutral, even to one who knows about them, save for the existence of an applicable statute. Thus, the basis of blame, if any, is inattention to one's duty as a citizen to see that the law gets complied with in all the situations to which it is supposed to apply. For example, manufactured food becomes adulterated or misbranded within the meaning of a statute, but in a way which involves no danger to health.

Condemning a person for lack of ordinary care in ascertaining facts at least does not involve the offense to justice sometimes involved in the ignorance-of-interpretation-of-statute cases of condemning him for failure to do the impossible. But otherwise, most of the points just made about ignorance of regulatory law apply: (1) the basis of moral blame will usually be thin and may be virtually nonexistent; (2) the likelihood of substantial social gain in stimulating greater care is dubious; (3) the social cost is a weakening of the moral force and, hence, the effectiveness of the threat of criminal conviction; and (4) the cost is unnecessary, since the legislature has always the alternative of a civil sanction.

D. Strict Liability

A large body of modern law goes far beyond an insistence upon a duty of ordinary care in ascertaining facts, at the peril of being called a criminal. To an absolute duty to know about the existence of a regulatory statute and interpret it correctly, it adds an absolute duty to know about the facts. Thus, the porter who innocently carries the bag of a hotel guest not knowing that it contains a bottle of whisky is punished as a criminal for having transported intoxicating liquor. The corporation president who signs a registration statement for a proposed securities issue not knowing that his accountants have made a mistake is guilty of the crime of making a "false" representation to the state blue-sky commissioner. The president of a corporation whose employee introduces into interstate commerce a shipment of technically but harmlessly adulterated food is branded as a criminal solely because he was the president when the shipment was made. And so on, *ad* almost *infinitum.*

In all such cases, it is possible, of course, that a basis of blameworthiness might have been found in the particular facts. Perhaps the company presidents actually *were* culpably careless in their supervision. Conceivably, even, the porter was culpably remiss in failing to see if he could hear a gurgle. But these possibilities are irrelevant. For the statutes in question, as interpreted, do not require any such defaults to be proved against a defendant, nor even permit him to show the absence of such a default in defense. The offenses fall within "the numerous class in which diligence, actual knowledge and bad motives are immaterial. . . ." Thus, they squarely pose the question whether there can be any justification for condemning and punishing a human being as a criminal when he has done nothing which is blameworthy.

It is submitted that there can be no moral justification for this, and that there is not, indeed, even a rational, amoral justification.

1. People who do not know and cannot find out that they are supposed to comply with an applicable command are, by hypothesis, nondeterrable. So far as personal amenability to legal control is concerned, they stand in the same posture as the plainest lunatic under the *M'Naghten* test who "does not know the nature and quality of his act or, if he does know it, does not know that the act is wrong."

2. If it be said that most people will know of such commands and be able to comply with them, the answer, among others, is that nowhere else in the criminal law is the probable, or even the certain, guilt of nine men regarded as sufficient warrant for the conviction of a tenth. In the tradition of Anglo-American law, guilt of crime is personal. The main body of the criminal law, from the Constitution on down, makes sense on no other assumption.

3. If it be asserted that strict criminal liability is necessary in order to stimulate people to be diligent in learning the law and finding out when it applies, the answer, among others, is that this is wholly unproved and prima facie improbable. Studies to test the relative effectiveness of strict criminal liability and well-designed civil penalties are lacking and badly needed. Until such studies are forthcoming, however, judgment can only take into account (a) the inherent unlikelihood that people's behavior will be significantly affected by commands that are not brought definitely to their attention; (b) the long-understood tendency of disproportionate penalties to promote disrespect rather than respect for law, unless they are rigorously and uniformly enforced; (c) the inherent difficulties of rigorous and uniform enforcement of strict criminal liability and the impressive evidence that it is, in fact, spottily and unevenly enforced; (d) the greater possibilities or flexible and imaginative adaptation of civil penalties, and their more ready enforceability; and (e) most important of all, the shocking damage that is done to social morale by open and official admission that crime can be respectable and criminality a matter of ill chance, rather than blameworthy choice.

4. If it be urged that strict criminal liability is necessary in order to simplify the investigation and prosecution of violations of statutes designed to control mass conduct, the answer, among others, is that (a) maximizing compliance with law, rather than successful prosecution of violators, is the primary aim of any regulatory statute; (b) the convenience of investigators and prosecutors is not, in any event, the prime consideration in determining what conduct is criminal; (c) a prosecutor, as a matter of common knowledge, always assumes a heavier burden in trying to secure a criminal conviction than a civil judgment; (d) in most situations of attempted control of mass conduct, the technique of a first warning, followed by criminal prosecution only of knowing violators, has not only obvious, but proved superiority; and (e) the common-sense advantages of using the criminal sanction only against deliberate violators is confirmed by the policies which prosecutors themselves tend always to follow when they are free to make their own selection of cases to prosecute.

5. Moral, rather than crassly utilitarian, considerations re-enter the picture when the claim is made, as it sometimes is, that strict liability operates, in fact, only against people who are really blameworthy, because prosecutors only pick out the really guilty ones for criminal prosecution. This argument reasserts the traditional position that a criminal conviction imports moral condemnation. To this, it adds the arrogant assertion that it is proper to visit the moral condemnation of the community upon one of its members on the basis solely of the private judgment of his prosecutors. Such a circumvention of the safeguards with which the law surrounds other determinations of criminality seems not only irrational, but immoral as well.

6. But moral considerations in a still larger dimension are the ultimately controlling ones. In its conventional and traditional applications, a criminal conviction carries with it an ineradicable connotation of moral condemnation and personal guilt. Society makes an essentially parasitic, and hence illegitimate, use of this instrument when it uses it as a means of deterrence (or compulsion) of conduct which is morally neutral. This would be true even if a statute were to be enacted proclaiming that no criminal conviction hereafter should ever be understood as casting any reflection on anybody. For statutes cannot change the meaning of words and make people stop thinking what they do think when they hear the words spoken. But it is doubly true—it is ten-fold, a hundred-fold, a

thousand-fold true—when society continues to insist that some crimes *are* morally blameworthy and then tries to use the same epithet to describe conduct which is not.

7. To be sure, the traditional law recognizes gradations in the gravity of offenses, and so does the Constitution of the United States. But strict liability offenses have not been limited to the interpretively-developed constitutional category of "petty offenses," for which trial by jury is not required. They include even some crimes which the Constitution expressly recognizes as "infamous." Thus, the excuse of the Scotch servant girl for her illegitimate baby, that "It was only such a leetle one," is not open to modern legislatures. And since a crime remains a crime, just as a baby is unalterably a baby, it would not be a good excuse if it were. Especially is this so since the legislature could avoid the taint of illegitimacy, much more surely than the servant girl, by simply saying that the "crime" is not a crime, but only a civil violation.

E. The Problem of Providing for Treatment

In determining that described conduct shall constitute a crime, a legislature makes necessarily the first and the major decision about the appropriate sanction for a violation of its direction. For it decides then that community condemnation shall be visited upon adjudged violators. But there remain hosts of questions about the degree of the condemnation and the nature of the authorized punishment, or treatment-in-consequence-of-violation.

Entangled with the problems of the appropriate aims to be pursued which are involved in these questions are problems of the appropriate assignment of powers to make decisions in carrying out the aims. To what extent should the legislature undertake to give binding directions about treatment which will foreclose the exercise of any later judgment or discretion? To what extent should it depend, instead, upon the judgment and discretion either of the sentencing court or of the correctional authorities who will become responsible for defendants after they are sentenced?

It is axiomatic that each agency of decision ought to make those decisions which its position in the institutional structure best fits it to make. But this, as will be seen, depends in part upon the criteria which are to guide decision.

1. The traditional criminal law recognizes different grades of offenses, such as felony and misdemeanor, and modern statutes recognize different degrees within the grades. If the criminal law were concerned centrally with reforming criminals, this would scarcely be appropriate: a confirmed petty thief may have much greater need of reformation than a once-in-a-lifetime manslaughterer. If the thesis of this paper is accepted, however, it follows that grading is not only proper, but essential; that the legislature is the appropriate institution to do the grading; that the grading should be done with primary regard for the relative blameworthiness of offenses (a factor which, of course, will take into account the relative extent of the harm characteristically done or threatened to individuals and, thus, to the social order by each type of offense); and that the grading should be determinative of the relative severity of the treatment authorized for each offense.

2. Given such a ranking of offenses, the question remains: how far up or down the scale of possible severity or lenity of treatment should the whole array be moved? Are comparatively severe punishments to be favored or comparatively lenient ones? Here is a question of public policy which is pre-eminently for the legislature. On this question, its cardinal aims should be its cardinal guide.

Punishments should be severe enough to impress not only upon the defendant's mind, but upon the public mind, the gravity of society's condemnation of irresponsible behavior. But the ultimate aim of condemning irresponsibility is training for responsibility. The treatment of criminals, therefore, should encourage, rather than foreclose, the development of their sense of responsibility. Allowance for the possibility of reformation, or formation, of character in the generality of cases becomes at this point, in other words, an overriding consideration. This consideration will point inexorably in the direction of eliminating capital punishment and minimizing both the occasions and the length of incarceration.

3. Should the legislature prescribe a single definite and unvarying form of treatment for each type of offense? The almost universal judgment of modern legal systems is that, ordinarily at least, it should not. Two types of considerations seem to underlie this judgment. The first is the need of making the treatment fit the crime. Statutory definitions of offenses are, of necessity, highly general categories covering a host of variant circumstances which are relevant to the blameworthiness of particular crimes. All the circumstances which are relevant in a particular case cannot be known until the case has been tried. The second type of consideration is the need of making the treatment fit the criminal, so as to take into account not only the kind of thing he did, but the kind of person he is. Only in this way can room be allowed for the effective play, on the basis of individualized judgment, of the criminal law's subordinate aims of reforming offenders or of disabling them where a special period of disablement seems to be needed. Both types of considerations indicate that discretion should be left to trial courts or correctional authorities, with respect both to the type of treatment—fine, imprisonment, probation, or the like—and to its extent or duration.

4. Should the legislature fix the maximum punishment, or the maximum severity of the treatment authorized, for particular types of crimes? Basic considerations of liberty as well as the logic of the aims of the criminal law dictate that it should. Men should not be put to death or imprisoned for a crime unless the legislature has sanctioned the penalty of death or imprisonment for that crime. Even with respect to penalties of an authorized type, the maximum of the permitted fine or term of imprisonment should be fixed by law. Only in this way can the integrity of the legislature's scheme of gradation of offenses and of the underlying principle that penalties should correspond in some fashion to the degree of blameworthiness of defendants' conduct be maintained. Only in this way can room be allowed for the beneficent operation of theories of reformation, while shutting the door to their tendencies toward cruelty.

5. Should the legislature prescribe the *minimum* punishment, or the minimum severity of the treatment to be meted out, for particular types of crimes? The problem here is to make sure that society does not depreciate the gravity of its own judgments of condemnation through the imposition by sentencing judges of disproportionately trivial penalties. Yet, the virtues of individualization have their claims, too. Perhaps a suspended prison sentence, with probation, may be the best form of treatment even for a convicted murderer, as it certainly may be for a convicted manslaughterer. A society which entrusts its juries with power to bring in a verdict of acquittal in cases of undoubted guilt ought to be able to trust its judges to exercise the lesser discretion of leniency in sentencing.

6. In cases in which convicted persons are to be sentenced to a term of

imprisonment, how should power be divided between the sentencing judge (or jury) and prison and parole authorities in determining the actual duration of the incarceration? This question can best be left to be considered when the problems of the criminal law are examined from the point of view of those agencies.

IV
THE PERSPECTIVE OF POLICE AND PROSECUTING ATTORNEYS

To shift from the perspective of the legislature to that of police and prosecuting attorneys is to shift from the point of view of formulation of general directions to that of their application. These law enforcement officers, moreover, have power only to determine how their own functions shall be carried out. Unlike the antecedent determinations of the legislature and the subsequent determinations of courts, their decisions carry no authority as general directions to others for the future. They have a lesser role to play, accordingly, in the conscious shaping of the aims of the criminal law.

Nevertheless, what enforcement officials do is obviously of crucial importance in determining how the criminal law actually works. Their problems and the policies they pursue in trying to solve them need to be studied for the purpose not only of learning how better to control their activities—familiar enough questions—but for the purpose also of a better understanding, which legislatures sadly need, of what responsibilities ought to be given them and of the consequences of unwise imposition of responsibility.

This is not the place to pursue these questions in detail. A few suggestions only will be ventured.

1. The breadth of discretion we entrust to the police and prosecuting attorneys in dealing with individuals is far greater than that entrusted to any other kinds of officials and less subject to effective control. This discretion presents obvious difficulties in securing the lawful and equal administration of law. It presents also less obvious, or less noticed, difficulties of transferring from the legislature to enforcement officials the *de facto* power of determining what the criminal law in action shall be.

2. To the extent that the activities of enforcement officials are confined to securing compliance with what have been described as the basic obligations of responsible citizenship, their discretion will tend to be reduced to the minimum which the necessities of the administration of law admit. If social morale is good, there will be community demand for enforcement of these obligations and community support of it, and it will be feasible to provide an enforcement staff reasonably adequate to its task. Under these circumstances, reliance upon enforcement only on private complaint or newspaper insistence will be minimized. The exercise of discretion by police and prosecutors will consist largely of making specifically professional, and inescapable, judgments concerning the sufficiency of the evidence to warrant further investigation or formal accusation, what charges to make, what pleas to accept, what penalties to ask for, and the like.

3. The stupidity and injustice of the thoughtless multiplication of minor crimes receives its most impressive demonstration in police stations and prosecutors' offices. Invariably, staffs are inadequate for enforcement of all the criminal statutes which the legislature in its unwisdom chooses to enact. Accordingly, many of the statutes go largely unenforced. To this extent, their enactment is rendered futile. But it proves also to be worse than futile. For statutes usually do not become a complete dead letter. What happens is that they

are enforced sporadically, either as a matter of deliberate policy to proceed only on private complaint, or as a matter of the accident of what comes to official attention or is forced upon it. Sporadic enforcement is an instrument of tyranny when enforcement officers are dishonest. It has an inescapable residuum of injustice in the hands even of the best-informed officers. A selection for prosecution among equally guilty violators entails not only inequality, but the exercise, necessarily, of an unguided and, hence, unprincipled discretion.

4. While the evils just described are common in the enforcement of most minor crimes, they are at their most acute in the sphere of regulation of conduct which is not intrinsically wrongful, and there a special phenomenon is likely to develop. Even though he ought not to seek the power in advance, a conscientious prosecutor, faced with the fact of more violators than he can prosecute, is likely to single out for prosecution those whom he regards as morally blameworthy, in default of any better basis of selection. Thus, he will negate the legislative judgment that all violators should be prosecuted, regardless of moral blame. But at the same time, he will create a *de facto* crime, the main element of which is withdrawn from proof or disproof by due process of law.

5. In the area of traditional crimes, enforcement officials have an opportunity to put the dominant aim of the criminal law to inculcate understanding of the obligations of responsible citizenship, and to secure compliance with them, into a meaningful relationship with its subsidiary aim of rehabilitating people who have proved themselves to be irresponsible. In the area of regulatory crimes, this is possible only if "wilfulness," as earlier defined, is an ingredient of criminality. The whole concept of curative-rehabilitative treatment has otherwise no relevance in this area.

V
THE PERSPECTIVE OF COURTS IN THE ASCERTAINMENT OF GUILT

Courts look both backward and forward in the application of law. They look backward to the relevant general directions of the Constitution and the statutes, as interpreted and applied in prior judicial decisions. They look backward to the historical facts of the litigation. But when the facts raise issues with respect to which the existing general directions are indeterminate, they are bound to look forward to the ends which the law seeks to serve and to resolve the issues as best they can in a way which will serve them. This, of course, is the strength of the judicial process—that it permits principles to be worked pure and the details of implementing rules and standards to be developed in the light of intensive examination of the interaction of the general with the particular. But it is a strength existing sometimes in the potentiality rather than in the realization. Notably has this been true in this country in the development of the substantive law of crimes.

The inherited criminal law was rich with principles and with potentialities for their reasoned and intelligible development. But the multiplication of statutory crimes and the inadequacy of judicial techniques of interpreting statutes, coupled with unimaginative and unintelligent use even of familiar common-law techniques, have shaken much of the law loose from these moorings.

It is possible to see the beginnings of this development in some unfortunate decisions in the area of customary crimes touching sensitive matters of sex and family law.

A well-known example is that of statutory rape and kindred offenses against immature girls. Here, the courts came widely to hold that when the legislature had specified a fixed age of consent, the man's belief in the girl's age, and even his utmost good faith and reasonableness in holding the belief, were irrelevant. They pictured the legislature, in other words, as saying to mankind: "If you choose to have intercourse with a willing female who may be over or under the age of consent, you will be playing a game with the law as well as with her. If she is of age, you win the law's game. If she is under age, you lose it and will be condemned as a felon, regardless of what she may have told you and regardless of the good reasons you may have had for believing her." When account is taken of the long tradition that ignorance of the fact excuses, it is evident that this interpretation was not a necessary one, if, indeed, it was even plausible. But it seems to have had important influence in encouraging the modern trend toward strict liability.

Similarly, in prosecutions for bigamy, and particularly when the bigamy statute was coupled with a presumption of the death of a missing spouse after a fixed period of unexplained absence, the courts tended to hold that a man or woman who remarried within the statutory period did so at the peril of criminal conviction if the spouse were actually alive. In effect, such courts said: "Good faith and reasonable inquiry have nothing to do with this. We read the legislature's presumption as not merely avoiding the necessity of specific proof of good faith when the presumption is applicable, but as barring such proof when it is inapplicable. We attribute to the legislature a purpose to discourage the remarriage of abandoned spouses as socially impolitic, by requiring those who attempt it to take a gambler's chance of becoming a criminal." Once again, obviously, the interpretation was not a necessary one. And once again, currency was given to the notion that people can commit crimes without really doing anything wrong at all.

Closely and vitally related to the failure of American courts to develop adequate principles of criminal liability and an adequate theory of the aims of the criminal law as guides in the interpretation of statutes has been their failure to come to grips with the underlying constitutional issues involved. This failure is the more surprising because of the obvious concern of the Constitution to safeguard the use of the method of the criminal law—especially, but not exclusively, on the procedural side—and the concern of the courts themselves, particularly in recent times, to give vitality to the procedural guarantees. What sense does it make to insist upon procedural safeguards in criminal prosecutions if anything whatever can be made a crime in the first place? What sense does it make to prohibit ex post facto laws (to take the one explicit guarantee of the Federal Constitution on the substantive side) if a man can, in any event, be convicted of an infamous crime for inadvertent violation of a prior law of the existence of which he had no reason to know and which he had no reason to believe he was violating, even if he had known of its existence?

Despite the unmistakable indications that the Constitution means something definite and something serious when it speaks of "crime," the Supreme Court of the United States has hardly got to first base in working out what that something is. From beginning to end, there is scarcely a single opinion by any member of the Court which confronts the question in a fashion which deserves intellectual respect. The Court began with a few dicta suggesting that a crime is anything which the legislature chooses to say it is. These were followed by a pair of narcotics cases, patently concerned with the evils of drugs rather than with the evil of disloyalty to a millennium of legal tradition. Then came, only a few

years ago, one of the most drastic of the Court's decisions, treating the whole matter as a *fait accompli.* Not until the last term, in *Lambert v. California,* did the Court discover that the due process clauses had anything to say about branding innocent people as criminals. But neither the majority nor the dissenting opinion in that case is persuasive of any need to qualify the second sentence in this paragraph.

The *Lambert* case involved a Los Angeles ordinance making it a criminal offense for any "convicted person," as defined, to be and remain in the city for more than five days without registering. The Court held that the application of this ordinance to one who had no actual or "probable" knowledge of it violated the due process clause of the fourteenth amendment. Yet, four members of the Court dissented. They were led by so sensitive a judge as Mr. Justice Frankfurter, who, pointing to the large body of legislation which he believed to be put in question by the majority's reasoning, expressed his confidence "that the present decision will turn out to be an isolated deviation from the strong current of precedents—a derelict on the waters of the law."

The opinion of the Court by Mr. Justice Douglas pinned its holding upon the fact that the conduct condemned by the ordinance was "wholly passive" and "unlike the commission of acts, or the failure to act under circumstances that should alert the doer to the consequences of his deed." Yet, it made no effort to analyze the nature of crimes of omission, as distinguished from those of commission. It spoke vaguely of "the requirement of notice" as "engrained in our concept of Due Process." But it cited only inapposite cases, left the unexplained suggestion that notice making for "probable" personal knowledge would be enough, and wholly ignored the fact that the theretofore unqualified doctrine of Anglo-American law has been that notice by due promulgation and publication of a statute is all that is required. On the issue of criminal intent, the opinion said that "we do not go with Blackstone in saying that 'a vicious will' is necessary to constitute a crime." More atrocious even than the rhetoric of this statement is its moral insensitivity and the intellectual inadequacy of the reasoning offered to support it. Why the views of Blackstone should be thus cavalierly overridden in interpreting a Constitution written by men who accepted his pronouncements as something approaching gospel was left unexplained. What the essential distinction is between those states of innocence which permit conviction of crime and those which do not was left to guesswork.

The dissenting opinion did not have the virtue even of the majority's muddy recognition that being a "criminal" must mean something. It contented itself with flat assertion that human beings may be convicted of crime under the Constitution of the United States even though they "May have had no awareness of what the law required or that what they did was wrongdoing." To this, one can say only, "Why? why? why?" The opinion gives only one answer, "So it has been decided. So it has been decided. So it has been decided." The replication has to be, "But this is wrong, wrong, wrong. And it will continue to be wrong so long as words have meaning and human beings have the capacity to recognize and the courage to resent bitter and unwarranted insult."

The importance of constitutional doctrine is not to be measured by the number of statutes formally invalidated pursuant to it or formally sustained against direct attack. Thinking in constitutional terms provides the points of reference which are necessary in building up a body of thought which is adequate to the task of statutory interpretation. Correspondingly, the absence of such basic thinking is likely to result in a hiatus of thought when interpretive problems present themselves. Thus, the small handful of pre-*Lambert* decisions upholding the constitutionality of strict criminal liability helped to breed a multitude of other decisions blandly assuming, with no effort at ratiocination, that it was a matter of indifference whether ambiguous statutory language were to be read as importing a requirement of "criminal" intent or dispensing with it, and permitting slight evidence to tilt the scales in favor of dispensation. Correspondingly, what will be chiefly important to watch about the *Lambert* case will be the strength of the push it gives to interpretations insisting upon the necessity of a genuinely criminal intent. One may guess that the push would have been stronger if the majority opinion had been more muscularly written.

What are likely to be crucial in the development of any body of statutory law are the presumptions with which courts approach debatable issues of interpretation. For it is these presumptions which control decision when a legislature has failed to address itself to an issue and to express itself unmistakably about it. If the interpretive presumptions of the courts are founded on principles and policies rationally related to the ultimate purposes of the social order, then statutory law will tend to develop the coherence and intelligibility, and the susceptibility to being reasoned about, which a body of unwritten law tends always to have. Otherwise, it will tend to become a wasteland of arbitrary distinctions and meaningless detail.

Legislatures in our tradition have depended heavily upon the assistance of courts in giving statutory law this kind of in-built rationality. The articulation and use of interpretive presumptions by the courts is an essential means of providing this assistance. It involves no impairment of legislative prerogative, but, on the contrary, facilitates the legislature's work rather than hinders it. It serves to focus issues, to sharpen responsibilities, and to discourage buck-passing. It gives assurance that a legislature's departure from generally prevailing principles and policies will be a considered one. This, in turn, requires the courts to confront the resulting constitutional questions, if any, with recognition of the deliberateness of the legislature's determination and of the need for taking full account of the reasons for the determination before overturning it.

The need of some improvement in the shoddy and little-minded thinking of American legislatures about the problems of the criminal law is great. But adequate improvement cannot come from that source alone. Only if the courts acknowledge their obligation to collaborate with the legislature in discerning and expressing the unifying principles and aims of the criminal law is it likely that a coherent and worthy body of penal law will ever be developed in this country. For the most part, American courts have, thus far, failed not only in the fulfillment, but even in the recognition of this obligation.

VI
THE PERSPECTIVE OF COURTS IN MAKING DECISIONS ABOUT TREATMENT

When an offender has been found guilty, the court's responsibility for the generalized statement of substantive legal doctrine is at an end. What ordinarily remains is only an individualized determination with respect to this particular defendant. This focus upon the defendant as an individual provides opportunities to be exploited. But it also points up tendencies to be resisted. For the defendant is a character in a much larger drama, and questions about his needs must not be allowed to push out of view questions about the effect of his treatment on other persons and on the well-being of society generally.

A. The Judgment of Conviction

If criminality is to be equated with antisocial conduct warranting the moral condemnation of society, then plainly the first and foremost function of the trial judge in every case, when a finding of guilty has been made, is to express to the defendant with all possible solemnity a judgment of condemnation of his conduct in society's behalf.

The trial judge, of course, can do this under existing law, as many do, when the defendant's offense is one which the community recognizes as blameworthy. But here we meet another of the hidden costs of the sacrifice of principle. For a conscientious judge who is called upon constantly to convict and to sentence defendants who have been guilty of bad luck more than anything else is forced to differentiate. Since he cannot, in honesty, tell such a defendant that his conduct is morally blameworthy, he is forced to draw a line among criminal defendants. This is not like drawing a line between genuinely criminal offenses of varying degrees of gravity. For this differentiation puts in question the very integrity and meaning of the concept of crime. The result may be that even the judge himself stops believing in the equation between criminality and blameworthiness.

A distinguished federal district judge said recently in private conversation that in entering judgments of conviction and passing sentence, he was careful always to refrain from expressing any view about the defendant's character or the morality of his conduct. One can respect the spirit of personal humility that lies behind this restraint. One can discern the main outlines of the supporting rationalization which the positivistic strain in American legal thought provides. One can understand why it is particularly easy for a federal judge, dealing with a considerably larger proportion of regulatory crimes than most state judges, to take such a view. Yet, it has still to be said that the practice described epitomizes the moral and intellectual debility of American criminal law. An able and sensitive judge does not consider that there is any difference between a criminal conviction and a civil judgment which it is worth while to try to communicate to the defendant. If this is so, what attention can ordinary people be expected to pay to the threat of a criminal as distinguished from a civil sanction?

The result, considered simply from the point of view of efficient social engineering, is a grievous waste. For all except the most hardened criminals, a judgment of community condemnation, solemnly and impersonally expressed, can be made a shaking and unforgettable experience. If legislatures had kept clean the concept of crime and sentencing judges were then enabled to tell a convicted criminal, in good conscience, that his conduct had been wrongful and deserved the condemnation of his fellow men, the very pronouncement of such a judgment would go far to serve the purposes of the criminal law by vindicating its threats and so to lessen the need for resort to other commonly less effective and invariably more expensive and oppressive forms of treatment.

B. The Sentence: Herein Also of the
Perspective of Prison and Parole Authorities

A judgment of conviction having been entered, the trial judge must next face the harsh realities of imposition of sentence.

If what has been said is correct, the judge, in doing this, should be guided by two main, and interrelated, objectives. First, is the overriding necessity of a sentence which, taken together with the judgment of conviction itself, adequately expresses the community's view of the gravity of the defendant's misconduct. Second, is the necessity of a sentence which will be as favorable as possible consistently with the first objective, to the defendant's rehabilitation as a responsible and functioning member of his community. The first objective stresses the interests of the community; but it does not ignore the interests of the defendant as an individual, since his rehabilitation requires his recognition of community interests and of the obligations of community life. The second stresses the interests of the defendant as an individual; but it does not ignore those of the community, since the community is interested in the defendant's realization of his potentialities as a human being and in the contributions he can make to community life.

The community's condemnation of the defendant's conduct can be expressed in four main ways: *first*, by the legislature's prior grading and characterization, in general terms, of the offense of which he has been found guilty; *second*, by the trial judge's formal expression of condemnation of the particular conduct, taking into account all the special circumstances of it; *third*, by a determination that the defendant shall be vulnerable to unpleasant consequences *in the future* if his behavior thereafter fails to conform to prescribed conditions; and, *fourth*, by a determination that the defendant shall *presently* and forthwith undergo unpleasant consequences, such as fine or imprisonment. Under modern statutes, the judge's exercise of discretion in sentencing will consist largely of choices about the use to be made of the third and fourth forms of condemnation. This paper will not attempt a detailed analysis of the judge's problems in making these choices, but a few broad suggestions in line with the general thesis of the paper may be appropriately made.

1. It is first to be observed that the best possibilities of an imaginative and effective reconciliation of the community's interests and the individual's in fixing sentences will lie ordinarily in the use of the third of the forms of condemnation just described. To declare that the defendant is to be vulnerable to future punishment can be, in itself, an impressive expression of the community's moral disapproval. At the same time, the conditional suspension of the punishment, whether it be a fine or term of imprisonment, can provide an environment favorable to rehabilitation, both by conveying to the defendant a sense of the community's confidence in his ability to live responsibly and by giving him a special incentive to do so. It would seem to follow that a suspended sentence with probation should be the preferred form of treatment, to be chosen always unless the circumstances plainly call for greater severity.

2. Of all the forms of treatment of criminals, prison sentences are the most costly to the community not only because of the out-of-pocket expenses of prison care, but because of the danger that the effect on the defendant's character will be debilitating rather than rehabilitating. It would seem to follow that if some form of present punishment is called for, a fine should always be the preferred form of the penalty, unless the circumstances plainly call for a prison sentence.

3. Once it is decided that a defendant should be sent to prison, a problem arises about the division of authority and responsibility between the sentencing court and the parole authorities in deciding the time of the prisoner's release— assuming, that is, that the view earlier advanced is accepted that prison sentences ought not to be for a fixed term, neither more nor less. The first aspect of this problem relates to the minimum length of the term. It was earlier urged that the legislature ought not to specify a fixed minimum term in such a way as to

deprive the sentencing judge of power to give a suspended sentence. But this was for the reason that the judge ought to have an opportunity to appraise the blameworthiness of the crime in the light of the particular circumstances of it. Should the judge, having made this appraisal, be empowered to fix a minimum prison term in such a way as to deprive the parole authorities of discretion to order an earlier release? Obviously, the judge is better qualified than the parole authorities to interpret the community's views of the blameworthiness of the defendant's conduct. Prima facie, therefore, it would seem that he ought to have the power to fix a minimum term, although the power should be used with caution, since its exercise will deprive the prisoner of an opportunity by his behavior in prison to justify an earlier parole.

4. Should the sentencing judge also have power to fix a maximum term shorter than the statutory maximum so as to deprive the parole authorities of discretion to keep the prisoner in confinement for the full statutory term? Undoubtedly there will be cases in which extenuating circumstances make the conduct of a guilty defendant less blameworthy than that of the general run of those who commit the same type of crime. This suggests that the judge, as the community's representative, should have the power to recognize these special circumstances in some fashion, either in his judgment of conviction or in his sentence. Yet, it will be observed that whereas the minimum term has the sole function of seeing that the community's condemnation of the defendant's conduct is adequately expressed, different, or at least additional, considerations enter into the fixing of the maximum term. The statutory maximum has as its prime function the fixing of a limit upon the period during which the prisoner may be subjected to administrative control. Judicial power to lower this maximum may be less essential than judicial power to see to the adequate expression of community disapproval.

5. In relation to both of the two points last made, a further and vitally important aspect of the problem of sentencing needs to be taken into account—namely, the necessity of avoiding anarchical inequality in the sentences handed down by different sentencing judges. The achievement of the purposes of the criminal law can never be satisfactorily approximated until this intractable problem is in some fashion reduced to minor, instead of major, proportions. The very ideal of justice is offended by seriously unequal penalties for substantially similar crimes, and the most immediate of its practical purposes are obstructed. Grievous inequalities in sentences are ruinous to prison discipline. And they destroy the prisoner's sense of having been justly dealt with, which is the first prerequisite of his personal reformation. Experience seems to show that large numbers of sentencing judges with power to fix both individualized minimum terms and individualized maximum terms will inevitably produce an indefensible heterogeneity of result. How can a reasonable degree of order be brought into this chaos?

6. Legal experience gives a relatively precise answer to the question just put. Consistency of result in similar cases can be secured either by the laying down of quite precise rules of decision (which here seems impossible), or by subjecting heterogeneous discretionary decisions to review and revision by a single tribunal, or in both ways. Appellate courts seem ill-adapted to the function of reviewing and revising the sentences of trial judges, besides being too preoccupied with other functions. The creation of a new authority, with the single responsibility of equalizing sentences initially imposed, to the end of assuring that they reflect uniform concepts of degrees of blameworthiness, is a tempting possibility. Short

of this expedient, the only institutional machinery presently available in most American legal systems is the parole board.

7. In an ideal system, perhaps, prison and parole authorities would receive prisoners from trial courts with sentences for predetermined, individualized maximum and, when appropriate, minimum terms. The correctional authorities would then have the sole responsibility of custody and treatment of each prisoner, with an eye single to determining, within those limits, first, what kind of custodial treatment would best promote the individual prisoner's growth in responsibility; and, second, when, after the minimum sentence, if any, had been served, growth had progressed to a point which made it proper to permit the prisoner to resume, on parole, the effort at responsible living. But if such a regime is to work effectively, prisoners must have some sense of reasonable equality, and hence justice, in the terms under which they are asked to work out their salvation. In the existing institutional structure, and in any alternative structure which seems feasible, parole boards seem to be the agency best qualified to take responsibility for bringing about this sense of equality. Occasional minimum sentences which have the special justification already indicated, would not seriously interfere with the discharge of this responsibility. But regular, judicially-tailored maximum sentences would.

THE STATE AND THE ACCUSED: BALANCE OF ADVANTAGE IN CRIMINAL PROCEDURE

ABRAHAM S. GOLDSTEIN

The principal objective of criminal procedure, like that of procedure generally, is to assure a just disposition of the dispute before the court. But because time, resources and the ability to determine what is just are limited, a procedural system inevitably represents a series of compromises. Justice to society is sometimes taken to require that a given case be used not only to deal with the situation immediately before the court but also to serve a larger public interest. In criminal cases, the accused may get relief, not so much out of concern for him or for the "truth," but because he is strategically located, and motivated, to call the attention of the courts to excesses in the administration of criminal justice. The underlying premise is that of a social utilitarianism. If the criminal goes free in order to serve a larger and more important end, then social justice is done, even if individual justice is not. For example, if the police beat an offender in order to extract a confession, the social interest is held to require that the confession be excluded from evidence, even if amply corroborated. The same is true, in varying extents in the several states, when evidence is illegally seized, or telephones "tapped," or counsel denied, or jurors selected improperly, or judges biased. In each of these cases, terminating the proceeding against the accused, regardless of his guilt or innocence, shifts the focus of deterrence from the accused to his prosecutors.

Though this idealized conception of procedure, as a means of shaping institutions involved in the administration of substantive law, has a place in civil cases as well as in criminal, it shows up most clearly and dramatically in the criminal cases. The reasons are several: the threat of imprisonment makes the criminal sanction an especially grave and terrifying one; an inherited tradition, reflected in constitutional law, makes more specific requirements for criminal cases than it does for civil; there is a general feeling that most cases find state and defendant mismatched—with the state having far the better of it in prestige and resources; and perhaps most important of all, the criminal trial serves complex psychological functions. In addition to satisfying the public demand for retribution and deterrence, it permits the ready identification of the same public, now in another mood, with the plight of the accused. Both demand and identification root deep in the view that all men are offenders, at least on a psychological level. And from the moment the offender is perceived as a surrogate self, this identification calls for a "fair trial" for him before he is punished, as we would have it for ourselves.

For centuries, the criminal trial has been held out as the most distinctive embodiment of societal interest in the "process" of administering law. In the presumption of innocence accorded the accused, in the requirement that the state prove him guilty beyond reasonable doubt, in the elaborate pretrial

Reprinted by permission of The Yale Law Journal Company and Fred B. Rothman & Company from *The Yale Law Journal,* Vol. 69, pp. 1149–1199.

evidentiary screens—arrest, preliminary hearing, and grand jury—through which the charge had to pass, in the rigorous pleading and evidentiary standards of the trial itself, it had given detailed content to an accusatorial system. By doing so, this formal system of criminal procedure had effectively resisted the seemingly inexorable logic which had, on the Continent, made state control of prosecution synonymous with reliance upon the accused as the principal source of the evidence against himself.

In the past generation, perhaps out of a feeling that our formal system of criminal procedure is more than adequate, the interest of the courts and commentators has shifted to other areas, usually constitutional in nature. Chief among them have been the problems of police excess in interrogation, search and seizure and wiretapping; the assurance of counsel to all; and the creation of an effective system of appeal for the indigent. Unfortunately, during the very period when tremendous strides were being made in dealing with these newly recognized problems, the bastion itself—the formal system of criminal procedure—was being eroded. In a series of "technical" decisions, each dealing in fragmentary fashion with limited parts of the total process, widespread changes were being wrought. These changes were designed to correct a serious imbalance allegedly existing in a process which gave to the accused "every advantage." In the words of a leading spokesman for the position, Judge Learned Hand in *United States v. Garsson:*

> While the prosecution is held rigidly to the charge, [the accused] need not disclose the barest outline of his defense. He is immune from question or comment on his silence; he cannot be convicted when there is the least fair doubt in the minds of any one of the twelve. . . . Our dangers do not lie in too little tenderness to the accused. Our procedure has been always haunted by the ghost of the innocent man convicted. It is an unreal dream. What we need to fear is the archaic formalism and the watery sentiment that obstructs, delays, and defeats the prosecution of crime.

This "hard-boiled" and "modern" view of criminal procedure has come to affect a myriad of issues in criminal cases, such as the place of the presumption of innocence; how much variance is fatal and how much not; how closely the grand and petit jury should be supervised by the courts; the scope of harmless error and plain error; and, perhaps most important, the availability of pretrial discovery of issues and evidence. It has done so principally by measuring the "formal" criminal procedure against its more efficient and flexible civil counterpart.

If Judge Hand's view represented an accurate appraisal of the formal system of criminal procedure, it would be difficult to join issue with his conclusion, except on broad philosophical grounds. But the fact is that his view does not accurately represent the process. Both doctrinally and practically, criminal procedure, as presently constituted, does not give the accused "every advantage" but, instead, gives overwhelming advantage to the prosecution. The real effect of the "modern" approach has been to aggravate this condition by loosening standards of pleading and proof without introducing compensatory safeguards earlier in the process. Underlying this development has been an inarticulate, albeit clearly operative, rejection of the presumption of innocence in favor of a presumption of guilt.

The purpose of this Article is to examine in some detail the two major problems of the criminal trial following indictment—that of the sufficiency of evidence to take a criminal case to the jury and that of disclosure, by prosecution and defense, of the issues and evidence to be presented by them at the trial. Each of the problems will be placed in the context of the entire process, principally in order to determine the lines which reform should take before it can become realistic to talk of removing "advantage" to the accused from the system.

PROOF BEYOND REASONABLE DOUBT

When the jury system first evolved in the seventeenth century into a method of trial by fact-witnesses, the procedural rights of the defendant were few in number. He had no right to counsel or even to a copy of the indictment against him. The freest use was made by the state of admissions elicited from him before trial, often under torture or the threat of it. And hearsay was regularly used as a means of establishing guilt. Before the century was out, there was added to these disadvantages the incompetency, because of interest, of the accused as a witness in his own behalf. Fairly clearly, the dominant strain in such a system of trial was the assumption that the accused was guilty and that it was of great importance to the state to prove him so.

Such an approach may well have served the needs of an expanding national state seeking to conserve its new gains and to deter as forcefully as possible any and all challenges to its authority. But with the consolidation of those gains in the eighteenth century, what had previously seemed essential instruments became oppressive ones. Grand and petit juries stepped into the breach. By refusing to return indictments or to find defendants guilty, they succeeded in considerable part in forcing a redress of the imbalance in favor of the state. And their actions directed attention to the substantive and procedural inadequacies of the criminal law. A whole series of institutions and practices, designed to safeguard the person accused of crime, appeared in response, principally in the nineteenth century. The spirit underlying these new developments was perhaps best reflected in the rule that the accused brought with him a "presumption of innocence" and that his guilt must be proved "beyond a reasonable doubt." Those two phrases symbolize today, as they did in their beginnings, the special place of the accused in our system of criminal procedure. They cast in evocative language the deeply-held feeling that the combination of all-too-fallible witnesses and serious sanctions requires that the sanctions should be imposed only where guilt seems virtually certain. They also suggest substantial advantage to the defendant and disadvantage to the prosecution. Yet, on analysis, it soon becomes clear that the degree of advantage or disadvantage depends upon the use to which those words are put. Those uses have been undergoing substantial change.

Conventionally, the phrases appear in the trial judge's instructions to the jury, much as they did a century ago. The jury is told that the defendant is presumed innocent; that the mere fact that he has been charged with crime is not to be taken as evidence against him; and that his guilt must be proved beyond reasonable doubt. Now and then, controversy has arisen about whether the presumption of innocence is to be treated by the jury as "evidence," or whether it is reversible error to omit all reference to the presumption or to water it down, or whether "proof beyond reasonable doubt" may be entirely eliminated from the charge. For the most part, however, there has been little tampering with either phrase at the jury stage. Whatever inroads have been made are found in the criteria fashioned by the courts to decide the question of sufficiency of evidence to take the case to the jury.

These criteria are applied by the trial judge in passing upon the motion for a judgment of acquittal at the close of the prosecution's case, or at the close of the entire case, or after the jury has returned its verdict. With rare exceptions, they are also used by the appellate court in deciding whether the trial judge erred in sending the case to the jury. The decision of trial and appellate judge is ordinarily described as a decision on a matter of law: Did the prosecution offer "enough" evidence to enable the jury to act rationally? Or, to use Judge Frank's terminology, is there enough F (facts) to permit application of R (rule of law)? The jury's decision is contrasted to that of the judge and is said to be on an issue of fact. Yet both, fairly clearly, involve a sifting of the evidence.

The judge sifts to delimit a zone within which the jury may act. He must take all facts offered in evidence by the prosecution as true and from those facts he must draw all reasonable inferences in favor of the prosecution. When, therefore, X testifies that he saw the accused aim at and shoot Y, and there is no question of defense or justification, the trial judge has no alternative but to submit the case to the jury, unless X or his testimony are inherently incredible. In this context of direct evidence of each element of the offense, the presumption of innocence means no more than that the prosecution must go forward first with the evidence and that the fact of indictment should not be taken as in any way determinative of guilt. "Proof beyond a reasonable doubt" can then mean only that the jury should be very certain that X is telling the truth—though it may also be viewed as a form of words inviting the jury to exercise its inherent power to dispense with law.

But when the prosecution's case, or any essential element of it, is built on circumstantial evidence, the role of the trial judge (and of the appellate court on review) in passing upon the sufficiency of evidence becomes much more significant. By definition, circumstantial evidence requires the assistance of an inference to make it probative of guilt. The handkerchief located at the scene of the crime must first be found to belong to the defendant; it must then be inferred, or proved, that it was in his possession at the time of the crime. There then remain the problems of placing the defendant at the scene of the crime at the time it was committed; and of making him the criminal, rather than a casual bystander. To the extent that a case is built up of a series of fragments of this kind, the trial judge may follow one of several courses: he may leave for the jury the problem of drawing inferences from each item of evidence, limiting his role to little more than ascertaining that there is "some" evidence of each element of the offense; or he may make an effort to trace inferences, or a sequence of inferences, flowing from each item of evidence to the point of determining whether it could be adopted by a rational man; or he may incorporate the standard of ultimate persuasion into the legal test of sufficiency of evidence. For example, in the civil context, he would try to assess whether the evidence is such that a reasonable jury could find it to preponderate in favor of the party bearing the burden of proof; in the criminal case, he would test the evidence to determine whether a reasonable jury could find that guilt had been proved beyond reasonable doubt.

Whichever approach is adopted, it seems fairly clear that none of the tests can be applied with precision or with confidence that any of them will materially affect the decision in any given case. Judges are too varied in personality, in perception, in analytical ability, and in their conception of themselves to make such abstract tests serve reliably in the many fact situations to which they will be applied. "The authoritative language of nice and scientific precision in which such conclusions are cast is after all only the language of delusive exactness. . . . [T]hroughout the field of circumstantial proof there is not a little room for considerations of policy and expediency to play a part in choosing between two very fallible and equally undemonstrable generalizations about the balance of probability."

It is precisely because "policy and expediency" do play a part in the decision whether to keep cases from the jury that the forms of words in which the legal tests are cast can be said to be important. The shade of meaning connoted by a word or phrase is itself a statement of policy which may tip the scales in the direction of acquittal or of further exposure to conviction. Whether the shades inherent in either the "presumption of innocence" or "proof beyond a reasonable doubt" shall be used is the substantive problem posed by cases dealing with sufficiency of evidence.

Almost from the time judges began to determine the sufficiency of the evidence in criminal cases, a development little more than a century old, they have included the standard of ultimate persuasion as part of their criterion of sufficiency. The earliest and the most common of the formulae is that set out in *Isbell v. United States,* holding it to be the trial judge's function to assure that the jury could reasonably find that the evidence of the prosecution negated "every other hypothesis but that of guilt." In effect, such a formula places both "presumption of innocence" and "proof beyond reasonable doubt" in the legal test and invites trial judges to give them a place among the "considerations of policy and expediency" inevitably accompanying their decisions in cases based on circumstantial evidence. More recently a formula seemingly less strict, but inclining in the same direction, was set forth in *Curley v. United States.* It imposed upon the judge the obligation to decide whether the prosecution's case would permit reasonable jurymen to conclude guilt beyond reasonable doubt.

The newest look, which promises to be an influential one because of the preeminence of its sponsors, has been developed most systematically by the judges of the Court of Appeals for the Second Circuit. Apparently a part of the correcting process foreshadowed in *Garsson,* it would eliminate from the judge's determination of when a case should be kept from the jury both the concept of "proof beyond reasonable doubt" and the presumption of innocence. Briefly stated, the Second Circuit rule, already followed in several other federal and state jurisdictions, confines "proof beyond reasonable doubt" to the role of an admonition to the jury regarding the assurance it should have before finding a man guilty. The *Isbell* language is permissible so long as its use is confined to the court's instructions to the jury. For the judge ruling on the sufficiency of the evidence, however, there is to be no distinction between civil and criminal cases. If there is substantial circumstantial evidence of each element of the offense, the case is to go to the jury.

The potential difference of the various tests, in application to similar facts, is illustrated by *Barton v. United States* and *Girgenti v. United States,* both of which involved charges of illicit possession or operation of a still. In *Barton,* the defendant and others were arrested just after arriving at the scene of an illegal distillery. Federal officers testified that they had heard the defendants discuss operation of a still, though it was uncertain whether they were discussing this one. In *Girgenti* too, the defendants were arrested when they arrived at the scene of the still. They had in their possession a hydrometer, old clothes and a revolver. The hydrometer was of the type used in testing the specific gravity of liquids heavier than water, particularly alcohol from mash.

The *Barton* court, adopting an approach similar to that of the Second Circuit and affirming a verdict against the defendant, said:

[T]he proximity of the accused to the place of the crime and [to] the unlawful apparatus used in the perpetration, may by a reasonable inference raise the presumption of possession, and that the party so found was guilty of a participation in the crime charged, which required the possession and use of the property. It is entirely a question for a jury whether this inference is ... sufficient to convict the defendant beyond a reasonable doubt.

The *Girgenti* court, apparently following *Isbell*, reversed the conviction and ordered acquittal, saying:

[T]he presence of the appellants at or near the premises where the still was in operation is not sufficient to sustain a conviction on counts charging them with possession of an unreigstered still or the manufacture of mash, in the absence of any testimony that they were in charge of, or were doing work in connection with, the still. The possession of old clothes ... and a revolver is as consistent with innocence of the offenses charged as with guilt. ... The unexplained possession of the hydrometer supports an inference that the appellants were concerned with testing liquor in some form, but was not in itself sufficient evidence to warrant the conclusion that they were connected with the operation of the still in question. To mention but a few of the possibilities, the appellants might have been purchasers of liquor, or sold liquor, or even had some connection with a still other than the one described in the indictment.

If words in opinions can be said to reflect or to shape attitudes, it seems fair to say that the *Isbell* rule, or the *Curley* rule, invite more careful judicial scrutiny of evidence in criminal cases than in civil. In contrast, the Second Circuit rule tells trial judges they are under no obligation to approach criminal cases as involving especially opprobrious or painful sanctions. Criminal prosecutions are not to be viewed as qualitatively different from the usual civil cases, even though society's interest in civil litigation may be no more than to provide an orderly means of resolving disputes.

By removing "proof beyond a reasonable doubt" from the legal test of the sufficiency of evidence, the Second Circuit rule has gone a long way toward completing the work begun by Thayer and Wigmore when they decreed that the "presumption of innocence" was no longer to have any evidentiary significance. For, if that presumption is to be more than a requirement that he who charges liability must prove it, it must be given content by judges in areas subject to their control. The instructions to the jury are, of course, one such area. But far more important, because far more subject to judicial control, is the power to keep cases from the jury. Assertion of that power, with its insistence upon a "fact" role for court as well as jury, serves not only to minimize "convicting the innocent" but also to keep the pressure on judge, prosecutor, and police to act as responsibly as possible in screening out cases not fit for trial. Placing the prestige of the judiciary directly on the scales in favor of strict standards of proof, it announces that the sufficiency of evidence will be ruled upon, deliberately, by a judge and will not simply pass into the anonymity of the general verdict.

Even if societal interests were put to one side and attention confined to the particular case, the serious nature of the criminal sanction would seem to be ample reason for insisting upon standards of proof more rigorous than those which prevail in civil cases. It has already been pointed out that no finding of fact in a case based upon circumstantial evidence is simply an exercise in computing whether there is "enough" evidence. Inevitably, mood and inclination play a considerable part. The perceptions of judge and jury, as witnesses of the witnesses, are as much influenced by the manner of men they are and the attitudes with which they set out to perceive as are the impressions of the witnesses themselves. Why, then, the seeming refusal to concede that the criminal case, being more serious, calls for an admonition to the judge comparable to that addressed to the jury?

The explanation which appears most plausible is that intimated by Thayer. It rests upon the assumption that "natural inference" indicates that he who is charged is guilty. This is, in turn, based upon the seeming plentitude of screens through which the charge against an accused must pass before he can be brought to trial. The large numbers of persons who do not pass through the screens—either because they have pleaded guilty or because there have been findings of insufficient evidence—appear to leave for the trial process only the guilty—indeed, those who are most adamant in denying their guilt. To accord this residuary group the benefit of a standard of proof more rigorous than in civil cases would seem, under the Thayer view, to be both inappropriate and undeserved.

This image represents only a small part of the reality. Largely overlooked in this "model" of the accused at trial are those defendants who deal in "good faith" with the system—those who have factual or legal defenses reasonably believed by them to be valid. From their ranks are drawn a substantial portion of the twenty-three to thirty-six per cent of defendants who actually stand trial and are acquitted. But even more important, in assessing the image, are the very limited protections afforded by the pretrial screening agencies—police, prosecutor, magistrate, and grand jury. The minimal standards of proof employed by these agencies give very little assurance that persons passed on by them to a later screen are indeed guilty of the offenses charged against them.

The Pretrial Screens

Arrest

The screening process begins the moment evidence of conduct designated criminal is discovered by policeman or private party. In the decision to make such conduct the basis of a formal charge, there exists the initial de facto screen which passes some persons further along the path towards ultimate adjudication of guilt or innocence, while taking others out of it. This decision first finds itself subjected to judicial scrutiny when the police officer seeks a warrant of arrest from a magistrate. If the officer arrests without a warrant, as he may for serious offenses, his decision will not be reviewed until the arrest has been consummated and its legality challenged. In both situations, the nature of the showing required of the officer is substantially the same. The arrest is legal if it is made upon "probable cause"—information which would have moved a reasonable man, under the circumstances, to believe that the crime in question had occurred and that it was committed by the accused. When the arresting officer is himself an eye-witness, no substantial problem arises. But when he acts on the basis of information supplied by others, his decision involves an embryo adjudication. He must weigh the probative value of the information, make judgments about the credibility of his informants, balance the probabilities, and determine the extent to which deviational conduct should be tolerated and law nullified.

The courts take note of the preliminary nature of the policeman's adjudication by requiring less formal, and less credible, evidence to validate his judgment than they require of the subsequent, more formal, screens. The word of the unidentified informer suffices, for example, if he has been shown to be reliable in the past. The lateness of the hour, the shape of the bag being carried, the reports of crimes in the neighborhood, the criminal records of the persons involved—all are permitted a weight in this determination which they would not receive at the trial itself. Such loose standards are entirely consistent with the primary concern of the police, at this early stage, which is to investigate, not adjudicate. But for that very reason, even the best enforced police evidentiary "screen" cannot be treated as a substantial one.

What makes the process of arrest even less rigorous a screen than it might be is the extent to which the illegal arrest may go unchallenged. Between the time of arrest and the appearance before a magistrate at a preliminary hearing (on the question of bail and of "probable cause" to hold for further proceedings), the alleged offender ordinarily need not be informed of his right to counsel, nor allowed access to counsel if he asks for it, nor supplied with counsel if he is indigent. If he does have counsel who knows of his arrest, a petition for habeas corpus might conceivably bring his release; but it is far more likely that he will have to defer his challenge until the preliminary hearing. In any event, since most persons arrested for crime neither know their rights nor have ready access to a lawyer, the deterrent effect of this remedy upon the illegal arrest is bound to be slight. The same is true, for a variety of reasons, of the civil suit for false arrest.

The Preliminary Hearing

Pressure on the arresting officer to act responsibly in screening the charges of crime would ordinarily come in the preliminary hearing before the magistrate. It is the magistrate who must determine whether the policeman's "reasonable belief," when made visible, constitutes "probable cause" to believe a crime has been committed; or a "prima facie" case; or sufficient evidence to warrant a jury's finding the accused guilty. Almost everywhere, however, the showing is held to be sufficient if the prosecution presents a skeletal outline of evidence admissible in court to support each element of the offense. This skeletal quality is virtually assured by certain grim facts. In most jurisdictions, no provision is made for appointment of counsel at this stage. Neither the due process clause of the fourteenth amendment nor state constitutional provisions have been held to require it. And most states make no statutory provision for appointment of counsel, though a considerable number require that he be advised of his right to retain counsel. Since, therefore, defense counsel is usually either not present, or insufficiently informed to play his role properly, it ordinarily falls to the magistrate, almost alone, to test the sufficiency of the evidence to warrant holding the accused for the grand jury, or for trial where there is no grand jury. Yet, most magistrates are either unskilled, or too busy, or too closely linked with police or prosecutor, or insufficiently mindful of the "judicial" nature of their role to perform this function adequately. And the sole review of the sufficiency of the evidence before them is the limited one afforded by habeas corpus, which looks only for some "legally competent evidence" to support the order committing the accused for trial. But even that is a limited safeguard because the unrepresented, or poorly represented, defendant may not learn until after his trial that there was insufficient evidence at the preliminary hearing to warrant passing the case on to trial. If the case has proceeded to trial, no remedy is available to the accused for the defect in the preliminary hearing. He must then look, on appeal, solely to the inadequacy of the evidence at trial.

In practical effect, therefore, the preliminary hearing in the United States doe⁵ not add significantly to the police evidentiary screen which has preceded it. As in the case of arrest, the point is not to suggest that the screening function of the preliminary hearing should be made more rigorous; or that every "error" requires a remedy. It is merely to indicate first, that the institutions empowered to do the screening job do it in quite limited fashion and, second, that the cumulation of noninterventionist attitudes serves to make very slight indeed the external pressures on policeman, prosecutor and magistrate to act as responsible screens. Entirely too much is left to self-discipline and tradition, which have been notoriously slow in developing in most American police forces and magistracies.

It would be misleading to leave the inference that there are not a substantial number of drop-outs at the arrest and preliminary hearing stages. What is not at all clear, however, is whether they are the result of the formal evidentiary screen, thereby reinforcing the probability of guilt, or whether they derive from something else—for example, the virtually undefined and unreviewable exercise of discretion by police and prosecutor not to proceed further, in accordance with criteria so subjective as to afford no assurance that the rule of law is being applied equally to all.

The Grand Jury

In perhaps half the states, mostly in the West, the preliminary hearing is the last formal screen device before trial. But in the remaining states and in the federal system, the grand jury stands as yet another screen. Though it may serve as an initiator of investigation and accusation, by far the greatest proportion of matters coming before it has already passed through arrest and preliminary hearing.

The grand jury is unquestionably the most celebrated of the pre-trial screening devices. Originally conceived as an extension of the royal authority over the citizen, it reached its greatest glory as a barrier against the state, refusing to indict for crime where the evidence was inadequate or the law creating the crime unpopular. During the nineteenth century, a great many jurisdictions set about to "judicialize" the grand jury proceeding, principally because the return of an indictment, without more, was recognized as bringing serious extra-legal sanctions with it. Beginning with a hearing restricted to the prosecution's case alone, with a firm ban on calling the defendant or his witnesses, most states soon authorized the grand jury to hear them if it chose. A considerable number enacted statutes providing that the grand jury was to hear only "legal evidence," or that it "ought" to indict only on the basis of such evidence. And those requirements were frequently enforced through the granting of motions to quash indictments based on no evidence at all, or no evidence as to an element of the crime, or "utterly insufficient" evidence. The nature of the judicial inquiry tended to resemble the manner in which courts now review the action of administrative agencies—to ascertain whether they are acting within the limits of their authority. The net effect of this development was to impose upon the prosecution the obligation to proceed more cautiously and circumspectly with the business of prosecuting crime than it might otherwise have done.

In the late '20's and early '30's, a complete change in judicial attitude toward the grand jury took place. There came to be increasing feeling, manifested most clearly in the report of the Wickersham Commission, that the grand jury was an inefficient "rubber stamp" for the prosecutor who conceived its investigations, directed its secret proceedings, and drafted its indictment.

Apart from its subpoena authority, which could conceivably be better lodged with the prosecutor who exercised the power de facto, the grand jury hearing seemed to serve no useful purpose. The adjudication of probable guilt would have to be made again by a petit jury after a fuller and fairer hearing than the grand jury could possibly provide. And besides, there was the preliminary hearing, which could be used to do the screening job hitherto done by the grand jury. There came to be increasing reluctance on the part of the courts to examine the sufficiency of the evidence before the grand jury. That body became its own judge of the kind of evidence it would hear and the amount and quality of evidence it would require for indictment.

United States v. Costello placed the imprimatur of the Supreme Court upon this conception of the grand jury. The Court held that an indictment based completely upon hearsay evidence is neither defective, dismissible on motion, nor ground for reversal of a conviction. The attempt by Justice Burton to place his concurrence on a narrower ground—that the hearsay was clearly reliable—and the failure of the Court to incorporate that ground into its opinion, indicated strongly that, henceforth, the federal grand jury was to police itself. Except for their very limited relationship to it before and during the proceedings, courts were no longer to interfere if the grand jury was "legally constituted and unbiased." The reason for this approach, fairly clearly stated in Costello, is that the accused will get his fair, "judicial," hearing at his trial. Due process, and the Supreme Court, require no more. Stated in somewhat more rhetorical fashion, why protect the defendant at the grand jury stage against an indictment based on little or no evidence when the exacting standards of the trial process will make such indictments meaningless?

The Relationships Among the Screens

In sum, the evidentiary standards of the pretrial screening process, implicitly relied upon by trial and appellate courts as a basis for relaxing trial standards, have themselves been relaxed in reliance upon the assumed vigor of the trial process. It by no means follows, however, that the pretrial process should be "judicialized" to assure that only the "really guilty" come to trial. Though a tightening of the screens might well decrease the danger that innocent men would be convicted, it might also distort other functions, such as investigation, which are perhaps equally important.

The point, simply stated, is that: the looseness of the pretrial screens makes questionable the move toward abandonment of the traditionally strict trial standards called for in Isbell and Curley. Only if the criminal sanction were to lose the special stigma associated with it in our society, or if the threat of imprisonment did not loom ominously in the background, or if there had been fewer instances in our history of conviction of innocent persons, would it be appropriate to treat the question of sufficiency of evidence in criminal trials in the same manner as in civil trials.

DISCLOSURE

Increased reliance upon the trial as the principal device for protecting the accused makes it imperative that the defense come to trial as well equipped as the prosecution to raise "doubt in the minds of any one of the twelve" men in the jury box. Particularly in a system based, as is ours, upon a single trial held on a single occasion, the parties must come to trial prepared to make the most of their presentation on that occasion. It is crucial, therefore, to determine which of the parties is specially advantaged by the system of disclosure currently employed. In Judge Hand's view, it will be recalled, the accused enjoys every advantage. Not only is the prosecution handicapped by the obligation to prove guilt beyond "the least fair doubt," it is further hampered in assembling the evidence to satisfy the obligation. "While the prosecution is held rigidly to the charge, . . . [the accused] need not disclose the barest outline of his defense. He is immune from question or comment on his silence. . . ."

Judge Hand is undoubtedly correct in tying proof of guilt or innocence to the problem of disclosure of issues and evidence. But he is quite wrong in his assessment of where the advantage lies. It has probably always been with the state, and is becoming even more so. Increasingly, the prosecution is being freed from restrictions on pleading and proof while the defendant and his case are, and always have been, far more accessible to the prosecution than Judge Hand's polemic would have it. To evaluate argument and counter-argument, it will be necessary to place the problem of disclosure in the perspective of the entire criminal procedural process, much as has been done with the problem of screening baseless charges.

"The Prosecution Is Held Rigidly to the Charge"

That persons accused of crime should be put on notice of the charge against them is fundamental in both a procedural and a substantive sense. Notice serves not only to assure maximal participation by the parties in the adversary trial but also to aid in fulfilling the function of that trial—deterring others from committing like crimes and instilling remorse in persons found guilty of the crime charged. Until fairly recently, notice (or disclosure) was afforded the accused by a series of devices. The indictment had to be drawn with precision; it could neither be explicitly amended nor would any variance be permitted between its allegations and the proof offered to support them. Only one offense could be charged in each count. If there were more, the count was "bad for duplicity."

These technical doctrines represented fairly crude devices for assuring that the decision of the magistrate or grand jury would be given effect—that, for example, the decision not to charge for larceny by trick but instead to charge for obtaining property by false pretenses would be respected. Moreover, defendants would be given as clear an idea of what they would have to meet at trial as could be supplied by pleadings alone. This heavy reliance on the pleadings was made necessary, of course, because there was virtually no other way in which the defendant could compel disclosure of the prosecution's case. An examination of pleading in modern criminal cases will show that the pleadings have lost their rigidity, and their specificity with it, while no compensatory increase has taken place in the amount of pretrial disclosure available to the defendant.

Indictment or Information

The Hand view of criminal pleading is, in large part, a reaction against the ridiculous lengths to which courts, armed with a constitutional principle, often carried the requirement that the indictment furnish the accused with notice of the charge against him. It has become a commonplace to inveigh against the pleading of that day by referring to dismissals of indictments because names were spelled incorrectly, or times and places stated inaccurately. Because of these "horribles," and because of the impact of legal realism on legal thinking generally, criminal pleading was made looser and more flexible. Indictments could now follow the language of the statute creating the crime, provided the statute contained the "essential elements of the offense." Though the cases continued to pay lip service to constitutional doctrine regarding specificity, indictments came to be drafted in more general terms. Any loss to the defendant in the way of notice could be made up to him when he moved for a bill of particulars.

But here, as in the analogous erosion of the preindictment screens, the implicit dependence upon the ready availability of particulars has proved to be unwarranted. Court after court has undercut the notice-giving function of the bill of particulars by refusing to grant it. Most often, the grounds for refusal have been that the defendant is not entitled to obtain the government's "evidence" in advance of trial; or to embark on a "fishing expedition"; or, ironically, to get details when he knows very well "what he did." Almost invariably, the shield for refusal has been the awareness of trial judges, because appellate courts have said it so often, that the application for a bill of particulars is "addressed to the sound discretion of the [trial] court."

Duplicity and Variance

In the wake of the indictment's decline in specificity has come the demise of the doctrine holding "bad for duplicity" any count which charged more than one offense. That doctrine had as its principal rationale the need for precise statement of the charge so that the accused could prepare his defense. Inevitably, however, the logic of the position that defects in the indictment could be "cured" brought with it the willingness to accept as a remedy for the "error" of duplicity something less than dismissal of the indictment. Not only were fewer pleadings classed as duplicitous, but in most jurisdictions, once the trial had begun, prosecutors were permitted to elect the one offense on which they intended to rely for conviction; in others, the indictment could be amended.

The concept of postindictment "cure" of an unfortunate pleading by the prosecution has also had an impact upon the doctrine of fatal variance between allegation and proof. Until recently, that doctrine prohibited any departure in the course of trial from the single offense alleged in each count; the prosecution was to be held strictly to the theory announced in the charging document. If the proof did vary, the prohibition against "amendment" of indictments, which denied to prosecutor or judge the power to add to what the grand jury had charged, prevented correction of the error.

Within the past generation, the rigors of both "variance" and "amendment" doctrine have been considerably relaxed. The Supreme Court held in *Berger v. United States* that the charge of one conspiracy, and the proof of more than one, was "harmless error" so long as the defendant was not "surprised"—that is, that the departure from the allegation had not materially prejudiced the accused in making his defense. Though the Supreme Court has not been altogether consistent in its decisions, this reasoning has been extended by the courts and legislatures to a wide variety of cases. Amendments as to form have been held permissible. And, in many jurisdictions, amendments as to substance are authorized by special statutory or constitutional provision. Evidencing the same trend are the cases holding that the prosecution may prove any "offense" of which the indictment does in fact give notice, even if the indictment indicates, on its face, that it is dealing with another, similar offense category.

Effective Notice to the Accused

Does this developing trend prejudice the defendant's preparation and trial of his case? There can be no question that notice of the facts and legal theories to be litigated is essential to the effective operation of an adversary system. Without such notice, each party is precluded from making the most of the facts potentially at his disposal or of legal research. If, for example, defense counsel does not learn until late in the trial that two conspiracies are involved rather than one, he faces the problem of belatedly mustering his proofs or of having to re-call witnesses—at best inefficient procedures making for disjointed testimony. Difficulties also arise with respect to objections by counsel to the admissibility of evidence, or cross-examination, or the preparation of instructions to the jury. What is the criterion of relevance by which counsel can object, and the trial judge rule, on admissibility? Toward what version of the facts should defense counsel's examination press the witnesses for the prosecution? What "law" should the parties seek to have the judge pass to the jury in his instructions? Only some "theory of the case" can furnish such a guide.

Perhaps in a system of "trial by intervals," such as characterizes German civil procedure and some of our own administrative proceedings, the importance of initial notice is minimized. Notice wanting on one occasion can be supplied on another. But in the single event trial, initial notice is essential. This does not mean, of course, that all the rigors of the early "issue" pleading need be revived, or that the "theory of the case" need be restricted to a single offense category. Indeed, a decent respect for the grand jury would seem to require that its indictment be taken to refer to any "legal theory," or "offense category," reasonably encompassed by the operative facts recorded in the indictment. Too strict an adherence to the initial pleading is probably more likely to frustrate the intention of the grand jury than to effectuate it. But notice of issues and facts adequate to enable the defense to prepare for trial is made all the more essential if such a view of pleading is adopted. The real question is: How is notice to be afforded the parties?

The reasonably expansible pleading, recognizing as it does the difficulties of precise initial statement of either facts or legal theories, moves in an inevitable direction. But unless it is accompanied by the means to prepare for the shifts in prosecution theories, factual and legal, the expansible pleading significantly aggravates the plight of the accused. Unfortunately, no such means is ordinarily available.

Discovery by the Defendant

The elimination of precise pleading, the general unavailability of particulars, and the increasing elasticity given to indictments all leave a good deal of room for "surprise" at trial. And not all such "surprise" is readily curable by granting a continuance. Civil procedure seeks to minimize this problem by permitting each party to inform himself to the utmost about the other's case—to sift legal issues and evidence in detail before trial through depositions, requests for admissions, and discovery of documents. This process has as its object the harnessing of the full creative potential of the adversary process, bringing each party to trial as aware of what he must meet as his finances and his lawyer's energy and intelligence permit.

Yet virtually no such machinery exists for the defendant accused of a crime. No deposition or admissions procedure is ordinarily available to him. Though a motion for discovery of documents before trial is technically available, attempts to invoke it are rarely successful. When they are, they usually enable the defendant to get only materials which are not central to his task of preparing a defense. For example, motions for leave to subpoena before trial commercial records of various sorts—in short, materials in the hands of nongovernmental persons involved in the prosecution—are often granted. Confessions, guns, bullets, chemical analyses and autopsy reports are also beginning to be made available, albeit reluctantly and in only a few jurisdictions. But the statement of a government witness—at best, a poor substitute for a deposition, since defense counsel was not there to cross-examine when it was made—is virtually unobtainable. The few federal cases making such statements available before trial, such as *Fryer v. United States,* have probably been overruled by the legislation which followed in the wake of *United States v. Jencks.* Even before that legislation was enacted, *Jencks had done little to open the government's files. It said no more than that defense counsel, at trial,* must be given access to prior statements of a witness *on the stand* regarding the subject matter of that witness's testimony. The case did not address itself either to the pretrial stage or to the statements, in government files at time of trial, of witnesses not testifying but potentially helpful to the defense. Only a handful of fairly limited due process cases deal with the latter problem—and none of them explicitly with the right to obtain such materials before trial.

If the defendant should wish to use his own resources in searching out those witnesses who have spoken to police, prosecutor, or grand jury, he will, more often than not, find that they have been advised not to discuss their testimony with him. Without the subpoena, he can do nothing effective to break the wall of silence. If he should try, he runs the risk of being charged with tampering with witnesses. Even his search for evidence at large is inevitably restricted because he has neither a crime laboratory nor vast identification and fingerprint files available to him. Most often, he has no investigative assistance whatever.

The one institution on the scene which might be used to afford the accused effective pretrial discovery of the prosecution's case is the preliminary hearing. But American courts have consistently refused to shape it in the mold of its British counterpart, in which the prosecution is obligated to make complete disclosure of the evidence it will use at trial. In its present form, the American preliminary hearing provides a minimal opportunity to discover the government's case and to confront and cross-examine witnesses. It requires only so much disclosure as is necessary to make out "probable cause" to believe that defendant committed the crime, or a "prima facie" case, or some other formulation of a minimal evidentiary burden.

Even this obligation can be evaded through subtle pressures designed to maximize waiver—for example, through failure to provide for appointment of counsel at this stage, thereby making it less likely that a hearing will be requested by the defendant. Where indictment by grand jury remains the general rule, continuance of the preliminary hearing until the grand jury has returned an indictment withdraws the limited opportunity for discovery at the preliminary hearing. For he who has already been indicted by a grand jury is not "entitled" to a preliminary hearing.

Once the case is placed in the grand jury's hands, it is shrouded with secrecy. Only under the most extraordinary circumstances may the defendant obtain the minutes of that body, though the government may use them for many purposes. And neither defendant nor his counsel sees, nor is given the opportunity to examine, the witnesses against him. True, in many states the names of witnesses before the grand jury are required by statute to be endorsed on the ensuing indictment. But, in most of them, witnesses whose names are not endorsed will be permitted to testify. And in the others, there is nothing the defendant can do to make the named witnesses talk to him or to get copies of their statements to the prosecutor.

In sum, if police or prosecution choose to withhold from the defendant their evidence or legal theories, or if they continue the preliminary hearing until indictment, the defendant has only the notice given him by the indictment, the occasional bill of particulars, and the even more occasional pretrial discovery. Is the prosecution similarly handicapped?

Discovery by the Government

Denial of pretrial discovery to the defendant is justified most often as a necessary counterweight to the alleged fact that the accused "need not disclose the barest outline of his defense [and] . . . is immune from question or comment on his silence." The justification is unsatisfactory for two entirely separate reasons. First, by assigning a central tenet of our accusatorial procedure to the bargain-counter, the defendant is made to pay dearly for his privilege of silence, whether or not he makes use of it. Second, and more immediately relevant, the Hand view grossly exaggerates the protection which this "immunity" affords.

Though the defendant still need not file a detailed responsive pleading in most states, more and more require that the defenses of alibi and insanity be pleaded specially before trial. Even at the trial, where the accused is most clearly immune from being called by the prosecution as its witness (or, in most jurisdictions, from having his failure to testify made the subject of comment by the prosecution), the protection means less to the defendant than appears: first, the accused will testify in his own behalf in most cases and thus subject himself to cross-examination; second, the prosecutor will rarely wish to make the accused his witness; third, the failure of the accused to testify is so conspicuous, particularly in this day of frequent invocation of the fifth amendment, that he is under the utmost pressure to take the stand to rebut the inference of guilt which will likely be drawn by the jury, whether or not his silence is explicitly called to their attention; finally, admissions made by the accused to the police before trial are freely and regularly used at the trial, placing defendants under pressure to take the stand to explain the admissions away.

If the accused's immunity at trial were all it is reputed to be, there would still remain his considerable amenability to interrogation before trial. Ordinarily, an accused person may be interrogated by the police up to the point of "coercion." So long as certain kinds of pressures—such as violence, threats of violence, intensive interrogation continuing over long periods of time, or promises of immunity—are not utilized, the ensuing admissions or confessions can ordinarily be used at trial. This remains true even where the accused has neither been advised of his right to remain silent nor permitted access to counsel. The *McNabb-Mallory* rule, excluding confessions obtained during the period before arraignment at a preliminary hearing, has had a mitigating effect in the federal courts. But no state court has followed it. Moreover, in both state and federal courts, leads obtained as a result of concededly inadmissible confessions or admissions may be used to find evidence which does not share the infection of the original source.

In state prosecutions, and in federal prosecutions in which the accused has been brought promptly before a magistrate, the police may use methods of interrogation involving trickery, fabricated evidence, subtle threats, violations of confidence, and a myriad other techniques for manipulating the fearful or suggestible. None of these conventional methods of interrogation is prohibited by law. None of them, alone, suffices to invalidate confessions or admissions following from its use. Each constitutes one among many factors to be considered in determining the complex issue of the "trustworthiness" or "voluntariness" of the confession. And because that issue has been arbitrarily limited to permit just such methods, police are invited to press to the limits of interrogation. Nor does the preliminary hearing, with its advice of rights to counsel and to silence, necessarily end exposure of the accused to these pressures. In most states, the accused apparently remains accessible to the police for questioning until final disposition of the case. The most impressive indication that our criminal procedure regularly acts on the assumption that the defendant is very much available and usable for self-incrimination is the overwhelming proportion of cases (75 to 90 per cent) which are decided by pleas of guilty. Such pleas quite obviously follow in considerable part from a breach in the wall of silence allegedly surrounding the defendant—whether because he has been cajoled to do so, or because he sees his interest best served in that way, or for more obscure reasons, is very difficult to say.

The availability of the accused for self-incrimination does not end with police interrogation. For, if he is that unusual accused who obstinately persists in remaining silent in the face of accusation at the police station, a substantial number of jurisdictions take his silence in the face of accusation as an adoptive admission—an admission by silence—the theory being that an innocent man must be expected to cry out his innocence in the face of accusation. And, virtually everywhere, the body of the accused may be used fairly freely to incriminate him. Although, on a theoretical level, such use of the body is not within the concept of self-incrimination, it remains a significant factor in assessing the total balance, or lack of it, between prosecution and accused. The accused's fingerprints and footprints may be taken; his blood and urine may be removed, provided the job is done scientifically; his handwriting and his voice may be used in most jurisdictions; he may be required to exhibit himself, in a line-up or otherwise, wearing particular kinds of clothing, though such exhibition may well increase the likelihood that he will be identified as the culprit.

When the grand jury investigation begins, most jurisdictions recognize the immunity of the accused from interrogation only if he has already been named a defendant by arrest, by information, or by earlier indictment. If the prosecutor chooses to defer arrest or formal charge and hales the target of his investigation before the grand jury as a "witness," that target need not, except in a few jurisdictions, be advised that it is he whose conduct is under scrutiny. As a result, he may testify where otherwise he might refrain from doing so. If he should assert complete immunity (for example, a privilege not to appear, or not to be sworn) on the ground that he is the accused *de facto,* most jurisdictions would deny the claim, thereby compelling him to testify or to virtually concede his indictment by invoking his privilege against self-incrimination.

Not only is the accused himself subject to considerable use by police and prosecution before trial, but every witness, his as well as the prosecution's, may be subjected to similar interrogation before trial. This may be done formally before a grand jury, which affords a full-fledged deposition procedure for the prosecution without the embarrassing presence of defendant or his counsel. Or it may be done informally at the police station, where the specter of being held as a material witness—or of being charged with one of many vaguely defined crimes as a means of detaining for questioning—offers a considerable inducement for cooperation. As if all this were not enough, extensive legislative and administrative subpoena power exists to assist the government in investigating virtually every major field of regulatory activity. These too may serve as discovery and trial preparation devices available to the government and unavailable to the defense.

Fairly clearly, pretrial discovery by the prosecution is far-reaching. And it cannot in any sense be said to be matched by what is available to the defendant or by what he can keep from the prosecution—even when his "immunity" from self-incrimination is thrown into the scales. While the possibility that the defendant may produce a hitherto undisclosed witness or theory of defense is always present, the opportunity for surprise is rendered practically illusory by the government's broad investigatory powers and by the requirement in many states that the defenses of alibi and insanity must be specially pleaded. The sum of the matter is that the defendant is not an effective participant in the pretrial criminal process. It is to the trial alone that he must look for justice. Yet the imbalance of the pretrial period may prevent him from making the utmost of the critical trial date. And the trial, in turn, has been refashioned so that it is increasingly unlikely that it will compensate for the imbalance before trial.

Implications for Reform

If a procedural system is to be fair and just, it must give each of the participants to a dispute the opportunity to sustain his position. It must not create conditions which add to any essential inequality of position between the parties but rather must assure that such inequality will be minimized as much as human ingenuity can do so. In the case of enforcement of the criminal law, it seems quite clear that our existing institutional arrangements, as construed by the courts, aggravate the tendencies toward inequality between state and accused. How can a halt be called to these tendencies?

Several tiers of solutions are necessary—some within the scope of this article and some without. Among the latter are the various measures now being taken to make the indigent accused "equal before the law"—such as providing him with counsel and trial transcripts—and those which should be taken, such as making public investigative resources available to the accused.

Most immediately relevant, however, is the creation of a free deposition and discovery procedure. For this would afford the accused the ability to draw upon all that the prosecution has gathered, compensating in part for all that the prosecution has learned from the accused and his witnesses. Every one of the many excellent arguments which carried the day for pretrial discovery in civil cases is equally applicable on the criminal side. If the trial is to be the occasion at which well prepared adversaries test each other's evidence and legal contentions in the best tradition of the adversary system, there can be no substitute for a deposition, discovery, and pretrial procedure. Whether this is accomplished through an expansion of the preliminary hearing, following the English model, or through incorporation of the discovery provisions of the Federal Rules of Civil Procedure, as in Professor Donnelly's proposed Puerto Rican Penal Code, is less important than that the job be done. If a choice is to be made, however, it should probably be for the Donnelly proposal since it draws upon a body of rules with which our courts are thoroughly familiar.

The argument customarily advanced in opposition to such a reform is that advice to the accused as to the details of the case against him will be an invitation to him to fabricate evidence, to suborn others to do so, or to intimidate the witnesses against him. Such a view implies that the presumption of innocence is inapplicable before trial. Indeed, its operational assumption is that all persons are guilty; since they expect to be convicted "for what they did," they can be expected to take any measures necessary to prevent conviction. This view builds a procedural system upon the assumption that virtually all are guilty when some twenty-three per cent to thirty-six per cent of persons who actually stand trial are acquitted. Moreover, it treats existing laws against lying, bribing, and intimidating witnesses as ineffective to deter persons charged with crime. In place of such assumedly ineffective criminal sanctions, it attaches a crippling procedural handicap to all defendants.

Since there is good reason to believe that the amount of perjury in civil cases is considerable, it seems questionable at best to allow full discovery in civil cases and deny it in criminal cases. It could, of course, be said that the severity of criminal snactions is so much greater than civil ones that the accused is more likely to tamper with the process than is the party to a civil case, or that the criminal "class" includes more persons disposed to violence than does the civil litigant class. But a moment's reflection indicates how suspect such hypotheses are. Even if we assume the accused to be more motivated or more disposed by personality to engage in such conduct, he, unlike his civil analogue, is already marked by the state as a criminal and hence is more likely to be under scrutiny. Moreover, the very real likelihood that charges of such misconduct against criminal defendants will be believed makes it all the more obvious that they must behave with the utmost circumspection.

But perhaps the most significant reason of all is the fact that the range of civil and criminal substantive law is too broad to permit the generalization that one involved in civil litigation is far less likely to suborn perjury or intimidate witnesses. It is difficult to believe that the defendant to charges of income tax evasion, false advertising, mail fraud, et cetera, will regularly tamper with justice on the criminal side of the court but that he will not do so when defending against the same or comparable charges on the civil side. Or that the petty thief accused of shoplifting will lie or intimidate but that the same person suing for an injury from an automobile collision will behave properly. Far more likely, "bad" people will do bad things on both sides of the court; the kind of people involved in litigation, and the stakes at issue, are central to the intimidation-bribery-perjury nexus, not their involvement on any one side of the court. It must be conceded, of course, that, at the margins, the pressure of a serious criminal charge may cause a given individual to engage in conduct which he would not consider if he were faced with a less serious civil charge, and that the personality types brought within certain criminal categories may present a significantly greater threat to the process. But since generalizations are necessary if systems of procedure are to be built, it seems fairly obvious that in most instances, the only approach to disclosure consonant with equality of opportunity and with the presumption of innocence is that used on the civil side of the court. It places its faith in the freest possible discovery as an aid to truth and as a means of searching out falsehood. But most important, it leaves to a more selective process than a blanket distinction between civil and criminal cases the development of techniques for coping with the special problems which may arise in some criminal cases.

The Protective Order

A number of problems will undoubtedly arise in the creation of such a system. Most important is the fear, well founded in certain limited classes of cases, that the defendant is dangerous and poses a real threat to the prosecution's witnesses. The almost identical problem is posed whenever a defendant who knows the identity of the complaining witness is released on bail pending trial; or when he has seen several of the prosecution's witnesses at a preliminary hearing; or when the nature of events leading up to the charge of crime informs him to the utmost about the nature of the case against him; or when, after a full trial, he is released on bail pending appeal. The law of bail stands four-square across the path to the easy assumption that he who is charged with crime is indiscriminately dangerous. It refuses to deny to all their liberty and their right to assist in preparing their defense because there are a few who may interfere with the process while it is at work. Even where the ban on excessive bail is manipulated to keep in prison those perceived as dangerous to public or process, the justification ordinarily reflects an attempt to cope with the incredibly complex problems of predicting the behavior of the accused while on bail.

It is likely, however, despite all that has been said, that there will arise cases in which free discovery by the defendant may be too dangerous. In such cases, it may be desirable to borrow from the Federal Rules of Civil Procedure the concept of the "protective order." This would authorize a trial court upon a proper showing to seal off information or identity of witnesses. It would do explicitly what is now done covertly at the bail stage. And in time it would undoubtedly lead to a more selective and discriminating case law than any we now have.

Special problems will surely follow in the wake of the "protective order." Where its effect is merely to seal off the identity of documents or of material which will eventually be disclosed at trial, the only interference with the defendant is that he will have to defer until trial the preparation of defensive matter responsive to, or discoverable from, such previously undisclosed material. Allowance of limited continuances may, of course, be necessary to enable the defendant to make use of such material.

Where, on the other hand, the effect of the protective order is to deny defendant access to material which the government is not likely to introduce at trial—for example, materials helpful to the defense—the prosecution's contentions will undoubtedly resemble those now regularly urged to support a claim of "government privilege." Disclosure will either make known the identity of an informer who would preferably remain unidentified; or it will involve "secrets" of some kind or other; or it will intrude upon the "work-product" of the government attorney; or it will interfere with the administration of justice in some undefined way. Here, the range of solutions developed in the case law generally for "government privilege" would seem adequate. If the court were persuaded that the matter should be privileged, and that nondisclosure would not seriously injure the defendant, then no price need be paid by the government. Where there is both a valid claim of privilege *and* injury to the defendant, the present case law makes the government pay a price—either of dismissing the case or of having an issue taken as decided against it. Where the claim of privilege is held to be invalid, disclosure could be compelled under penalty of contempt.

Discovery by the Defendant—Right or Privilege

If full discovery were adopted, it would perhaps be open to the prosecution to claim that it would not have as much access to the defendant himself as he would have to all the prosecution's witnesses. This would, of course, be true—subject to all of the qualifications on the extent of that inaccessibility. Three responses may be made to this line of argument—none of which consigns all defendants to outer darkness, as does the present approach.

The first, and probably the most desirable, would allow the defendant his immunity—as a mark of the maturity of our state and the consummate respect it pays to the dignity of the individual, both for his own sake and for the benefit of a society seeking to impress upon its police and prosecutors the high obligation to proceed against a citizen only when they have independent evidence of his crime. History teaches that too ready availability of the accused as the source of the evidence against him inevitably tempts the state to intrude too much. And the inherent inequality in investigative resources, as between state and accused, suggests also that the defendant does not get so much on the total scale when his limited immunity is left him.

The second response would demand of the accused who wishes to participate in a balanced and intelligent procedural system that he pay a price for such participation: that he waive his special status as an accused, though not his status as witness, in return for full rights of discovery. He would still have the privilege of the witness to refuse to answer particular incriminating questions. But the questions could be put to him at depositions or at trial. And his refusal to answer, or to take the stand, could be made the subject of comment.

Yet a third response remains. As a condition of enjoying full rights of discovery, the accused could be required to waive all immunity from self-incrimination regarding the crime charged, at the time he enters his plea of not guilty. He would then become as much subject to deposition, discovery and testimony at trial as is any witness in a civil case. The choice would be his to make—to participate in either a civil or criminal type procedural system. In all three approaches, the remedy of the protective order would remain to deal with the exceptionally threatening situation.

About all that can reasonably be said against the second or third suggestions is that the mere existence of the option may make for invidious comparison between those defendants who elect the civil-type procedure and those who insist upon their privilege or immunity. The argument is reminiscent of another day when some resisted the restoration of competency to defendants. Then, too, it was urged that if any defendant were permitted to take the stand, it would create an adverse effect upon those defendants who did not choose to do so. The second and third suggestions seem to call for less in the way of invidious comparison. And in both cases, there is too much to be gained by defendants as a class to warrant denying them the opportunity to get the fairest and most efficient trial our procedural reformers have been able to develop.

CONCLUSION

The "procedural revolution" of the twentieth century followed inevitably from the legal realists' attack upon the procedural formalism of the prior century. Uncritical reverence for the forms of another day was supplanted by a more discriminating and instrumental view of procedure as an integral part of the substantive law. It became clear that the effectiveness of a court's statement of "the law" is a function of many variables—chief among them the manner in which relevant institutions channel to them the materials for decision, the forms of words in which legel criteria are stated, and the vigor with which those criteria are worked out at each stage by all those concerned with the process. In the field of civil procedure, the heritage left by the legal realists was a happy one—flexibility, concern for the substantive ends to be served by a procedural system, discriminating efficiency, and maximal opportunity to all to make use of the legal process to obtain the information necessary for resolving the dispute between the parties.

But when those who did so much to shape the procedural revolution on the civil side turned their attention to criminal procedure, albeit as writers of case law not of codes, the results were unfortunate. The modifications fashioned by them on the basis of allegedly rigorous analysis and in the interest of flexibility and efficiency have all worked to the very serious disadvantage of the defendant. This has occurred not because the modifications are intrinsically undesirable but rather because they have been fragmentary in nature and were introduced without any real appreciation of the requirements of the total procedural system.

If the flexibility of pleading and proof introduced by the procedural reformers at the trial stage were matched by a compensatory zeal for improving the pretrial disclosure devices, or if the pretrial screens could be expected to leave for trial only those who are guilty, it would be difficult to avoid joining the "modernizers," though there would still remain the question why the state could not afford to try the obviously guilty by the strictest possible standards of proof; or whether it is not as important that the process be "fair" as that the guilty be brought to book. Unfortunately, however, the relationships among the parts remain unnoticed in entirely too much of the case law. Judicial supervision of the quantum of proof necessary to convict is being relaxed at the very time when pretrial standards of proof are being removed from meaningful judicially enforced standards. And pleading is being loosened at the very time that judicial attitudes towards pretrial discovery and bills of particulars remain hard.

However much he can be said to benefit from the widely publicized decisions in certain areas of constitutional law, the hypothetical "accused" can find little to please him in current developments in the criminal trial process. Those developments reflect entirely too little concern about the inherent inequality of litigating position between the expanding state and even the most resourceful individual, much less the vast majority of resourceless ones. And even more fundamentally, they reflect subtle erosion of the accusatorial system, relieving police and prosecutor in many instances of the pressures necessary to maintain their actions at the optimum level of responsibility.

TWO MODELS OF THE CRIMINAL PROCESS

HERBERT L. PACKER

There are two more or less separable complexes of issues which need to be investigated as one approaches the central question of the limits of criminal law. One complex of issues concerns what may be called the ideology of the criminal law, such as questions about the nature and purposes of criminal punishment. This is generally recognized as relevant to what I have termed the central question. There does not seem to be an equivalent recognition of the relevance of the other complex of issues, which concerns what may be called the processes of the criminal law. The major premise of this Article is that the shape of the criminal process has an important bearing on questions about the wise substantive use of the criminal sanction. Its minor premise is that important trends in the development of the criminal process that are now underway make the task of appraising the uses of the criminal sanction an especially timely one.

We will start by considering the spectrum of choices that is at least in theory open in fixing the shape of the criminal process and by proposing a device for identifying and appraising the poles and the distance between them. The device, a pair of models, will then serve as a framework for considering the dynamism that appears to characterize present-day trends in the evolution of the criminal process. Finally, after a summation of the trends and an attempt to evaluate their continued potency, some tentative suggestions will be advanced about the relevance of the criminal process to the elaboration of criteria for the substantive invocation of the criminal sanction.

I. VALUES AND THE CRIMINAL PROCESS

A. Why Build Models?

People who commit crimes appear to share the prevalent impression that punishment is an unpleasantness that is best avoided. They ordinarily take care to avoid being caught. If arrested, they ordinarily deny their guilt and otherwise try not to cooperate with the police. If brought to trial, they do whatever their resources permit to resist being convicted. And, even after they have been convicted and sent to prison, their efforts to secure their freedom do not cease. It is a struggle from start to finish. This struggle is often referred to as the criminal process, a compendious term that stands for all the complexes of activity that operate to bring the substantive law of crime to bear (or to avoid bringing it to bear) on persons who are suspected of having committed crimes. It can be described, but only partially and inadequately, by referring to the rules of law that govern the apprehension, screening, and trial of persons suspected of crime. It consists at least as importantly of patterns of official activity that correspond only in the roughest kind of way to the prescriptions of procedural

From *The University of Pennsylvania Law Review,* vol. 11, 1964, pp. 1–23. Copyright © 1964 by *The University of Pennsylvania Law Review.* Reprinted by permission.

rules. As a result of recent emphasis on empirical research into the administration of criminal justice, we are just beginning to be aware how very rough the correspondence is.

At the same time, and perhaps in part as a result of this new accretion of knowledge, some of our lawmaking institutions—and particularly the Supreme Court of the United States—have begun to add measurably to the prescriptions of law that are meant to govern the operation of the criminal process. This accretion has become, in the last few years, exponential in extent and velocity. We are faced with an interesting paradox: the more we learn about the Is of the criminal process, the more we are instructed about its Ought and the greater the gulf between Is and Ought appears to become. We learn that very few people get adequate legal representation in the criminal process; we are simultaneously told that the Constitution requires people to be afforded adequate legal representation in the criminal process. We learn that coercion is often used to extract confessions from suspected criminals; we are then told that convictions based on coerced confessions may nͻt be permitted to stand. We discover that the police in gathering evidence often use methods that violate the norms of privacy protected by the fourth amendment; we are told that evidence so obtained must be excluded from the criminal trial. But these prescriptions about how the process ought to operate do not automatically become part of the patterns of official behavior in the criminal process. Is and Ought share an increasingly uneasy co-existence. Doubts are stirred about the kind of criminal process we want to have.

The kind of criminal process we have is an important determinant of the kind of behavior content that the criminal law ought rationally to comprise. Logically, the substantive question may appear to be anterior: decide what kinds of conduct one wants to reach through the criminal process, and then decide what kind of process is best calculated to deal with those kinds of conduct. It has not worked that way. On the whole, the process has been at least as much a Given as the content of the criminal law. But it is far from being a Given in any rigid sense.

The shape of the criminal process affects the substance of the criminal law in two general ways. First, one would want to know, before adding a new category of behavior to the list of crimes and therefore placing an additional burden on the process, whether it is easy or hard to employ the criminal process. The more expeditious the process, the greater the number of people with whom it can deal and, therefore, the greater the variety and, hence, the amount of antisocial conduct that can be confided in whole or in part to the criminal law for inhibition. On the other hand, the harder the process is to use, the smaller the number of people who can be handled by it at any given level of resources devoted to staffing and operating it. The harder it is to put a suspected criminal in jail, the fewer the number of cases that can be handled in a year by a given number of policemen, prosecutors, defense lawyers, judges and jurymen, probation officers, etc. A second and subtler relationship exists between the characteristic functioning of the process and the kinds of conduct with which it can efficiently deal. Perhaps the clearest example, but by no means the only one, is in the area of what have been referred to as victimless crimes, *i.e.,* offenses that do not result in anyone's feeling that he has been injured so as to impel him to bring the offense to the attention of the authorities. The offense of fornication is an example. In a jurisdiction where it is illegal for two persons not married to each other to have sexual intercourse, there is a substantial enforcement problem (or would be, if the law were taken seriously) because people who voluntarily have sexual intercourse do not often feel that they have been victimized and therefore do not often complain to the police. Consensual transactions in gambling and narcotics present the same problem, somewhat exacerbated by the fact that we take these forms of conduct rather more seriously than fornication from the standpoint of the criminal law. To the difficulties of apprehending a criminal when it is known that he has committed a crime are added the difficulties of knowing that a crime has been committed. In this sense the victimless crime always presents a greater problem to the criminal process than does the crime with an ascertainable victim. But this problem may be minimized if the criminal process has at its disposal measures that are designed to enhance the probability that the commission of such offenses will become known. If suspects may be entrapped into committing offenses, if the police may arrest and search a suspect without evidence that he has committed an offense, if wiretaps and other forms of electronic surveillance are permitted, it becomes easier to detect the commission of offenses of this sort. But if these measures are prohibited and if the prohibitions are observed in practice, it becomes more difficult, and eventually there may come a point at which the capacity of the criminal process to deal with victimless offenses becomes so attentuated that a failure of enforcement occurs.

In both of these ways, the characteristics of the criminal process bear a relationship to the central question of what the criminal law is good for. Both a general assessment of whether that process is a high-speed or a low-speed instrument of social control and a series of specific assessments of its fitness for the handling of particular kinds of antisocial behavior are called for if we are to have a basis for elaborating the criteria that ought to affect the invocation of the criminal sanction. How can we provide ourselves with an estimate of the criminal process that pays due regard to its static and dynamic elements? There are, to be sure, aspects of the criminal process that vary only inconsequentially from place to place and from time to time. But its dynamism is clear—clearer today, perhaps, than ever before. We need to have an idea of the potentialities for change in the system and the probable direction that change is taking and may be expected to take in the future. We need to detach ourselves from the welter of more or less connected details that make up an accurate description of the myriad ways in which the criminal process does operate or may be likely to operate in midtwentieth-century America so that we can begin to appraise the system as a whole in terms of its capacity to deal with the variety of substantive missions we confide to it.

One way to do this kind of job is to abstract from reality, to build a model. In a sense that is what an examination of the constitutional and statutory provisions that govern the operation of the criminal process would produce. This, in effect, is the way analysis of the legal system has traditionally proceeded. The method has considerable utility as an index of current value choices; but it produces a model that will not tell us very much about some important problems that the system encounters and that will only fortuitously tell us anything useful about how the system actually operates. On the other hand, the kind of model that might emerge from an attempt to cut loose from the law on the books and to describe, as accurately as possible, what actually goes on in the real-life world of the criminal process would so subordinate the inquiry to the tyranny of the actual that the existence of competing value choices would be obscured. The kind of criminal process we have depends importantly on certain value choices that are reflected, explicitly or implicitly, in its habitual functioning. The kind of model we need is one that permits us to recognize explicitly the value choices that underlie the details of the criminal process. In a word, what we need is a *normative* model, or rather two models, to let us perceive the normative antinomy that runs deep in the life of the criminal law. These models may not be labelled Good and Bad, and I hope they will not be taken in that sense. Rather, they represent an attempt to abstract two separate value systems that compete for attention in the operation of the criminal process. Neither is presented as either corresponding to reality or as representing what the criminal process ought to be. The two models merely afford a convenient way to talk about the operation of a process whose day-to-day functioning involves a constant series of minute adjustments between the competing demands of two value systems and whose normative future likewise involves a series of resolutions, of greater or lesser magnitude, of the tensions between mutually exclusive claims.

I call these two models the Due Process Model and the Crime Control Model. In the next section I shall sketch their animating presuppositions, and in succeeding sections I shall present the two models as they apply to a selection of representative problems that arise at successive stages of the criminal process. As we examine in succession this sampling of stage and substage of the criminal process on which the models operate, we will move from the description of the model stages to two further inquiries: first, where on a spectrum between the extremes represented by the two models do our present practices seem approximately to fall; second, what appears to be the direction and thrust of current and foreseeable trends along each such spectrum?

There is a risk in an enterprise of this sort that is latent in any attempt to polarize. It is, simply, that values are too various to be pinned down to yes or no answers. When we polarize, we distort. The models are, in a sense, distortions. The attempt here is only to clarify the terms of discussion by isolating the assumptions that underlie competing policy claims and examining the conclusions to which those claims, if fully accepted, would lead. This Article does not make value choices, but only describes what are thought to be their consequences.

B. *Values Underlying the Models*

In this section we shall develop two competing systems of values, the tension between which accounts for the intense activity now observable in the development of the criminal process. The models we are about to examine attempt to give operational content to these conflicting schemes of values. Like the values underlying them, the models are polarities. Just as the models are not to be taken as describing real-world situations, so the values that underlie them are not to be regarded as expressing the values held by any one person. The values are presented here as an aid to analysis, not as a program for action.

1. Some Common Ground

One qualification needs to be made to the assertion of polarity in the two models. While it would be possible to construct models that exist in an institutional vacuum, it would not serve our purposes to do so. We are not postulating a criminal process that operates in any kind of society at all, but rather one that operates within the framework of contemporary American society. This leaves plenty of room for polarization, but it does require the observance of some limits. A model of the criminal process that left out of account relatively stable and enduring features of the American legal system would not have much relevance to our central task. For convenience, these elements of stability and continuity can be roughly equated with minimal agreed limits expressed in the Constitution of the United States and, more importantly, with unarticulated assumptions that can be perceived to underlie those limits. Of course, it is true that the Constitution is constantly appealed to by proponents and opponents of many measures that affect the criminal process. And only the naive would deny that there are few conclusive positions that can be reached by appeal to the Constitution. Yet assumptions do exist about the criminal process that are widely shared and that may be viewed as common ground for the operation of any model of the criminal process. Our first task is to clarify these assumptions.

First, there is the assumption implicit in the ex post facto clause of the Constitution that the function of defining conduct that may be treated as criminal is separate from and anterior to the process of identifying and dealing with persons as criminals. How wide or narrow the definition of criminal conduct must be is an important question of policy that yields highly variant results depending on the values held by those making the relevant decisions. But that there must be a means of definition that is in some sense separate from and anterior to the operation of the process is clear. If that were not so, our efforts to deal with the phenomenon of organized crime would appear ludicrous indeed (which is not to say that we have by any means exhausted the potentialities for dealing with that problem within the limits of this basic assumption).

A related assumption that limits the area of controversy is that the criminal process ordinarily ought to be invoked by those charged with the responsibility for doing so when it appears that a crime has been committed and that there is a reasonable prospect of apprehending and convicting its perpetrator. Although the area of police and prosecutorial discretion not to invoke the criminal process is demonstrably broad, it is common ground that these officials have no general dispensing power. If the legislature has decided that certain conduct is to be treated as criminal, the decision-makers at every level of the criminal process are expected to accept that basic decision as a premise for action. The controversial nature of the occasional case in which that is not the role played by the relevant decision-makers only serves to highlight the strength with which the premise holds. This assumption may be viewed as the other side of the ex post facto coin. Just as conduct that is not proscribed as criminal may not be dealt with in the criminal process, so must conduct that has been denominated as criminal be so treated by the participants in the process.

Next, there is the assumption that there are limits to the powers of government to investigate and apprehend persons suspected of committing crimes. I do not refer to the controversy (settled recently, at least in broad outline) as to whether the fourth amendment's prohibitions against unreasonable searches and seizures applies to the states with equal force as to the federal government. Rather, I refer to the general assumption that there is a degree of scrutiny and a degree of control that have to be exercised with respect to the activities of law enforcement officers, that the security and privacy of the individual may not be invaded at will. It is possible to imagine a society in which not even lip service is paid to this assumption. Nazi Germany approached but never quite reached this position. But no one in our society would maintain that every individual may be taken into custody at any time and held without any limitation of time during the process of investigating his possible commission of crimes, or that there should be no form of redress for violation of at least some standards for official investigative conduct. Although this assumption may not appear to have much in the way of positive content, its absence would render moot some of our most hotly controverted problems. If there were not general agreement that there must be some limits on police power to detain and investigate, the very controversial provisions of the Uniform Arrest Act, permitting the police to detain for questioning for a short period even though they do not have grounds for making an arrest, would be a magnanimous concession by the all-powerful state rather than, as it is now perceived, a substantial expansion of police power.

Finally, there is a complex of assumptions embraced within terms like "the adversary system," "procedural due process," "notice and an opportunity to be heard," "day in court," and the like. Common to them all is the notion that the alleged criminal is not merely an object to be acted upon, but an independent entity in the process who may, if he so desires, force the operators of the process to demonstrate to an independent authority (judge and jury) that he is guilty of the charges against him. It is a minimal assumption. It speaks in terms of "may," not "must." It permits but does not require the accused, acting by himself or through his own agent, to play an active role in the process; by virtue of that fact, the process becomes or has the capacity to become a contest between, if not equals, at least independent actors. Now, as we shall see, much of the space between the two models is occupied by stronger or weaker notions of who this contest is to be arranged, how often it is to be played, and by what rules. The Crime Control Model tends to deemphasize this adversary aspect of the process; the Due Process Model tends to make it central. The common ground, and it is an important one, is that the process has, for everyone subjected to it, at least the potentiality of becoming to some extent an adversary struggle.

So much for common ground. There is a good deal of it, even on the narrowest view. Its existence should not be overlooked because it is, by definition, what permits partial resolutions of the tension between the two models to take place. The rhetoric of the criminal process consists largely of claims that disputed territory is "really" common ground; that, for example, the premise of an adversary system "necessarily" embraces the appointment of counsel for everyone accused of crime, or conversely, that the obligation to pursue persons suspected of committing crimes "necessarily" embraces interrogation of suspects without the intervention of counsel. We may smile indulgently at such claims; they are rhetoric and no more. But the form in which they are made suggests an important truth: that there *is* a common ground of value assumption about the criminal process that makes continued discourse about its problems possible.

2. Crime Control Values

The value system that underlies the Crime Control Model is based on the proposition that the repression of criminal conduct is by far the most important function to be performed by the criminal process. The failure of law enforcement to bring criminal conduct under tight control is viewed as leading to the breakdown of public order and thence to the disappearance of an important condition of human freedom. If the laws go unenforced, which is to say, if it is perceived that there is a high percentage of failure to apprehend and convict in the criminal process, a general disregard for legal controls tends to develop. The law-abiding citizen then becomes the victim of all sorts of unjustifiable invasions of his interests. His security of person and property is sharply diminished and, therefore, so is his liberty to function as a member of society. The claim ultimately is that the criminal process is a positive guarantor of social freedom. In order to achieve this high purpose, the Crime Control Model requires that primary attention be paid to the efficiency with which the criminal process operates to screeen suspects, determine guilt, and secure appropriate dispositions of persons convicted of crime.

Efficiency of operation is not, of course, a criterion that can be applied in a vacuum. By "efficiency" we mean the system's capacity to apprehend, try, convict, and dispose of a high proportion of criminal offenders whose offenses become known. In a society in which only the grossest forms of antisocial behavior were made criminal and in which the crime rate was exceedingly low, the criminal process might require many more man-hours of police, prosecutorial, and judicial time per case than ours does, and still operate with tolerable efficiency. On the other hand, a society that was prepared to increase substantially the resources devoted to the suppression of crime might cope with a rising crime rate without sacrifice of efficiency while continuing to maintain an elaborate and time-consuming set of criminal processes. However, neither of these hypotheses corresponds with social reality in this country. We use the criminal sanction to cover an increasingly wide spectrum of behavior thought to be antisocial, and the amount of crime is very large indeed. At the same time, while precise measures are not available, it does not appear that we are disposed in the public sector of the economy to increase very drastically the quantity, much less the quality, of the resources devoted to the suppression of criminal activity through the operation of the criminal process. These factors have an important bearing on the criteria of efficiency and, therefore, on the nature of the Crime Control Model.

The model, in order to operate successfully, must produce a high rate of apprehension and conviction and must do so in a context where the magnitudes being dealt with are very large, and the resources for dealing with them are very limited. There must then be a premium on speed and finality. Speed, in turn, depends on informality and on uniformity; finality depends on minimizing the occasions for challenge. The process must not be cluttered with ceremonious rituals that do not advance the process of a case. Facts can be established more quickly though interrogation in a police station than through the formal process of examination and cross-examination in a court; it follows that extrajudicial processes should be preferred to judicial processes, informal to formal operations. Informality is not enough; there must also be uniformity. Routine stereotyped procedures are essential if large numbers are being handled. The model that will operate successfully on these presuppositions must be an administrative, almost a managerial, model. The image that comes to mind is an assembly line or a conveyor belt down which moves an endless stream of cases, never stopping, carrying the cases to workers who stand at fixed stations and who perform on each case as it comes by the same small but essential operation that brings it one step closer to being a finished product, or, to exchange the metaphor for the reality, a closed file.

The criminal process, on this model, is seen as a screening process in which each successive stage—prearrest investigation, arrest, postarrest investigation, preparation for trial, trial or entry of plea, conviction, and disposition—involves a series of routinized operations whose success is gauged primarily by their tendency to pass the case along to a successful conclusion.

What is a successful conclusion? One that throws off at an early stage those cases in which it appears unlikely that the person apprehended is an offender and then secures, as expeditiously as possible, the conviction of the rest with a minimum of occasions for challenge, let alone postaudit. By the application of administrative expertness, primarily that of the police and prosecutors, an early determination of probable innocence or guilt emerges. The probably innocent are screened out. The probably guilty are passed quickly through the remaining stages of the process. The key to the operation of the model as to those who are not screened out is what I shall call a presumption of guilt. The concept requires some explanation, since it may appear startling to assert that what appears to be the precise converse of our generally accepted ideology of a presumption of innocence can be an essential element of a model that does correspond in some regards to the real-life operation of the criminal process.

The presumption of guilt allows the Crime Control Model to deal efficiently with large numbers. The supposition is that the screening processes operated by police and prosecutors are reliable indicators of probable guilt. Once a man has been investigated without being found to be probably innocent, or, to put it differently, once a determination has been made that there is enough evidence of guilt so that he should be held for further action rather than released from the process, then all subsequent activity directed toward him is based on the view that he is probably guilty. The precise point at which this occurs will vary from case to case; in many cases it will occur as soon as the suspect is arrested or even before, if the evidence of probable guilt that has come to the attention of the authorities is sufficiently strong. But in any case, the presumption of guilt will begin to operate well before the "suspect" becomes a "defendant."

The presumption of guilt is not, of course, a thing. Nor is it even a rule of law in the usual sense. It simply exemplifies a complex of attitudes, a mood. If there is confidence in the reliability of informal administrative factfinding activities that take place in the early stages of the criminal process, the remaining stages of the process can be relatively perfunctory without any loss in operating efficiency. The presumption of guilt, as it operates in the Crime Control Model, is the expression of that confidence.

It would be a mistake to think of the presumption of guilt as the opposite of the presumption of innocence that we are so used to thinking of as the polestar of the criminal process and which, as we shall see, occupies an important position in the Due Process Model. The presumption of innocence is not its opposite; it is irrelevant to the presumption of guilt; the two concepts embody different rather than opposite ideas. The difference can perhaps be epitomized by an example. A murderer, for reasons best known to himself, chooses to shoot his victim in plain view of a large number of people. When the police arrive, he hands them his gun and says: "I did it, and I'm glad." His account of what happened is corroborated by several eyewitnesses. He is placed under arrest and led off to jail. Under these circumstances, which may seem extreme but which in fact characterize with rough accuracy the factfinding situation in a large proportion of criminal cases, it would be plainly absurd to maintain that more probably than not the suspect did not commit the killing. But that is not what the presumption of innocence means. It means that until there has been an adjudication of guilt by an authority legally competent to make such an adjudication, the suspect is to be treated, for reasons that have nothing whatever to do with the probable outcome of the case, as if his guilt is an open question. The presumption of innocence is a direction to officials how they are to proceed, not a prediction of outcome. The presumption of guilt, however, is basically a prediction of outcome. The presumption of innocence is really a direction to the authorities to ignore the presumption of guilt in their treatment of the suspect. It tells them, in effect, to close their eyes to what will frequently seem to be factual probabilities. The reasons why it tells them that are among the animating presuppositions of the Due Process Model, and we will come to them shortly. It is enough to note at this point that the presumption of guilt is descriptive and factual; the presumption of innocence is normative and legal. The pure Crime Control Model finds unacceptable the presumption of innocence although, as we shall see, its real-life emanations are brought into uneasy compromise with the dictates of this dominant ideological position. For this model the presumption of guilt assures the dominant goal of repressing crime through highly summary processes without any great loss of efficiency (as previously defined), for in the run of cases, the preliminary screening processes operated by the police and the prosecuting officials contain adequate guarantees of reliable factfinding. Indeed, the position is a stronger one. It is that subsequent processes, particularly of a formal adjudicatory nature, are unlikely to produce as reliable factfinding as the expert administrative process that precedes them. The criminal process thus must put special weight on the quality of administrative factfinding. It becomes important, then, to place as few restrictions as possible on the character of the administrative factfinding process and to limit restrictions to those that enhance reliability, excluding those designed for other purposes. As we shall see, the desire to avoid restrictions on administrative factfinding is a consistent theme in the development of the Crime Control Model.

For this model the early administrative factfinding stages are centrally vital. The complementary proposition is that the subsequent stages are relatively unimportant and should be truncated as much as possible. This, too, produces tensions with presently dominant ideology. The pure Crime Control Model has very little use for many conspicuous features of the adjudicative process and in real life works a number of ingenious compromises with it. Even in the pure model, however, there have to be devices for dealing with the suspect after the preliminary screening process has resulted in a determination of probable guilt. The focal device, as we shall see, is the plea of guilty; through its use adjudicative factfinding is reduced to a minimum. It might be said of the Crime Control Model that, reduced to its barest essentials and when operating at its most successful pitch, it consists of two elements: (a) an administrative factfinding process leading to exoneration of the suspect, or to (b) the entry of a plea of guilty.

3. Due Process Values

If the Crime Control Model resembles an assembly line, the Due Process Model looks very much like an obstacle course. Each of its successive stages is designed to present formidable impediments to carrying the accused any further along in the process. Its ideology is not the converse of that underlying the Crime Control Model. It does not deny the social desirability of repressing crime, although its critics have been known to claim so. Its ideology is composed of a complex of ideas, some of them based on judgments about the efficacy of crime control devices. The ideology of due process is far more deeply impressed on the formal structure of the law than is the ideology of crime control; yet, an accurate tracing of the strands of which it is made is strangely difficult. What follows is only an attempt at an approximation.

The Due Process Model encounters its rival on the Crime Control Model's own ground in respect to the reliability of factfinding processes. The Crime Control Model, as we have suggested in a preliminary way, places heavy reliance on the ability of investigative and prosecutorial officers, acting in an informal setting in which their distinctive skills are given full sway, to elicit and reconstruct a tolerably accurate account of what actually took place in an alleged criminal event. The Due Process Model rejects this premise and substitutes for it a view of informal, nonadjudicative factfinding that stresses the possibility of error: people are notoriously poor observers of disturbing events—the more emotion-arousing the context, the greater the possibility that recollection will be incorrect; confessions and admissions by persons in police custody may be induced by physical or psychological coercion, so that the police end up hearing what the suspect thinks they want to hear rather than the truth; witnesses may be animated by a bias or interest that no one would trouble to discover except one specially charged with protecting the interests of the accused—which the police are not. Considerations of this kind all lead to the rejection of informal factfinding processes as definitive of factual guilt and to the insistence on formal, adjudicative, adversary factfinding processes in which the factual case against the accused is publicly heard by an impartial tribunal and is evaluated only after the accused has had a full opportunity to discredit the case against him. Even then the distrust of factfinding processes that animates the Due Process Model is not dissipated. The possibilities of human error being what they are, further scrutiny is necessary, or at least must be available, lest in the heat of battle facts have been overlooked or suppressed. How far this subsequent scrutiny must be available is hotly controverted today; in the pure Due Process Model the answer would be: at least as long as there is an allegation of factual error that has not received an adjudicative hearing in a factfinding context. The demand for finality is thus very low in the Due Process Model.

This strand of due process ideology is not enough to sustain the model. If all that were at issue between the two models was a series of questions about the reliability of factfinding processes, we would have but one model of the criminal process, the nature of whose constituent elements would pose questions of fact, not of value. Even if the discussion is confined for the moment to the question of reliability, it is apparent that more is at stake than simply an evaluation of what kinds of factfinding processes, alone or in combination, are likely to produce the most nearly reliable results. The stumbling-block is this: how much reliability is compatible with efficiency? Granted that informal factfinding will make some mistakes that will be remedied if backed up by adjudicative factfinding, the desirability of providing this backup is not affirmed or negated by factual demonstrations or predictions that the increase in reliability will be x percent or x plus n percent. It still remains to ask how much weight is to be given to the competing demands of reliability (a high degree of probability in each case that factual guilt has been accurately determined) and efficiency (a process that deals expeditiously with the large numbers of cases that it ingests). Just as the Crime Control Model is more optimistic about the unlikelihood of error in a significant number of cases, it is also more lenient in establishing a tolerable level of error. The Due Process Model insists on the prevention and elimination of mistakes to the extent possible; the Crime Control Model accepts the probability of mistakes up to the level at which they interfere with the goal of repressing crime, either becuase too many guilty people are escaping or, more subtly, because general awareness of the unreliability of the process leads to a decrease in the deterrent efficacy of the criminal law. On this view reliability and efficiency are not polar opposites but rather complementary characteristics. The system is reliable *because* efficient; reliability becomes a matter of independent concern only when it becomes so attenuated as to impair efficiency. All of this the Due Process Model rejects. If efficiency suggests shortcuts around reliability, those demands must be rejected. The aim of the process is at least as much to protect the factually innocent as it is to convict the factually guilty. It somewhat resembles quality control in industrial technology: tolerable deviation from standard varies with the importance of conformity to standard in the destined use of the product. The Due Process Model resembles a factory that has to devote a substantial part of its input to quality control. This necessarily reduces quantitative output.

This is only the beginning of the ideological difference between the two models. The Due Process Model could disclaim any attempt to provide enhanced reliability for the factfinding process and still produce a set of institutions and processes that would differ sharply from those posited by the demands of the Crime Control Mode. Indeed, it may not be too great an oversimplification to assert that in point of historical development the doctrinal pressures that have emanated from the demands of the Due Process Model have tended to evolve from an original matrix of concern with the maximization of reliability into something quite different and more far-reaching. This complex of values can be symbolized although not adequately described by the concept of the primacy of the individual and the complementary concept of limitation on official power.

The combination of stigma and loss of liberty that is embodied in the end result of the criminal process is viewed as being the heaviest deprivation that government can inflict on the individual. Furthermore, the processes that culminate in these highly afflictive sanctions are in themselves coercive, restrict-ing, and demeaning. Power is always subject to abuse, sometimes subtle, other times, as in the criminal process, open and ugly. Precisely because of its potency in subjecting the individual to the coercive power of the state, the criminal process must, on this model, be subjected to controls and safeguards that prevent it from operating with maximal efficiency. According to this ideology, maximal efficiency means maximal tyranny. And, while no one would assert that minimal efficiency means minimal tyranny, the proponents of the Due Process Model would accept with considerable equanimity a substantial diminution in the efficiency with which the criminal process operates in the interest of preventing official oppression of the individual.

The most modest-seeming but potentially far-reaching mechanism by which the Due Process Model implements these antiauthoritarian values is the doctrine of legal guilt. According to this doctrine, an individual is not to be held guilty of crime merely on a showing that in all probability, based upon reliable evidence, he did factually what he is said to have done. Instead, he is to be held guilty if and only if these factual determinations are made in procedurally regular fashion and by authorities acting within competences duly allocated to them. Further-more, he is not to be held guilty, even though the factual determination is or might be adverse to him, if various rules designed to safeguard the integrity of the process are not given effect: the tribunal that convicts him must have the power to deal with his kind of case ("jurisdiction") and must be geographically appropriate ("venue"); too long a time must not have elapsed since the offense was committed ("statute of limitations"); he must not have been previously convicted or acquitted of the same or a substantially similar offense ("double jeopardy"); he must not fall within a category of persons, such as children or the insane, who are legally immune to conviction ("criminal responsibility"); and so on. None of these requirements has anything to do with the factual question of whether he did or did not engage in the conduct that is charged as the offense against him; yet favorable answers to any of them will mean that he is legally innocent. Wherever the competence to make adequate factual determinations lies, it is apparent that only a tribunal that is aware of these guilt-defeating doctrines and is willing to apply them can be viewed as competent to make determinations of legal guilt. The police and the prosecutors are ruled out by lack of capacity in the first instance and by lack of assurance of willingness in the second. Only an impartial tribunal can be trusted to make determinations of legal as opposed to factual guilt.

In this context of legal guilt lies part of the explanation for the apparently quixotic presumption of innocence of which we spoke earlier. A man who after police investigation is charged with having committed a crime can hardly be said to be presumptively innocent, if what we mean is factual innocence. But if any of a myriad of legal doctrines may be appropriately invoked to exculpate this particular accused, it is apparent that as a matter of prediction it cannot be said with any confidence that more probably than not he will be found guilty.

Beyond the question of predictability this model posits a functional reason for observing the presumption of innocence: by forcing the state to prove its case against the accused in an adjudicative context, the presumption of innocence serves to force into play all the qualifying and disabling doctrines that limit the use of the criminal sanction against the individual, thereby enhancing his opportunity to secure a favorable outcome. In this sense the presumption of innocence may be seen to operate as a kind of self-fulfilling prophecy. By opening up a procedural situation that permits the successful assertion of defenses that have nothing to do with factual guilt, it vindicates the proposition that the factually guilty may nonetheless be legally innocent and should therefore be given a chance to qualify for that kind of treatment.

The possibility of legal innocence is expanded enormously when the criminal process is viewed as the appropriate forum for correcting its own abuses. This notion may well account for a greater amount of the distance between the two models than any other. In theory the Crime Control Model can tolerate rules that forbid illegal arrests, unreasonable searches, coercive interrogations, and the like if their enforcement is left primarily to managerial sanctions internally imposed. What it cannot tolerate is the vindication of those rules in the criminal process itself through the exclusion of evidence illegally obtained or through the reversal of convictions in cases where the criminal process has breached the rules laid down for its observance. The availability of these corrective devices fatally impairs the efficiency of the process. The Due Process Model, while it may in the first instance be addressed to the maintenance of reliable factfinding techniques, comes eventually to incorporate prophylactic and deterrent rules that result in the release of the factually guilty even in cases in which blotting out the illegality would still leave an adjudicative factfinder convinced of the accused's guilt.

Another strand in the complex of attitudes that underlies the Due Process Model is the idea—itself a shorthand statement for a complex of attitudes—of equality. This notion has only recently emerged as an explicit basis for pressing the demands of the Due Process Model, but it appears to represent, at least in its potential, a most powerful norm for influencing official conduct. Stated most starkly, the ideal of equality holds that "there can be no equal justice where the kind of trial a man gets depends on the amount of money he has."

The factual predicate underlying this assertion is that there are gross inequalities in the financial means of criminal defendants as a class, that in an adversary system of criminal justice, an effective defense is largely a function of the resources that can be mustered on behalf of the accused, and that a very large proportion of criminal defendants are, operationally speaking, "indigent" in terms of their ability to finance an effective defense. This factual premise has been strongly reinforced by recent studies that in turn have been both a cause and an effect of an increasing emphasis upon norms for the criminal process based on the premise.

The norms derived from the premise do not take the form of an insistence upon governmental responsibility to provide literally equal opportunities for all criminal defendants to challenge the process. Rather, they take as their point of departure the notion that the criminal process, initiated as it is by government and containing as it does the likelihood of severe deprivations at the hands of government, imposes some kind of public obligation to ensure that financial inability does not destroy the capacity of an accused to assert what may be meritorious challenges to the processes being invoked against him.

The demands made by a norm of this kind are likely by its very nature to be quite sweeping. Although its imperatives may be initially limited to determining whether in a particular case the accused was injured or prejudiced by his relative inability to make an appropriate challenge, the norm of equality very quickly moves to another level on which the demand is that the process in general be adapted to minimize discriminations rather than that a mere series of *post hoc* determinations of discrimination be made or makeable.

It should be observed that the impact of the equality norm will vary greatly depending upon the point in time at which it is introduced into a model of the criminal process. If one were starting from scratch to decide how the process ought to work, the norm of equality would have nothing very important to say on such questions as, for example, whether an accused should have the effective assistance of counsel in deciding whether to enter a plea of guilty. One could decide, on quite independent considerations, that it is or is not a good thing to afford that facility to the generality of persons accused of crime. But the impact of the equality norm becomes far greater when it is brought to bear on a process whose contours have already been shaped. If our model of the criminal process affords defendants who are in a financial position to consult a lawyer before entering a plea the right to do so, then the equality norm exerts powerful pressure to provide such an opportunity to all defendants and to regard the failure to do so as a malfunctioning of the process from whose consequences the accused is entitled to be relieved. In a sense that has been the role of the equality norm in affecting the real-world criminal process. It has made its appearance on the scene comparatively late and has therefore encountered a situation in which, in terms of the system as it operates, the relative financial inability of most persons accused of crime sharply distinguishes their treatment from the small minority of the financially capable. For that reason its impact has already been substantial and may be expected to be even more so in the future.

There is a final strand of thought in the Due Process Model whose presence is often ignored but which needs to be candidly faced if thought on the subject is not to be obscured. That is a mood of skepticism about the morality and the utility of the criminal sanction, taken either as a whole or in some of its applications. The subject is a large and complicated one, comprehending as it does much of the intellectual history of our times. To put the matter *in parvo,* one cannot improve upon the statement by Professor Paul Bator:

> [I]n summary we are told that the criminal law's notion of just condemnation and punishment is a cruel hypocrisy visited by a smug society on the psychologically and economically crippled; that its premise of a morally autonomous will with at least some measure of choice whether to comply with the values expressed in a penal code is unscientific and outmoded; that its reliance on punishment as an educational and deterrent agent is misplaced, particularly in the case of the very members of society most likely to engage in criminal conduct; and that its failure to provide for individualized and humane rehabilitation of offenders is inhuman and wasteful.

This skepticism, which may be fairly said to be widespread among the most influential and articulate of contemporary leaders of informed opinion, leads to an attitude toward the processes of the criminal law which, to quote Mr. Bator again, engenders

> a peculiar receptivity towards claims of injustice which arise within the traditional structure of the system itself; fundamental disagreement and unease about the very bases of the criminal law has, inevitably, created acute pressure at least to expand and liberalize those of its processes and doctrines which serve to make more tentative its judgments or limit its power.

In short, doubts about the ends for which power is being exercised create pressure to limit the discretion with which that power is exercised.

The point need not be pressed to the extreme of doubts about or rejection of the premises upon which the criminal sanction in general rests. Unease may be stirred simply by reflection on the variety of uses to which the criminal sanction is put and by judgment that an increasingly large proportion of those uses may represent an unwise invocation of so extreme a sanction. It would be an interesting irony if doubts about the utility of certain uses of the criminal sanction prove to contribute to a restrictive trend in the criminal process that in the end requires a choice among uses and finally an abandonment of some of the very uses that stirred the original doubts.

There are two kinds of problems that need to be dealt with in any model of the criminal process. One is what the rules shall be. The other is how the rules shall be implemented. The second is at least as important as the first. As we shall see time and again in our detailed development of the models, the distinctive difference between the two models is not only in the rules of conduct that they lay down, but also in the sanctions that are to be invoked when a claim is presented that the rules have been breached and, no less importantly, in the timing that is permitted or required for the invocation of those sanctions.

As I have already suggested, the Due Process Model locates at least some of the sanctions for breach of the operative rules in the criminal process itself. The relation between these two aspects of the process—the rules and the sanctions for their breach—is a purely formal one unless there is some mechanism for bringing them into play with each other. The hinge between them in the Due Process Model is the availability of legal counsel. This has a double aspect: many of the rules that the model requires are couched in terms of the availability of counsel to do various things at various stages of the process—this is the conventionally recognized aspects; beyond it, there is a pervasive assumption as to the necessity for counsel in order to invoke sanctions for breach of any of the rules. The more freely available these sanctions are, the more important is the role of counsel in seeing to it that the sanctions are appropriately invoked. If the process is seen as a series of occasions for checking its own operation, the role of counsel is a much more nearly central one than is the case in a process that is seen as primarily concerned with expeditious determination of factual guilt. And if equality of operation is a governing norm, the availability of counsel to some is seen as requiring it for all. Of all the controverted aspects of the criminal process, the right to counsel, including the role of government in its provision, is the most dependent on what one's model of the process looks like, and the least susceptible of resolution unless one has confronted the antinomies of the two models.

I do not mean to suggest that questions about the right to counsel disappear if one adopts a model of the process that conforms more or less closely to the Crime Control Model, but only that such questions become absolutely central if one's model moves very far down the spectrum of possibilities toward the pure Due Process Model. The reason for this centrality is to be found in the shared assumption underlying both models that the process is an adversary one in which the initiative in invoking relevant rules rests primarily on the parties concerned, the state and the accused. One could construct models that placed central responsibility on adjudicative agents such as committing magistrates and trial judges. And there are, as we shall see, marginal but nonetheless important adjustments in the role of the adjudicative agents that enter into the models with which we are concerned. For present purposes it is enough to say that these adjustments *are* marginal, that the animating presuppositions that underlie both models in the context of the American criminal system relegate the adjudicative agents to a relatively passive role and therefore place central importance on the role of counsel.

One last introductory note. What assumptions do we make about the sources of authority to shape the real-world operations of the criminal process? What agencies of government have the power to pick and choose between their competing demands? Once again, the limiting features of the American context come into play. Ours is not a system of legislative supremacy. The distinctively American institution of judicial review exercises a limiting and, ultimately, a shaping influence on the criminal process. Because the Crime Control Model is basically an affirmative model, emphasizing at every turn the existence and exercise of official power, its validating authority is ultimately legislative (although proximately administrative). Because the Due Process Model is basically a negative model, asserting limits on the nature of official power and on the modes of its exercise, its validating authority is judicial and requires an appeal to supralegislative law, to the law of the Constitution. To the extent that tensions between the two models are resolved by deference to the Due Process Model, the authoritative force at work is the judicial power, working in the distinctively judicial mode of invoking the sanction of nullity. That is at once the strength and the weakness of the Due Process Model: its strength because in our system the appeal to the Constitution provides the last and the overriding word; its weakness because saying no in specific cases is an exercise in futility unless there is a general willingness on the part of the officials who operate the process to apply negative prescriptions across the board. It is no accident that statements reinforcing the Due Process Model come from the courts while at the same time facts denying it are established by the police and prosecutors.

* * * * * * * *

THE SUPREME COURT AND RESTRICTIONS
ON POLICE INTERROGATION

LAWRENCE HERMAN

I. INTRODUCTION

This article concerns one of the major problems of criminal procedure: the scope and effect of constitutional restrictions on the interrogation of persons suspected of crime.

A woman has been viciously beaten and raped in a deserted alley. Now, at the police station, she looks at "mug shots," but she is unable to identify her assailant. She can give the police only the most general description. He was probably under thirty, of medium height and weight, and either a swarthy Caucasian or a light-skinned Negro. The description is hardly enough to warrant an arrest, but the police mechanism does not depend on such technical concepts as probable cause. Within a few hours, four men are taken into custody and booked "for investigation of rape." Each lives in the vicinity of the crime; each fits the general description; each has been convicted or suspected of rape or attempted rape; and each, in his turn, will be interrogated.

The interrogation room is windowless. Windows in a police station require bars; bars suggest imprisonment; and the thought of imprisonment is a deterrent to confession. The room is bare of distracting ornamentation and pictures; there is no telephone; there are no small objects to finger in relief of tension; the absence of ashtrays indicates that smoking is prohibited. The room is furnished with a desk and several straight-back chairs. The chairs discourage slouching or leaning. They are placed close together. The desk does not intrude between them. Interrogator and subject will face each other man to man.

Adjoining the interrogation room is a room from which other law-enforcement officers may observe the interrogation through a two-way mirror. No friend or representative of the suspect will be permitted in either the interrogation room or the observation room. The interrogation concerns only the subject and his interrogator. When the subject is brought into the interrogation room, he finds his interrogator in conservative civilian dress. The interrogator displays neither pencil nor paper. He appears disinterested in taking notes. He gives an impression of patience, an impression of having an unlimited amount of time for the interrogation. Should the subject ask to see an attorney, he may be met with the advice that truth is cheap and that he can save an attorney's fee by telling the truth. Should the subject decline to answer questions, he may be informed that he has a privilege of silence, but that silence carries an inference of guilt. The interrogation is already under way. The interrogator's techniques are effective, and they produce a confession. Because the confession contains an accurate description of the victim and the scene of the crime, the case is solved. Without the confession the case probably would not have been solved. Precisely

From *The Ohio State Law Journal*, Vol. 25, 1964, pp. 449–500. Reprinted by permission of *The Ohio State Law Journal* and the author.

which techniques of interrogation were used and how they produced a case-
-solving confession may be disputed at the subject's trial. It is not unlikely that
the subject will claim that he was beaten or that he was subjected to other
impermissible pressures or inducements. If the claims are made, they will be
denied by the interrogator.

Because confessions can be very important in the criminal process and
because interrogations are conducted in secret, it might be expected that
legislatures, the source of comprehensive codes of substantive and procedural
criminal law, would prescribe controls for the police interrogation stage. Sur-
prisingly, they have not done so. It is true, of course, that in most states a
person who is arrested is entitled to a prompt preliminary hearing; that in some
states he has a statutory right not to be held incommunicado; and that in two
jurisdictions he must be advised of his privilege of silence. But with these
exceptions, it has been correctly observed that "in the Anglo-American law there
is no regular provision for police examination of a person suspected of crime." In
the face of legislative silence, courts have attempted to resolve the problems of
police interrogation by creating certain exclusionary rules. Until January 1963,
the significant restrictions were the *McNabb-Mallory* rule at the federal level, and
the coerced confessions rule at both state and federal levels. The *McNabb-Mallory*
rule is unrelated to what happened during the interrogation. At least in theory,
its focal point is the failure of the police to bring the arrestee before a magistrate
without unreasonable delay. The confessions rule, however, relates directly to
what happened during the interrogation. Although the question is said to be
whether the confession was "voluntary," the rule has developed with an emphasis
on opprobrious police conduct. The *McNabb-Mallory* rule, in its origin and
present application, is a rule of statutory interpretation. The confessions rule,
however, is a due process requirement, and, until recently, it was regarded as the
only federal constitutional restriction on police interrogation.

In January 1963, in *Wong Sun v. United States,* the Supreme Court held
inadmissible incriminating statements made shortly after an unconstitutional
arrest. Thereby the Court suggested a fourth-amendment restriction on police
interrogation. Less than five months later, in *Haynes v. Washington,* the Court
held a confession inadmissible because the police had refused "to allow a suspect
to call his wife until he confessed." Thereby the Court changed the contour of
the confessions rule. Before the effect of these decisions could be felt, the Court
added two new dimensions to constitutional restrictions on police interrogation.
In *Massiah v. United States* and *Malloy v. Hogan,* respectively, the Court held
that the sixth-amendment right to counsel barred the admissibility of a post-
indictment confession obtained in the absence of counsel, and that the fifth-
amendment privilege against self-incrimination applied to the states through the
due process clause of the fourteenth amendment. Then, on the last day of the
1963 term, came what may prove to be the most significant decision ever made
in the area of criminal procedure. In *Escobedo v. Illinois,* a case in which most
of the previous restrictions coalesced, the Court held that the right to counsel
extended to the police interrogation stage of the criminal proceeding.

A preliminary assessment of the impact of all of these decisions, but
particularly of *Escobedo,* is the subject of this article. Development of the
problem in terms of a chronology of the cases would put *Wong Sun* first.
However, because the coerced confessions rule has been the traditional constitutional limitation on police interrogation, and because many aspects of the recent
decisions derive from dissatisfaction with the operation of that rule, consider-

ation will first be given to the due process restriction barring the admissibility of coerced confessions.

II. THE COERCED CONFESSIONS RULE

As developed by English courts, the confessions rule was designed to increase the accuracy of the guilt-determining process by excluding from evidence confessions obtained under pressure which, as viewed retrospectively and unscientifically by judges, was sufficient to create a fair risk of falsity. The rule and its rationale were adopted by the Supreme Court in 1884:

> But the presumption upon which weight is given to such evidence, namely, that one who is innocent will not imperil his safety or prejudice his interests by an untrue statement, ceases when the confession appears to have been made either in consequence of inducements of a temporal nature, held out by one in authority, touching the charge preferred, or because of a threat or promise by or in the presence of such person, which, operating upon the fears or hopes of the accused, in reference to the charge, deprives him of that freedom of will or self-control essential to make his confession *voluntary* within the meaning of the law.

From 1884 through 1940, the rule remained substantially unchanged, and, although the word "voluntary" was used to describe admissible confessions, it was clear that the test of admissibility was whether the confession was obtained under reliability-impairing circumstances. However, in 1941, in *Lisenba v. California,* a different tack was taken. Although the Court stated that "the aim of the rule that a confession is inadmissible unless voluntarily made is to exclude false evidence, five sentences later the Court observed that "the aim of the requirement of due process is not to exclude presumptively false evidence but to prevent fundamental unfairness in the use of evidence whether true or false." Of the two statements, the latter has proved the more durable. Although the Court has continued to mask its decisions with the test of voluntariness, and although the decisions can be harmonized with a theory of reliability, a police-methods theory has emerged. In *Spano v. New York,* it was stated:

> The abhorrence of society to the use of involuntary confessions does not turn alone on their inherent untrustworthiness. It also turns on the deep-rooted feeling that the police must *obey the law* while enforcing the law; that in the end life and liberty can be as much endangered from *illegal methods* used to convict those thought to be criminals as from the actual criminals themselves.

The point was reiterated in *Blackburn v. Alabama,* where the Court added:

> Thus a *complex of values* underlies the stricture against use by the state of confessions which, by way of convenient shorthand this court terms involuntary, and the role played by each in any situation varies according to the particular circumstances of the case.

Haynes v. Washington clearly demonstrates the extent of the restriction imposed by the police-methods theory. Shortly after a filling station robbery had been reported, petitioner was seen in the area by several policemen. After stating that he lived nearby, he walked to a house, fumbled with the screen door, then returned to the police car and stated, "You got me, let's go." He admitted the robbery and, en route to the police station, identified the filling station. At the

police station he was interrogated for about thirty minutes and he made a second
oral confession. The next morning he made a third oral confession and it was
transcribed. Shortly thereafter, he was taken to the office of a deputy prosecutor
where he made a fourth confession which was also transcribed. Although Haynes
refused to sign the transcribed confession, he did sign the transcript of the
confession given earlier that morning. Prior to signing the confession, he had
been held incommunicado for about sixteen hours, contrary to state law, and,
although he had requested permission to call his wife on the morning following
arrest, he was told that "when I had made a statement and cooperated with
them that they would see to it that as soon as I got booked I could call my
wife." Apparently at no time had Haynes been advised of a right to remain silent
or to consult counsel. On the other hand, Haynes made no claim of physical
abuse, lack of food or sleep, or prolonged interrogation.

Using the traditional jargon of voluntariness, a five-judge majority held the
confession inadmissible.

> Confronted with the express threat of continued incommunicado detention
> and induced by the promise of communication with and access to family
> Haynes understandably chose to make and sign the damning written
> statement; given the unfair and inherently coercive context in which made,
> that choice cannot be said to be *the voluntary product of a free and
> unconstrained will,* as required by the Fourteenth Amendment.

In no case of an adult defendant prior to *Haynes* had a confession "secured by
so mild a whip" been held inadmissible. Unlike the "composite defendant" of
prior cases, Haynes was not mentally subnormal, young, or naive and impressionable. To the contrary, he was an adult, of at least average intelligence, who,
in the eleven years preceding his trial, had been convicted of drunken driving,
resisting arrest, being without a driver's licence, breaking and entering, robbery,
breaking jail, and taking a car. Moreover, he had volunteered a threshold
confession. Measuring the result in *Haynes* by its facts, it is a good bet that a
majority of the present Court would hold inadmissible the confessions found to
have been admissible in such cases as *Lisenba v. California, Gallegos v. Nebraska,
Stroble v. California,* and *Stein v. New York. Haynes* clearly stands at the
periphery of the confessions rule.

In the hands of the current majority, the confessions rule operates with a
doctrinal sweep that permits little, if any, police pressure to obtain a confession.
Yet, police interrogation depends in large part upon an application of pressure
which is made effective by isolating the accused from those who give him
strength. Under *Haynes,* therefore, productive interrogation (interrogation followed by a constitutionally admissible confession) is, *in theory,* substantially
jeopardized. I stress the words "in theory" because, in the area of criminal
procedure, law in the Supreme Court cases frequently does not reflect the reality
of law in its operational aspects at the police station and in its doctrinal aspects
in state and lower federal courts. If it is clear that a confession is essential to
conviction, it is unlikely that the police will refrain from hard interrogation. If
the police are forced to choose between no-conviction-because-no-confession and
the more remote risk that a conviction will not be sustained because of coercive
interrogation, the latter is the likely choice.

Moreover, the sweep of the confessions rule is mitigated in practice by the
Court's own adherence to the terminology of voluntariness which hides the
values now underlying the confessions rule. The doctrine emphasizes police

conduct as is made abundantly clear by *Haynes.* The terminology of the rule, with a substantial assist from Mr. Justice Frankfurter's treatise in *Culombe v. Connecticut,* emphasizes the interrogee's reaction. The reaction, measured by the terminology of voluntariness, is, at best, a mixed question of law and fact. To be sure, the fact is of constitutional dimension, but it is still a fact. The result is that the fact-finding process cuts against the grain of the theory by dealing with the wrong issue. Further, because the issue frequently involves contradictory testimony, there arises a question of credibility, a contest between the defendant (whose guilt is manifested by his confession) and the police. Whether the question is resolved by judge or jury, it will in most cases be resolved against the defendant and he will be convicted. If he does not appeal, the matter is ended. If he does appeal, he runs up against the reluctance of appellate courts to overturn findings of fact and the impossibility of adequate policing by the Supreme Court. Although he does have a federal habeas corpus remedy, he is in jail during the pendency of the proceedings and whether the proceedings prove fruitful rests in large part upon whether the federal court has in mind the very standard from which its attention is diverted by the terminology of voluntariness. Thus, the result probably is an uneasy compromise in which the operation of the rule lags behind theory and thereby encourages the police to undertake the sort of interrogation that the theory prohibits. If the Court continues vigorously to proscribe "mild whips," as in *Haynes,* and particularly if the Court abandons the terminology of voluntariness, the theory of the confessions rule may filter down to other courts, and the area of compromise may shrink. But, unless the confessions rule has been made obsolete by recent developments, there will still be some compromise and there will still be productive police interrogation.

III. FOURTH-AMENDMENT RESTRICTIONS ON POLICE INTERROGATION

Until the decision in *Wong Sun v. United States,* it had generally been assumed that the fourth amendment had little impact on police interrogation, and a substantial majority of courts had refused to suppress confessions as derivatives of an unlawful arrest. In *Wong Sun,* six or seven federal narcotics agents, acting without probable cause, broke into the house of petitioner Toy and followed him into a bedroom. When Toy reached into a drawer, an agent drew a gun, pulled Toy's hand out of the drawer, arrested him, and then handcuffed him. Interrogated in the bedroom, Toy made incriminating statements and thereafter led the agents to the house of Yee where the agents found narcotics. Toy was then brought before a United States Commissioner for a preliminary hearing and was released on his own recognizance. Several days later, in the office of the Narcotics Bureau, Toy was again interrogated and he made further incriminating statements. At Toy's trial, the court accepted into evidence the narcotics, the statements made in the bedroom, and the statements made in the federal office. Toy was found guilty and his conviction was affirmed by the court of appeals. In the Supreme Court, the conviction was reversed on the ground that the bedroom statements and the narcotics were the derivatives of an unconstitutional arrest. Regarding the statements, the Court, following *Silverman v. United States,* held that the protection of the fourth amendment and the purpose of the exclusionary rule apply to verbal as well as physical evidence.

In determining whether *Wong Sun* is a significant restriction on police interrogation, there arises the preliminary question whether *Wong Sun* applies to the states. Although microscopic analysis of different parts of the opinion yields different conclusions, the matter has probably been put to rest by the generally unnoticed per curiam decision in *Traub v. Connecticut.* In *Traub,* the defendant was arrested without probable cause of the offense of arson and was taken to a police station where, after interrogation, he confessed. Following conviction, he appealed on the ground that his confession was inadmissible because it had been obtained after an unlawful arrest or during an unlawful detention or both. The Connecticut court, relying on the appellate court decision in *Wong Sun,* held that "the existence of an illegal arrest and detention does not automatically render inadmissible confessions made after the arrest or during the period of detention. Traub then filed a petition for a writ of certiorari, and the Supreme Court, in a unanimous decision, vacated the judgment and remanded the case for reconsideration in the light of *Wong Sun* and *Ker v. California.* In *Ker,* the Court had held that fourth-amendment questions in state courts were to be governed by federal standards. Consequently, *Traub* must be taken as establishing that the *Wong Sun* rule is applicable to the states.

However, the decision of the Connecticut court on remand indicates that pressing problems remain. The court held that *Wong Sun* created no absolute, fourth-amendment barrier to admissibility; that a confession is inadmissible under *Wong Sun* only if there is a causal relationship between the illegal detention and the confession; and that this rule of inadmissibility is the only change made by *Wong Sun* in the coerced confessions rule. A slightly different rationale in favor of admissibility was used in *Hollingworth v. United States.* The court held that the gauge of admissibility is still the voluntariness of the confession, and that, in *Wong Sun,* the Court held only that the unlawful arrest made the confession involuntary.

On the other hand, in several state and federal cases, confessions not claimed to have been involuntary have been held inadmissible under *Wong Sun* apparently solely because they were obtained shortly after an unconstitutional arrest or search. Typical of the uneven treatment accorded *Wong Sun* is *Commonwealth v. Palladino.* There, immediately after an arrest assumed by the court to have been unconstitutional, the defendant made certain statements. About an hour after his arrest, he made additional statements at a police station. The court held that what the defendant said immediately after arrest was inadmissible, but that what he said an hour later was admissible.

The picture, then, is one of judicial disagreement over the meaning of the *Wong Sun* rule (a disagreement that parallels the theory-practice gap under the confessions rule), and the blame must be borne entirely by the unsurpassedly vague opinion of Mr. Justice Brennan in *Wong Sun.* The ambiguities have been explored in detail elsewhere and need not be considered here. It is sufficient for present purposes to note that isolated passages of the opinion support all of the subsequent, divergent decisions. Until the rule is clarified by the Supreme Court, it will probably have little impact on police interrogation, and, at this juncture, appraisal can be made only in the alternative. If the *Wong Sun* result is based on a test of voluntariness, it adds nothing to the confessions rule. Similarly, it will prove to be illusory if it is based on a causal relationship between the unconstitutional arrest and the confession. Because it is highly unlikely that many arrestees will know that the arrest is improper, it will be impossible to establish a causal relationship between the illegality of the arrest and the confession.

If, however, the *Wong Sun* rule rests exclusively on the unconstitutionality of the arrest, as some commentators have suggested, the rule may have drastic consequences for police interrogation. Available evidence indicates that the police frequently arrest on less than probable cause. Consequently, unless the constitutional standard of probable cause is watered down in subsequent cases, a stringent interpretation of the *Wong Sun* rule against the state will make inadmissible a confession obtained after a dragnet arrest or after the so-called "arrest on suspicion" or "arrest for investigation." The result will be a second giant step toward the end of "productive" police interrogation. This step, it should be noted, has nothing to do with the accuracy or reliability of the guilt-finding process. But it has everything to do with the constitutional value of privacy—the right to be free from governmental restraint unless the state has probable cause to take action—a value which is hard to accommodate with present procedures of police interrogation.

IV. THE PRIVILEGE AGAINST SELF-INCRIMINATION

In 1908, in *Twining v. New Jersey,* eight judges of the Supreme Court held that the fifth amendment's privilege against self-incrimination did not apply to the states. Thirty-nine years later, in *Adamson v. California,* five judges of the Supreme Court adhered to *Twining.* Both cases involved comment on the defendant's failure to testify at trial, and, in spite of sweeping language in both opinions, there was some reason to believe that the court would not tolerate more severe sanctions. However, in *Cohen v. Hurley,* five judges held that New York could constitutionally disbar an attorney who, on grounds of self-incrimination, refused to testify at a judicial inquiry into ambulance chasing. In a dissenting opinion, Mr. Justice Brennan argued that the privilege should be applied to the states will full force; that there was no historical or logical basis for partial application; and that, in fact, there had already been a partial application. In support of the last point, he observed:

> The case before us presents, for me, another situation in which the application of the full sweep of a specific is denied, although the court has held that its restraints are absorbed in the Fourteenth Amendment for some purposes. Only this Term we applied, admittedly not in terms but nevertheless in fact the privilege against compulsory self-incrimination guaranteed by the Fifth Amendment to invalidate a state conviction obtained with the aid of a confession, however true, which was secured from the accused by duress or coercion. *Rogers v. Richmond,* 365 U.S. 534; and see *Bram v. United States,* 168 U.S. 532.

In the critical comment that followed *Cohen,* no notice was taken of Mr. Justice Brennan's obvious effort to effect an engagement between the privilege against self-incrimination and the coerced confessions rule. Indeed, most lawyers, judges, and commentators, if pressed on the matter, probably would have said that the point was a cute forensic device but otherwise not meritorious. For all practical purposes, the point was ignored until, infused by the vote of Mr. Justice Goldberg, it became a cornerstone of Mr. Justice Brennan's opinion in *Malloy v. Hogan.*

In 1959, William Malloy was convicted of the misdemeanor of gambling in Hartford, Connecticut. About sixteen months later, he was ordered to testify at a judicial inquiry into gambling. Asked a series of questions concerning his arrest and conviction, he invoked the privilege against self-incrimination, was committed for contempt, and sought his release through a petition for habeas corpus in which he specifically raised the federal constitutional issue. The superior court denied relief and Malloy appealed to the Supreme Court of Errors. Although the latter court stated that the federal constitutional privilege was inapplicable to state proceedings, it recognized that some restrictions were imposed by the due process clause of the fourteenth amendment. However, relying on both state and federal cases, the court held that Malloy had not sufficiently demonstrated a risk of incrimination. Relief was denied, but Malloy's petition for certiorari was granted by the Supreme Court.

Three issues were presented to the Court: whether the fifth-amendment privilege applied to the states; if so, whether it applied with full, federal constitutional content; and whether the privilege had been violated. The Court answered all three questions in the affirmative. Only the first and second answers will be considered herein.

In support of his contention that the fifth amendment's privilege against self-incrimination applied to the states, counsel for the petitioner made a deceptively simple, three-step argument: (1) the fourth and fifth amendments are "so intertwined as to be complementary," (2) the fourth amendment applies to the states through the due process clause of the fourteenth amendment; (3) therefore, the fifth amendment should be applied to the states. Counsel for Connecticut, however, conceded an even more persuasive argument: that underlying the confessions rule was the privilege against self-incrimination, and that the Court, in the guise of the confessions rule, had been applying the privilege as a bar to state inquiry. In a statement that magnificently pointed up one prosecutor's view of the relationship between the various possible constitutional restrictions on police interrogation, counsel for Connecticut observed:

> Underlying the decisions excluding coerced confessions is the implicit assumption that an accused is privileged against incriminating himself, either in the jail house, the grand jury room, or on the witness stand in a public trial. The principal motivation for incommunicado coercion by the police is the effort to circumvent the suspect's right of silence which will be available to him in the formal proceedings. cf. *Culombe v. Connecticut,* 367 U.S. 568, 571. The principal reason for excluding confessions coerced by the police is to preserve the right of silence available in later proceedings.
>
> Even if an accused could be compelled to testify against himself in a trial, there would still be some motive for attempting to pry a confession from him before he had counsel. The coerced confession cases, therefore, also tend to preserve the right to counsel. Yet no federal right to have counsel present at all official interrogations has been recognized by the Court. See *In re Groban,* 352 U.S. 330; *Anonymous v. Baker,* 360 U.S. 287. So it is not merely protection of the right to counsel that is involved, but preservation of the right of silence. It is fundamentally inconsistent to suggest, as the Court's opinions now suggest, that the State is entirely free to compel an accused to incriminate himself before a grand jury, or at the trial, but cannot do so in the police station. Frank recognition of the fact that the Due Process Clause prohibits the States from enforcing their laws by compelling the accused to confess, regardless of whether such compulsion occurs, would not only clarify the principles involved in confession cases, but would assist the States significantly in their efforts to comply with the limitations placed upon them by the Fourteenth Amendment.

And the Court took him at his word. Although the Court might have distinguished *Twining* and *Adamson,* or might have disagreed with their rationales outright, it chose to do neither. Rather, the Court, speaking through Mr. Justice Brennan, stated that "Decisions of the Court since *Twining* and *Adamson* have departed from the . . . view expressed in those cases. We discuss first the decisions which forbid the use of coerced confessions in state criminal prosecutions." Following analysis of cases through *Haynes v. Washington,* the Court asserted:

> [T]he American system of criminal prosecution is accusatorial, not inquisitorial, and . . . the Fifth Amendment privilege is its essential mainstay. . . .
> Since the Fourteenth Amendment prohibits the States from inducing a person to confess through "sympathy falsely aroused" [citing *Spano v. New York*] or other like inducement far short of "compulsion by torture" [citing *Haynes*], it follows *a fortiori* that it also forbids the states to resort to imprisonment, as here to compel him to answer questions that might incriminate him. The Fourteenth Amendment secures against state invasions the same privilege that the Fifth Amendment guarantees against federal infringement—the right of a person to remain silent unless he chooses to speak *in the unfettered exercise of his own will.*

In a dissenting opinion, Mr. Justice White, joined by Mr. Justice Stewart, took no issue with what might have seemed to some a shotgun wedding of the privilege to the confessions rule. His point was that the record did not disclose a risk of incrimination. Only Mr. Justice Harlan, joined by Mr. Justice Clark, was moved to complain that "[I]n none of the cases cited in which was developed the full sweep of the constitutional prohibition against the use of coerced confessions at state trials was there anything to suggest that the Fifth Amendment was being made applicable to state proceedings." However, even he was forced to note that "[the coerced confession cases] do, it seems to me, carry an implication that coercion to incriminate oneself, even when under the form of law . . . is inconsistent with due process."

The significance of *Malloy* lies not in the belief that the privilege is something new to state criminal procedure. To the contrary, all states have recognized the privilege as a matter of local law. What is significant is that, by necessary inference from Mr. Justice Brennan's opinion, the privilege, as a matter of constitutional law, applies at the police station. If the privilege gives the defendant greater protection than is accorded by the confessions rule, the latter has become obsolete in determining the admissibility of confessions. The critical questions then, are two: (1) What is the test for determining whether the police have obtained a confession in violation of the privilege; and (2) does the privilege give more or less protection than the confessions rule?

In attempting to ascertain the test to be used in deciding whether the privilege has been violated by police interrogation, a stumbling block is immediately encountered: most of the federal self-incrimination cases do not involve police interrogation. The paucity of case law may be attributed to two factors. First, until *Malloy,* there was no well settled rule, even in federal courts, that the privilege applied at the police station. Second, the creation of the *McNabb-Mallory* rule made it unnecessary in most cases to consider the confession problem in any terms other than delay. Indeed, since the decision in *McNabb,* the Court has reviewed only one federal case involving the confessions rule. Accordingly, if a case-law test is sought, reliance must be placed both on the many cases that do not involve police interrogation and on the few cases that do.

An examination of the cases that do not involve police interrogation discloses three basic fact situations that deserve comment. In the first, the court must decide whether the information sought by the government is within the protection of the privilege, that is, whether the information is testimonial as opposed to demonstrative, or whether the information tends to incriminate. These cases are irrelevant to the problem under consideration because by hypothesis the instant problem involves an oral or written confession, a clearly incriminating, testimonial utterance.

In the second group of cases, the state imposes a sanction upon the defendant for exercising his privilege. Here, the only question is whether the sanction is an impermissible compulsion. The cases involve such questions as whether a doctor may be prohibited from performing medical duties because he refused to divulge information when applying for a military commission, and whether a discharge in bankruptcy may be conditioned upon an incriminating explanation of lost assets. Although the cases are obviously distinguishable from cases involving police interrogation, they raise a question that may also be relevant in the context of police interrogation: whether the police conduct leading to the confession constitutes an impermissible compulsion.

In the third group of cases, the defendant answers some questions, but invokes the privilege as to others. Here, the only question is whether the defendant has waived the privilege. The same question may be relevant to a determination of whether the privilege has been violated by police interrogation.

Separation of the questions in terms of compulsion and waiver should not be taken as an indication that the terms are unrelated. Even though inquiry has not yet been made into the content of the terms, it is clear that they overlap. If, yielding to impermissible pressure, the defendant confesses, both terms may be applied. The defendant has been compelled to incriminate himself and he has not waived his privilege. On the other hand, pressure may be lacking to such an extent that an argument of compulsion would be frivolous. At the same time, it could be argued that the defendant had not waived his privilege. Perhaps he did not know that he had a privilege; perhaps he was tricked into making a statement; or perhaps he did not realize the incriminating import of his statements. Whatever the situation, if the argument of non-waiver is permissible, and if, as permitted, it is broad enough to cover the case, the traditional law of confessions has been shattered. An examination of the few self-incrimination/confessions cases indicates that the devastation may already have occurred.

Three cases must be noted, *Bram v. United States, Brock v. United States,* and *Escobedo v. Illinois.* In *Bram,* the defendant, an American seaman, was suspected of murdering his captain, and was interrogated by a detective in Halifax, Nova Scotia. Prior to the interrogation, the defendant's clothing was removed for inspection. While the defendant was nude, the detective told him that a fellow-sailor claimed to have observed him commit the murder in the captain's cabin. When Bram was informed that the fellow-sailor had been standing at the wheel, he replied, "He could not see me from there." This denial was accepted into evidence for its implication of guilt, and Bram was convicted. The Supreme Court, however, held the statement inadmissible under the self-incrimination clause of the fifth amendment.

Much of the opinion is couched in the language of the confessions rule, and, in view of the fact that Bram had been stripped prior to the interrogation, the case may represent nothing more than a recognition that an interrogee who is stripped may reasonably fear a beating. However, the Court also stressed the fact that the statement resulted from an accusation:

> But the situation of the accused, and the nature of the communication made to him by the detective, necessarily overthrows any possible implication that his reply to the detective could have been the result of a purely voluntary mental action; that is to say, when all the surrounding circumstances are considered in their true relations, not only is the claim that the statement was voluntary overthrown, but the impression is irresistibly produced that it must necessarily have been the result of either hope or fear, or both, operating on the mind.
>
> It cannot be doubted that, placed in the position which the accused was when the statement was made to him that the other suspected person had charged him with crime, the result was to produce upon his mind the fear that if he remained silent it would be considered an admission of guilt, and therefore render certain his being committed for trial as the guilty person, and it cannot be conceived that the converse impression would not have naturally arisen, that by denying there was hope of removing the suspicion from himself.

Although the quoted passage is not irreconcilable with the confessions rule, it can be interpreted as a rejection of all confessions that result from interrogation, all confessions, that is, except those that are volunteered. Such an interpretation would flow from a deep-seated distrust of the techniques of interrogation. That the Court entertained such a distrust is clear from its reference to the statement in *Brown v. Walker* regarding the origin of the privilege:

> if an accused person be asked to explain his apparent connection with a crime under investigation, the ease with which the questions put to him may assume an inquisitorial character, the temptation to press the witness unduly, to browbeat him if he be timid or reluctant, to push him into a corner, *to entrap him into fatal contradictions* . . . made the system so odious as to give rise to a demand for its total abolition.

However, to question the techniques of interrogation and to say that the privilege bars the admissibility of a confession that is not volunteered is not to establish with any precision a test for determining when the privilege has been violated. Nor is a test established by regarding a confession as volunteered only if the defendant desires to confess. As noted above, a determination of whether the privilege has been violated may be made by either of two overlapping tests: whether the defendant was compelled to incriminate himself, and whether the defendant waived his privilege. In *Bram,* primary emphasis appears to have been placed on the compulsion test. However, there is nothing in *Bram* that constitutes a rejection of the waiver test. Moreover, because it is required that a waiver be voluntary, the same result would have been reached under either test. In short, insofar as the articulation of a test is concerned, *Bram* is probably a standoff.

In *Brock v. United States,* federal revenue agents discovered an illicit still near a house. Looking through a window, they observed the defendant sleeping. One of the agents, pretending to be a fellow-moonshiner, said, "Come down to the still and help us." The defendant, still asleep, said, "No, I am not going down there today." The agent then stated that a blower had broken and that help was needed. The defendant replied in his sleep, "You . . . wouldn't help me last night, and I am not going to help you today." This statement was accepted into evidence at his trial, and the defendant was convicted. On appeal, the statement was held inadmissible by the United States Court of Appeals for the Fifth Circuit:

> Evidence obtained at the end of a whip is no less voluntary than that derived by insidious and more subtle means where the opportunity to exercise the right against self-incrimination is absent. Before a man can be compelled to testify against himself, he must have a fair chance to exercise his right under the Fifth Amendment.

The court thus blended the language of compulsion with the language of waiver. The principal ingredient, however, is waiver. If the agents had simply overheard incriminating statements made in sleep, it could not fairly be argued that they had compelled the remarks. Even though they induced the statements in *Brock,* they used no pressure. What must be emphasized, then, is that the defendant was unaware that he was making a statement, that it was incriminating and that it was being recorded in the agent's memory. In sum, the defendant had no opportunity to assert or waive his privilege. However, it should be noted that the incriminating statements in *Brock* probably would have been inadmissible as involuntary even under the confessions rule. Consequently, although *Brock* suggests the waiver test, it, too, is probably no more than a standoff.

In *Escobedo v. Illinois,* the defendant was arrested on suspicion of murder and was interrogated during a fifteen hour period. He made no incriminating statements and was released on a writ of habeas corpus obtained by his attorney. Eleven days later, he was re-arrested and was taken to the police station. He requested an opportunity to see his attorney but the request was denied. Shortly after the defendant's arrival at the police station, his attorney arrived and demanded to see him. The demand was refused. At one point, the attorney saw the defendant through an open door and made a gesture which the defendant interpreted as an admonition of silence. This was the only contact between attorney and client at the police station.

During the interrogation, the defendant was accused by a co-defendant of firing the gun. He replied, "I didn't shoot Manuel, you did it," thereby admitting some knowledge of the crime. The admission was apparently used as a wedge and the defendant made further incriminating statements. At no time did anyone at the police station advise the defendant of his rights. Although the defendant had consulted counsel during the period between arrests, the record disclosed only that counsel had told the defendant "to tell the officers in a nice way that [he] was sorry but that [he] could not talk to them until [he] had the advice of [his] lawyer." The record did not disclose that the attorney had specifically advised the defendant of his privilege against self-incrimination.

After the defendant's conviction had been affirmed by the Supreme Court of Illinois, the Supreme Court of the United States granted certiorari. In his brief, the defendant argued that the confession was inadmissible under the confessions rule and that it was inadmissible under a right-to-counsel theory. In support of his confessions-rule argument, the defendant stressed, as part of the "totality of the circumstances," that he had not been advised of the privilege, and that, as in *Bram,* incrimination resulted from the defendant's attempt to deny an accusation of guilt. In support of his right-to-counsel argument, the defendant claimed that the presence of counsel was necessary to effectuate the privilege. Thus, although the Court did not have before it the form of the privilege argument, it did have the substance.

As will be discussed in detail later, the Court, in an opinion by Mr. Justice Goldberg, held the confession inadmissible on a right-to-counsel theory. However, the privilege argument did not go unnoticed:

> the purpose of the interrogation was to 'get him' to confess his guilt despite his constitutional right not to do so. At the time of his arrest and throughout the course of the interrogation, the police told petitioner that they had convincing evidence that he had fired the fatal shots. Without informing him of his absolute right to remain silent in the face of this accusation, the police urged him to make a statement.

If, after *Malloy v. Hogan*, there was any basis to question the applicability of the privilege at the police station, *Escobedo* answers the question. The privilege is applicable. Moreover, by inference from *Escobedo*, the privilege supplants the confessions rule as a test for determining the admissibility of confessions obtained by the police. On the facts of *Escobedo*, the confession could have been held inadmissible under the confessions rule. Indeed, *Escobedo* probably was a stronger case for inadmissibility than *Haynes v. Washington*. Like Haynes, Escobedo had been held incommunicado. Unlike Haynes, Escobedo was twenty-two years old and of Mexican extraction. Apparently he had no prior criminal record, he had not made a threshold confession, he was interrogated while handcuffed in a standing position, he was nervous and upset during the interrogation, he had not slept well for a week prior to the interrogation, he was cut off from the only person who had previously given him advice, and part of the interrogation was conducted by a Spanish-speaking policeman who grew up in the defendant's neighborhood and who knew the defendant's family. The major part of the defendant's brief was devoted to the confessions rule, the traditional test for the admissibility of confessions. The Court, however, ignored the test and used instead a right-to-counsel/privilege approach. Although the opinion purports to rest on sixth-amendment grounds, the privilege is not just another item under the heading of right to counsel. To the contrary, the privilege is one of the bases of the right-to-counsel argument. The defendant so urged in his brief, and Mr. Justice Goldberg so stated in his opinion. Responding to the contention that it would be more difficult to obtain confessions if the interrogee were given an opportunity to consult counsel, Mr. Justice Goldberg stated that "our Constitution, unlike some others, strikes the balance in favor of the right of the accused to be advised by his lawyer of his privilege against self-incrimination."

However, to say that, as a result of *Escobedo,* the privilege has supplanted the confessions rule is not to say that the privilege accords greater protection. Consideration still must be given to the test for determining whether a confession has been obtained in violation of the privilege. To this problem two parts of the *Escobedo* opinion are relevant. After launching a vigorous attack on the reliability of methods of criminal-law enforcement that depend on confessions, Mr. Justice Goldberg stated:

> We have also learned the companion lesson of history that no system of criminal justice can, or should, survive if it comes to depend for its continued effectiveness on the citizens' *abdication through unawareness* of their constitutional rights. . . . If the exercise of constitutional rights will thwart the effectiveness of a system of law enforcement, then there is something very wrong with that system.

In a footnote, Mr. Justice Goldberg continued:

> The accused may, of course, *intelligently and knowingly waive his privilege against self-incrimination* and his right to counsel either at a pre-trial stage or at the trial. . . . But no knowing and intelligent *waiver of any constitutional right* can be said to have occurred under the circumstances of this case.

From these quotations, there is reason to suggest that, in future cases, the admissibility of a confession obtained by the state will depend upon whether the defendant waived his privilege against self-incrimination. But under what circumstances can it be said that the privilege has or has not been waived? What is the meaning or content of waiver? As it bears on these questions, Mr. Justice Goldberg's opinion is susceptible to a number of interpretations.

As already noted the opinion sets out in detail the factors that would have been relevant to a confessions-rule determination. These factors are also relevant to the problem of waiver. If the defendant was subjected to pressures impermissible under the confessions rule, it can hardly be argued that he voluntarily waived his privilege against self-incrimination. On the other hand, if waiver exists in every case in which such pressure is absent, the privilege accords no greater protection than the confessions rule, and the impact of *Escobedo* on the law of confessions will be negligible. It is possible to argue that minimal pressure, insufficient for invalidation under the confesions rule, would be sufficient for a finding that the defendant had not voluntarily waived the privilege. The argument, however, borders on the frivolous not only because it involves an impossible, metaphysical comparison but also because the confessions rule, as applied in *Haynes,* allows almost no latitude for pressure. Consequently, it must be concluded that the theory of waiver, if tested by voluntariness, represents no addition to the protection of the confessions rule.

Voluntariness, however, is not the only requirement for a finding of waiver. If a waiver is to be effective, it must also be "intelligent" and "knowing." In *Escobedo* it was said that such a waiver did not occur "under the circumstances of [the] case." Why? Different answers of the drastically different impact, may be derived by implication from Mr. Justice Goldberg's opinion.

The first answer is an easy one: Escobedo did not know that he had a constitutional privilege and therefore he could not knowingly waive it. No one at the police station warned him of his rights. Although he had consulted counsel before his second arrest, and although counsel had told him to remain silent, the record did not reflect that counsel had specifically advised him of his constitutional privilege. Nor could counsel's gesture at the police station be taken as such advice. If, in future cases, *Escobedo* is limited to this answer, then it adds only the following small morsel to the confessions rule: the defendant must be advised of his constitutional privilege before he is interrogated. Such a warning is now required by a Texas statute and by the Uniform Code of Military Justice, and there is some evidence that neither in Texas nor in the military jurisdiction has the requirement impaired productive interrogation. A constitutionally required warning probably would have no greater effect.

The second answer is a more difficult one: Escobedo was not advised of his constitutional privilege at that critical point in the interrogation when he was accused by a co-defendant of firing the fatal shots. Therefore, and without regard to any previous warning, he did not knowingly waive his privilege when, in an effort to deny the accusation, he admitted incriminating knowledge of the incident which was thereafter used to obtain additional information from him. The factual component of this answer is correct, and the legal component finds some support in Mr. Justice Goldberg's opinion:

> At the time of his arrest and throughout the course of the interrogation the police told petitioner that they had convincing evidence that he had fired the fatal shots. Without informing him of his *absolute right to remain silent in the face of this accusation,* the police urged him to make a statement.

In a footnote, Mr. Justice Goldberg added:

> Although there is testimony in the record that petitioner and his lawyer had previously discussed what petitioner should do in the event of interrogation, there is no evidence that they discussed what petitioner should, or could, do in the face of a false accusation that he had fired the fatal bullets.

Finally, in a capsulization of the salient facts of the case, Mr. Justice Goldberg noted that "the police [had] not *effectively* warned him of his absolute constitutional right to remain silent."

If, in subsequent decisions, this answer to the waiver question proves correct, then a tremendous restriction will be imposed upon police interrogation. The entire thrust of police interrogation is to put the defendant in an emotional state in which his instinct for self-preservation is dulled and (building upon the passage already quoted) in which the defendant, through temporary unawareness, abdicates his constitutional privilege against self-incrimination. If, at the critical points in the interrogation, it is required that the defendant be advised of his privilege of silence, the fluidity of the interrogation will be interrupted, and the defendant, emboldened by both the interruption and the advice, may remain silent. The result will be that the police will obtain far fewer confessions than they now obtain. In all probability, only the volunteered confession, the confession made by one who, with knowledge of his rights, desires to confess, will be admissible. Under this interpretation of *Escobedo,* the privilege will give far more protection than the confessions rule.

The third answer is even more difficult: when he made his abortive denial, Escobedo did not know that he was incriminating himself because he did not realize the legal significance of his statement. Consequently, he did not knowingly and intelligently waive the privilege. Again, the factual component of the answer is correct and, again, the legal component has a basis in Mr. Justice Goldberg's opinion. As has already been noted, some emphasis was placed on the facts that Escobedo was not "effectively warned . . . [by the police] of his absolute constitutional right to remain silent," and that the pre-interrogation advice of counsel did not include instructions regarding Escobedo's response to an accusation that he had fired the gun. Moreover, it was observed that:

> Petitioner, a layman, was undoubtedly unaware that under Illinois law an admission of mere complicity was legally as damaging as an admission of firing the fatal shots. . . . The guiding hand of counsel was essential to advise petitioner of his rights in this delicate situation.

The most effective warning would, of course, advise the defendant of the significance of what he was about to say, and that he had a right to make no statement. Obviously, the police hoped that, in response to the accusation of what might be regarded as a more serious offense, Escobedo's denial would be pregnant with an admission of a lesser offense. Indeed, this is a recommended technique of interrogation, just as it is a recommended technique of interrogation to minimize the moral seriousness of the offense charged. In either case, it is quite likely that the defendant does not realize the importance of what he is saying, and the police intend to capitalize on his unawareness. Consequently, if in subsequent cases it is held that such unawareness vitiates waiver, a restriction of enormous dimension will circumscribe police interrogation: recommended and highly effective techniques of interrogation will be forbidden. Again, the likely result will be the inadmissibility of all confessions that are not volunteered, the privilege will give far greater protection than the confessions rule, and effective interrogation will be constitutionally impermissible.

Of the three possible interpretations of *Escobedo,* the first interpretation is certainly viable, unless *Escobedo* is meaningless on the fifth-amendment point. The important question, therefore, is whether either of the remaining interpretations will be adopted by the Court. The question is important not only because an answer will shed new light on the privilege but also because the answer will determine the role that the defendant's attorney must be accorded during the police interrogation.

In his dissenting opinion, Mr. Justice White reads the majority opinion as standing for more than the first interpretation:

> The Court may be concerned with a narrower matter: the unknowing defendant who responds to police questioning because he mistakenly believes that he must and that his admissions will not be used against him. *But this worry hardly calls for the broadside the Court has now fired.* The failure to inform an accused that he need not answer and that his answers may be used against him is very relevant indeed to whether the disclosures are compelled. Cases in this Court, to say the least, have never placed a premium on ignorance of constitutional rights.

There is no indication in the dissenting opinion of the cases that Mr. Justice White had in mind. One can guess, however, that they concern the right to counsel because it is in those cases that the Court has most vigilantly guarded against the waiver of constitutional rights. For example, in *Glasser v. United States,* the defendant, formerly an Assistant United States Attorney, objected to the trial court's suggestion that his attorney be appointed to represent a co-defendant. Thereafter, when the co-defendant indicated that he would accept appointed counsel, the appointment was made, and the defendant remained silent. The Court held that by his silence the defendant did not waive his right to the effective assistance and undivided loyalty of his attorney. In *Von Moltke v. Gillies,* the defendant, charged with wartime espionage, purportedly waived her right to counsel and pleaded guilty. Four judges were convinced that the record disclosed no intelligent waiver; three judges held that the right had been waived; and two judges found the record incomplete. Because a majority of the Court was unwilling to affirm, the case was remanded for further findings. However, the plurality opinion of Mr. Justice Black, concurred in by Mr. Justice Douglas, merits consideration:

> The fact that an accused may tell [the trial judge] that he is informed of his right to counsel and desires to waive this right does not automatically end the judge's responsibility. To be valid such waiver must be made with an apprehension of the nature of the charges, the statutory offenses

included within them, the range of allowable punishments thereunder, possible defenses to the charges and circumstances in mitigation thereof, and all other facts essential to a broad understanding of the whole matter. A judge can make certain that an accused's professed waiver of counsel is understandingly and wisely made only from a penetrating and comprehensive examination of all the circumstances under which such a plea is tendered.

In *Carnley v. Cochran,* the Court, in holding that the trial judge had not adequately protected the rights of an unrepresented defendant, stated:

it appears that, while petitioner was advised [by the trial judge] that he need not testify, he was not told *what consequence might follow if he did testify.* He chose to testify and his criminal record was brought out on his cross-examination. For defense lawyers, it is commonplace to weigh the risk to the accused of the revelation on cross-examination of a prior criminal record, when advising an accused whether to take the stand in his own behalf. For petitioner, *the question had to be decided in ignorance of this important consideration.*

If the right to counsel cases furnish an appropriate analogy, they fully support the suggestion that *Escobedo* should be read for all three interpretations of the waiver theory. This suggestion is reinforced by the fact that in recent cases, including *Escobedo,* the Court has surrounded the pre-trial stage with safeguards traditionally associated only with the trial. Insofar as the privilege is concerned, the accused need not testify for any purpose unless he chooses to do so. He cannot be called as a witness without his consent. Before consenting to testify, he will have been primed by his attorney for cross-examination. Moreover, the attorney can by objection protect his client against trick questions and abusive cross-examination. If the substance of these safeguards is available at the police interrogation stage, the privilege has been accorded all of the interpretations discussed above, and productive police interrogation is, in theory, at an end.

However, once again the words "in theory" are relevant. It is quite likely that state and lower federal courts will attempt to narrow the scope of *Escobedo.* Impetus for a restrictive interpretation will undoubtedly come from the impact of a broad interpretation. Because the possibilities of restrictive interpretation must be assessed on the basis of the opinion as a whole, a consideration of these possibilities will be deferred until the right-to-counsel aspect has been discussed. For now, it is sufficient to observe that the critical question for future resolution is this: how *effective* a privilege against self-incrimination does a majority of the present Court want? The answer to that question will resolve the constitutional theory of police interrogation.

V. RIGHT TO COUNSEL

In 1958, in the cases of *Crooker v. California* and *Cicenia v. Lagay,* the Court was faced with the question of whether there was a constitutional right to counsel at the police station. In *Crooker,* the defendant was a thirty-one-year old college graduate who, during one year of law school, had studied criminal law. Prior to interrogation, he was advised by a policeman of his privilege against self-incrimination. After the police had denied his request to consult a named attorney, he was interrogated. By answering some questions and refusing to answer others he indicated that he understood his privilege. Ultimately he confessed to murder. The Court, in a five-to-four decision, first held the confession to be voluntary. Then, applying the prevailing standard of *Betts v. Brady,* the Court held that the confession was not inadmissible for want of counsel. The Court rejected as too broad the defendant's argument that the right to counsel was absolute and independent of the existence of special circumstances. This argument, the Court observed, would result in the invalidation of a conviction even though the defendant did not confess. The test applied by the Court was whether the existence of special circumstances at the interrogation so prejudiced the defendent at his trial as to require the presence of counsel at the interrogation. Finding no special circumstances, the Court held the confession admissible. Quite clearly, the Court evaluated the right to counsel as of the outset of the interrogation, and the fact that the defendant thereafter confessed was not regarded as a special circumstance.

In *Cicenia,* decided on the same day as *Crooker,* the Court held that a confession was not rendered inadmissible by a refusal to permit the defendant to consult retained counsel. After *Crooker* and *Cicenia,* there was every reason to believe that the admissibility of a confession was to be tested by the confessions rule and not by a requirement of counsel. Although the absence of counsel was, under the confessions rule, relevant to a determination of voluntariness, the absence of counsel was not per se an invalidating factor.

One year later, in *Spano v. New York,* a capital case, a unanimous Court held inadmissible a post-indictment confession obtained under pressure after the police had refused to permit the defendant to consult his retained lawyer. Chief Justice Warren, a dissenter in *Crooker* and *Cicenia,* wrote the majority opinion, the rationale of which was that the confessions rule had been violated. However, Justices Black, Douglas, Brennan, also dissenters in *Crooker* and *Cicenia,* and Justice Stewart concurred on the basis of a right-to-counsel theory. Said Mr. Justice Stewart:

> Under our system of justice an indictment is supposed to be followed by an arraignment and a trial. At every stage in those proceedings the accused has an absolute right to a lawyer's help if the case is one in which a death sentence may be imposed. Indeed the right to the assistance of counsel whom the accused has himself retained is absolute, whatever the offense for which he is on trial.

Although *Spano* was decided under the confessions rule, a majority of the Court—Mr. Justice Stewart and the dissenters in *Crooker* and *Cicenia*—now favored a sixth-amendment theory of the admissibility of post-indictment confessions. A small breach had been made in the wall of *Crooker* and *Cicenia.* The breach was enlarged a bit in *Gideon v. Wainwright. Crooker* and *Cicenia* had been decided during the ascendancy of *Betts v. Brady.* Indeed, the special circumstances test of *Betts* was an important part of the *Crooker* rationale. The overruling of *Betts* in *Gideon* thus sapped *Crooker* and *Cicenia* of more of their vitality.

Another blow was delivered toward the end of the 1963 term in *Massiah v. United States* when the Court held inadmissible, specifically on sixth-amendment grounds, incriminating statements obtained after indictment and in the absence of retained counsel. Mr. Justice Stewart, writing for a six-judge majority, relied on his concurring opinion in *Spano:*

> It was said that a Constitution which guarantees a defendant the aid of counsel at . . . trial could surely vouchsafe no less to an indicted defendant

under interrogation by the police in a completely extrajudicial proceeding. Anything less, it was said [by Mr. Justice Douglas in a separate concurring opinion], might deny a defendant 'effective representation by counsel at the only stage when legal aid and advice would help him.'

By its stress on the need for counsel at the pre-trial stage and on the relationship between representation by counsel at trial and at the pre-trial stage, the rationale of *Massiah* is broad enough to encompass a right to appointed counsel as well as to retained counsel. If *Gideon* is added to *Massiah,* it is clear that a post-indictment confession is inadmissible whether counsel is absent as the result of an investigative end-run, as in *Massiah,* or whether counsel is absent because he has not yet been appointed.

A question left unanswered by *Massiah* is whether a post-indictment confession is inadmissible solely for the reason that it was elicited in the absence of counsel. In *Massiah,* the confession was obtained by electronic eavesdropping, and the defendant did not know that his words were being recorded by government agents. If his attorney had advised him not to make any statements, the advice was nullified not only by the defendant's willingness to talk but also by the government's use of electronic deception. Consequently, on its facts *Massiah* was a fairly strong case for an extension of the right to counsel. The question remains, however, whether the statements would have been inadmissible if Massiah had known that his words were being recorded. In his dissenting opinion, Mr. Justice White argued that the test of admissibility should continue to be one of voluntariness under the confessions rule. As viewed by the dissenting opinion, the majority opinion emphasized only the absence of counsel and not the defendant's knowledge. This interpretation is buttressed by the majority's reliance on *Spano,* a case in which the defendant was interrogated at the police station in the absence of his attorney but after his attorney had warned him not to make any statements. Obviously, Spano knew that he was speaking to law enforcement officers. Thus, there is a substantial basis for predicting the inadmissibility of all post-indictment confessions obtained by agents of the state in the absence of counsel. Because the presence of counsel will make it impossible to obtain a confession, the result of *Massiah,* as a practical matter, is that all post-indictment confessions are inadmissible. However, and also as a practical matter, it is unlikely that *Massiah* will have much impact on criminal procedure. Excepting cases in which an indictment is based on weak evidence or in which the government needs additional information for the apprehension of co-defendants, there is no need for post-indictment inter-rogation. From an investigative standpoint, the critical stage is the police interrogation prior to preliminary examination by a committing magistrate. *Massiah* does not compel the conclusion that there is an absolute right to counsel at that stage. *Escobedo,* however, probably does.

The facts of *Escobedo* have already been stated in detail. For present purposes, it is sufficient to note that *Escobedo* bears a striking factual resem-blance to *Cicenia.* In both cases, counsel had been retained prior to interrogation; the interrogation was conducted in the absence of counsel; the police denied the defendant's requests to see counsel; and counsel's efforts to see his client were similarly rebuffed. In *Cicenia,* the confession was held admissible. In *Escobedo,* it was held inadmissible:

> We hold, therefore, that where, as here, the investigation is no longer a
> general inquiry into an unsolved crime but has begun to focus on a

particular suspect, the suspect has been taken into police custody, the police carry out a process of interrogations that lends itself to eliciting incriminating statements, the suspect has requested and has been denied an opportunity to consult with his lawyer, and the police have not effectively warned him of his absolute constitutional right to remain silent, the accused has been denied 'the Assistance of Counsel' in violation of the Sixth Amendment . . . and that no statement elicited by the police during the interrogation may be used against him at a criminal trial.

This holding, incorporating some of the important facts of the case, can be taken as a hint that the right to counsel at the police station is to be determined by a test of special circumstances analogous to the test announced in *Betts v. Brady* regarding counsel at trial. The *Betts* test "had a troubled journey throughout the years" and existed "in form while its substance [was being] substantially and steadily eroded." It was discarded in *Gideon v. Wainwright* in favor of an absolute right to be represented by counsel at trial. Consequently, the first question raised by *Escobedo* is whether the right to counsel at the police station is absolute (in the sense of excluding a confession obtained in the absence of counsel if the right has not been waived) or whether the right to counsel depends on a search for elusive special circumstances. In spite of the hint referred to above, Mr. Justice Goldberg's opinion supports a conclusion that the right is absolute.

Two main themes run through the opinion. The first is that the right to counsel at the police station makes effective the privilege against self-incrimination. The second is that the right to counsel at the police station makes effective the right to counsel at trial. If the right to counsel is evaluated only in the context of the privilege, then whether the right to counsel is absolute depends upon the meaning of the privilege and the necessity for protection of the privilege through the presence of counsel. The meaning of the privilege has already been considered and three interpretations have been suggested: that the defendant is entitled to a warning at the outset of the interrogation; that he is entitled to a warning at the critical point in the interrogation; and that he is entitled to know the legal significance of what the police expect him to say. Under the first interpretation, it is difficult to argue that the presence of counsel is necessary for protection of the privilege. It is not at all unlikely that an understandable warning could and would be given before the interrogation by someone other than counsel—a policeman, for example. Thus, if the defendant is entitled to a warning only at the beginning of interrogation and if the right to counsel is based on this interpretation of the privilege, the presence of counsel is not necessary, the right to counsel is not absolute, and *Escobedo* is nothing more than a grand illusion.

Under the second and third interpretations of the privilege, the communication could be made by someone other than counsel. In theory, therefore, the right to counsel would not be absolute. However, it is unlikely that either the second or the third communication would be made by anyone other than counsel to the detriment of productive interrogation. Consequently, as a practical matter, the right to counsel would be absolute. As has been suggested above, a strong argument can be made that all three interpretations of the privilege are correct. Accordingly, the right to counsel would be absolute. However, until the Court resolves the problem of interpreting the privilege, the right to counsel, to the extent that it depends on the privilege, must remain in some doubt.

In the second theme that runs through Mr. Justice Goldberg's opinion, the right to counsel at the police station is regarded as protecting the right to counsel at trial:

> This was the 'stage when legal aid and advice' were most critical to petitioner. It was a stage surely as critical as was the arraignment in *Hamilton v. Alabama*, 368 U.S. 52, and the preliminary hearing in *White v. Maryland*, 373 U.S. 59. What happened at this interrogation could certainly 'affect the whole trial' since rights 'may be as irretrievably lost, if not then and there asserted, as they are when an accused represented by counsel waives a right for strategic purposes.' . . .
>
> In *Gideon v. Wainwright*, we held that every person accused of a crime, whether state or federal, is entitled to a lawyer at trial. The rule sought by the State here, however, would make the trial no more than an appeal from the interrogation; and the 'right to use counsel at the formal trial [would be] a very hollow thing [if], for all practical purposes, the conviction is already assured by pre-trial examination.'

Under this view of right to counsel at the police station, it is obvious that the right must be regarded as absolute. Moreover, the analogy between interrogation and trial is highly relevant to an interpretation of the privilege. At the trial, if the defendant cannot help himself by testifying, competent counsel will insist that he exercise his privilege. Even if the defendant waives his privilege, he will be thoroughly prepared for direct examination and he will be protected from improper cross-examination by the presence of counsel. The analogy between interrogation and trial thus suggests that the privilege be given the second and third interpretations discussed above. As has already been noted, to the extent that the right to counsel is regarded as protecting the privilege, the right must be treated as absolute under either of these interpretations. Consequently, the problem presented by *Escobedo* may be stated as follows: at the police station is the defendant entitled only to a warning of his rights (by anyone) at the outset of interrogation or is he entitled to all of the safeguards provided by the presence of counsel at trial? On the basis of *Escobedo* alone, it is reasonable to predict that a majority of the present Court espouses the trial analogy, and a consideration of the antecedents to *Escobedo* dictates the same answer.

In *Crooker v. California*, it will be remembered, the defendant had studied law for one year and his program included a course in criminal law. Toward the beginning of the interrogation, he was advised by a police lieutenant that he need not say anything. Apparently both before and after the warning he refused to answer certain questions. In spite of Crooker's awareness of his rights, four judges, all of whom concurred in *Escobedo*, would have held the confession inadmissible because it had been obtained in the absence of counsel. Writing for the dissenters, Mr. Justice Douglas insisted that "the right to have counsel at the pretrial stage is often necessary to give meaning and protection to the right to be heard at the trial itself." In addition, said Mr. Justice Douglas, the presence of counsel would at least minimize two problems inhering in the interrogation process: the defendant's inability to prove coercion in the face of contradictory testimony by his interrogator, and the risk that, at the trial, the interrogator might inaccurately relate the substance of an oral confession. The dissenting opinion in *Crooker* was cited in the brief dissenting opinion in *Cicenia v. Lagay*.

In *Ashdown v. Utah*, decided on the same day as *Crooker*, the defendant was taken into custody for interrogation and was advised that she did not have to make a statement and that she had a right to counsel. She did not request counsel. While she was being interrogated, two relatives were denied permission to see her. In an opinion in which the absence of counsel was mentioned but not discussed, seven judges held the confession voluntary and admissible. Justices Douglas and Black, relying on their dissent in *Crooker,* dissented in an opinion in which it was asserted that the record did not establish either that counsel had been waived or that the defendant "had elected to talk."

In *Spano v. New York,* the link between counsel at the police station and counsel at the trial was clearly articulated in the concurring opinions of Justices Douglas and Stewart. Without referring to the privilege against self-incrimination, Mr. Justice Douglas stated:

> This is a case of an accused, who is scheduled to be tried by a judge and jury, being tried in a preliminary way by the police. This is a kangaroo court procedure whereby the police produce the vital evidence in the form of a confession which is useful or necessary to obtain a conviction. They in effect deny him effective representation by counsel.

And Mr. Justice Stewart noted that "our Constitution guarantees the assistance of counsel to a man on trial for his life. . . . Surely a Constitution which promises that much can vouchsafe no less to the same man under midnight inquisition in the squad room of a police station. As was previously discussed, the same link between counsel at interrogation and counsel at trial was emphasized in *Massiah v. United States.*

Considered in the light of its antecedents, *Escobedo* must be taken as establishing at the interrogation stage all of the safeguards provided by the presence of counsel at trial. However, it should be noted that in *Cicenia, Spano,* and *Escobedo* the defendant had retained counsel prior to interrogation and had requested permission to consult counsel during the interrogation. In *Crooker,* the defendant had demanded to see a named attorney. In none of the cases, therefore, would it have been necessary for the state to provide counsel at the interrogation. Thus, the second question raised by *Escobedo* is whether an indigent defendant is entitled to counsel upon request. An affirmative answer is fully supported by *Gideon v. Wainwright* and by the rationale of *Escobedo* that the presence of counsel at the interrogation makes effective both the right to representation by counsel at trial and the privilege against self-incrimination. Neither *Gideon* nor the rationale of *Escobedo* permits any meaningful distinction between the indigent and the affluent.

In *Escobedo,* as in *Crooker, Cicenia* and *Spano,* the defendant specifically requested an opportunity to consult counsel. Is such a request essential, or will silence be taken as a waiver? If the defendant knows that he has a right to consult counsel, will a waiver be inferred from his silence or from a statement that he does not desire counsel? The opinion in *Escobedo* suggests only the following: if the right to counsel is as important as Mr. Justice Goldberg indicates, the Court will not be quick to draw inferences of waiver. Clearly, if the defendant is unaware of his rights, a request is not essential and silence will not be taken as a waiver. This conclusion follows from the right-to-counsel cases discussed previously as an analogue to the privilege/waiver problem. Moreover, as the plurality opinion in *Von Moltke v. Gillies* demonstrates, even if the defendant is aware of the right to counsel and purports to waive it, the waiver will be ineffective unless the defendant is aware of the importance and scope of the assistance of counsel. If the record discloses only a naked awareness of the right, it is highly unlikely that a waiver will be inferred.

In his dissenting opinion in *Escobedo,* Mr. Justice Stewart argued that there was no right to counsel prior to indictment:

> [T]he institution of formal, meaningful judicial proceedings by way of indictment, information, or arraignment marks the point at which a criminal investigation has ended and adversary litigative proceedings have commenced. It is at this point that the constitutional guarantees attach which pertain to a criminal trial. Among those guarantees . . . is the guarantee of the assistance of counsel.

In essence, Mr. Justice Stewart relied on the specific terminology of the sixth amendment ("criminal prosecutions") and insisted that the prosecution began only with indictment. Because Mr. Justice Stewart had written the opinion in *Massiah,* an anticipatory reply from Mr. Justice Goldberg was necessary. Leading from strength, Mr. Justice Goldberg noted that in *Massiah* considerable emphasis had been placed on the relationship between effective representation at trial and representation at pre-trial stages. If, in order to insure effective representation at trial, it is necessary to have counsel after indictment and before trial, it is no less necessary to have counsel at the police station before indictment. Indeed, because post-indictment interrogation is unusual and pre-indictment interrogation is typical, from the defendant's standpoint it is far more important to have counsel at the police station. In short, Mr. Justice Stewart had painted himself into a corner in *Massiah* from which he could extricate himself only by a highly formalistic reading of the sixth amendment. Moreover, Mr. Justice Stewart's position is weak for two additional reasons, neither of which was urged by Mr. Justice Goldberg. The first is that, although the phraseology of the fifth amendment limits the privilege against self-incrimination to a criminal case, the Court has applied the privilege to such pre-indictment procedures as legislative inquiries and grand-jury investigations. If an effective privilege can be achieved only through the presence of counsel, the right to counsel must arise prior to indictment. The second reason is that the Court had already held that a right to counsel existed at a pre-indictment stage. In *White v. Maryland,* a capital case, the defendant, unrepresented by counsel, pleaded guilty at the preliminary hearing. Although this plea was not controlling for purposes of the trial, it was admitted as evidence. In a unanimous per curiam decision, the Court held that the preliminary examination was a critical stage in the proceeding, that the defendant should have had counsel, and that the plea was inadmissible as evidence of guilt.

Had Mr. Justice Goldberg been content to rely on the trial analogy, he could have been criticized only for not making a complete argument. However, he was not content. In what appears to be an attempt to establish a factual, as well as doctrinal, analogy between *Escobedo* and *Massiah,* he stated:

> The interrogation here was conducted before petitioner was formally indicted. But in the context of this case, that fact should make no difference. When petitioner requested, and was denied, an opportunity to consult with his lawyer, the investigation had ceased to be a general investigation of 'an unsolved crime.' Petitioner had become the accused, and the purpose of the interrogation was to get him to confess his guilt despite his constitutional right not to do so. . . . It would exalt form over substance to make the right to counsel, under these circumstances, depend

on whether at the time of the interrogation, the authorities had secured a formal indictment. Petitioner had, for all practical purposes, already been charged with murder.

Two restrictive interpretations may be given to this factually correct statement. First, it may be said that the *Escobedo* rule does not apply if the interrogee has been arrested only "on suspicion." This statement, however, collides with the *Wong Sun* rule. The words "on suspicion" suggest an arrest that is unconstitutional for want of probable cause. In such a case it is likely that a subsequent confession is inadmissible on fourth-amendment grounds. Consequently, even if the first interpretation is valid, it still leads to a cul-de-sac of inadmissibility.

The second interpretation is that *Escobedo* applies only if there is "strong" probable cause to believe that the interrogee committed the offense. It would follow that, although *Wong Sun* and *Escobedo* ride tandem in some cases, neither would govern a case in which only "ordinary" probable cause existed. This interpretation probably involves an unworkable distinction in terms of quanta of probable cause. Even if the distinction is workable, at some point in the interrogation "strong" probable cause must arise because, by hypothesis, the interrogee will give some indication of a willingness to confess. At that point, the *Escobedo* rule would apply. The second interpretation, therefore, results only in delayed application.

A third interpretation may be given to Mr. Justice Goldberg's statement. It is that the statement is meaningless. If the right to counsel at the police station preserves the right to representation at trial and makes effective the privilege against self-incrimination, it is illogical to distinguish the case of the prime suspect from the case of any other suspect. In each case the right to counsel serves the same purpose in the same way. To suggest that the right to counsel arises only when the investigation begins to focus on the interogee is to play hocus-focus with the right to counsel and to obliterate the very arguments urged to support the result in *Escobedo*. Consequently, although it may be inferred from Mr. Justice Goldberg's statement that only a prime suspect has a constitutional right to counsel, the inference should be ignored.

In *Haynes v. Washington,* it was observed by way of disclaimer that "... detection and solution of crime is, at best, a difficult and arduous task requiring determination and persistence. . . . [W]e do not mean to suggest that all interrogation of witnesses and suspects is impermissible." But after *Wong Sun, Malloy,* and *Escobedo,* what is the scope of permissible interrogation? In all probability, *Wong Sun* severely limits the class of persons who may be interrogated. If the interrogee is within the class, *Malloy* and *Escobedo* give him the privilege against self-incrimination, and *Escobedo* makes it effective through a requirement of counsel. The total theoretical impact of these cases is that productive police interrogation is a dead letter. Unless the defendant wants to confess, his natural reluctance must be overcome. To this extent, police interrogation is, and has to be, inherently coercive. Effective coercion comprehends increased pressure by the interrogator and diminished resistance on the part of the person interrogated. But pressure is impermissible under the privilege and diminished resistance is unlikely if counsel is present. Through a series of cases, each of which chips away at the scope of permissible interrogation, the Court has held, in effect, that productive interrogation is impermissible.

It is unlikely, however, that the theoretical impact will be felt immediately in practice. The opinion in *Escobedo* simply furnishes too many possibilities for convenient avoidance, each of which has to be resolved through litigation. It is to be expected that law enforcement officers, state courts, and lower federal courts will seize upon each of the ambiguities in *Escobedo* as a basis for distinction. In one case the basis will be that the police advised the defendant of his rights at the outset of interrogation. In another case it will be that the defendant was a mere suspect when he confessed. In still another case the basis will be that coercive circumstances were absent (remember that *Escobedo* could have been decided under the confessions rule) or that the defendant voluntarily waived his privilege and his right to counsel. All in all, the cases will resemble in tenor those lower federal court decisions in the wake of *McNabb* in which it was held that the *McNabb* rule applied only if some coercion was present. They will also resemble in tenor those decisions in the wake of *Mallory* in which it was held that a particular delay was reasonable even though a confession was obtained during that period and even though it was likely that the delay was motivated by a desire to interrogate. Undoubtedly, *Escobedo* will be resisted as *McNabb* and *Mallory* were resisted. *McNabb* was decided in 1943. After twenty-one years and three subsequent clarifying Supreme Court decisions, the battle is still being fought. *Escobedo,* therefore, can hardly be regarded as more than a skirmish.

VI. CONCLUSION

The Supreme Court must have decided *Escobedo* with full realization that police interrogation is essential to the solution of some crimes and that, if the theory of *Escobedo* is ever translated into action, police interrogation is at an end. Why was the Court ready to sacrifice police interrogation? The answer to this question involves two factors: dissatisfaction of the inconsistency of giving to the accused at trial a privilege against self-incrimination made effective by the presence of counsel, and, at the same time, at the critical stage of police interrogation, denying to the accused both the full reach of the privilege and the protection of counsel.

Insofar as counsel is concerned, and without regard to the privilege, it is apparent that *Escobedo* represents a shift in emphasis. At the trial the participation of counsel serves the due process value of preserving the accuracy of the guilt-finding process. Because "truth machines" are not available, we maintain the adversary system as the method best calculated to keep to a minimum erroneous determinations of guilt. Obviously, the system contemplates roughly equivalent adversaries, and the only surprising thing about *Gideon v. Wainwright* is that it was so long in coming. However, at the police interrogation stage, the reliability preservative has traditionally been the confessions rule. Absent a consideration of the privilege, the argument that effective representation at trial requires the presence of counsel at the interrogation stage must be based on one of two assumptions: that effective representation at trial means winning, or that the presence of counsel at interrogation in some way increases the reliability of the guilt-determining process. The first assumption must be rejected as without constitutional or other basis. The second assumption may or may not be true. Mr. Justice Jackson observed in *Watts v. Indiana* that "any lawyer worth his salt will tell the suspect in no uncertain terms to make no statement to police under any circumstances." Advice regarding the privilege will frustrate inquiry and, in many cases, will detract from the reliability of the guilt-determining process. On the other hand, if the interrogee does submit to interrogation, the presence of counsel is a substantial hedge against pressure, unfair questions, and inaccuracies in either the recording or recollection of oral statements. Moreover, the presence of any third party at the interrogation minimizes the credibility problem that arises when the defendant's claim of coercion is resisted by the testimony of the interrogator that no pressure was used. In short, whether the presence of counsel at the interrogation enhances accuracy or reliability will depend upon the facts of a particular case, upon the details of what happened at the interrogation. Consequently, insistence upon the presence of counsel in all cases is simply an insistence upon the barrier to confession imposed by an effective privilege against self-incrimination, and a root-and-branch rejection of all confessions that are not volunteered. Why should the Court reject such confessions? One possible answer is indicated in *Escobedo:*

> We have learned the lesson of history, ancient and modern, that a system of criminal law enforcement which comes to depend on the 'confession' will, in the long run, be less reliable and more subject to abuses than a system which depends on extrinsic evidence independently secured through skillful investigation.

Abusive police conduct does exist to some extent, but the extent is difficult to determine. If one theme runs through the coerced confession cases, it is that the Court does not know what happened at the police station. The defendant claims that he was beaten or threatened or was promised some benefit. All of these claims are denied by the police. A reviewing court, faced with a finding of fact against coercion, is forced to speculate, to state that thirty-six hours of interrogation are "inherently coercive," and to insist that "the effect of such massive official interrogation must have been felt." The blame lies not with judges. They know that abusive practices exist and they also know that abuse seldom appears clearly from the record. The blame lies not with the defendant. He is forced to rely on his own testimony because no third party was permitted to attend the interrogation. The blame does lie with the police. For years, the police have insisted that productive interrogation can take place only in private and that an interrogee will not confess if he is aware of the presence of third persons. In practice, privacy has become secrecy, and the details of the interrogation are almost always in doubt. Steps could have been taken to maintain privacy but to avoid secrecy. The presence of a third person, unobserved, could have been provided for, but the police did not do so, and legislatures did not undertake effective control. It was not that control was impossible. The relevant literature is full of such suggestions as substituting a judicial interrogation for the police interrogation; providing that police interrogation take place within time limits and only after preliminary examination; and requiring that all interrogations be filmed. In the absence of legislatively prescribed controls, the burden fell on the courts. Because due process was involved, the Supreme Court was drawn into the picture only to be frustrated by the problem of proof under the confessions rule. The solutions available to legislature were not directly available to the Court, but the Court was not without its weapons. Regarding federal procedure, the Court, as a supervisory matter, fashioned the *Mallory* exclusionary rule, the purpose of which was to solve the problem of proof by the blunt tool of minimizing, if not putting to an end, the opportunity for interrogation. The states, however, not bound by *Mallory,* refused to attach exclusionary rules to their own "prompt arraignment" statutes. The state cases, therefore, continued to be governed by the confessions rule with all of its attendant weaknesses. Ultimately, the Court, in *Escobedo,* found that it was forced to circumscribe state interrogation as it had been forced to circumscribe federal interrogation in *Mallory,* and, as in *Mallory,* the Court used a necessarily blunt device: the privilege against self-incrimination made effective by the required presence of counsel. The result is that the Court will no longer be forced to guess whether a confession is "voluntary" or "involuntary" under the confessions rule. Unless a confession is obtained under circumstances consistent with an effective privilege against self-incrimination, it is inadmissible even if "voluntary." The result may well be undesirable, but the police (by their insistence on secrecy), the state legislatures (by their failure to act effectively), and the state courts (by their failure to give meaning to prompt arraignment statutes) have brought it on themselves.

In his dissenting opinion in *Escobedo,* Mr. Justice White stated:

> I do not suggest for a moment that law enforcement will be destroyed by the rule announced today. The need for peace and order is too insistent for that. But it will be crippled and its task made a great deal more difficult, all in my opinion, for unsound, unstated reasons, which can find no home in any of the provisions of the Constitution.

However, there may be a way out. Even assuming the broadest interpretation of *Escobedo,* the Court might approve less restrictive procedures if delineated by state legislation, enforced by state courts, and adhered to by state police. For this approach to be successful, however, it will be necessary to distinguish the operation of the privilege against self-incrimination at the police station from its operation in other proceedings. As matters now stand, an effective privilege against self-incrimination is an insuperable barrier to interrogation, and our crucial question is this: how effective a privilege can we afford?

POLICE INTERROGATION AND THE PRIVILEGE
AGAINST SELF-INCRIMINATION

WALTER V. SCHAEFER

Under *Escobedo v. Illinois* it is the fifth amendment privilege against self-incrimination that gives rise to the right to council during police interrogation, and in this article I should like to look directly at that privilege. The chief difficulty with the privilege is that it runs counter to our ordinary standards of morality. Parents try hard to inculcate in their children the simple virtues of truth and responsibility. Yet in the enforcement of the criminal law a different set of values has come to prevail. Perhaps to prepare our children for adult life we should carefully instruct them never to answer any questions if the answers may reveal misconduct—but I don't think so.

In criminal matters, everyday practices somehow become unseemly. The concept of an accusatorial system becomes dominant, and that concept evokes the vision of a majestic government engaged in formal contest with the suspect. Surely, our rhetoric teaches, the government cannot ask the suspect about his conduct. Rather it must prove its case by "evidence independently secured." Formal conceptions of the trial have recently been extended to pre-trial investigations, and they seem to prevail over society's interest in securing the truth. Under this concept of an accusatorial system, no sanction, not even the natural inference that the suspect may have something to hide, can be imposed upon a failure to respond to an orderly, civilized inquiry.

Other nations have not departed so far from the idea that asking questions is a reasonable way to get answers, and it seems to me that the burden rests upon those who advocate an entirely accusatorial system to justify its divergence from everyday morality and common sense. It is the privilege against self-incrimination that gives our criminal procedure its conceptual, accusatory flavor; and it is important to examine the considerations that have been advanced to justify it. It has been urged that the privilege (1) prevents the use of torture and other abuses, (2) promotes initiative on the part of the police, (3) protects the innocent, (4) ensures dignity of the legal process, (5) secures an area of privacy, and (6) prevents inquisition into political and religious beliefs. These considerations must be appraised in terms of the provisions of the American Law Institute's Model Code of Pre-Arraignment Procedure. Those provisions contemplate a complete record of the interrogation as a method for enforcing the requirement that questioning be conducted in a fair and civilized manner.

As we examine the justifications advanced to support the privilege, you will note that even at this late period in our history, it remains a doctrine in search of a reason. As Professor Kalven has said, it "is the product of a tangled and complex history of abuses many of which have been corrected today by other legal safeguards. . . . [T]he law and the lawyers despite endless litigation over the privilege have never made up their minds just what it is supposed to do or just whom it is intended to protect." As we shall see, the Supreme Court has experienced this difficulty.

It is appropriate to begin with Dean Wigmore's views. He did not favor the privilege against self-incrimination and urged that it "should be kept within limits the strictest possible." Since the privilege was a part of the Constitution, however, he undertook to justify it. His justification was a blend of practical and historical considerations going largely to the integrity and efficiency of the administrative system. He said:

> The exercise of the power to extract answers begets a forgetfulness of the just limitations of that power. The simple and peaceful process of questioning breeds a readiness to resort to bullying and to physical force and torture. If there is a right to an answer, there soon seems to be a right to the expected answer,—that is, to a confession of guilt. Thus the legitimate use grows into the unjust abuse; ultimately, the innocent are jeopardized by the encroachments of a bad system. Such seems to have been the course of experience in those legal systems where the privilege was not recognized.

Dean Wigmore also feared that without the privilege the prosecution would have no incentive to seek other evidence, and quoted the remark attributed by Sir James Stephen, the draftsman of the Indian Code, to an Indian official: "It is far pleasanter to sit comfortably in the shade rubbing red pepper in a poor devil's eyes than to go about in the sun hunting up evidence."

The shadow of the rack was the main support that Dean Wigmore saw for the existence of the privilege. Professor Maguire, however, saw another possibility:

> Deprived of assurance that the prosecutor can probe for a suspect's information by decent, orderly questioning, police are tempted to bully their prisoner into admissions suggesting lines of investigation usable to turn up other evidence of guilt. The privilege may *encourage* torture rather than the reverse.

In any event the common law doctrine of involuntariness, now incorporated in the due process clauses of the Constitution, can take care of gross police misconduct and of more subtle kinds as well. When the process of interrogation becomes visible, as it would under the requirements of the Model Code, it seems to me that we will have proceeded far toward eliminating abusive police practices. But the central point is that the expanded doctrine of involuntariness makes it possible to consider the value of the privilege apart from its historical association with torture.

Dean Wigmore's other thought was that the privilege stimulates the police to search for other evidence, apart from statements of the accused. It is difficult to know just what other evidence he had in mind. Of course there are scientific methods of crime detection, but every criminal does not leave fingerprints, and ballistics testimony is not involved in many cases. Heavier emphasis upon identification testimony seems undesirable to me, because my experience leads me to distrust that kind of evidence.

If the privilege serves as a significant protection to the innocent, it is hardly appropriate that "it should be kept within limits the strictest possible," as Dean Wigmore suggested. To the extent that it operates to prevent torture and other forms of compulsion, it protects the innocent. Beyond that, however, its effectiveness in this respect is doubtful. Wigmore saw the privilege as protecting the innocent only indirectly, through its operation upon the morality and efficiency of the system of criminal law administration. The critical question, of course, is not whether the privilege may protect an innocent man now and then; prohibiting all criminal prosecution, I suppose, would be a more effective way to do that. If the privilege is to be justified as a protection of the innocent, it must protect them in a way that does not also protect the guilty.

In *Grunewald v. United States* the Supreme Court said: "Recent reexamination of the history and meaning of the Fifth Amendment has emphasized anew that one of the basic functions of the privilege is to protect *innocent* men. Griswold, The Fifth Amendment Today, 9-30, 53-82." Dean Griswold had indeed advanced this argument in support of the privilege. But he later stated, in a lecture at Northwestern University law school, that he felt that it was a mistake to defend the privilege as a protection of the innocent:

> Others have said, and I think they are right, that the privilege protects the guilty more often than it does the innocent. It was a mistake, I now think, to undertake to defend the privilege on the ground that it is basically designed to protect those innocent of crime, at least in any numerical sense.

Last year, in *Griffin v. California,* protection of the innocent was again advanced as a justification of the privilege. There the Court struck down the provision of the constitution of California which authorized both judicial and prosecutorial comment on the failure of the accused to take the witness stand. The heart of the opinion is the following quotation from Mr. Justice Field's discussion of the purpose of the 1878 federal statute that prohibits such comment:

> [T]he Act was framed with a due regard also to those who might prefer to rely upon the presumption of innocence which the law gives to everyone, and not wish to be witnesses. It is not everyone who can safely venture on the witness stand though entirely innocent of the charge against him. Excessive timidity, nervousness when facing others and attempting to explain transactions of a suspicious character, and offenses charged against him, will often confuse and embarrass him to such a degree as to increase rather than remove prejudices against him. It is not everyone, however honest, who would, therefore, willingly be placed on the witness stand. The statute, in tenderness to the weakness of those who from the causes mentioned might refuse to ask to be a witness, particularly when they may have been in some degree compromised by their association with others, declares that the failure of the defendant in a criminal action to request to be a witness shall not create any presumption against him.

After this quotation, the Court added: "If the words 'Fifth Amendment' are substituted for 'act' and for 'statute,' the spirit of the Self-Incrimination Clause is reflected."

Early this year in *Tehan v. Shott,* the Supreme Court decided that the prohibition against comment upon the claim of the privilege was not to be applied retroactively to the cases of California defendants, who had been convicted before the new constitutional doctrine of *Griffin v. California* was announced. The Court candidly recognized that an "important factor" in its decision was that "a retrospective application of *Griffin v. California* would create stresses upon the administration of justice : . . so devastating as to need no elaboration." It indicated that newly articulated constitutional doctrines would be applied retroactively if they substantially affected the determination of guilt or innocence. But, the Court then announced that "the basic purposes that lie behind the privilege against self-incrimination *do not relate to protecting the innocent from conviction . . .*" and that the privilege "is not an adjunct to the ascertainment of truth." The constitutional prohibition against comment on the claim of the privilege thus remains, although the primary ground upon which it was read into the Constitution has been disavowed.

The simple fact is that in criminal matters a claim of privilege against self-incrimination unmistakably suggests guilt. As Professor McNaughton has said in his edition of Volume 8 of Wigmore:

> The layman's natural first suggestion would probably be that the resort to privilege in each instance is a clear confession of crime. . . . In *most* instances (a characterization of disturbingly little use in a *particular* instance) this is probably the true significance of silence. But silence by the accused also, as a matter of logic, may imply fear of exposure of matters related only remotely to the charges, fear of impeachment by proof of bad character evidence (especially prior convictions), or fear that his demeanor on the witness stand will do his innocence a fatal disservice.

The first of these alternative inferences relates to the proverbial married man who, if he is compelled to speak, will be forced to reveal indiscretions or worse. Although I can sympathize with him, I see no reason why our rules of law should be shaped to accommodate him. As for the nervous defendant, I would agree with Professor Meltzer that such a defendant stands a better chance if he testifies, than if he risks the inference that will flow from his silence. The most significant of Professor McNaughton's alternatives is the second—the fear of impeachment by proof of prior convictions. But the risk that prior convictions will be brought out at trial might be dealt with legislatively, as in England, where since 1898 the introduction of prior convictions for impeachment has been prohibited unless the defendant has introduced testimony about his good character, impugned the character of prosecution witnesses, or testified against a co-defendant.

Evidence of prior crimes is properly admissible when it tends to establish guilt as, for example, when it shows motive or plan, or negatives mistake or accident. When the credibility of a defendant who has taken the witness stand is impeached by showing that he has committed other crimes, the focus is shifted from the facts of the case to the defendant's bad character; and the danger is great that the jury may convict the defendant because he is a bad man, rather than because he has committed the crime with which he is charged. The customary safeguard against this danger is an instruction to the jury that the defendant's criminal record may be considered only as it bears upon the weight to be given to the defendant's testimony. Concerning this practice, Dean Griswold has said:

> We accept much self-deception on this. We say that the evidence of the prior convictions is admissible only to impeach the defendant's testimony, and not as evidence of the prior crimes themselves. Juries are solemnly instructed to this effect. Is there anyone who doubts what the effect of this evidence in fact is on the jury? If we know so clearly what we are actually doing, why do we pretend that we are not doing what we clearly are doing?

When the accused takes the stand in his own behalf, he should, in my opinion, be subject to impeachment only by proof of past crimes which directly bear on testimonial deception, such as perjury. Past convictions not in this category should not be admissible unless they are relevant for some purpose other than impeachment. The Uniform Rules of Evidence so provide, as did the Model Code of Evidence. The contrary and current practice lies close to the borders of the due process clause, and it should be eliminated.

It has also been said that "the existence of the privilege confers upon the criminal trial—and for that matter, upon every investigatory proceeding—an aspect of dignity, humanity, and impartiality which the contrasted inquisitorial process is too apt to lack." This suggestion has a distinctly reminiscent quality. Sir James Stephen and others had first argued that to permit accused persons to testify in their own behalf would destroy the dignity of the English trial. Sir James later admitted his error, and we have moved so far from that view today that a defendant now has a right under the due process clause to testify. It seems to me that the fear that without the privilege trials would lack dignity is equally misplaced.

Somewhat similar justifications were advanced in *Tehan v. Shott,* in which the court said that the privilege reflects "the concern of our society for the right of each individual to be let alone." The privilege shows "our respect for the inviolability of the human personality and of the right of each individual 'to a private enclave where he may lead a private life.' " Dean Griswold had earlier expressed much the same thought when he said: "We in this nation have inherited a great sense of freedom. . . . The essence of this, I suggest, requires that we continue to recognize and respect 'the right to be let alone.' "

That the protection of privacy is not a purpose of the privilege is demonstrated by the fact that a witness may constitutionally be granted immunity from prosecution and then be required to testify, under penalty of imprisonment for contempt, if he refuses to do so. All concern for personal dignity disappears when the prospect of prosecution is removed. If privacy were our guide, moreover, we would be hard put to explain why a grocery list, or an automobile repair bill, is protected from disclosure if it incriminates, while disclosure of the most personal entries in a diary may be compelled if they do not incriminate. In a civil case the refusal of a party to come forward with evidence at his command, however intimate or personal it may be, routinely gives rise to an adverse inference, and it is hard to see why privacy, or the "private enclave," should be given greater protection in a criminal setting.

It has been said that "the American system of criminal prosecution is accusatorial, not inquisitorial, and the Fifth Amendment privilege is its essential mainstay." This sort of statement seems to me more suitable for Law Day speeches than for analytical judicial opinions. To characterize our system as accusatorial and then to derive consequences from that characterization involves the risk of losing sight of the objectives of the system. The goal of criminal procedure should be the conviction of the guilty and the prompt acquittal of the innocent with as little disruption of other human values as possible. The problem is to decide what human values are to be disrupted, and how much. The label "accusatorial" does not help to decide these questions. Our system of civil procedure is "adversary," but has not barred the introduction of discovery procedures designed to aid in the difficult job of ascertaining the truth.

Moreover, undue emphasis upon the accusatorial aspects of our system has an embarrassingly parochial quality. Most nations of the world do not rely upon a system that is wholly accusatorial, nor do they go to the other extreme.

Instead they require that the silence of an accused be noted for consideration in the ultimate determination of guilt or innocence. They neither require that he take an oath nor do they employ contempt as a sanction for his failure to answer. These rules seem to me to follow natural assumptions. The silence of the accused is noted and taken into account because of the strength of the inference of guilt that flows from his failure to respond; the refusal to administer an oath to the accused, or to force him to answer, reflect spiritual and physical aspects of the law of self-preservation invoked by John Lilburn before the Star Chamber. The epithet "inquisitorial" evokes the image of historic abuses that are not relevant to an obligation to respond to orderly inquiry.

I have deferred to the last what I think is the most important ground upon which some have sought to justify the privilege against self-incrimination. The Supreme Court has said that the privilege "registers an important advance in the development of our liberty—'one of the great landmarks in man's struggle to make himself civilized.' " The Court has also adopted Dean Griswold's statement that the privilege is "an expression of the moral striving of the community . . . . a reflection of our common conscience . . . ." These characterizations seem rather broad and sweeping when they are applied to a case like Escobedo's. But Dean Griswold was not talking about that sort of case. He was considering the role of the privilege as a protection against inquisitions into political and religious beliefs.

There is no doubt that the privilege played a leading role in the struggle to achieve religious and political liberty, both in England and in the American colonies. Lilburn and Udal before the Star Chamber and William Bradford in the Colonies were the great heroes in the development of the privilege. That the abuses of the Star Chamber and Court of High Commission in England, and of the prerogative courts of Governor and Council in the colonies in probing and suppressing religious and political dissent must not be forgotten was dramatically shown by what Leonard Boudin called the "revival of the *ex officio* oath" by congressional committees during the McCarthy period. Their hearings, Boudin said, were "accompanied by all the objectionable features of the inquisition; absence of formal charges, dragnet inquiry into beliefs, opinions and association," and the rest.

The point that must be emphasized is that the history of the privilege is "noble" primarily because of the nature of the substantive crimes for which self-accusation would ensure punishment. If publishing a book is evidence of a capital crime, Lilburn and Udal's guilt was beyond dispute. As Bentham noted,

> [W]hat evidence more satisfactory could have been given of it, than (their) inability to deny it with any prospect of success? . . . (W)hat of injustice there was . . . the seat was in the substantive branch of the law; it consisted in the converting into a capital crime the act of him who makes known, to use the words of the Scripture, "the reason of the faith that is in him."

As Professor Pittman says, in both England and the colonies the privilege was primarily "a defensive weapon . . . against laws and proceedings that did not have the sanction of public opinion," and its fundamental momentum was toward the protection of diverse political and religious beliefs and their free expression. Dean Griswold ultimately rested his justification for the privilege on this ground. He said in 1960 that, "it is enough to say that the privilege is available to protect those who are guilty only of heretical or unpopular beliefs." As Leonard Boudin said in the 1950's: "The privilege is now returned to its original function—the protection of first amendment freedoms—since the direct protection has now failed."

The continuing validity of this argument is difficult to assess. At the time Boudin and Griswold wrote, the efforts of the Court in seeking to restrict legislative inquiry into belief and association were halting and unsure. Several recent developments indicate, however, that the conclusion that the first amendment direct protection has failed may have been premature.

Protection for unpopular and heretical political and religious ideas is now in the process of being remitted to the first amendment, where, in my opinion, it belongs. Two recent decisions of the Supreme Court give rise to this thought. The first is the 1962 case of *Gibson v. Legislative Investigation Comm.* in which the Court held that a state commission could not punish someone who refused to disclose membership lists in the NAACP, because no sufficient connection or "nexus" was initially made, as a "foundation" for inquiry, between the NAACP and particular "subversive activities" about which the state might legitimately inquire.

In the course of its opinion the Court reaffirmed the existence of a "First Amendment privilege" not to respond to questions. The broad standard announced was that "it is an essential prerequisite to the validity of an investigation which intrudes into the area of constitutionally protected rights of speech, press, association and petition that the State convincingly show a substantial relation between the information sought and a subject of overriding and compelling state interest." The Court emphasized that before inquiry may proceed, an "adequate foundation" consisting of a connection or nexus of substantial ties between the organization about which information is sought, and particular "subversive activities" must be established. "To permit legislative inquiry to proceed on less than an adequate foundation would be to sanction unjustified and unwarranted intrusions into the very heart of the constitutional privilege to be secure in associations in legitimate organizations engaged in the exercise of First and 14th Amendment rights. . . ."

Gibson provides support to those who have long sought limits upon legislative inquiry apart from the privilege against self-incrimination. The opinion implies three facets to the emerging "First Amendment privilege." First, the opinion clearly requires a first amendment equivalent to the fourth's probable cause limitation on threshold inquiry. This is framed in terms of an "adequate foundation" for any specific demand. Second, by requiring that the state "convincingly show" an "overriding and compelling state interest" in the subject of inquiry, and a sufficient nexus or connection between that subject and the information sought, the opinion provides a substantive limit on the power of compelled state inquiry. There is an indication that the Court intends to police those limits. Third is the assertion of the inviolability of personal belief. It is significant, I think, that battles such as *Gibson* have all concerned association, a derivative aspect of free speech. The realm of pure thought or belief seems too sanctified for even the most callous commission to invade.

The second case is *Griswold v. Connecticut,* which held that Connecticut's statute prohibiting the dissemination of birth-control information violates the "emanations of the penumbras" of the Bill of Rights, especially the first, fourth and fifth amendments, which create "zones of privacy" which the state may not invade. Because of its vagueness, the opinion is susceptible of interpretation and expansion to suit anybody's predilections. But the significance of the case lies in the spotlight it turns on the Court's concern over privacy and the ingenuity employed in preventing a possible invasion.

These considerations show that the argument for the privilege against self-incrimination as a protection of first amendment freedoms is diminishing in significance. It is my belief that the proper place for devising solutions to abuses of freedom of speech and association is the amendment which is primarily intended to protect against them. To maintain the fifth amendment's privilege against self-incrimination as a first amendment shield does a disservice to both.

Sometimes it seems to me that our difficulties in solving problems stem from the fact that we are too close to them. The problems of the past always seem so much easier than those that confront us now. I would venture that to a legal historian writing a hundred years from now, the current problem—that of police interrogation—will fall into place simply as another skirmish in the long war to make the judicial process an instrument for the ascertainment of the truth. There have been many engagements in that war. In *Slade's* case, decided in 1602, a rear guard action was fought against the then novel institution of trial by jury. The defendant set up older methods of trial as aspects of "due process" and argued that wager of law was his "birthright." The right of parties to testify, both in civil and in criminal cases, was also challenged. Sir James Stephen argued that to permit a defendant to testify in his own behalf in a criminal case would "degrade our criminal jurisprudence by converting it into an inquisitorial system." In my own time the battle has centered upon pretrial discovery procedures in civil cases. That engagement has been won against the protest that to permit pretrial discovery would convert our adversary system into something else. Now the movement clearly discernible, is toward pretrial discovery in criminal cases. That movement, of course, is inhibited by the privilege against self-incrimination. The argument for a proposal that the prosecution afford pretrial discovery of what it expects to prove at the trial is always countered by the argument that discovery should not be a "one-way street."

Interrogation before a judicial officer is central to the drive for broader discovery in criminal proceedings. The idea is by no means novel. The national concern in the 1920's and '30's over third degree practices stimulated a number of such proposals, principally those of Dean Pound and Professor Kauper, and legislation was urged in several states. Perhaps because constitutional doctrines did not then, as now, threaten the extinction of police questioning, the proposals met with public indifference or hostility. The police were especially hostile, although perhaps to take as typical these words of the Los Angeles Chief of Police about a California proposal would be unfair: "That bill was backed by the Communist Party of America, by the Constitutional Rights Committee of the Los Angeles Bar Association, the sob sisters, the prison reformers and all that type of individual, who wanted to see the law defeated, who wanted to set at naught the work of the peace officers of the state."

Although proposals for interrogation before a magistrate have been made and repeated throughout this century, their impact has been limited. One reason for the failure of legal scholars and the public to view these suggestions as serious proposals for legislation may have been the difficulty of supplying a sufficient number of magistrates to do the job. In an earlier lecture I indicated my reasons for concluding that an expansion of the number of judicial officers is justified, even apart from their possible role in presiding over interrogation. A more serious reason for the general indifference is that these proposals seem to require a constitutional amendment. That step, with all its attendant practical difficulties, should not be lightly undertaken. Today, the *Escobedo* decision has focused attention on the interrogation problem, and it seems to me that the time has come for intensive public consideration of an idea which has been part of the body of legal literature for a long time.

Interrogation conducted either by or before a judicial officer affords a rational adjustment of the concern of society for effective law enforcement and its concern for a fair system of criminal procedure. The goal of that interrogation should not just be the securing of a confession; its objective should also be to secure the suspect's version of the facts at an early stage of the proceedings. If there are weaknesses in his story, they can be demonstrated at the trial, if he is subsequently brought to trial. At present, the hearsay rule prohibits a defendant from introducing his prior consistent statements except to rebut the charge that his testimony is a "recent concoction." Thus he can not put before the trier of the fact self-serving statements that he may have made to the police or others. I would suggest that in this particular the hearsay rule should be modified so that a defendant may have the advantage of a prior consistent denial or explanation.

The judicial officer before whom the interrogation takes place should, before questioning begins, determine the existence of the grounds for detention or arrest described in the Model Code of Pre-Arraignment Procedure. This determination would prevent unwarranted interference with the liberty of the citizen who has given no cause for alarm. Today the police are encouraged to delay in bringing the suspect before a magistrate, because effective questioning is ended at that point. With judicially supervised interrogation, prompt production would be encouraged, for it would be only before the magistrate that admissible statements could be obtained.

As required by the Model Code, a record of the interrogation should be kept. While it may not be a matter of vital concern, it would seem desirable that the questions be put by police officers, rather than by the magistrate. The officers will know what information is relevant and what direction the inquiries should take. Such a procedure would also minimize the risk that the magistrate might come to feel responsible for the successful outcome of the interrogation from a police point of view.

Such a system of judicially supervised interrogation would go far toward eliminating police misconduct, and it would afford fully adequate protection to the rights of individual citizens. If this system were limited by prevailing constitutional doctrine, however, it would not, in my opinion, adequately protect the interests of the public. The privilege against self-incrimination as presently interpreted precludes the effective questioning of persons suspected of crime. I agree that a suspect should not be compelled to answer and that a defendant in a criminal case should not be required against his will to take the witness stand. But in my opinion it is entirely unsound to exclude from consideration at the trial the silence of a suspect involved in circumstances reasonably calling for explanation, or of a defendant who does not take the stand. It therefore seems to me imperative that the privilege against self-incrimination be modified to permit comment upon such silence. To avoid over-enthusiastic comment by a prosecutor, it might be wise to provide that only the judge may comment.

Before any suspect is questioned, he should be advised, as the Model Code requires, that he need not answer. But he should also be advised that if he is subsequently charged, his failure to answer will be disclosed at his trial. The only sanction upon a suspect's refusal to respond to questioning before a judicial officer should be to permit the trier of fact to consider that silence for whatever value it has in determining guilt or innocence.

Because judicially supervised interrogation as here proposed would permit effective questioning of all suspects, whether counseled or not, it would tend to eliminate discrimination between the knowledgeable and the naive, without at the same time eliminating interrogation. This proposal will not guarantee the elimination of all improper police conduct, but neither does the system as it exists under *Escobedo*. An additional safeguard is desirable, like that of the proposed Code, which places upon the prosecution the burden of establishing that evidence which it offers is not the product of any statement of the accused procured by improper means.

This proposal seems to me to supply a rational adjustment of the needs of society and those of the individual. More important, however, than the details of this or any other proposal, is the necessity that the problem be discussed and considered so that we may ultimately have the kind of law that we want and need.

CONSTITUTIONAL LIMITATIONS ON DETENTION FOR INVESTIGATION

GERALD H. ABRAMS

One of the major constitutional issues in the field of law enforcement in the United States is whether police officials may stop and detain for investigation. This law enforcement method typically involves a restriction of freedom on less than probable cause and without a warrant. Police officials generally pursue this type of action when they observe individuals under suspicious circumstances. The constitutionality of this activity depends on an interpretation of the fourth amendment, which provides:

> The right of the people to be secure in their persons, houses, papers, and effects, against unreasonable searches and seizures, shall not be violated, and no Warrants shall issue, but upon probable cause, supported by oath or affirmation, and particularly describing the place to be searched, and the persons or things to be seized.

The thesis of this article is that the historical background of the amendment and the relevant decisions teach that the first clause of the amendment should be considered as subsidiary to the warrant clause. Although recent authorities have sustained a power to detain as being reasonable under the fourth amendment, an appropriate standard of legality should include the specific guarantees of the warrant clause as well as reasonableness. Detention on suspicion, therefore, arguably bypasses two basic applicable safeguards: (1) the requirement of probable cause and (2) the normal requirement of obtaining a warrant.

The conclusion is reached that a detention for investigation constitutes a significant invasion of privacy. This view is based on an analysis of the privilege against self-incrimination, as it relates to a detention on suspicion, and on a consideration of the policy of the fourth amendment. This author concludes, therefore, that a general power to detain on less than probable cause is unconstitutional, but that a carefully limited power to detain relating to the gravity of the crime is justified.

Part I of this article studies the historical background of the fourth amendment. Part II consists of an analysis of the amendment as it applies to detention for investigation. In Part III the applicability of the privilege against self-incrimination to detention situations is considered.

I. HISTORY OF THE FOURTH AMENDMENT

A full comprehension of the pertinent constitutional issues depends in part upon an understanding of the historical background of the fourth amendment. The amendment was passed to prohibit particular abuses, and its standards, probable cause and the necessity of warrants, have roots in the common law.

From *Iowa Law Review,* Vol. 52, 1967, pp. 1093–1119. Reprinted by permission of *Iowa Law Review* and the author.

A. Events in England

The concept of probable or reasonable cause was well established by the end of the seventeenth century. Hale, the leading exponent of the common law, stated that any individual could arrest another if, in fact, a felony was committed and there was probable cause to believe the person to be arrested had committed the crime. A constable had the additional authority to arrest felons on complaint that stated reasonable grounds.

In the late seventeenth and early eighteenth centuries justices of the peace had full authority to issue warrants for the apprehension of criminals. Indeed, it was thought that the best practice was to obtain a warrant, and that summary arrest of felons should only be made when there was a possibility of escape. Hale stated that a justice could issue warrants on the basis of testimony because, "he is a competent judge of the probabilities."

During a long period of English history, the King and Parliament had authorized arrests and searches under general warrants, which did not describe with particularity the person to be seized or the place to be searched. Despite the development in the seventeenth and eighteenth centuries of common-law principles of arrest founded on probable cause and condemnatory of general warrants, arrests of the broadest type continued under new statutes and by usage. In England and the American colonies citizens challenged the legality of the general warrant. Against this background, the fourth amendment was adopted.

The Secretary of State in England customarily issued general warrants for arrest and search in seditious libel cases. In 1762, a warrant issued to four messengers provided that "strict and diligent search for the authors, printers and publishers of a seditious and reasonable paper, entitled, The North Briton, No. 45, . . . and them, or any of them, having been found to apprehend and seize, together with their papers." By the authority of this document, a number of arrests and seizures were made. Led by Wilkes, a member of Parliament, the persons affected challenged the legality of the warrant in a number of court cases. Leech, a printer, was arrested by three messengers under the authority of the so-called "No. 45 warrant." He brought suit for false arrest and alleged that these officers acted without any lawful or probable cause. Since there was no seizure of his property, his suit raised the precise issue of the legality or justification of the warrant for a body arrest. After a jury verdict for the plaintiff Leech, the case was appealed to the King's Bench. In affirming the judgment, Chief Justice Mansfield stated:

> As to the validity of the warrant, upon the single objection of the uncertainty of the person, being named or described—The Common Law, in many cases, gives authority to arrest without warrant, more especially, where taken in the act: and there are many cases where particular Acts of Parliament have given authority to apprehend, under general warrants . . . . But here it is not contended, that the Common Law gave the officer authority to apprehend; nor that there is an Act of Parliament which warrants this case. . . . Therefore it must stand upon principles of the Common Law . . . . It is not fit, that the receiving or judging of the information should be left to the discretion of the officer. The magistrate ought to judge; and should give certain directions to the officer. This is so, upon reason and convenience . . . .

This case and others, including the famous *Wilkes v. Wood* and *Entick v.*

Carrington cases, reaffirmed the common-law principle that general warrants are invalid as to both arrest and search. They received great notoriety and in response to public acclaim, the House of Commons passed a bill outlawing general warrants except if provided for by an Act of Parliament.

B. Events in the Colonies

Prior to the American Revolution, the English subjected the American colonies to a number of trade restrictions and beginning in 1760 these tariffs were strictly enforced. The resistance of the colonies to the English trade policy included an attempt to limit the authority of the customs officials. Searches were conducted by customs officers pursuant to writs of assistance. Issuance of a writ did not depend on a factual showing based on sworn testimony. Pursuant to a writ's authority, an officer could, at will, search any house during the daytime and any ship during day or night for goods, wares, or merchandise. Since it was not returnable at a specific time, it was in substance a general search warrant of unlimited legal duration.

James Otis, in a widely heralded argument before the Massachusetts Supreme Court of Judicature, contended that writs of assistance were contrary to the common law. His argument rested on the premise that only search warrants issued upon oath and good ground of suspicion were valid. Since writs of assistance made the customs officials judges of the facts, they were illegal. The Massachusetts court upheld the legality of the writ and it thereafter issued from time to time.

Attempts by customs officials to seize merchandise pursuant to writs of assistance caused the colonists to riot and demonstrate. The widespread objection of the colonists to the use of general warrants is evidenced by some of the documents of the period. A document published by colonists in 1772 charged that one of the basic violations of colonial rights by the British was the exercise of general search powers by the customs officials. In the Petition of the Colonial Congress to the King, one of the listed grievances was that, "The officers of the customs are empowered to break open and enter houses, without the authority of any civil magistrate, founded on legal information."

C. Events after Independence

Not until the last days of the Constitutional Convention, which convened in 1787 to draft the new constitution, was a motion made to establish a committee to consider a bill of rights. This motion was defeated and the proposed constitution went to the States without a bill of rights. The omission of a bill of rights was a central argument used by the anti-Federalists in a vigorous attack against adoption of the proposed constitution. It was argued that unless the federal government was prohibited from indulging in certain deprivations, the people would be subjected to tyranical rule not unlike the British experience.

Examination of contemporary sources shows that the danger of arbitrary arrest and search pursuant to general warrants, or warrants not founded on oath, was mentioned in connection with the necessity for a bill of rights. One popular pamphlet stated:

> There is no provision by a bill of rights to guard against the dangerous encroachments of power in too many instances to be named: but I cannot pass over in silence the insecurity in which we are left with regard to warrants unsupported by evidence—the daring experiment of granting *writs of assistance* in a former arbitrary administration is not yet forgotten in the

Massachusetts; nor can we be so ungrateful to the memory of the patriots who counteracted their operation, so soon after their manly exertions to save us from a detestable instrument of arbitrary power, to subject ourselves to the insolence of any petty revenue officer to enter our houses, search, insult and seize at pleasure.

The rights of individuals ought to be the primary object of all government, and cannot be too securely guarded by the most explicit declarations in their favor . . . .

Ratification of the Constitution was in part conditioned upon subsequent adoption of a bill of rights. During the first session of Congress, Madison moved the adoption of a bill of rights and laid nine proposals before the House of Representatives. In pertinent part, his proposals provided that:

The rights of the people to be secured in their persons, their houses, their papers, and their other property, from all unreasonable searches and seizures, shall not be violated by warrants issued without probable cause, supported by oath or affirmation, or not particularly describing the places to be searched, and the persons or things to be seized.

After committee consideration, Madison's proposals were put before the entire House. The revised version of the search and seizure provision was as follows:

The rights of the people to be secured in their persons, houses, papers and effects, shall not be violated by warrants issuing without probable cause, supported by oath or affirmation, and not particularly describing the place to be searched, and the persons or things to be seized.

Elbridge Gerry said that he presumed that there was a mistake in the wording and moved to amend to have it read "the right of the people to be secure in their persons, houses, papers and effects against unreasonable searches and seizures shall not be violated by warrants issuing . . . ." This motion was passed. The final motion was to delete "by warrants issuing" and insert "and no warrants shall issue." This change would have created two independent clauses. The motion was voted down. A committee of three was selected to arrange all of the amendments as passed by the House. When they reported back to the House, the fourth amendment consisted of the two independent clauses that had previously been rejected. No explanation for the change appears in the records of the Congress.

D. Historical Conclusion

The text of the amendment is comprised of two independent clauses; the first prohibits unreasonable searches and seizures, and the second lays down constitutional guidelines for the issuance of warrants. With the idea of two separate guarantees, the conclusion easily follows that the Constitution prohibits only unreasonable searches and seizures and hence permits reasonable ones. However, such an oversimplified interpretation is contrary to the historical background of the fourth amendment.

Analysis of the legislative history of the fourth amendment indicates that there is no apparent explanation for its wording. Madison's first proposal was directed at general warrants alone. Even after the House amended to insert "unreasonable searches and seizures," this phrase was totally subordinate to the warrant clause. The motion to revise the amendment into two independent clauses was defeated; yet, unexplainably, the amendment was adopted in its present form. Textually, therefore, the fourth amendment according to the annals of Congress is either a mistake or totally inexplicable, or both.

Since the legislative history is ambiguous, historical background is especially relevant in discovering the intent of the framers. The colonists had been subjected to the tyranny of British customs officials acting under writs of assistance. This was one of the causes of the Revolutionary War. "[N]or, although with grievances of their own, were they [the colonists] unobservant of what was going on in England. 'Wilkes and Liberty' was a familiar cry in Boston as well as in London." These events were not forgotten during the debates on the adoption of the Constitution. It was recognized that unlimited search and seizure was a weapon of arbitrary government. Early Americans strenuously argued that it was mandatory to enact a constitutional amendment that protected the individual from abuses perpetrated under general warrants. Therefore, it seems clear that Madison and his colleagues intended the fourth amendment to be a statement declaring illegal, for all times, searches and seizures under discretionary warrants.

The right that was protected was a right that could be violated through the use of illegal warrants. In light of the colonists' experience, it would have been ludicrous for them to prohibit arbitrary activity only if it was perpetrated pursuant to a warrant. The framers probably did not intend to permit the circumvention of the constitutional protection by the simple method of acting without a warrant. They logically intended to require all arrests to be made pursuant to warrants issued by magistrates under appropriate constitutional safeguards. The requirements of probable cause, supported by sworn testimony, for the issuance of special warrants are at the core of the fourth amendment.

II. FOURTH AMENDMENT AS IT APPLIES TO DETENTION FOR INVESTIGATION

Interpretation of the fourth amendment guarantees involves the reconciliation of individual rights and law enforcement needs. Perhaps one of the most difficult issues arising under the amendment is the legality of a detention for investigation. This police method typically involves a restraint of freedom on less than probable cause and without a warrant. It has been argued that the sacrifice of these basic safeguards is necessary for the prevention of crime.

The phrase detention for investigation describes a broad category of police activity. The police practices under this category include: (1) the stopping of individuals on the street, (2) the stopping of moving vehicles, and (3) the holding of people for the purposes of interrogation. These detentions are typically temporary, from a few minutes to a few hours, and for that reason differ from a formal arrest. The fourth amendment applies to seizures of the person. Any constitutional issue, therefore, is not reached until a restraint of freedom is established.

A. Determination of a Restraint of Freedom

The possible evidentiary tests to determine a restraint of freedom are: (1) whether the officer's conduct indicates he has restrained the individual, (2) whether the individual understands that he is restrained, and (3) whether a reasonable man under the circumstances would believe he was restrained. Synthesis of relevant decisions indicates that the courts have adopted a combination of tests one and two. If the officer's conduct clearly indicates that the individual is restrained, the courts do not inquire into the individual's state of mind. Thus, an officer forcing a car to stop along the side of the road would appear to establish a restraint of freedom. However, if the policeman's conduct presents ambiguity as to the existence of a restraint, then the state of mind of the individual is controlling. This is a sound approach, for it is the citizen's right to be protected from intrusion which is prohibited by the fourth amendment. If he believes that he is in custody, then all of the legal protections that flow from that consequence should be his.

It might be argued that rather than considering the subjective state of mind of the individual, an objective, reasonable man test should be employed. Proponents of this test argue that the police will be intolerably burdened if they have to guess what is in every foolish or irrational mind. However, the Bill of Rights was enacted to protect every man and although the police may be burdened from time to time, the subjective test seems appropriate and required. As a practical matter, however, the jury may employ an objective test anyway, since it is likely that the defendant's testimony will not be credited unless it is reasonable. Therefore, the subjective test will probably not unduly burden the police.

Several detention for investigation situations raise difficult problems as to whether there is a restraint of freedom. Consider, for example, the case of a policeman who approaches a citizen who is walking on a public sidewalk. The policeman does not announce any coercive order, but his uniform and inherent authority will surely affect the individual. The citizen may feel entirely free and willing to stop and answer questions. Thus, should the citizen stop, it would be difficult to discern whether the "stop" was coerced or volunteered. This is, and should be, a question for the trier of the facts. The United States Supreme Court has recognized that responsible citizens have an obligation to cooperate with the police. Although treatment of the nature of the "stop" as a question of fact permits ambiguity, it does not eliminate the possibility of voluntary cooperation.

B. Detentions for Investigation as Seizures
within the Fourth Amendment

Even if there is a restraint of freedom, there is the further question as to whether or not such restraint is a seizure within the fourth amendment. Some cases have permitted detentions for investigation on the ground that they are not seizures. According to these decisions, a showing of probable cause is not required. The courts, however, have not articulated clearly under what circumstances, and on what bases, this power may be exercised. The main thrust of their reasoning is that although both involve a restriction of freedom, there is a valid, but admittedly thin line between detention and arrest. The distinction turns on the purpose and length of the restriction—whether or not it is a short detention solely for investigation.

The attempt to differentiate seizure and detention on the basis of the purpose of a restriction would appear to be unsound. The fourth amendment was passed to prohibit arbitrary interference with freedom. From the individual's view, it matters not for what purpose his right to come and go has been curtailed. If purpose is not a valid criterion, the duration of a restriction of freedom per se certainly cannot serve as a basis for holding that the fourth amendment does not apply to detentions for investigation. Time, standing alone, is too arbitrary. Many courts take this view and hold that all restraints of freedom, however brief, for whatever purpose, and however they are denominated, "stops" or "detentions," are seizures within the fourth amendment.

C. Constitutional Standard of Legality

Recent authorities have held that all detentions are seizures, but have concurrently asserted that under the fourth amendment a broad test of reasonableness is appropriate. Under this standard, detentions of different types have been upheld. The critical question of what is the proper criterion of constitutionality under the fourth amendment is thereby raised.

The Model Code of Pre-Arraignment Procedure states "[T]here can be no doubt that the Fourth Amendment's guarantee against 'unreasonable seizure of the person' is applicable to any official exercise of custody over the person." The legality of the Model Code's proposed statutory authority to detain for investigation depends, according to the Reporters of the Code, on whether the detention is in principle unreasonable. Under Section 202(2), "a person observed in circumstances which suggest that he has committed or is about to commit a felony or misdemeanor . . . may be detained for a period of not more than 20 minutes if such action is reasonably necessary to enable an officer to determine the lawfulness of the person's conduct." During the detention the officers may seek identification and cooperation; they may verify by readily available information any identification or account that the person renders.

Without agreeing with the Code's conclusion that its proposal is constitutional, one may state that insofar as the Reporters carefully define and limit the power to detain, their approach is sound. However, some recent cases, relying on the reasonableness approach of the Code, have failed to articulate clear standards for police action, thus giving too broad a discretion to law enforcement officials. For example, in *Gilbert v. United States*, the Ninth Circuit Court of Appeals stated that "[A]ny official exertion of custody over the person is a seizure within the Fourth Amendment and may be sustained if it is not unreasonable." Legality is determined by a review of the totality of the circumstances. The detention must be based on reasonable grounds and not be arbitrary or harassing. Under this broad test, the amount of evidence at the agent's command is only one fact among many to be considered.

The United States Supreme Court has not ruled directly on the constitutionality of detention for investigation. However, there are decisions that are relevant to the standard of legality under the fourth amendment. These cases emphasize the specific guarantees of the warrant clause and cast doubt on the reasonableness doctrine. To that extent they implicitly suggest that detention on less than probable cause is unconstitutional.

Henry v. United States, perhaps the leading United States Supreme Court case in the area, involved a conviction for the unlawful possession of property stolen from an interstate shipment. FBI agents stopped a car in which Henry, the defendant-petitioner, and Pierotti, a co-defendant, were riding with some stolen merchandise. Prior to the stop, the agents had some evidence, but there was a substantial question whether or not this would have supported probable cause. The prosecution did not contend that the officers' action was a lawful exercise of the right to detain for investigation. Instead, before the Supreme Court and the lower courts as well, the government conceded that an arrest occurred when the car was stopped. Affirmance of the conviction was sought on the ground that the arrest and the incidental search were based on probable cause. The Supreme Court rejected the government's contention and found that the evidence did not amount to probable cause. The Court, using the opportunity to make some important observations concerning the fourth amendment and the right of police to detain for investigation, stated that "when the officers interrupted the two men and restricted their liberty of movement, the arrest, for purposes of this case, was complete." Justice Douglas, speaking for a majority of seven, suggested that the fourth amendment permits arrests only for offenses committed in the officers' presence or on reasonable ground to believe the person has committed or is committing a felony. For, according to the Justice, "the requirement of probable cause has roots deep in our history . . . and arrest on mere suspicion collides violently with the basic human right of liberty."

The Court's reasoning warrants close examination. One should consider whether under *Henry* every temporary restriction of freedom is an arrest within the fourth amendment, or whether the *Henry* rationale is limited by its facts. Here, the agents had some reason to suspect that the occupants of a moving vehicle were carrying stolen merchandise. The officers stopped the car, overheard some incriminatory remarks, searched the vehicle, and discovered cartons that turned out to be stolen. Justice Douglas held that at the point of the stop, the arrest was complete within the meaning of the amendment. This conclusion seems sound. When the agents decided to stop the vehicle, it was clear that they would ascertain whether or not the occupants were in possession of stolen merchandise and, if they were, would make an arrest. Factually, the stop, arrest, and search were simultaneous events and, therefore, their legality should depend on the prior existence of probable cause.

Thus, although the facts of *Henry* did not present a difficult problem, the Court emphasized the importance of the requirement of probable cause in protecting people from arbitrary government. It would seem that the Court will carefully examine every situation involving a restriction of freedom and most likely will require the police to make a showing of probable cause as justification for the interference with liberty.

Carroll v. United States, in which Chief Justice Taft announced his oft-quoted dictum that the fourth amendment prohibits only unreasonable searches and seizures, supports this analysis nevertheless. There, the issue was the legality of a search and seizure without a warrant of a motor vehicle that was stopped on a public highway. The officers had evidence that the occupants were carrying contraband liquor and the search of the car proved that their suspicions were correct. Again, the stop, search, and arrest were factually indistinguishable. Therefore, it was entirely appropriate for the court to premise its decision on the idea that it was necessary for the government to establish probable cause prior to the stopping of the car. However, the Supreme Court went on to make this statement:

> It would be intolerable and unreasonable if a prohibition agent were authorized to stop every automobile on the chance of finding liquor and thus subject all persons lawfully using the highways to the inconvenience and indignity of such a search. Travellers may be so stopped in crossing an international boundary because of national self protection reasonably requiring one entering the country to identify himself as entitled to come in, and his belongings as effects which may be lawfully brought in. But those lawfully within the country, entitled to use the public highways, have a right to free passage without interruption or search unless there is known to a competent official authorized to search, probable cause for believing that their vehicles are carrying contraband or illegal merchandise.

Under the facts in *Carroll,* it was perhaps unnecessary to make a statement that so vividly supported the constitutional requirement of probable cause. The fact that the Court did say this all the more suggests the Court's belief in the importance of protecting citizens from capricious intrusions by government officials by requiring a showing of probable cause.

In the most recent case, *Rios v. United States,* the government argued that the police had the power to detain for investigation. There, officers on less than probable cause approached a taxicab while it was stopped at a red light. A conflict developed in certain portions of the testimony, but it was undisputed that the defendant was found in the cab with narcotics. The conflict in the testimony concerned the sequence of events, whether the defendant voluntarily revealed the narcotics as the officers approached, or whether the officers discovered the contraband after restraining the defendant. Since it appeared that the district court may have rested its denial of the motion to supress on the silver platter doctrine, which was overturned in *Elkins v. United States,* the Court remanded for a complete factual hearing and stated:

> But the Government argues that the policeman approached the standing taxi only for the purpose of routine interrogation, and that they had no intent to detain the petitioner beyond the momentary requirements of such a mission. If the petitioner thereafter voluntarily revealed the package of narcotics to the officers' view, a lawful arrest could then have been supported by their reasonable cause to believe that a felony was being committed in their presence. The validity of the search thus turns upon the narrow question of when the arrest occurred, and the answer to that question depends upon an evaluation of the conflicting testimony of those who were there that night.

Some have argued that *Rios* implies an acceptance of the prosecution's argument because of the remand. However, the Court's action in the light of the factual dispute may be construed as a rejection of the Government's contention that the police may detain for investigation. The Court's action means that only if the agents saw the narcotics prior to any restraint, thus giving rise to probable cause, would the arrest be deemed legal.

Henry, Rios, and *Carroll* involved restraints of the person and each opinion, with varying degrees of emphasis, suggests that within a particular situation probable cause is required. The fourth amendment doctrine of reasonableness has been mainly applied by the Supreme Court to certain search situations. In these cases there existed probable cause, but for policy reasons the Court permitted an exception to the normal requirement of obtaining a warrant. Law enforcement officials need not obtain a warrant in all cases to search a moving car because of the danger that the vehicle would leave the jurisdiction before a warrant could be secured. An arrested person may be searched in order to protect the arresting officer, to deprive the arrested person of potential means of escape, or to avoid destruction of evidence. In such cases the proper limits of the search may be defined by a test of reasonableness. Even in these instances, however, the doctrine of reasonableness must be carefully limited so that the guarantees of the warrant clause are not rendered nugatory. In *Chapman v. United States,* police without a warrant searched a house that reeked with the odor of mash. One might argue that this search was reasonable under the circumstances, but this is not the test under the fourth amendment. In declaring the search illegal, the Supreme Court stated:

No reason is offered for not obtaining a search warrant except the inconvenience to the officers and some slight delay necessary to prepare papers and present the evidence to a magistrate. These are never very convincing reasons and, in these circumstances, certainly are not enough to by-pass the constitutional requirement. No suspect was fleeing or likely to take flight. The search was of permanent premises, not of a movable vehicle. No evidence or contraband was threatened with removal or destruction, except perhaps the fumes which we suppose in time would disappear.

III. PRIVILEGE AGAINST SELF-INCRIMINATION AS IT APPLIES TO DETENTION FOR INVESTIGATION

The main object of a detention for investigation is interrogation. Thus, substantial self-incrimination problems are raised. It is appropriate, then, to consider this factor in balancing the individual interests against the police needs as to the legality of detention for investigation under the fourth amendment.

Normally, an officer will request name, address, and an account of activities from a suspect who is detained on the street for investigation. Two critical legal issues pertain here: (1) under the circumstances does the fifth amendment apply, and (2) if it does, can the police nevertheless require the suspect to supply his name and address? Resolution of the issue depends on the applicability of *Miranda v. Arizona.*

The holding of *Miranda* is summarized, in pertinent part, as follows:

The prosecution may not use statements, whether exculpatory or inculpatory, stemming from custodial interrogation of the defendant unless it demonstrates the use of procedural safeguards effective to secure the privilege against self-incrimination. By custodial interrogation, we mean questioning initiated by law enforcement officers after a person has been taken into custody or otherwise deprived of his freedom of action in any significant way. As for the procedural safeguards to be employed, unless other fully effective means are devised to inform accused persons of their right of silence and to assure a continuous opportunity to exercise it, the following measures are required. Prior to any questioning, the person must be warned that he has a right to remain silent, that any statement he does make may be used as evidence against him, and that he has a right to the presence of an attorney, either retained or appointed.

Analysis of *Miranda* begins with a consideration of *Escobedo v. Illinois.* In *Escobedo* the Court announced a new test for when the right to counsel under the sixth amendment accrues. Justice Goldberg, for the Court, stated:

We hold only that when the process shifts from investigatory to accusatory—when its focus is on the accused and its purpose is to elicit a confession—our adversary system begins to operate, and, under the circumstances here, the accused must be permitted to consult with his lawyer.

With this statement the Court attempted to draw a clear, workable distinction between the accusatory and investigative processes. This distinction was intended to allow the police to investigate crime by interviewing witnesses and by using other proper investigative techniques, yet at the same time, to place a control on methods used to obtain confessions. However, the language of the

Court raised several interpretative problems: (1) what was the meaning of the terms "focus" and "purpose," and (2) whether a subjective or objective test was to be employed in determining the existence of the requisite focus or purpose.

The Court in *Miranda* did not rely on a focus-purpose test but instead, developed the in-custody standard as meaning deprived of freedom in any way. The Court examined various police training manuals that stressed the importance of removing the suspect from family, friends, and familiar surroundings, all of which would support his will to resist the interrogators. These manuals also described various psychological strategems that could be used during interrogation to induce the suspect to confess. Each of the four cases before the Court entailed this type of interrogation. Each of the four defendants was arrested for a crime and taken to unfamiliar surroundings, where he was questioned in a police dominated, incommunicado atmosphere. The Court commented that such interrogation environments are "created for no purpose other than to subjugate the individual to the will of his examiner."

After this review, Chief Justice Warren concluded that the "very fact of custodial interrogation" establishes compulsion within the meaning of the fifth amendment. Therefore, according to the Court, the protection afforded the individual by the privilege against self-incrimination is as broad as the ability of the police to compel answers. This compulsion is presumed whenever law enforcement officials question an individual who is in custody or deprived of his freedom in any way. In these situations the *Miranda* warnings must be given to dispel the inherent compulsion and to enable the suspect to waive his constitutional rights knowingly.

Does a typical on-the-street detention of an individual fall within the *Miranda* compulsion rationale? The police do not detain for investigation solely "to subjugate the individual to the will of his examiner" and thus obtain a confession. Typically, in a detention on suspicion case it is not clear that a crime has been committed. The police seek truthful, but possibly incriminating, information and intend the prevention of crime. Nor is this the type of circumstance in which law enforcement officials can readily employ the psychological stratagems that the Court disapproved in its opinion.

Nevertheless, on-the-street detention shares certain common characteristics with station house interrogation. A detention may place the individual in an incommunicado, police dominated atmosphere. The person who is restrained on the street is cut off from his lawyer and, perhaps, his friends. Indeed, the possible absence of a readily available telephone may put the individual at a greater disadvantage than if he were in a station house. Two policemen surrounding an individual on the street may dominate and instill fear in the same way that two policemen may at the police station. If a suspect understands he is in the custody and under the control of the police, regardless of location, it is natural for him to feel obliged to answer questions.

One might argue that because of its short duration, a detention for investigation is distinguishable from a typical custodial interrogation. Although arguably the pressure on the individual increases with the passage of time during an interrogation, some cases suggest that there is compulsion within the meaning of *Miranda* during short interrogations of ten or twenty minutes. In the initial shock of confrontation the suspect may be particularly prone to say something that is incriminatory.

On-the-street detention under certain circumstances may have enough of the characteristics of station house interrogation for a court to conclude that there is compulsion within the meaning of *Miranda*. However, one should consider the applicability of the privilege against self-incrimination to detention situations with regard to a second rationale of *Miranda.*

The Court distinguished between the accusatory and investigative processes. This division is reflected in Chief Justice Warren's discussion of the principles embodied in the privilege against self-incrimination. These principles are: (1) "the respect a government . . . must accord to the dignity and integrity of its citizens," and (2) as a part of this respect "our accusatory system of criminal justice demands that the government seeking to punish an individual produce the evidence against him by its own independent labors, rather than by the cruel, simple expedient of compelling it from his own mouth." So viewed, *Miranda* is an affirmation of the *Escobedo* distinction between the investigative and accusatory process. The Court stated that "after a person has been taken into custody or otherwise deprived of his freedom of action in any significant way . . . is what we meant in *Escobedo* when we spoke of an investigation which had focused on the accused."

The action of stopping and questioning a person in suspicious circumstances is properly part of the accusatory process. Although the sole object of the police may not be to obtain a confession, the main purpose of the stop is nevertheless interrogation. To the individual, this is a critical stage of a proceeding that may result in formal arrest and indictment. The statements he might make, whether falsely exculpatory or self-incriminating, are just as significant as those made after arrest.

All this may be true as to a man observed in suspicious circumstances, but should this analysis apply with equal force to eyewitnesses? The answer to this problem is not entirely clear. Consider, for example, two witnesses who observed a hit and run accident. If the police freeze the situation, they have restrained the freedom of these individuals. However, it is clear that in this instance a police interrogation will be directed at securing truthful information and not self-incriminatory evidence. The purpose of the questioning is to discover what these witnesses observed. It is difficult to classify these individuals as accuseds. The policy of *Miranda* in protecting suspects would not appear to apply to this case.

In one paragraph of the *Miranda* opinion the Court discusses on-the-street interrogation. However, the relevance of the language is solely to the problem of obtaining evidence against the accused who is in custody. The Court stated:

> [W]hen an individual is in custody on probable cause, the police may, of course, seek out evidence in the field to be used at trial against him. Such investigations may include inquiry of persons not under restraint. General on-the-scene questioning as to facts surrounding a crime or other general questioning of citizens in the fact-finding process is not affected by our holding. It is an act of responsible citizenship for individuals to give whatever information they may have to aid law enforcement. In such situations, the compelling atmosphere inherent in the process of in-custody interrogation is not necessarily present.

This statement clearly permits some questioning of witnesses without the delivery of the *Miranda* warnings. As a practical matter, the presence of police at the scene of a crime will oblige witnesses to remain. Therefore, to that extent, the *Miranda* opinion may be interpreted as allowing a minimal restriction of freedom without the required warnings. However, the Court's statement that in such situations a compelling atmosphere is not necessarily present suggests that in some on-the-street situations the holding of *Miranda* will apply. If this is possible as to witnesses, it is likely as to suspects; the greater the likelihood of adducing self-incriminatory statements, the greater the need for the *Miranda* guarantees.

If the fifth amendment and all of the procedural safeguards developed by the Supreme Court in *Miranda* are fully applicable to on-the-street detention in suspicious circumstances, the utility of the detention power becomes questionable as a practical matter. There cannot be an attorney on every street corner. On the other hand, there may be a distinction between eliciting a name and address, and seeking an account of a man's behavior. As to the latter, there can be no doubt that the privilege can be claimed. One must closely consider, however, whether or not a suspect may refuse on constitutional grounds to supply his name and address. This inquiry is especially important because of identification of individuals is apparently the basic justification of a detention.

The first issue is whether an individual may always refuse to supply his name and address. The Supreme Court in *Malloy v. Hogan, Miranda,* and *Schmerber v. California* stated that "the privilege [against self-incrimination] is fulfilled only when the person is guaranteed the right to remain silent unless he chooses to speak in the unfettered exercise of his own will." Taking this standard literally, the essence of the privilege is choice rather than information. Thus, it is possible that a suspect may always refuse on constitutional grounds to supply his name and address upon request and stand mute before police officers.

It is hard to believe, however, that the Court means that a person may refuse to answer when there is no chance whatsoever that the statement would tend to incriminate him. Perhaps, the implication of the Court's language is that suspects have the absolute right to refuse to answer and that witnesses may refuse to answer only if the answer might tend to incriminate. But in *Malloy* the Court suggested that witnesses and defendants receive the same protection under the amendment. In any event, even if the privilege does not mean that a person has a right to silence, substantial self-incrimination problems remain. Although the factual variations are innumerable, a refusal to supply an address will be clearly justified in many cases. Knowledge of a man's name might be incriminating if the suspect were using an alias or if it would provide police with an investigative shortcut that would aid in building the prosecution's case.

However, there is an argument for excepting this information from constitutional protection. The fifth amendment is not an absolute. The importance of the privilege is in establishing and maintaining a fair state-individual balance. Therefore, the giving of name and address by a suspect is arguably a minimal invasion compared to the time and energy likely to be necessary to find him again.

In *Schmerber,* the Court justified the compelled withdrawal of blood and the introduction of the chemical analysis into evidence on the basis of the distinction between real and testimonial evidence. Practically speaking, this was highly incriminatory material, far more incriminatory than the facts of a man's name and address. In addition, the Court suggested that certain identification techniques, such as fingerprinting and photographing, might be valid. A suspect is not likely to be more damaged by supplying name and address than by being fingerprinted and photographed, all of which may lead the prosecution to valuable testimony. Therefore, judging by the Court's action in *Schmerber,* a suspect possibly would not be permitted to refuse to give his name and address to police officers.

IV. CONCLUSION

The major question of the constitutionality of the police power to detain is beclouded if it is phrased as whether or not under certain circumstances a detention for investigation is reasonable. Reasonableness is not a proper criterion of constitutionality under the fourth amendment. Such a vague standard vests law enforcement officials with the same type of discretion as existed under general warrants. The doctrine of reasonableness should not be employed to circumvent the specific protections of the warrant clause. The power of the police to stop and detain without a warrant and without probable cause constitutes a manifest exception to the specific guarantees of the fourth amendment.

Although the Supreme Court has made limited exceptions to the normal requirement of obtaining warrants, it never has sustained a restraint of an individual on less than probable cause. Therefore, the basic problem is whether or not there is clear and convincing justification for the Supreme Court to make an exception to the requirement of probable cause and to sustain a general power of detention for investigation.

Cogent analysis of the pertinent constitutional issue depends on a clear understanding of what is, and what is not, involved. Frequently, supporters of the constitutionality of a power to detain in suspicious circumstances attempt to prove police need for this authority by citing sympathetic eyewitness crime circumstances.

Consider a situation in which the police receive a report of a killing and arrive at a designated corner to find six people standing near a bloody corpse. May the officers order these individuals to remain for purposes of investigation? This is a different case from stopping a man in suspicious circumstances. Here, there is probable cause to believe that a crime has been committed and that these people have material information pertaining to the crime. Identification of these individuals is necessary to preserve valuable investigative leads. Information that might be supplied by these witnesses could lead to an immediate arrest of the criminal. These considerations may justify a carefully defined exception to the normal requirement of obtaining a warrant.

After laying aside eyewitness situations, the proponents of the power to detain in suspicious circumstances may rest their case on several commonsense factors. There is a need to identify people in suspicious circumstances, or it will be difficult to find them again. This is especially true in our large urban centers where people are anonymous. A short period of detention also allows the police to seek an account of the suspect's activities, make an investigation, and formulate an informed decision as to arrest.

Thus, the concept of voluntary cooperation, it is argued, cannot be stretched to cover all investigative situations. The proponents of the power say, and one must agree, that it is impossible without a coercive command to secure the cooperation of a man driving a car or of a group of people thundering down the street. There is a hiatus between voluntary cooperation and arrest on probable cause. The issue is whether or not it should be filled with a power to detain.

The right to be secure from unwarranted intrusions is a basic characteristic of a free society. Justice Jackson has stated:

These, I protest, are not mere second-class rights but belong in the catalog of indispensable freedoms. Among deprivations of rights, none is so effective in cowing a population, crushing the spirit of the individual and putting terror in every heart. Uncontrolled search and seizure is one of the first and most effective weapons in the arsenal of every arbitrary government. And one need only briefly to have dwelt and worked among a people possessed of many admirable qualities but deprived of these rights to know that the human personality deteriorates and dignity and self-reliance disappear where homes, persons and possessions are subject at any hour to unheralded search and seizure by the police.

Besides the obvious interference with freedom, the right to come and go as one pleases, a detention for investigation also raises basic self-incrimination problems. An analysis of *Miranda* suggests that its compulsion rationale is applicable to a detention in suspicious circumstances. Such a detention is a substantial invasion of privacy. Therefore, a broad exception to the specific guarantees of the fourth amendment may not be justified and a general power to detain on less than probable cause may be unconstitutional.

It appears appropriate to carve out a limited exception in the detention area along the lines suggested by Justice Jackson's dissent in *Brinegar v. United States,* that is, with reference to the gravity of the crime. Consider the following example: "A police car is called late at night to investigate a reported fight and killing. Two blocks away from the address to which they are headed, the officers see a man running in the opposite direction." Here, there is probable cause to believe a serious crime has been committed, an emergency, and some reasonable evidence, though not amounting to probable cause, that the individual is implicated. In such a case, it would seem proper to uphold a short detention. Even if *Miranda* applied, there would be practical utility to the stop, since such an investigation might produce either eyewitnesses capable of making an identification or the suspect's name and address, which could be obtained possibly pursuant to an appropriate statutory procedure. This exception would cover the compelling situations that might justify exercise of a power to detain. The validity of the distinction would be tested on a case to case basis. It seems that this exception is preferable to conferring upon the police broad authority to stop an individual on suspicion.

THE LAW AND PRACTICE OF
FIELD INTERROGATION

WAYLAND D. PILCHER

A workable, qualitative definition of the term "field interrogation" is almost impossible to devise. We will have to be content, then, with a descriptive definition. For the purposes of this article, a field interrogation is any situation in which a police officer asks questions, pertaining to a crime or a suspected crime, of a citizen prior to the time when the citizen is taken, by force or consent, to a police station for further processing. The terms "field stop" and "field contact" are to be considered as synonymous with the term "field interrogation."

It would seem, at first glance, that the term "field interrogation" should be susceptible of a fairly accurate definition. But first glances can be deceptive. There are several revealing and important reasons why any definition of the term "field interrogation" must be, at least in some degree, arbitrary.

The necessity to be arbitrary in the definition of the term "field interrogation" arises primarily because there are so few clear-cut cases where the practice of field interrogation has been examined, analyzed, or defined. At the root of this definitional problem is the wide disparity between the criminal law, as developed by appellate courts, and police practice. To the police officer, an arrest and a field interrogation are entirely distinct concepts. Each has its own purpose, and the techniques used in the streets are quite different. Generally, from the policeman's standpoint, he "arrests" a person when he takes this person to the police station to be charged with a specific crime. On the other hand, he is engaged in the practice of "field interrogation" when he "checks out" a person to determine who he is, what he has been doing, and attempts to obtain an explanation of his actions. Our appellate courts apparently have not made this distinction until very recently. Instead, the courts, when they have faced the real issues at all, have talked in terms of "arrest."

Once the term "arrest" is used by an appellate court it is immediately handicapped. In the first place, the traditional concept of arrest is encrusted with the barnacles of an ancient time which has long since passed. Our present concept of arrest was fairly accurately described by Matthew Hale before 1676. In feudal England, law enforcement, or at least the bringing of an accused person before a magistrate, was the responsibility of the people in the community and the citizens were organized in groups of hundreds in order to apprehend the perpetrator of a crime. In theory, when a crime was perpetrated and the person suspected of committing the crime was attempting to evade capture, the general populace was supposed to evoke a "hue and cry" to pursue the criminal in much the same manner that the posse operates in a western movie.

Such a system of apprehending criminals apparently worked satisfactorily in

Reprinted by Special Permission of the *Journal of Criminal Law, Criminology and Police Science* (Northwestern University School of Law), Copyright © 1967, Volume 58, Number 4.

a static, rural society where each person in the community was intimately acquainted with every other person. The system described above eventually evolved into the Justice of the Peace system wherein the Justice of the Peace was not only a magistrate but also had the responsibility of preserving the peace within his jurisdiction and was the chief law enforcement officer. But the Justice of the Peace system proved inadequate in the face of urbanization and a marked increase in criminal activity.

As cities began to develop, a system of night watchmen was evolved. The actual authority of the night watchman is somewhat vague, but apparently his only function was to take into custody persons who were suspicious or who were committing a crime and hold such persons until dawn, when they could be handed over to the regular law enforcement apparatus. At the same time there developed in England a system of rewards and pardons to encourage citizens to apprehend criminals and bring them before a judicial officer for the criminal process to commence. The first organized police force in the Anglo-American heritage was not established until 1829 when the London metropolitan police force was created by act of Parliament over vigorous opposition. Thus, as one writer states:

. . . the law of arrest was developed in the context of a citizen enforcement system where arrests were often motivated by greed for "blood money," private vendetta, or hope of pardon for the arresting person's own crime.

The development of arrest law was probably also influenced by the post arrest predicament of the arrested person in early England. Persons charged with serious offenses were rarely admitted to bail and conditions in the jails of the time were horrible. Jails were run as a private business and fees were charged for the most elementary "privileges." Those persons arrested who did not have the means to purchase better accommodations were huddled together, often in irons, in dark, filthy, rooms and in close proximity to depravity and disease. Under such conditions, an arrest could be, and often was, equivalent to a death sentence.

The concept of the individual citizen as a law enforcer is not merely of interest to medieval scholars; it is very much alive in some parts of the United States today. For example, the State of Texas completely revised its Code of Criminal Procedure in 1965, and this "modern" code provided the individual citizen with exactly the same authority to make arrests without warrant as the authority granted to the peace officer, with one exception.

It is part of our judicial heritage that courts do not determine abstract questions of law. Therefore, field interrogation situations which are decided by courts usually are cast in the context of a situation where the field interrogation has in fact played a part in an arrest, a subsequent charge, and a trial. Furthermore, the discussion of field interrogation practices then arises under a motion to suppress, an objection to the introduction of evidence, or a discussion of the existence or nonexistence of probable cause to make the arrest. Unfortunately, at least at the trial court level, the prosecutor is usually faced with meeting the defense attorney on these grounds and attempting to convince the court that: (a) probable cause for an arrest did exist, or (b) the evidence in issue was obtained prior to the time that an arrest occurred. The crucial questions in field interrogation suffer from being presented in this light.

In the first place, in most field contacts, probable cause, in a classic sense, does not exist. The traditional elements of probable cause are (1) that the peace officer knows a specific crime has been committed and (2) that the peace officer has probable cause to believe that a specific individual has committed the specific crime. If these elements are present, then the officer would more than likely simply arrest the individual, charge him, and there would be no field interrogation problem. As a result, the line is usually drawn on the rather artful definition of what is an arrest; the defense attorney naturally insists that the arrest occurred at the very instant the person was stopped and the prosecution insists with equal vigor that the arrest occurred at some nonspecific time after the individual was approached by the peace officer. With very few exceptions the courts tend to fall into this definitional trap. Therefore, we have numerous courts which hold that the slightest interference with a person's freedom of movement is an "arrest," and a large number of other decisions which define an arrest as "the taking into custody a person so that he may answer for a crime." Thus, the critical issues involved in the practice of field interrogation are obscured by the semantic battle over the definition of "arrest."

Neither of these definitions reaches the essential issues which are involved in the field interrogation. Each of these definitions tends to beg the question, and a court's decision automatically follows from its choice of definition. To say that a peace officer must have probable cause to make an arrest at the very first instant where a citizen's full freedom of locomotion is impeded in any way can lead to some fantastic results. For example: let us assume that an officer is informed that a person has just been killed in a particular room in a particular building. The officer rushes in and finds it full of people. Most people would be willing to concede, at this point, that the officer has probable cause to believe that a crime has been committed; however, he has absolutely no idea that any specific person in this room has committed the crime. It would follow then that the officer must stand there totally helpless while the people in the room with the dead body silently file out, leaving eventually no one left but one confused and frustrated police officer and one dead body.

On the other hand, the definition of arrest as the taking of a person into custody to answer for a crime can lead to some equally fantastic results. This latter definition, if applied logically, would authorize an officer to take people into custody and theoretically detain them for an unknown length of time. There would be no arrest unless the officer's purpose in taking the individual was to charge him with a crime. The odious "dragnet" fits very comfortably in this latter definition. In addition, this latter definition of arrest makes the determination of whether or not an arrest has occurred resolve around the subjective intent of a police officer. It is submitted that the officer's subjective intent is not a particularly desirable point at which to determine such a crucial question of an arrest, even when it is mitigated by the general rule that the officer's intent can be determined from extraneous evidence and is not dependent solely upon his word as to what was his intent.

It is the author's suggestion that the very critical question involving individual liberties and protection of society against crime are not served by leaning on artificial and obscure definitions.

Another reason for the lack of legislative and judicial attention to the question of field interrogation is the simple fact that such attention was irrelevant in the many jurisdictions which did not have an exclusionary rule, and where a person who was unlawfully detained or arrested had no remedy other than a theoretical cause of action against the arresting officer for false arrest or false imprisonment. However, recent decisions by the Supreme Court of the

United States, especially in the cases of *Mapp v. Ohio, Miranda v. Arizona,* and *Wong Sun v. United States* have made the initial contact between the police officer and the citizen not only relevant, but in many situations critical.

Prior to any further discussions relating to field interrogation it is necessary that we examine the Constitution of the United States with relation to the right of an individual to be free from arrest. After all, if the Constitution requires that no individual can be detained in any manner unless the officer has classic probable cause to make an arrest without a warrant, then any future discussion of balancing of public interest with individual rights is irrelevant. The Fourth Amendment to the United States Constitution reads as follows:

> The right of the people to be secure in their persons, houses, papers and effects, against unreasonable searches and seizures, shall not be violated, and no warrants shall issue, but upon probable cause, supported by oath or affirmation, and particularly describing the place to be searched, and the persons or things to be seized.

It seems clear that the framers of this particular amendment did not have in mind arrest and searches as we think of them today. Historically, the framers of the Constitution placed the Fourth Amendment in the Bill of Rights to prohibit general warrants and writs of assistance. The writs of assistance were widely used and abused in the thirteen colonies. They were writs which authorized the officers to search anywhere at anytime for contraband. Furthermore, these writs were for an indefinite period of time, usually for the life of the sovereign who was then reigning. At one point in the drafting of the Fourth Amendment it only contained the latter portion, which spoke specifically of warrants. The insertion of the first part of the amendment against "unreasonable searches and seizures" probably was not intended to impose additional standards, but to serve merely as a preface to the prohibition of general warrants. However, there seems little doubt that the Supreme Court has, and probably correctly so, given life and meaning to the first portion of the Fourth Amendment by interpreting the amendment to carry an overriding requirement of "reasonableness" to the entire field.

In the process of imposing this penumbra of reasonableness to searches and seizures the Court has also emasculated the rather simplistic argument that the Constitution prohibits only unreasonable searches and seizures; that a reasonable search is constitutional. This type of argument is invalid, or more accurately a simple truism, because it overlooks the fact that "unreasonable" as applied to searches and seizures is a word of art and has, over the decades, obtained a specific legal meaning over and above the meaning as applied in general usage.

It should be noted at this point that the Fourth Amendment does not use the word "arrest" at all. Instead it uses the word "seizure" which is, in effect, much broader than the word "arrest." Few people would argue that no person could ever be "seized" in the sense of being detained unless "probable cause" existed. We have many examples of this outside of the criminal field. A quarantine to protect the community from contagious disease, the picking up of a lost child on the streets, the detention of a person who is entering the United States from a foreign country or the restraint of a person who is attempting to commit suicide are all examples of detentions which are "reasonable" but which do not involve an arrest.

One may well wonder how the whole concept of "probable cause" arose to apply to situations where an officer stops a person on the street for the purpose of investigating a crime. Apparently, the rationale runs something like this: (1) the Fourth Amendment states that no warrant shall issue but upon probable cause particularly describing the person to be seized; (2) this applies to warrants of arrest as well as search warrants; and (3) obviously the standard required to arrest a person without a warrant must be at least as high as the standard required to arrest a person with a warrant. Thus we have reached the rather ironic situation in which a constitutional provision which was originally designed to prohibit governmental authorities from ransacking houses and personal effects anytime they wanted to has now been interpreted, by some persons at least, to also prohibit police officers from stopping an individual who, at 2:00 in the morning, breaks and runs at the first sight of a patrol car.

ARREST VERSUS DETENTION

At this point we will deepen our inquiry and ask some of the more fundamental questions which arise when a police officer stops a citizen on the street. Basically, the issues boil down to the following questions: Is there any significant difference between a detention and an arrest? If there are valid distinctions, are there sufficient policy reasons to recognize and authorize the police to draw their own distinctions between detention and arrest?

First, let us ask ourselves just what happens to a person who is placed under "arrest," regardless of exactly how the word is defined or exactly when the arrest occurs. Let us assume that a person is walking down a street in a city and a peace officer, with more than adequate probable cause, approaches and places him under arrest. The individual is very probably searched on the spot, and then taken to a police station where he is booked on some charge. He may be interrogated at this point if he waives his right to counsel, as required by *Miranda v. Arizona,* and even if he is not interrogated, he is placed in jail unless he makes bond. He is given the opportunity to have a preliminary hearing to determine whether or not there is "probable cause" to hold him pending indictment or other procedure to bring him to trial. If such probable cause exists, he either remains in jail, or out on bond, until he is tried by a judge or a jury. At this point he is found guilty or innocent of the crime as charged and he is either released or retaken into custody. Let us further assume that this particular individual is not guilty of the crime with which he is charged and he is released after a not guilty finding by the trier of fact.

On the other hand, let us take a situation where a person is "detained." In this circumstance he is stopped on the street, usually asked to identify himself and give some explanation of what he has been doing and his movements in the neighborhood. He may even be required to stand by while the officer investigating or detaining him checks with the police station to see if he is wanted. There might possibly even be a further detention while witnesses to a crime attempt to identify him. If the individual is under suspicion of committing a major crime and he has an alibi he might even be taken to the police station and held there until his alibi can be checked. Under many circumstances he will probably be searched to a greater or lesser extent. We will assume once again that the individual is innocent of the crime, if any, of which he is suspected and that he is released from his detention.

It cannot be too strongly emphasized at this point that we are not discussing the detention of a person that a police officer picks up at random. In all cases relating to field interrogation or detention we are assuming that the police officer has certain facts which draw his attention to the individual being detained or interrogated in the field, but these facts fall short of classic probable cause to make an arrest. The author knows of no responsible authority who advocates authorizing police officers to pick a citizen at random off the street, detain him, interrogate him or confine him in any way unless there were some circumstances which set this particular individual apart from the general public.

In order to make this latter point especially clear, perhaps it would be best to outline the type of situation which the author is speaking about when he uses the word detention. A good example occurred while the author was serving as Police Legal Advisor to the Police Department of the City of Corpus Christi, Texas and was one in which he specifically suggested that the officers detain a person without making an arrest. The circumstances of the detention were as follows: At 1:00 A. M., an individual knocked on the door of a citizen and asked if this particular citizen could spare a bandage. The person who knocked on the door was bleeding rather profusely from a cut of unknown origin on his hand. The homeowner, who was a city official, called the police and reported the incident while his wife obtained a bandage for the injured person. When a patrol car approached the house, two persons, not counting the injured party, were sitting out in front in an automobile. As soon as the patrol car came into view, the two individuals, both young males, drove off at a high rate of speed. They got approximately three-fourths of a block when they were stopped by another patrol car coming from the other direction. The type of clothing worn by these three young men and the type of car they were driving rather clearly indicated that they did not live in the neighborhood in which they were found. When questioned separately, the individuals gave at least two names to the police officers and came up with three conflicting stories as to what they were doing at this particular place and at this particular time of night. None of the persons would give any information as to how the injured individual cut his hand. All three of the persons were held on the street for approximately 30 minutes while the police officers checked with headquarters to determine whether or not any crime, such as burglary, had occurred that night to the knowledge of the police department in which a person suffered a cut on the hand. While this check was being conducted, another patrol car examined two nearby schools which were the source of frequent cases of burglary or vandalism. Neither the check by the patrol car nor the check through headquarters indicated that these particular people had been involved in any specific crime. The young men were permitted to leave after they had identified themselves finally to the satisfaction of the patrolmen and after the injured party had been given first aid. It should be noted that all three of these individuals were distinctly held against their will, although no force was necessary, and it should be further noted that the officers at the scene had no "probable cause" to make an arrest for a specific crime.

This type of detention apparently meets the approval of a rather significant majority of commentators. A relatively recent article states:

"The stop, contrasted with an arrest, is relatively short, less conspicuous, and less humiliating to the person stopped and offers much less chance for police coercion. Moreover the attempts to apply a single standard of probable cause to all interferences is likely to lead to a standard either so diluted that the individual is not adequately protected or so strict that much apparently reasonable police investigation is unlawful."

Professor Wayne R. La Fave has asked a number of extremely pertinent questions relating to field interrogations. He asks whether it makes any difference that the field interrogation typically results in a much shorter period of detention than an actual arrest. Does it make any difference that the suspect will not have an arrest record, or that the suspect will not consider himself under arrest? He also inquires whether or not the person subjected to field interrogation has suffered as much damage to his reputation as an actual arrest. He apparently concludes that there is a good deal of difference between a detention and an arrest and he observes, "A conversation with a policeman on the street corner is not likely to be mistaken by the public as an arrest as is the actual taking of the suspect to the station for further questioning."

Another writer has observed that "The London Police, who have been proclaimed as models for American police agencies, have been stopping several hundred thousand people a year and asking to see the contents of bags they are carrying or inquiring as to the possession of other property which might have been stolen."

Still another author goes to the extreme of postulating the proposition that a policeman's authority to conduct a field interrogation is in reality an exercise of the detained individual's affirmative right to be given an opportunity to be heard before he is arrested. Presumably this "right" is based on some sort of free speech rationale rather than on the more familiar right to remain silent as contained in the Fifth Amendment.

Even among the writers who belittle the distinction between arrest and detention there is usually a concession that there is a difference in (a) the limitation on the length of a detention, (b) the lack of an arrest record, and (c) the fact that the detained person can truthfully answer "no" if asked if he has ever been arrested. This latter element is becoming more and more important in our society today when individuals must fill out all types of forms, many of which ask questions relating to the person's "police record." However, the suggestion that there is a valid distinction between an arrest and a detention in fact, if not in law, does not mean to imply that an interrogation, no matter how short, by a police officer on the street is totally innocuous. When a person is stopped on the street and asked questions by a police officer there is undoubtedly a good deal of pressure on this individual to respond to the police officer's questions. After all, what are a person's alternatives when he is faced with the situation where he is the subject of a field interrogation? In practice, he has only five alternatives: (1) He can confess to a crime, (2) he can offer his identification and give plausible reasons for being present and give an explanation of his recent movements, (3) he can attempt to flee, (4) he can tell a lie, or (5) he can refuse to answer any questions at all. To a thoughtful person a confession or flight are obviously out of the question. This conduct will only tend to confirm the police officer's original suspicion, whatever that may have been, which caused the officer to single the person out in the first place. This, in effect, leaves a person only three alternatives: cooperate, refuse to answer any question, or lie.

Regardless of the legal effect of a refusal to answer, the practical effect of such a refusal will be to confirm an officer's suspicion. A lie is dangerous because it can be used as a factor in probable cause to make an arrest if it is detected and will, at least, heighten the officer's suspicion. Thus, as a practical matter, a person detained has no satisfactory alternative but to identify himself and attempt to convince the police officer that he is an upstanding citizen with nothing to fear from the law.

By way of summary, then, what are the distinctions between a detention and an arrest? First, the detention or custody is limited. It is true that in some rare instances field interrogation or field detention will go beyond the few minutes which it normally takes. However, even at it most extreme, a field detention is likely not to take anywhere near the time that a formal arrest will consume. We must bear in mind that a traditional arrest usually carries with it a processing period during which the individual under arrest is fingerprinted, has his picture taken and is usually interrogated unless he refuses to answer any questions. Of course, almost every state requires that the individual be released on bond or taken "immediately" before a magistrate. But the bond procedure can consume 30 to 45 minutes, counting the time that the person under arrest gets in touch with a bondsman and has all of the paper signed.

Secondly, a person who is subjected to a field detention and a field interrogation does not have on his record, which will be with him for the rest of his life, the fact that he has been charged with a crime. In most states a person who is arrested, no matter how capriciously, is still saddled with that vague and indefinable thing which scares employers away—a "police record." The individual has this albatross hanging around his neck regardless of the outcome of his trial—even though he may be totally exonerated and even collect damages from the peace officer who illegally arrested him. It is true that some police departments maintain informal or "nonofficial" records of field interrogations which they feel will be significant in the future. But this is an entirely different process than the maintenance of an official arrest record.

Thirdly, since a detained person has virtually no idea that he has in fact been "arrested," in spite of some courts' definitions, he can truthfully answer "no" to the inevitable question, "Have you ever been arrested or convicted of any crime other than a traffic offense?"

Finally, we must consider the detained person's reputation. It is almost inconceivable that a person who has been the subject of a field interrogation does any significant damage to his reputation when his friends and neighbors see him talking to a police officer on the street corner. Any damage to reputation under such circumstances is certainly far less than the damage which might occur if these same friends and neighbors saw the individual being taken off, handcuffed, in the back seat of a police car. This difference in damage to reputation is particularly important if the crime under investigation is one involving extreme emotional reactions from the neighborhood, such as child-molesting, homosexual activity, or the like.

The fact that the actual distinction between an arrest and a detention is a real distinction is a far cry from saying that the distinction is significant enough to treat the arrest differently from the field interrogation in terms of public policy. One of the most vigorous foes of field interrogation and detention is Professor Caleb Foote. Although he laces his works with a great deal of emotionalism, he nevertheless makes some points which can hardly be ignored. He challenges, to begin with, the necessity for any type of general detention statute or practice which is separate from the traditional law of arrest. And, as might be suspected, he insists that arrest is "an actual restraint of the person to be arrested," which occurs at the moment an individual is no longer a free agent to do as he pleases.

Professor Foote insists that we do not have enough information to determine the necessity of field interrogation. He states: "factual assumptions made about police arrest practices today necessarily rest upon political philosophy or armchair speculation seasoned with the number of persons arrested but usually this only reflects cases experiences or undocumented police claims." He is, of course, correct that criminal law, especially as it involves the work of the police officer on the street, has suffered and is still suffering from a gross lack of concrete, reliable data. But the social sciences cannot remain static because our methods of information-gathering do not fit in the admirable and convincing matrix which the physical sciences have managed to develop.

Professor Foote argues that the need for field interrogation and detention would disappear if we have more and better trained police officers. He states:

> The chief disadvantages of these alternatives are that they cost money and require the exercise of political and administrative statesmanship whereas enacting new arrest laws offers the illusion of doing something about crime without financial or political complications and has a natural appeal to political expediency. I suspect that in police work, as elsewhere, one generally gets no more than he pays for, and that legislation of police power is a wholly inadequate substitute for responsible police fiscal and personnel policy.

> The importance of seeking alternatives within the present legal framework is emphasized when one examines the impact of police arrest practices upon our constitutional respect for privacy. The right to be let alone—to be able to sit in one's own house or drive one's own car or walk the streets without unwarranted police intrusion—is surely one of the most important factors to be weighed in achieving a balance between individual liberty and public necessity. Ironically, it is this factor about which we know the least. Although we are often inadequate, we collect at least some data on the number of crimes reported, the number of crimes cleared by arrest and the mortality between charge and conviction. We also have figures purporting to state the number of persons arrested but usually this only reflects cases where the police have booked, fingerprinted and charged the suspect. We cannot even guess at the true arrest rate because we have no data on the number of people whose liberty is restrained but who after investigation are released without charge. Under these circumstances to try to make an intelligent evaluation of how the right of privacy fares under present conditions and how proposed changes in the law would affect it is very much like trying to compute batting averages when one knows only the number of hits for each player but has no data on the number of times at bat.

Professor Foote sidesteps the problems of the hypothetical emergency situation, such as the right of the police to temporarily detain a person found near a fresh corpse, by stating: "Whatever the law may be in such situations, the reasonableness of the police action is conditioned by an immediate crisis and would have no general application. Then he refers to Mr. Justice Jackson's dissenting opinion in the case of *Brinegar v. United States,* where the Justice appears to approve of a situation in which police officers might throw a roadblock around a neighborhood and search every outgoing car when this is "the only way to save a threatened life and detect a vicious crime," whereas he would disapprove of "a roadblock and universal search to salvage a few bottles of bourbon and catch a bootlegger." The fact that Professor Foote himself draws a distinction between emergency situations and everyday police problems seems to be flatly contradictory to his position that the Constitution permits only one single standard of probable cause. Once it is admitted that a police officer may take certain steps in an "emergency" situation, but that the officer may not take the same steps in a "non-emergency" situation, it is obvious that the authority of the police officer to arrest or detain a person depends on the type, degree, or even existence of an emergency. Therefore, the whole scope of the inquiry ceases to be whether or not the officer has the authority to detain a person, but rather the essential question is—under what type of "emergency" circumstances may an officer detain a person?

One engaged in library research in the field of police detention is struck by the fact that there is almost no dialogue between the persons who want to strictly limit the policeman's authority to detain a person and those advocates of broadening the officer's authority to make a detention. There are numerous articles, of course, but they are in effect monologues which are, this author suspects, largely directed at people who have already become convinced. In other words, the scholarly debators are simply not speaking the same language at all.

Those authors who tend to advocate broadening a policeman's authority to detain a person usually stress the "practicalities" of on-the-spot police work. They can point to numerous situations where reasonableness and common sense would dictate that a police officer make a detention, but where the circumstances are such that the officer would normally be beyond his authority in making such a detention. These advocates usually fail to come to grips with the legal and constitutional issues which are involved in any exercise of authority by a police officer in the field other than to say, perhaps, "well, the Constitution of the United States only prohibits unreasonable searches and seizures and thereby permits searches and seizures which are reasonable."

On the other hand, those individuals who advocate strictly limiting a police officer's power tend to avoid concrete discussions of hypothetical, or even real, situations where a police officer could be expected to act "reasonably" and use good common sense. These advocates prefer instead to discuss the legalistic issues involved and to become enmeshed in esoteric discussions of "arrest" and "probable cause."

What is too often overlooked is that no constitutional right, privilege or guarantee is absolute. The whole idea of law, as a decisional process, is an attempt to apply certain principles to everyday life to the extent that they are meaningful and pliable. The task of building Utopias is left to the philosopher. The task of the working lawyer is to develop certain principles and practices which will guarantee the maximum of public order and crime prevention and at the same time permit the maximum of constitutional freedoms to the individual citizen.

Specific Issues

So far, the problem of field detention and interrogation have been discussed in somewhat general terms. It would be useful, now, to examine some of the more narrow and specific issues which will arise in a field interrogation or detention situation.

USE OF FORCE

One of the issues which courts and legislatures have been particularly reluctant to face is the question of what force, if any, a police officer should be authorized to use in a detention less than an arrest. Neither the Uniform Arrest Act nor the "Stop and Frisk" law of New York mention the question of force. Very few courts have been faced with this question, since experience seems to show that only an infinitesimal group of people attempt to resist a mere street stop. Furthermore, it is this author's very firm suspicion, based on two years' on-the-street work and observation with police departments, that in those rare instances where the police must use force in what would ordinarily be a field detention situation, the officer has a tendency to take the position that he approached the resisting individual initially for the purpose of making an arrest, usually for some vagrancy type offense.

However, the fact that the use of force in a field detention situation is seldom clearly placed in issue during the course of trial does not mean that the question of force is not an important one to which we should address our attention. About the only legislative enactments, in the criminal law area, which specifically deal with force are the merchant detention statutes designed to combat shoplifting. In addition, the provision of the American Law Institute's Code of Pre-Arraignment Procedure, which has not been enacted by any state, also clearly faces the issue of force in a field interrogation or detention context. Both the ALI code and the typical merchant detention statute state that the person who is detaining or stopping an individual may use all reasonable force short of deadly force.

It is quite understandable why legislatures and courts are loathe to face the issue of force. A field detention, virtually by definition, is the stopping of a person when there is no probable cause to believe the person who is the subject of the stop has committed a crime. It seems rather extreme, therefore, to authorize a police officer to forcefully wrestle with an individual and perhaps handcuff him for the purpose of asking that individual his name and address and what he has been doing.

Some writers evade the issue of force by stating that all the police officer is doing is walking up and asking a person a question in much the same way a private individual would do. Therefore, the implication is that the police officer is doing no more than any other individual could do, thus the question of force, if not irrelevant, tends to fade away. In other words, if A, a private citizen, stops B on street and asks of him directions to the bus station, it is quite possible that B would simply continue on his way without answering at all. A would probably classify B as an extremely rude person; however, we simply do not consider the question of how much force A may be permitted to use against B in order to obtain an answer to his question because force, in such a context, is simply unthinkable. Therefore, to equate a police officer with the private citizen in a field detention situation is to lose touch with reality.

The author has observed more than 400 field stops in two different states and he has never seen a situation where force has been necessary. It is almost inconceivable that the type of questions which were asked during these field stops, and some of the questions were rather searching, would have been tolerated by the detained person unless they were being asked by a police officer. The only conclusion which can be drawn from these observations is that the presence of a police officer, no matter how pleasant his demeanor, implies the potential use of force—force at least to effectuate the stop if not to compel the answers.

Another method of evading the question of force in a detention situation is to take the position that any force used was, in fact, for some purpose other than detaining an individual. An excellent example of this technique is found in the case of *High v. State.* In this case the police officers were informed by a passing motorist that a disturbance was taking place at a certain location. The officers rushed to the location and saw a car driving away with one person in it. They stopped the car and found that the driver was intoxicated. There was apparently no evidence, such as erratic driving, to indicate that the driver was intoxicated prior to the time he was stopped by the officers. The Supreme Court of Tennessee upheld the conviction for driving while intoxicated. It held that the stopping of the automobile was not a technical arrest and that the officers simply stopped the car for the purpose of quelling the disturbance of which they had been informed and found that the driver was intoxicated. The court rather unimaginatively overlooked the fact that there was no disturbance to quell at the time the officers stopped the car and, as a matter of fact, no disturbance ever took place in the presence of the officers other, perhaps, than the disturbance which may have occurred during the course of taking the driver into custody for the offense of driving while intoxicated.

The only case to face the issue of force squarely is *Cannon v. State.* In this case the defendant followed a woman to her house and accused her of speeding while she had been driving an automobile. The defendant was obviously drunk. Two officers arrived and took the defendant, against his will, to the police station for an intoxication test. He apparently failed the test and was charged with driving while intoxicated. It was the theory of the state that he was not placed under arrest until after he had failed his test for intoxication and that the intervening detention was authorized by Delaware's version of the Uniform Arrest Act. The defendant contended that the detention statute did not authorize the use of force and contemplated only voluntary detention. The Delaware Supreme Court, without much discussion, rejected such a contention out of hand. The court held that such a construction of Delaware's detention statute would make the statute meaningless.

It is obvious that the Delaware Supreme Court in the *Cannon* case articulated the proper rule of law. It is admittedly offensive to contemplate force being used against a private citizen when the private citizen is not being placed under arrest based on probable cause. The necessity of force will occur in extremely rare instances in the field detention context. But even so we should face the fact that a field detention authorization must carry with it the right of the officer to use force in making a detention. If such authorization is not present then we have not given the officer the tool which he needs to gain the maximum benefit from a field detention and interrogation authority. Indeed, a detention statute without the right to use force may lead to a situation where the general public, which has relatively little to fear with or from a field detention statute, will be subjected to being stopped and questioned, but the small corps of criminals at whom the detention statute is primarily aimed, will have no reason to fear it since they know they will not be required to pay any attention to the officer when he approaches them. This would lead to the further result that the general public would be limited in their freedom and there would be no corresponding gain to society as a whole.

PRIVILEGE AGAINST SELF-INCRIMINATION

Another issue involved in a field detention and interrogation is the question of the detainee's right not to answer the questions on the basis that the answers might incriminate him. There seems to be absolutely no question that a person who is subjected to a field interrogation cannot be required to answer questions of an incriminatory nature. Any other interpretation of a statutory or common law right of field detention would be squarely contrary to the Fifth Amendment's protection against self-incrimination. However, there does seem to be some question as to the effect of a person's refusal to answer the police officer's question. This question is usually framed in the context of whether or not the refusal to answer questions can be taken into consideration as one of the factors or elements in determining probable cause to make an arrest for a specific offense.

It has been held that flight from an officer to avoid answering questions can be a factor in determining probable cause. By the same token, contradictory stories given in rapid succession, and obvious lies can also be taken into consideration in determining probable cause. Chief Justice Traynor of the California Supreme Court stated, as dictum, in the case of *People v. Simon* that "there is, of course, nothing unreasonable in an officer's questioning persons outdoors at night [citing authorities] and it is possible that in some circumstances even a refusal to answer would, in the light of other evidence, justify an arrest." There are, of course, other authorities that do not agree; they state that an exercise of a person's privilege against self-incrimination cannot be used as a factor in determining probable cause.

The only provision of the ALI's Model Code of Pre-Arraignment Procedure which was specifically rejected was the provision which would permit a failure to comply with an obligation imposed by the code to be used in determining probable cause for an arrest. It was the intention of the drafters, as shown by the commentary accompanying the draft, to permit the refusal to answer authorized questions by police officers to be used as a factor in determining probable cause.

States which have adopted the Uniform Arrest Act provide that any person, questioned by an officer, who fails to identify himself or explain his actions to the satisfaction of the officer may be detained further for a period of detention not to exceed two hours. The statutory wording seems to indicate quite clearly that a refusal to answer the officer's questions, even on the basis of a privilege of self-incrimination, could result in the individual being taken to the police station and held there until he does answer the officer's questions or until two hours expire. However, research does not reveal any case with that specific holding. In fact, no cases from the states which have adopted the Uniform Arrest Act have been found which even discuss the effect of a failure to answer the officer's questions.

There is authority for the proposition, of course, that while the Constitution does not require a person to incriminate himself, the Constitution does not state that the exercise of the privilege cannot be used for any other purpose. Recent decisions of the Supreme Court seem to indicate that the purposes for which an invocation of the privilege against self-incrimination are used have been severely limited, although the court has not overruled the above stated principle in its entirety. Nevertheless, the court has been especially alert and sensitive to any situation in which the use of the privilege against self-incrimination could be interpreted as an admission of guilt. It would seem, therefore, that the use of the privilege against self-incrimination in a context where a detained person refuses to answer any of the officer's questions would fall in the "admission of guilt" category and be held to be constitutionally protected; in other words, a refusal to answer questions during field interrogation cannot be used as a factor in determining subsequent probable cause to make an arrest.

Thus far we have been discussing a situation in which a detained person refuses to answer any of the police officer's questions, except perhaps for name and address. A different conclusion might be reached if a detained person answered most of the officer's questions but refused to answer certain questions relating to a specific subject. Under such circumstances, if the officer considered refusal to answer a portion of his questions in his determination of probable cause to make an arrest, his determination might be upheld. True, he would be implying that the detainee was admitting guilt by his refusal to answer certain questions and would therefore be subject to the previously outlined constitutional objections. On the other hand, such conduct on the part of the detained individual might come closer to the "contradictory or evasive answer" category which has been recognized as a factor in probable cause.

The field research did not disclose a single instance where a detained person absolutely refused to answer any of the police officer's questions. On those rather rare instances when answers were refused, the subject matter usually did not involve probability of a crime, but rather third persons whom the detainee preferred not to name. Most instances of refusal occurred when the officer asked the detainee where he had been and he replied that he had been to see his girlfriend. When the officer would inquire as to her name and address, presumably for the purpose of verification, the detained individual would refuse to answer, perhaps out of chivalry or perhaps out of wisdom.

It is the author's opinion that an officer who has so little probable cause to make an arrest that the refusal of a person to answer his questions will swing the decision one way or the other, in all likelihood has a pretty weak arrest to begin with. A reviewing court would probably find "insufficient probable cause" without a detailed and careful examination of the constitutional issues involved. It is also the author's conclusion, based upon field research, that a person who answers questions with extreme reluctance almost invariably attracts the full attention of the questioning officer to the extent that the officer starts attempting to find probable cause to make an arrest. Even when probable cause is not found, the person who answered the questions evasively or with extreme reluctance can almost certainly be assured that he will be under some type of surveillance. The time and duration of this surveillance will, of course, depend on numerous circumstances. Therefore, even if a refusal to answer the officer's questions does not constitute probable cause for an immediate arrest, such refusal to answer is seldom to the detainee's advantage.

LENGTH OF DETENTION

The length of a field detention is an issue of particularly vital importance. Various statutory enactments permit a detention for any period of time ranging from twenty minutes, in the case of the ALI Code of Pre-Arraignment Procedure, to two hours in the case of the Uniform Arrest Act. Other statutes, such as New York's "Stop and Frisk Act," and the common law right to field detention, do not contain any specific time period for the detention. Presumably cases falling in the latter category could result in a detention for a "reasonable" period of time.

In discussing the length of detention, the conflicting balance of values is rather obvious. On one hand, it is quite obvious that a field detention is especially capable of police abuse. In addition, those persons who advocate a field detention of some type stress the fact that the invasion of a person's right to free mobility is so slight as to justify the use of field detention as a law enforcement tool. On the other hand, if the length of detention is made so short as to dilute the effectiveness of such a detention as a law enforcement aid, then very little has been gained by authorizing such detention.

One argument against having any specific period of detention named at all is that any time limit set by a statutory enactment will be considered by the officer as the usual length of time which he can detain a person and, therefore, there will be a tendency for officers to detain persons for the maximum period of time even when the use of this maximum period of time is not necessary. This conduct on the part of the police officer would, in the author's opinion, be especially true in those cases where the officer, by virtue of his experience and "street wisdom," feels intuitively that the individual he is detaining has committed some crime, but the officer just can't quite "pin anything on him." On the other hand, the phrase "for a reasonable period of time" can be interpreted many ways under certain circumstances. This might result in a field detention statute being used as an excuse for a general investigative custody for a number of hours. Such a use would, of course, be contrary to the general purpose of field interrogation statutes which are primarily designed to authorize the police officer to obtain the name, address and explanation of actions from the individual who has been stopped. Naturally there will be some cases where the officer, using reasonableness and common sense, will desire to detain a person for a more protracted length of time pending a further investigation. However, the field research done by the author, coupled with his field experience, indicate that the need for an extended detention is an extremely rare event. This field research and subsequent experience, which will be described in some detail hereafter, indicate that the vast majority of field detentions consume less than six minutes. Indeed, the only field detention observed by the author which exceeded thirty minutes occurred in the City of Chicago when the police department's highly touted computer broke down and, as a result, an individual was detained for almost an hour until the clerical staff at headquarters could determine whether or not the detained person was wanted for an offense. He was.

Any detention statute should have a maximum length of detention expressed therein and that length of detention should be approximately thirty minutes. Such a period of time would be sufficient to cover the overwhelming majority of situations in which a field detention would be desirable. In addition, the existence of a thirty-minute time limit would clearly indicate to the officer that the statute is designed to permit only the most minor of detentions and is not to be used as an excuse to take a person into custody while an investigation is in process. A thirty-minute time period would also tend to cancel out those situations where the individual police officer, for one reason or another, decided to hold a detained person for the full time alloted by the statute. Even where this abuse does occur, a detention for a half-hour is a relatively minor invasion of a person's general right to free locomotion.

EXCLUSIONARY RULE

The vexing question always arises regarding what remedy would be available if a person has been detained beyond the thirty-minute maximum time period advocated in this article. For example, though no exclusionary rule governing violations of the ALI twenty minute limitation has yet been drafted, conceivably the drafters could take the position that *all* evidence obtained during the stop—that taken before the expiration of twenty minutes as well as that taken thereafter—should be excluded because the stop, considered as a whole, was illegal. This would be, to say the least, a most unfortunate and, indeed, unfair rule. We would then have a situation where the search of a person, which almost always occurs very early in the stop, would result in the discovery of legally admissible evidence, but if the detained person gave a prolonged explanation regarding his conduct or his possession of the contraband, then this evidence, which was originally valid and admissible, would, at the 21st minute of detention, suddenly become inadmissible. Such a "now you see it, now you don't" rule of exclusion is unnecessary, impractical, and logically inconsistent. An exclusionary rule which covered only those items discovered as a result of a search *after* the maximum period of detention had elapsed might be acceptable, but evidence obtained as the result of the search during the permissible time period should be admissible, regardless of subsequent circumstances. If the officer exceeds the period of detention, such violations of the statute can more effectively be dealt with by use of other disciplinary techniques which will be subsequently discussed.

SCOPE OF QUESTIONS

Another issue involved in a field interrogation situation relates to the types of questions which may be asked a detained person. This issue has been created primarily as a result of the Supreme Court's decisions in the *Escobedo* and *Miranda* cases.

The *Miranda* case will be discussed at some length hereafter to determine if it applies to a field interrogation situation at all. However, assuming that the *Miranda* case could apply to a field interrogation, the issue remains as to whether or not *Miranda* would apply to every field interrogation.

It seems valid to classify field interrogation into three broad categories. The first is where a police officer has some reason to believe that the detained party has committed a crime. Perhaps the belief is not of such a nature as to constitute probable cause, but at least the officer has, prior to the stop, a very specific situation or set of circumstances about which he desires to question the detained person. In the second, it is believed that the person to be detained has done something, or his presence is so out of character with the neighborhood, that the officer desires a *general explanation* regarding the individual's *movements*. Finally, we have the circumstance wherein a detained person may be a *witness* to a crime or have information relating to a specific crime which the peace officer feels would be valuable. Of course, these three general categories of detentions are very broad and each category is capable of being broken down into an almost infinite variety of sub-categories.

There seems to be little doubt that no *Miranda* warning would be required in the third class of field interrogation involving a witness. This is the type of interrogation in which there is no thought, at least initially, that the detained person has committed a crime or is guilty of any other unlawful conduct. Indeed, the *Miranda* case itself excludes this type of questioning from the requirement of a warning. The second category of field interrogation would, at first glance, also seem to be outside the scope of the *Miranda* decision. After all, there is no probable cause for an arrest and, there is in fact no "custody" or arrest as those terms have been used and interpreted by a majority of the cases. Furthermore, the officer is usually not concentrating his questions upon a specific crime or circumstance but rather is asking the individual for nothing more than his name, address and explanation of his presence and actions.

We must remember, however, that the field stop, if properly used, is not a "random sampling" of persons in the community. Under court decisions which validate the common law field interrogation and the stop and frisk statutes, an officer is authorized to make a stop only when an individual's conduct raises a certain degree of suspicion in the officer's mind that the person stopped has committed, is committing, or is about to commit a crime. Therefore, a person subjected to a field stop is being investigated as a suspect for a crime even though the exact nature of the crime may be unknown to the officer at the time of the stop. True, the detained individual is not the "focus of suspicion" that he would be if the officer had extraneous evidence to the fact that the detained person had committed a specific crime, but this does not remove the fact that the detained person is suspected of doing something illegal. Nevertheless, the author believes that the *Escobedo* and *Miranda* cases would not apply to this second category of field detention. *Escobedo* and the four cases decided in *Miranda* all involved circumstances where individuals were very clearly under arrest and had been in fact taken to places of detention. The interrogators in those cases employed techniques which were designed to obtain confessions from the individual involved to be used in evidence against him in a specific case which was under investigation. The field interrogation, on the other hand, is not designed so much to obtain a confession of a specific crime as it is to determine or obtain information relating to the detained person's conduct. As long as the interrogation officer confines himself to such questions as "what are you doing out here at this time of the morning?", there is little likelihood that he would be required to give the *Miranda* warning at this first approach to the individual to be detained.

The first category of field stop, that of questioning a person with relation to his guilt concerning a specific crime or series of crimes, is an entirely different matter. Here we have a situation where the "focus of suspicion" is relatively firm and it would appear that if *Miranda* applies to questioning away from the stationhouse at all, it would apply in this type of circumstance. Hence, the officer would be required to give the *Miranda* warning if he wanted to use the individual's statements as evidence against the individual in a criminal case. In addition, we can predict with a relatively high degree of accuracy that the Supreme Court is going to be rather sensitive to investigative techniques which can be reasonably construed as designed to evade the *Miranda* decision. Approaching a person whom a police officer believes has committed a specific crime and interrogating him with relation to that specific crime on a street corner under the disguise of a field stop might very easily be interpreted as such an evasion.

In summation, no warnings are necessary under the *Miranda* decision to persons who have been subjected to a field stop except in those cases where the interrogation relates to a specific crime which an officer has probable cause to believe, or at least suspects, that the detained person has committed.

RECORDS OF THE STOP

Another issue involved in field stops is whether the police ought to record the detention. This issue probably has an emotional content which far exceeds its true importance. The New York "Stop and Frisk" Act, as well as the Uniform Arrest Act, are quite specific in stating that field detentions should not be recorded as arrests in any official police record. On the other hand, the ALI Model Code of Pre-Arraignment Procedure requires each field stop to be recorded and sets forth in some detail the information to be kept. The importance of record keeping insofar as the general public is concerned is perhaps exemplified by a public controversy which broke out in the City of Chicago in the winter of

1965—66. That police department's policy is to conduct field stops even though Illinois has no enabling legislation and the Illinois courts have not clearly sustained a peace officer's common law authority to make field detentions. In spite of the fundamental issues which surround field interrogations, the opponents of such a departmental policy opposed most vigorously the Chicago police department's practice of making notations of field stops and then retaining them for a thirty-day period. If newspaper support is any indication of general public approval, it would appear that the people of Chicago approve the practice of field stops even in spite of their alleged "illegality"; nevertheless, even the newspapers which generally supported the policy of a field interrogation expressed discomfort over the record-keeping practice.

Those states which prohibit the keeping of records of field stops do so, presumably, in an attempt to make the consequences of such a stop as innocuous as possible. In fact, as indicated earlier, the lack of a detained person's "police record" as the result of the stop is one of the primary points which distinguishes a field interrogation from an arrest. A good deal of public sentiment can be aroused by charging that police departments are compiling dossiers on individuals to be used for some vague, future and unknown (but presumably sinister) purpose.

Police officials, on the other hand, support the idea of keeping records which are to be maintained for a limited period of time on a number of grounds. First, such records provide leads if it should be later determined that a crime was committed in a certain neighborhood. The theory is that the investigating officers would check the field stop records to find out which suspiciously acting persons were in the general area of the crime at the time it was committed. Police officers, especially administrators and supervisors, can also use the field interrogation records as a method of supervision and internal control of the patrolmen under their command. In short, they can have some indication of which patrolmen are aggressively checking their beats and which ones are dragging their feet.

Most importantly, records of field stops are invaluable to police supervisors when a citizen complains that he was rudely approached or otherwise mistreated during the course of a field interrogation. In a large metropolitan police department it would be next to impossible to determine which officers were involved in the complaint unless there was a record of the incident. We can only presume that this latter use of records be maintained. This presumption is reinforced when we notice that there is, among other information to be recorded, information of witnesses present during the field stops and whether or not the detained person objected to the stop. It is also worthy of note that the ALI drafters went to rather elaborate precautions to limit potential abuse of the field stop, yet did not see fit to require that the records kept of the field stop be destroyed after a limited period of time. Under the ALI provisions these records could be maintained indefinitely. The only conclusion which can be drawn from this circumstance is that the ALI drafters did not consider maintenance of records to be a significant source of unwarranted exercise of police powers.

It is the author's opinion that field stops should not be recorded as arrests and should not be considered as "a police record." By "police record" we mean that an authorized person in a police position who was checking on a specific individual would not be routinely informed of any field stops. Beyond this limitation, the keeping or nonkeeping of records is largely a false issue. It would appear that if the lack of records would make a policy of field interrogation more palatable to a particular community, records should not be kept, not for a law enforcement or legal reason, but from the standpoint of public acceptance and police department public relations.

THE SEARCH

Of the various issues which may arise in the course of a field interrogation, probably the most critical and controversial issue is that of a search of the detained person. This is a vital issue because a person arrested after a field stop is frequently arrested for the possession of contraband which is discovered as a result of a search. In addition, it is one of the most difficult issues to grapple with. The overwhelming majority of authorities seem to approve of the idea of permitting police officers to make field stops and conduct inquiries. However, there is a much more substantial difference in opinion when the inquiry includes a search.

One line of reasoning holds fast to the idea that absolutely no search of a person is constitutionally permissible unless that search is conducted under the authority of a search warrant or as an incident to a lawful arrest. It naturally follows, according to this rationale, that if a field stop is not an arrest, then there can be no search of a person until such time as an arrest has occurred. The dissent in the case of the *People v. Rivera* took this position. Justice Fuld predicated his dissent on the basis that a search without consent and without a warrant is constitutional only if it is an incident to a lawful arrest. He brushed aside any suggestions that a frisk is distinguished from a search by pointing out that neither the Fourth Amendment nor the law of torts distinguishes between a cursory search and an elaborate one. He then stated: "This is nothing but exercise in semantics; a search by any other name is still a search." It is, perhaps, interesting to note that the judge dissented only on the question of the right of an officer to search as an incident to a field stop. The highest court in New York was unanimous in agreeing that officers had a common-law authority to stop and question an individual.

Another writer also doubts that a search of any nature is permissible. He appears to base this conclusion on the fact that arrests without warrants are well known and have been traditionally used whereas searches without warrants have been more strictly proscribed. He states that a very important distinction exists between arrests and searches, and adds: "Whereas the basic postulate is that a search without warrant is *per se* unreasonable and is to be tolerated only in certain circumstances . . . arrest without warrant is hardly treated as exceptional." And a recently published, comprehensive analysis of street stops also expresses doubt that gradations of search are constitutionally permissible.

In general, a majority of the authorities approving a street stop at all would authorize a cursory search, "a frisk," for the self-protection of the police officer. While such a modified search does not fit neatly into a traditional view of search and seizure law, it does conform more closely to the realities of the street. As one author states, "Hale, Hawkins and Blackstone never saw a 4 inch automatic pistol, but to officers who have, it does not seem unreasonable to search a person being questioned who may be armed." A 1964 article points out that 26% of the police officers killed in the four previous years were making an arrest or transporting prisoners. Another 18 were killed investigating reports of suspicious persons, and 63 were killed interrupting robberies or burglaries, even though the officer did not know, in all cases, that he was in fact interrupting a crime in progress.

There appears to be virtually no suggestion from any responsible source that a police officer be authorized to make a general evidentiary search incident to a field interrogation. The Uniform Arrest Act, New York's "Stop and Frisk Act," and the ALI Proposed Code of Pre-Arraignment Procedure all strictly tie the authority of an officer to make a search of any kind incident to a field stop to the officer's need for protection. This same limitation is also contained in the case law of those states, notably California, which recognize a police officer's right to stop and question an individual as a part of that state's common law. Thus far, the author has not been able to find any state which recognizes a statutory or common-law right to stop and question persons, but prohibits the police officer from conducting any type of search of him.

There is a distinct tendency, however, for the courts to scrutinize a search with considerably more care than they review the probable cause to investigate a stopped person's activity. An excellent example of this is the case of *People v. Rodriguez*. In this case a motion to suppress evidence of policy slips was granted. The policy slips were uncovered while a police officer was frisking an individual for weapons. The court reasoned that a cursory search, or patting down of the outside clothing to determine whether or not a person was carrying a weapon would not have revealed policy slips, hence the court held that this type of search must, by the very nature of the evidence uncovered, have been beyond the frisk which was contemplated under the New York statute and was an unlawful search.

Another such case is *People v. Simon*. In this case a police officer saw the defendant and another person walking in a warehouse district late at night. The officer stopped and searched the defendant and, in the course of said search, found a quantity of marijuana. Defendant was charged with illegal possession of that drug. The California Supreme Court set the information aside and released the defendant. Chief Justice Traynor pointed out that under California law a search may be before or after an arrest but probable cause must exist prior to the search or it is invalid. In this case, the officer simply stopped the defendant and thoroughly searched him before he asked defendant to identify himself or explain his conduct. The Court pointed out that there is nothing unreasonable in an officer's questioning of a person who is outdoors late at night. However, in this case the type of search indicated that the officer was engaged in a general search for evidence without probable cause, which is, of course, unlawful. A later California case, also written by Chief Justice Traynor, does clearly recognize the right of an officer to request a suspect to "submit to a superficial search for concealed weapons."

In summation, the majority of the authorities which have faced the issue of the search seem to take the position that even though the constitutional language relating to searches has no exceptions, courts, in the light of experience, have engrafted certain exceptions such as a search incident to an arrest by consent. These authorities tend to engage in a balancing of social values and reach the conclusion that, " ... as long as the frisk is strictly limited, this invasion seems outweighed by the necessity to protect the questioning policeman."

This general rationale is also well summarized in the commentary to the stop and frisk provision of the ALI Model Code of Pre-Arraignment Procedure:

> ... an officer, if he reasonably believes his safety so requires, may search a person stopped pursuant to this section. He may search only to the extent necessary to discover any dangerous weapon which may on that occasion be used against him. The search envisioned here should not usually be more intensive than "an external feeling of the clothing" that is,

the traditional "frisk." The subsection also authorizes a search of the immediate surroundings of the person for the same purpose and under the same limitations. By immediate surroundings, the draft intends to designate any place (for example, a lady's handbag) where a weapon may be concealed, and which during the interview remains in easy reach of the person.

The Reporters included this authority to search with some reluctance. Many people would find being subjected even to the limited search authorized by this subsection offensive and humiliating. Nevertheless, the important purpose which this section as a whole is intended to serve would be frustrated if no search were authorized. Police officers will not, and should not, be asked to risk an encounter with a person who may be armed unless they can protect themselves by "frisking" the person at the outset. Where the authority to stop has been recognized, the search for dangerous weapons has also generally been recognized as a necessary concomitant to it.

The draft seeks to minimize as far as possible the recourse to such searches by limiting their scope to the specific need which is their justification. The very extensive search which may accompany an arrest is clearly not within the terms of this provision.

Thus far, we have discussed a number of authorities which take the position (a) that no search at all is permissible under any circumstances which constitute less than probable cause to make an arrest, and (b) that some type of limited search, for the protection of the officer involved, is permissible. A third alternative has been suggested. It would authorize police officers to conduct a limited search for deadly weapons and would go further by not permitting into evidence any item recovered by the search except weapons. Presumably the reasoning behind such a suggestion is that the authority of a police officer to frisk an individual for deadly weapons would not be abused by being used as an excuse to conduct a general search of the detained person for other types of contraband. In other words, it would remove any motive for the officer to conduct a thorough search for items other than weapons since the other items could not be used in obtaining a conviction.

At first blush such a proposal sounds rather attractive. It would allow the officer to protect himself and greatly reduce the temptation to abuse the authority to frisk. However, such a proposal, like most simplistic solutions to extremely complex problems, can lead to some illogical situations. In general, if this proposal were followed we may encounter a situation of a police officer making a perfectly proper frisk and uncovering what could very well be evidence of a major crime, but immunity would be accorded the stopped person because the seized evidence was not an instrumentality dangerous to the officer. Indeed, we could easily reach the point where a police officer would not stop persons whom the officer suspects are guilty of possessing narcotics, burglary tools, stolen property or other contraband out of fear that he might accidently find some of this contraband on the person during the frisk and thereby taint its validity. This possibility is not merely a product of the author's imagination. In fact, one case now pending before the Supreme Court involving New York's "Stop and Frisk Act" is just such an example.

The question naturally arises: If there is so little judicial or scholarly opposition to the authority of a police officer to stop an individual and ask an explanation of his movements, why do we then find a rather significant opposition to the right of a law enforcement officer to conduct a frisk as an incident to the street stop? It is this author's opinion that some of the concern relating to a frisk is based on the very real potential for abuse in a field situation.

To begin with, most openminded students of the problems related to field interrogation can easily see the distinction between a field stop and arrest. There is a relatively clear distinction between a four or five minute conversation with a policeman on a street corner, as in the case of a field stop, and, on the other hand, an arrest in which the individual is taken to a police station, charged with a crime, fingerprinted, "mugged," and in general caught up in the entire criminal law process. However, the distinction between a frisk and a more thorough search is an even finer distinction than that between a field stop and an arrest. It is quite easy to define a frisk as the patting down of the outer clothing for the purpose of determining by touch the existence of a concealed weapon. However, in actual field practice, a police officer will frequently face situations in which a simple "frisk," to be effective for self-protection, may turn into a reasonably thorough search—even assuming the good faith of the police officer. For example, cold weather, when people are wearing numerous garments and heavy clothing, creates something of a problem. Even the educated fingers of a veteran police officer have difficulty in checking for knives and small weapons beneath extremely bulky clothing. Requiring an individual to unbutton his topcoat, then checking the various layers of clothing for a reasonably available weapon can have all the appearances of a rather thorough search. Such a search is certainly necessary to protect the officer in some instances, but it also goes considerably beyond the mere patting down of the outer clothing as discussed by the courts. Hatbands, boot tops, and collar linings are favorite places for concealment of certain types of sharp bladed weapons, yet it is extremely difficult to check these parts of a person's clothing by simply running a hand over them, and this is especially true if the weapon is made of flexible material such as leather or plastic, or a safety razor.

The most common confiscated weapon which the author has seen in two years' field experience with police departments is a small Spanish or Italian automatic pistol, which sells for $8–$15 and which fits in an adult male's hand without being seen. Such weapons, while lacking in accuracy and precision, are extremely effective at point-blank range. Yet this is the type of weapon which an officer is supposed to protect himself against by patting down the outer clothing.

In addition to the sophistication and increasing availability of commercial weapons, the officer in the street must contend with an occasional ingenious homemade weapon. The author has seen a homemade "zip gun" capable of firing a single .22 or .25 caliber bullet which was designed and constructed to be concealed in a common cigarette lighter. From outward appearances, this weapon would have a very low threshold of reliability and accuracy but it did work when tested. Therefore, in the hands of a certain type of person, the very act of casually lighting a cigarette could spell death or serious injury to a police officer.

Another troublesome problem in defining the limits of a frisk is the question of items being carried by the detained individual. There is a very real threat to officers making street stops under certain circumstances when the detained individual is carrying open boxes, grocery sacks or even handbags. This is an especially relevant problem in view of the fact that the carrying of some such items very late at night and in certain portions of a city would be the very type of circumstance which would attract a police officer's attention to the individual in the first place.

The purpose of the preceding discussion is not to develop any definite line between a frisk and a search. Rather, the purpose is to demonstrate that a peace officer, in order to protect himself, is going to have to engage in some type of search which will exceed the casual patting down of the outer clothing. In balancing the degree of intrusion of the freedom of personal movement over and against the effectiveness of a law enforcement technique, we must not delude ourselves into believing that the degree of intrusion, insofar as the frisk is concerned, can be effectively limited to a fleeting three or four second patting down of outer clothing.

There is still an additional reason why the frisk of the person causes more concern than the original stopping of the individual. The statutory and common-law authority of a police officer to stop an individual on the street is based on "reasonable suspicion" that the individual stopped has commited, is about to commit, or is going to commit a crime. While it is conceded that the term "reasonable suspicion" has not been the subject of extensive case law, nevertheless a reading of the few cases which have interpreted and analyzed this and similar terms indicates that the appellate courts have some general concept of what these terms mean and the circumstances to which they apply. In general these terms mean that a person must be engaged in some type of conduct or be in some circumstances which remove him from the general class of ordinary citizens in the same area at the same time and, further, that these circumstances must suggest to a reasonably prudent officer that the individual is engaged, or is about to engage, in some illegal act. While such a criterion is necessarily vague, it would appear that it is no more vague or incapable of review than the classic concept of "probable cause to arrest."

It should be noticed, however, that the statutory authority for an officer to make a frisk as an incident to a street stop is dependent on the officer's "reasonable belief that he is in danger." Yet research has not revealed a single case in which the officer's "belief that he is in danger" was ever subjected to appellate review. This presumably means that the authority of an officer to frisk an individual, which can be a much more serious intrusion of the individual's liberty than the original stop, is going to be based on the criterion of whether or not the officer has a right to stop the individual. It is understandable that a judge would be somewhat hesitant to review the officer's judgment as to whether or not he was in danger. After all, it is the police officer's life which is at stake and a judge would be naturally hesitant to review this highly personal decision. But if the authority of an officer to make a frisk is to be constitutionally upheld and properly applied and opposition to the frisk abated somewhat, the courts are going to have to grapple with the question of standards which justify a frisk.

The concept of "reasonable belief of danger" is going to have to be determined and developed by case law in conformance with our common law tradition. But it appears that the very first question which must be decided prior to the development of case law is whether or not the courts are going to require objective criteria or take into account generally surrounding circumstances which do not necessarily apply to a specific individual being stopped. In other words, does an officer have to testify to certain movements or conduct on the part of the specific individual stopped in order to justify a belief in danger, or will the court take into consideration the general character of the neighborhood, the time of day, the availability of assistance to the officer, the general type of crime which the detained person is suspected of committing and other circumstances of a like nature? The author believes that general circumstances such as those mentioned must be taken into account in determining "reasonable belief of danger." Any attempt to require some suspicious movement—such as the reaching for a glove compartment or a hip pocket on the part of the individual detained—would not comport with the reality of the streets.

At this point, we should realistically face the fact that we are actually not talking about the protection of citizens from the intrusion of a frisk but are discussing admissibility of evidence. There is not the slightest doubt that an officer who believes that he may be in danger, based on any conceivable criteria, is going to conduct a frisk. If the officer feels his life is at stake he will protect himself first and the question of admissibility of evidence will have extremely low priority. However, the judicial development of some case law, at least to the extent of crystalizing the concept of "reasonable belief of danger," will reassure those individuals who may have reservations about granting a police officer the authority to conduct a frisk. At least it will indicate that the criteria to conduct the frisk will be subject to judicial review and not left to the whim of each individual police officer.

There is one final reason why some persons might have reservations about authorizing a frisk as opposed to authorizing a field stop. This involves the question of the detained person's reputation or embarrassment. It is relatively easy for a well-trained police officer to conduct a short field stop involving a short period of questioning of an individual and make such a practice inconspicuous to the other persons in the vicinity. However, a frisk is more difficult to conceal from other citizens, especially when it also includes checking of shopping bags or the more heavy-handed frisk necessary for heavy or bulky clothing. Associated with the question of reputation is the attitude of the person who has been stopped. The field research for this article, has been that individuals who are merely questioned almost never raise objections to being stopped, especially if the interrogating officer's demeanor is one of politeness and efficiency. Almost every objection of any degree observed has been in a situation where the detained person was subjected to a field stop. Indeed, this author's personal experiences while residing in the City of Chicago bear out the field observation. He was subjected to a field stop by Chicago police officers on two occasions. During both incidents it was quite understandable that his conduct, when viewed by a police officer from a distance of a block or so away, could be considered suspicious. Under both circumstances, a short explanation of that conduct satisfied the officers that the seemingly suspicious conduct was, in fact, reasonable and innocuous. The author departed from both field stops with a generally favorable impression of the officers concerned, especially their politeness and alertness. However, if the field stop had resulted in a frisk of either the person or an automobile, the author strongly suspects his own feelings would have been less favorable and some degree of resentment would have been present.

A corollary to the question of reputation is the fact that a frisk is much more subject to abuse by police officers than a field stop. Assuming that a police officer desires to harass a particular individual and this harassment took the form of stopping the individual at every conceivable opportunity, it would no doubt be annoying and somewhat damaging to the individual's standing and reputation in his community. However, if the harassment took the form of a thorough frisk, it could become extremely oppressive, especially if the officer managed to conduct the frisk in open view and in relatively crowded public places. This type of harassment by conducting frequent personal searches is not a figment of some civil libertarian's overactive imagination. It exists today, in varying degrees, to the extent that a slang expression has been developed to cover the situation. Harassment by frequent personal stops and searches is known in one big city as "jacking-up" an individual. This practice of "jacking-up" a citizen is usually accomplished by means of unlawful detentions and searches. Any statutory or common-law scheme to add new tools to the arsenal of law enforcement officers must be especially constructed to assure that it does not, at the same time, legalize a presently existing abuse.

MIRANDA AND THE FIELD INTERROGATION

One of the more pressing constitutional problems involved in the area of field interrogation is the question of what effect, if any, the recent decision of the Supreme Court in *Miranda* has on field stops. There is an assumption, which is probably valid, that the requirement that a person be warned of his right to silence, that any statement he makes may be used against him, that he is entitled to an attorney either of his own selection or appointed for him if he cannot afford one, would hamper the use of the field stop as a technique to uncover crime. Certainly, an exercise of the full *Miranda* ritual would have a tendency to alarm a citizen whose suspicious conduct resulted from completely and innocuous motives. It is the judgment of the author that *Miranda* does not apply to the typical field interrogation. However, this case has such importance and potentially far-reaching effect on the process of criminal investigation that it will be discussed separately and in some detail, apart from other constitutional issues.

To begin with, all four of the cases which were decided by the Supreme Court in the *Miranda* opinion involved persons who had been arrested and taken to the police station and interrogated for the purpose of obtaining a confession. In each of the cases, a confession was obtained after lengthy detention and interrogation at the station house. Before examining the language of the court, it is of interest to note that Mr. Chief Justice Warren, who wrote the majority opinion, does not use the word "arrest" in the opinion. He therefore avoids the semantic and definitional difficulty which has been the stumbling block of many other courts and which was discussed at the very outset of this article. Instead of using the word "arrest" the majority almost always uses the word "custody." Therefore, for our purposes, it behooves us to examine some of the language of the majority opinion to determine whether or not an interference with a person's freedom to move about the streets for the purpose of inquiring of the individual his name, address, and explanation of actions is the type of "custody" to which *Miranda* is addressed.

In the very first paragraph of the majority's opinion, we find the statement ". . . we deal with the admissibility of statements obtained from an individual who is subjected to custodial police interrogation . . ." The Court then points out that in each of the cases before it law enforcement officials took the defendant into custody and interrogated him at the police station. By way of introduction to the rationale of the majority's opinion, Mr. Chief Justice Warren stated:

Our holding will be spelled out with some specificity in the pages which follow but briefly stated it is this: the prosecution may not use statements, whether exculpatory or inculpatory, stemming from custodial interrogation of the defendant unless it demonstrates the use of procedural safeguards effective to secure the privilege against self-incrimination. *By custodial interrogation, we mean questioning initiated by law enforcement officers after a person has been taken into custody or otherwise deprived of his freedom of action in any significant way.*

It is submitted that the word "custody" means that an individual has been taken physically from the street or other place and confined. This interpretation of the word "custody" is reinforced by additional quotations which will follow. But the Court also indicated that the *Miranda* rule would have to be followed in any other situation which deprived a person of his freedom of action "in any significant way." At this point in the opinion it is not clear what the Court means by being deprived of freedom of action in any significant way. This statement implies that *Miranda* is applicable to situations in which the suspect is not actually confined in a police station or jail, but, by the same token, it also implies that there can be a deprivation of freedom of action in an insignificant way, to which *Miranda* would not apply. As the opinion progresses we find the following:

> The Constitutional issue we decide in each of these cases is the admissibility of statements obtained from a defendant questioned while in custody and deprived of his freedom of action. In each, the defendant was questioned by police officers, detectives, by a prosecuting attorney *in a room in which he was cut off from the outside world.*

The Court then observed that all four cases were similar in that "They all thus share salient features—*incommunicado interrogation of individuals in a police dominated atmosphere,* resulting in self-incriminating statements without full warnings of constitutional rights." The Court added that "An understanding of the nature and setting of this in-custody interrogation is essential to our decisions today."

At this point the Court goes into a discussion of reports of physical abuse of prisoners in order to obtain confessions, primarily the Wickersham report of 1931 and three Law Review articles dated 1930, 1932 and 1936. The Court then points out that "Interrogations still take place in privacy," and that "Privacy results in secrecy and this in turn results in a gap in our knowledge as to what in fact goes on in the interrogation room." The Court next discusses at some length two well known and widely used manuals of police interrogation wherein the authors discuss psychological techniques of gaining the confidence of the suspect and obtaining a confession thereby. The Court then states: "Even without employing brutality, the 'third degree' or the specific strategems described above, the very fact of custodial interrogation exacts a heavy toll on individual liberty and trades on the weakness of the individuals." The majority also observed: "It is obvious that such an *interrogation environment* is created for no purpose other than to subject the individual to the will of his examiner. This atmosphere carries its own badge of intimidation. To be sure, this is not physical intimidation, but it is equally destructive to human dignity. *The current practice of incommunicado interrogation* is at odds with one of our nation's most cherished principles—that the individual may not be impelled to incriminate himself." The Court at a later point states: "We have concluded that without proper safeguards the process of in-custody interrogation of persons suspected or accused of a crime contains inherently compelling pressures which work to undermine the individual's will to resist and to compel him to speak where he would not otherwise do so freely."

As the opinion progresses, its application to field interrogation based on reasonable suspicion becomes less certain. We find a statement to the effect that, "the principles announced today deal with the protection which must be given to the privilege against self-incrimination when the individual is first subjected to police interrogation while in custody at the station or otherwise deprived of his freedom of *action in any way."* The preceding quotation very clearly supports the earlier implication that the word "custody" means confinement at a police station but instead of talking in terms of deprivation of freedom of action in any *significant* way which the court discussed early in the opinion, we now find the opinion turning to the deprivation of freem of action in *any* way. Of course, if this preceding statement is interpreted to be the holding of the court in *Miranda,* certainly the field stop is a deprivation of freedom of action "in any way." If this apparent contradiction in the opinion were not enough, in the very next paragraph we find the court saying that "investigation [of a crime] may include inquiry of persons not under restraint." And then the court said:

> General on-the-scene questioning as to facts surrounding a crime or other general questioning of citizens in the fact-finding process is not affected by our holding. It is an act of responsible citizenship for individuals to give whatever information they may have to aid in law enforcement. In such situations the compelling atmosphere inherent in the process of in-custody interrogation is not necessarily present.

The preceding quotation could easily be interpreted as applying to witnesses only and not to a person who is suspected of committing a crime. However, such an interpretation is weakened because the Court attaches a footnote at the end of the foregoing quotation. This footnote cites with approval the police practice of visiting ". . . the house or place of business of a *suspect* and there questioning him, probably in the presence of a relative or friend."

It is submitted that this latter quotation rather effectively destroys the idea that the general non-custodial investigation of crime referred to in the *Miranda* quotation applies only to witnesses. Based on the preceding quotations, it is the author's conclusion that *Miranda* was striking at what the Court considered the inherently coercive circumstances and atmosphere of a place of confinement and does not apply to general inquiries made in public places and in public view which do not have the attributes of a jail or station house. *Miranda,* therefore, does not apply to the typical field interrogation.

There are situations, of course, which could develop in the field which would bring about an atmosphere and circumstances similar to a station house questioning and in which *Miranda* would apply. For example, a person is stopped and a general field interrogation, or the evidence obtained as a result of a frisk, indicates that the detained person has been guilty of a major crime. If he is placed in a police car and interrogated at significant length by police officers with relation to the individual's guilt of the crime, the circumstances would not be significantly different from the inherently coercive in-custody interrogation which was generally condemned by *Miranda.* Then too, a police station is not the only place where a person can be taken into physical custody and "cut off from the rest of the world." If a police officer stops an individual in a store on suspicion of shoplifting, and takes him to some isolated room in the back of the store and proceeds to interrogate him for the purpose of obtaining a confession, there can be relatively little doubt that *Miranda* would apply. Examples such as the two which have just been mentioned would be exceedingly rare, however, and to apply *Miranda* would have little effect on the general practice of field interrogation. In summation, the entire thrust of the rationale of *Miranda v. Arizona* is such that it does not apply to field interrogations so long as the stop is for a relatively short period of time, is conducted in public, or in a non-police dominated atmosphere, and the questioning, at least initially, is confined to the general conduct of the individual and is not an interrogation relating to the individual's involvement in a specific crime for the purpose of obtaining a confession.

FIELD RESEARCH

In order to obtain factual data for this article, the author made arrangements with the Chicago Police Department to ride with various units of that department's Patrol Division in November and December of 1965, and in April and May of 1966.

Method

The information set forth hereafter in this article resulted from observation in Task Force Areas 6, 1, and 4 and in Patrol Districts 11, 2, 20, and 16. The author would report to the relevant area or district headquarters at 6:00 P. M. after a supervisory officer had been notified that an observer would be present. The author would then be assigned to one unit for the night's observation. The officers involved were given an explanation of the purpose of the observer's presence and were requested to conduct themselves as though they were on a routine patrol mission. (The possible effect on the police officers' conduct due to the presence of the observer is discussed hereafter.) The author would accompany the officers during the entire eight-hour shift, making notes on certain stops which were made. The data contained herein includes only those contacts in the field which were not primarily concerned with the apprehending of a particular person for the commission of a specific criminal act. The type of police activity under investigation in this report is the stopping of individuals who were allegedly engaged in "suspicious" activity and operates under the various labels such as "field challenge," "field interrogation," "stop and frisk," and "stop and quiz."

Explanation of data

The phrase "total persons contacted" represents the number of persons the officer spoke to in an official capacity. For example, if an automobile with three occupants was stopped and only the driver was asked to identify himself, one person was counted as "contacted." If all occupants were questioned or asked to identify themselves, three persons were counted as "contacted."

The phrase "vehicles stopped" is self-explanatory; it also includes a few instances (less than ten) when persons were questioned after being observed in a parked car.

The phrase "frisk of a person or car" means, in relation to a person, the running of the officer's hands over the outside of a person's clothing as a check for concealed weapons. If during the course of a frisk the officer felt an object which, in his opinion, could have been a weapon, the incident is counted as a frisk, even though the officer went into the person's clothing after feeling the object. The frisk of a car is defined as a superficial shining of a flashlight inside the automobile to observe items which would be in plain view; it also includes the shining of lights under the seats and other potential hiding places which are accessible without rearranging any items in the car.

The phrase "search of a person or car" is defined, in relation to an individual, as the examining of the inside of a person's pockets or minutely examining a piece of clothing; for example, taking a person's hat off and turning the sweatband inside out. Basically, any physical investigation which extended beyond the feeling of a subject's outer clothing is counted as a search. The looking inside of packages or sacks is not counted as a search unless the officer shifted the contents of the parcel around or lifted some items of the parcel in order to examine all of the contents of the package. Any such rearranging of the contents of a parcel is counted as a search. A search of an automobile is defined as any conduct which goes beyond a superficial checking of the interior of an automobile. The opening of glove compartments, trunks, or boxes inside a car are examples of searches. Any time the officer felt it necessary to rearrange any of the contents of an automobile it was counted as a search.

The phrase "approval" represents the number of persons who affirmatively congratulated the officers for being alert or expressed their appreciation of the officer's presence.

The phrase "Protest 1" represents the number of persons who did not verbally protest at being stopped, but who displayed objective signs of annoyance or inconvenience.

The phrase "Protest 2" represents the number of persons who were visibly upset at being questioned and expressed such disapproval verbally.

Using the definitions contained above, the data obtained is as follows:

Total persons contacted, 297;
Vehicles stopped, 129;
Persons arrested, 11;
Frisk of persons or cars, 187;
Search of person or car, 142;
Approval, 4;
Protest 1, 8; and
Protest 2, 7.

Validity of data

The most difficult problem in this type of field survey is the interpersonal relationship between the police officer and the observer. As stated earlier, each unit was requested to carry out its function as though the observer was not present. The author is under no delusion that the request was complied with entirely. However, even though the observer is an "outsider" there are some techniques which can be used to minimize the possible distortive effect of the observer's presence: (A) The author always rode the entire shift with a single unit. After a few hours in the close confines of a patrol car, the officers would begin to become more accustomed to the observer's presence and this would, in turn, tend to make the observations more valid. (B) The normal practice would be to ride with a different unit each night until the observer found a team which seemed to be comfortable with him and the observer with them; then the observer would ride with that unit for the balance of the time he was in the particular area or district. (C) The observer attempted to show by his actions that he knew how to conduct himself in a field contact situation; the author's previous experience with another police department in another state tended to relieve the officers' natural apprehension that the observer might do something foolish in a potentially delicate situation. (D) In all of the author's relationships with the officers, he operated on the theory that establishing a good rapport was his job, thus taking the burden off the officer to keep the observer "entertained."

Although we must assume that the presence of a non-policeman had an effect on the conduct of the officers, it does not automatically follow that the officers' altered conduct will always reflect favorably on the police department or the field contact practice. For example, one night the author accompanied two officers who were so polite to the public that they actually gave the appearance of being obsequious. It is interesting to note that almost half of the "Protest 2" incidents occurred in that one tour of duty. Of course, it is possible that this was just a coincidence or a "bad night." On the other hand, it is psychologically valid to state that a grovelling police officer will get a large share of complaints because he does not command the respect of the people with whom he is dealing. In addition, the number of "searches" was considerably higher than the author anticipated. Perhaps this resulted from the officers' attempt to impress the observer with the very thorough job which they were doing.

There is another reason for believing that the observer's presence did not seriously distort the collected data. With the single exception pointed out above, the officers with whom the observer rode conducted themselves in fundamentally the same manner. If the presence of an observer was radically altering police conduct, it follows that more than three dozen policemen would have to react to an observer's presence in a uniform manner and would have to keep up the "act" for more than 300 hours. The author finds such a suggestion somewhat difficult to accept.

General observations

The average length of time a citizen was detained by a field stop was between two and three minutes. One person was detained about 20 minutes until the victim of an armed robbery arrived and made a negative identification. One driver was detained for more than 45 minutes while a name check was being made. This delay occurred on a Friday night while there was a computer malfunction; the person was arrested when it was reported that his driver's license had been revoked. Other than these two instances a detention did not last over five or six minutes and, of course, the overwhelming majority were much less than that.

The author was impressed at the length to which most officers went in order to keep from drawing attention to the fact that a person was being questioned. The officers would stand quite close to the detained individual in order to speak in low tones. Very few of the frisks or searches of a person were conducted in the traditional "hands-on-the-wall" manner. The normal technique used, even for a search, was for an officer to stand directly in front of the detained individual and conduct his frisk from this position. The only movement which the detained person was required to make was to hold his arms out from his sides a few inches in order that the officer could feel under the armpits and the chest pockets. This technique of frisking is not in accordance with good police practice and is, in fact, dangerous to the officer since it places him in a vulnerable position in the event that the frisked person decides to attack the officer. Nevertheless, this kind of frisking technique was almost invariably used since it can be done in a very inconspicuous manner by an experienced officer.

The normal technique of a frisk or search of the person is to require the individual to place his hands on a vehicle or wall and to extend his feet out from the object which is supporting his hands. The only times this frisk was observed during the course of the author's observation was in certain situations where more than two persons were being frisked or where the detained person gave some distinctly objective sign that he had a weapon. Examples of this latter category occurred when an individual would reach under the seat of his car or would put his hand in his pocket when the officers identified themselves as policemen and would be hesitant in removing his hand when ordered to do so.

A number of the officers explained to the observer that the attempts to make the stop as inconspicuous as possible were done to keep from drawing a crowd which could potentially create a problem for the officer on the street. While such a motive may not be based on the highest principles of civil liberties, it does minimize the embarrassment factor.

The fact that a field stop, especially accompanied by a frisk or search is humiliating to some degree, is recognized by a general policy followed by the officers in the field in Chicago. Males are almost never subjected to field stops when accompanied by females. The theory behind such a policy is that a man, either alone or accompanied by other men, will not normally object to being stopped and frisked. However, the same man, in the same circumstances, accompanied by a wife or girl friend, will feel that his masculine role as a protector is challenged by such a field stop and thus he may offer objection or resistance. This writer observed three instances of field stops involving females, but in only one instance was a female involved to the extent that she was listed under a category of "total persons contacted."

Most of the persons contacted were involved in some type of "suspicious activity" which was discernible to the observer. Of course, the term "suspicious activity" is, to a large extent, a subjective evaluation. And, we must remember, that the observer was not a trained police officer nor familiar with the neighborhoods in which he rode. Of the 297 persons contacted, 243 of them were engaged in some type of conduct which the author would classify as "suspicious." Most of the suspicious activity involved attempts, in varying degrees, to evade police officers as soon as the individuals recognized a police car, or involved persons who might be fairly classed as loitering or lurking in back alleys, dark doorways or similar locations late at night.

The author did notice that the number of field stops is a factor in the supervisory control of patrolmen in the Task Force. This is quite readily understandable, especially for a unit such as the Task Force which is given a considerable independence and which does not answer routine calls. This is not meant to imply that a "quota" system exists, in the strict sense of the word. Nevertheless, in each Task Force area headquarters a monthly list is posted in a prominent place on the bulletin board which indicates, among other things, the number of field stops which each Task Force officer has made. In addition, there does appear to be pressure on the patrolmen to "show some activity." In areas of a high crime rate and dense population, this system, insofar as the observer could determine, causes little problems. However, in some relatively quiet districts this real or imagined pressure could lead to a number of field contacts in which there is no suspicion of any kind. This author also observed, that in the relatively quiet residential areas, an officer would patrol for five or six hours without making any field stops and then, as his tour of duty came to a close, would stop two or three people within the course of an hour whose only suspicious activity appeared to be their presence in the neighborhood. Such conduct can only be classified as an abuse of the field stop technique. It is strongly suggested that any police department using the field stop practice should make it scrupulously clear to the officers involved that stops should be made only in reasonably suspicious circumstances and that there is not going to be the slightest hint of a "quota" system by which the officers' efficiency or competence is to be judged.

The data set forth is not intended to be a definitive study, based on scientific methods, of the field interrogation practice of the Chicago Police Department. Rather, the data is descriptive and to some degree subjective even though a conscious effort was made to obtain a balanced view of the field interrogation method by selecting districts and areas of varying crime rates and ethnic groups. The statistics contained above indicate that 3.6% of the persons stopped were eventually arrested, all as a result of information or physical evidence obtained by virtue of the detention. Statistics from the Task Force rate of arrests of "field challenges" indicate that out of more than 250,000 field contacts, the arrest rate was approximately 3.2%. This close relationship between the author's sample data and the total statistics indicate that his experience and observation offer a statistically valid insight into one police department's experience and practice—especially if we use the figures contained herein as a general guide and do not attempt to use them as highly precise tools.

The collection of this data naturally gives rise to the question of whether or not the advantages of a systematic field interrogation program outweigh its disadvantages. In the final analysis, such a question is based on a person's concept of values rather than on some mathematical formula. Nevertheless, we can make some generalizations.

The value of a field interrogation program exceeds the 3.6% of the arrests made because it keeps persons with a criminal inclination on the defensive. Any police department that follows a practice of centering its attention only on responses to crimes already committed places itself in a position, not of preventing crime, but of reacting to criminal activity. Such a practice gives the criminal the initiative in that he is almost totally free to determine the time, place, and circumstance under which he will commit a crime. But a well planned and a well conceived program of field interrogation leaves the criminal without all of the options. An aggressive and controlled program of patrol to determine who is on the streets, what the explanation for their presence is (assuming the individual is engaged in some unusual activity), will throw an indeterminable variable into any preconceived plan to commit a crime. In addition, such a practice of field interrogation is designed to give the general public, including the vast majority of law-abiding citizens, the feeling of police "presence." This will in turn, hopefully, help to instill in the general public a confidence in the alertness and efficiency of the police department.

As indicated previously, there was very little abuse observed in the course of the original stop. The data indicates that, on the average, the patrol units which were under observation stopped about one person an hour. Considering the general nature of criminal activity in the city of Chicago, this number of stops per hour is not excessive.

The foregoing data and observations indicate, however, that the field interrogation practice does have some disadvantages. The data indicates that approximately 5% of the individuals contacted show visible signs of anger or resentment at the intrusion. It can be assumed that an unknown number of additional people were more successful in hiding their feelings about their detention. Nevertheless, it is the author's impression, based on observing the demeanor and manner of speech of persons detained during the course of the field survey, that an overwhelming majority of the individuals stopped cooperated willingly with the police officer, if not out of a sense of civic duty at least with the attitude that this temporary delay be ended as quickly as possible. The observer also noted that all but one of the protests occurred in predominantly Negro districts of Chicago. It is likely, therefore, that field interrogation practice, in all probability, adds to the general deterioration in the relationship between policemen and minority groups.

Already noted, the extent of the search in many instances was surprising. Over one-third of the field detentions resulted in searches which far exceeded even that which proponents of "stop and frisk" advocate. Certainly the searches, except in two or three instances, went far beyond the type of search which would be necessary to protect a police officer. Slightly more than one-half of these extensive searches were made in high crime rate, Negro areas which had been the scene of large scale rioting the year before (1964). Most of the officers in these districts were quite candid in explaining that they were aware the search was unlawful and that no conviction could be supported on the basis of evidence obtained by the search. However, they further explained that the purpose of these extensive searches was to confiscate firearms in the event of future riots and that a conviction for unlawful carrying of a firearm was largely irrelevant. Such conduct also widens the gap between police officers and the Negro minority, especially in the vicinity of Chicago's Eleventh District. On the other hand, the officers' prediction of future riots in the summer of 1966 did prove accurate and the author feels certain that the same officers who had to face the rioters felt quite justified in previously removing a number of firearms from the area of the riots.

In general, the "field challenge" practice of Chicago's police department has advantages which outweigh the disadvantages. It is submitted, however, that the number of extensive searches is not only unlawful, but unnecessary, and that such a practice of extensive searching be discontinued or at least not be permitted to hide under the cloak of legitimate field interrogation practice. If the Chiago police department decides to conduct clearly unlawful general searches in areas of potential rioting, then the department should, as a matter of policy, do so openly and explicitly. In this way the courts and the municipal officials responsible for such a policy can clearly and cleanly be judged by the responsible citizenry. To conduct general searches under the guise of field interrogation does not make the searches any more lawful, and such a practice endangers, through abuse, the legitimate use of the tool of field interrogation.

It is interesting to note that out of the approximately 300 persons subjected to a field stop, not one single individual indicated in any way that he would not answer the police officer's question. The author heard a number of highly unskillful lies, but observed no one who chose to resort to silence.

CONCLUSION

It appears that the primary opposition to authorizing temporary police detentions is the fact that such authority is capable of abuse by police officers. This fear has some validity and cannot be brushed aside easily. But an effective law enforcement tool should not be completely negated because it is subject to potential abuse.

In dealing with the problem of abuse of authority, it is suggested that attention be directed toward the potential abuse rather than the authority itself. Thus far the technique of the courts in handling abuse of police authority has been through the exclusionary rule which prohibits the introduction of illegally seized evidence—a technique that, in the main, has been ineffective. It is ineffective because it does not actually prevent the abuse itself but only strikes at a consequence of the abuse. For instance, if police officers kick in the door of a person's home in the middle of the night and ransack it without probable cause, and if, in fact, the officers find no incriminating evidence, there can be no doubt that a very gross abuse of police authority has occurred—and yet there is no evidence to exclude. By the same token, even if some contraband is found, when the prosecuting attorney learns of the method by which the evidence was obtained, there is little likelihood that a charge will be placed against the home owner for possession of contraband. Once again the courts' exclusionary technique becomes a futility.

Traditional civil suits against police officers are largely ineffective because of the difficulty of satisfying a judgment in a substantial amount against a relatively impecunious policeman.

As regards remedial action by disciplinary measures directed at the offending officer, this seems quite unrealistic to contemplate when consideration is given to the fact that the officer in our hypothetical case actually obtained highly incriminating evidence even though his conduct was illegal. This places the police administrator in the awkward position, as far as the general public and his subordinates are concerned, of disciplining a policeman who caught a criminal. In addition, a competent defense attorney would almost certainly get a good deal of mileage at the trial of the case against the possessor of the contraband out of the fact that the evidence against him was obtained in a manner so grossly abusive as to result in a policeman's discharge or suspension.

The author's recommendation is that the governmental agency by whom the offending officer is employed should be made civilly liable for abuses in field detention *arising out of malice, bad faith, or gross negligence.* It is suggested that a field detention statute carry with it this creation of civil liability against the agency employing the police officer.

In order to make civil liability meaningful, it is further suggested that a certain sum of money be assumed as damages in case of such abuse—perhaps a sum in the neighborhood of $500.00, plus reasonable attorney's fees. A provision should also be included which would permit the plaintiff to collect a higher amount upon proof of actual damage. This concept of a minimum is necessary, however, because in the ordinary situation an individual subjected to police misconduct either has not suffered any actual damage or else the damages which he has suffered are so speculative as to be extremely difficult to prove. This recommendation is made with the full knowledge that, initially, at least, this statutory liability would result in a rash of ill-founded and even fraudulent lawsuits.

The author is confident that a governmental agency, faced with the prospect of a budget-wrecking series of lawsuits, would very quickly and very vigorously establish and enforce criteria and standards for field interrogations, and would also resort to a wide range of administrative sanctions to insure that the criteria are followed. If this result occurred, the courts would be impelled to accept the principle that civil rights and liberties can be adequately protected by police administration without court interference.

It must be emphasized that the civil liability suggested herein is only for abuses which are the result of malice, bad faith, or gross negligence. The fact that a police officer simply made an error in judgment, would not be the basis for liability. In other words, it is contemplated that no action would lie if unwarranted motives were absent, as when the officer had legitimate "reasonable suspicion" as a basis for the original stop.

Field detention interrogation is both a constitutional and a necessary tool in the fight against crime. It must, however, be used with discretion, and for the legitimate purposes for which it was intended. The police officer in the street must take seriously the admonition of the great French statesman, Talleyrand, when he said, "above all, not too much zeal."

POLICE DISCRETION NOT TO INVOKE THE CRIMINAL PROCESS: LOW-VISIBILITY DECISIONS IN THE ADMINISTRATION OF JUSTICE

JOSEPH GOLDSTEIN

Police decisions not to invoke the criminal process largely determine the outer limits of law enforcement. By such decisions, the police define the ambit of discretion throughout the process of other decisionmakers—prosecutor, grand and petit jury, judge, probation officer, correction authority, and parole and pardon boards. These police decisions, unlike their decisions to invoke the law, are generally of extremely low visibility and consequently are seldom the subject of review. Yet an opportunity for review and appraisal of nonenforcement decisions is essential to the functioning of the rule of law in our system of criminal justice. This Article will therefore be an attempt to determine how the visibility of such police decisions may be increased and what procedures should be established to evaluate them on a continuing basis, in the light of the complex of objectives of the criminal law and of the paradoxes toward which the administration of criminal justice inclines.

I

The criminal law is one of many intertwined mechanisms for the social control of human behavior. It defines behavior which is deemed intolerably disturbing to or destructive of community values and prescribes sanctions which the state is authorized to impose upon persons convicted or suspected of engaging in prohibited conduct. Following a plea or verdict of guilty, the state deprives offenders of life, liberty, dignity, or property through convictions, fines, imprisonments, killings, and supervised releases, and thus seeks to punish, restrain, and rehabilitate them, as well as to deter others from engaging in proscribed activity. Before verdict, and despite the presumption of innocence which halos every person, the state deprives the suspect of life, liberty, dignity, or property through the imposition of deadly force, search and seizure of persons and possessions, accusation, imprisonment, and bail, and thus seeks to facilitate the enforcement of the criminal law.

These authorized sanctions reflect the multiple and often conflicting purposes which now surround and confuse criminal law administration at and between key decision points in the process. The stigma which accompanies conviction, for example, while serving a deterrent, and possibly retributive, function, becomes operative upon the offender's release and thus impedes the rehabilitation objective of probation and parole. Similarly, the restraint function of imprisonment involves the application of rules and procedures which, while minimizing escape opportunities, contributes to the deterioration of offenders confined for reformation. Since police decisions not to invoke the criminal

Reprinted by permission of The Yale Law Journal Company and Fred B. Rothman & Company from *The Yale Law Journal,* Volume 69, pp. 543–589.

process may likewise further some objectives while hindering others, or, indeed, run counter to all, any meaningful appraisal of these decisions should include an evaluation of their impact throughout the process on the various objectives reflected in authorized sanctions and in the decisions of other administrators of criminal justice.

Under the rule of law, the criminal law has both a fair-warning function for the public and a power-restricting function for officials. Both post- and pre-verdict sanctions, therefore, may be imposed only in accord with authorized procedures. No sanctions are to be inflicted other than those which have been prospectively prescribed by the constitution, legislation, or judicial decision for a particular crime or a particular kind of offender. These concepts, of course, do not preclude differential disposition, within the authorized limits, of persons suspected or convicted of the same or similar offenses. In an ideal system differential handling, individualized justice, would result, but only from an equal application of officially approved criteria designed to implement officially approved objectives. And finally a system which presumes innocence requires that preconviction sanctions be kept at a minimum consistent with assuring an opportunity for the process to run its course.

A regularized system of review is a requisite for insuring substantial compliance by the administrators of criminal justice with these rule-of-law principles. Implicit in the word "review" and obviously essential to the operation of any review procedure is the visibility of the decisions and conduct to be scrutinized. Pretrial hearings on motions, the trial, appeal and the writ of habeas corpus constitute a formal system for evaluating the actions of officials invoking the criminal process. The public hearing, the record of proceedings, and the publication of court opinions—all features of the formal system—preserve and increase the visibility of official enforcement activity and facilitate and encourage the development of an informal system of appraisal. These proceedings and documents are widely reported and subjected to analysis and comment by legislative, professional, and other interested groups and individuals.

But police decisions not to invoke the criminal process, except when reflected in gross failures of service, are not visible to the community. Nor are they likely to be visible to official state reviewing agencies, even those within the police department. Failure to tag illegally parked cars is an example of gross failure of service, open to public view and recognized for what it is. An officer's decision, however, not to investigate or report adequately a disturbing event which he has reason to believe constitutes a violation of the criminal law does not ordinarily carry with it consequences sufficiently visible to make the community, the legislature, the prosecutor, or the courts aware of a possible failure of service. The police officer, the suspect, the police department, and frequently even the victim, when directly concerned with a decision not to invoke, unlike the same parties when responsible for or subject to a decision to invoke, generally have neither the incentive nor the opportunity to obtain review of that decision or the police conduct associated with it. Furthermore, official police records are usually too incomplete to permit evaluations of nonenforcement decisions in the light of the purposes of the criminal law. Consequently, such decisions, unlike decisions to enforce, are generally not subject to the control which would follow from administrative, judicial, legislative, or community review and appraisal.

Confidential reports detailing the day-to-day decisions and activities of a large municipal police force have been made available to the author by the American Bar Foundation. These reports give limited visibility to a wide variety of police decisions not to invoke the criminal process. Three groups of such decisions will be described and analyzed. Each constitutes a police "program" of nonenforcement either based on affirmative departmental policy or condoned by default. All of the decisions, to the extent that the officers concerned thought about them at all, represent well-intentioned, honest judgments, which seem to reflect the police officer's conception of his job. None of the decisions involve bribery or corruption, nor do they concern "obsolete," though unrepealed, criminal laws. Specifically, these programs involve police decisions (1) not to enforce the narcotics laws against certain violators who inform against other "more serious" violators; (2) not to enforce the felonious assault laws against an assailant whose victim does not sign a complaint; and (3) not to enforce gambling laws against persons engaged in the numbers racket, but instead to harass them. Each of these decisions are made even though the police "know" a crime has been committed, and even though they may "know" who the offender is and may, in fact, have apprehended him. But before describing and evaluating these nonenforcement programs, as an agency of review might do, it is necessary to determine what discretion, if any, the police, as invoking agents, have, and conceptually to locate the police in relation to other principal decisionmakers in the criminal law process.

II

The police have a duty not to enforce the substantive law of crimes unless invocation of the process can be achieved within bounds set by constitution, statute, court decision, and possibly official pronouncements of the prosecutor. *Total enforcement,* were it possible, is thus precluded, by generally applicable due-process restrictions on such police procedures as arrest, search, seizure, and interrogation. *Total enforcement* is further precluded by such specific procedural restrictions as prohibitions on invoking an adultery statute unless the spouse of one of the parties complains, or an unlawful-possession-of-firearms statute if the offender surrenders his dangerous weapons during a statutory period of amnesty. Such restrictions of general and specific application mark the bounds, often ambiguously, of an area of *full enforcement* in which the police are not only authorized but expected to enforce fully the law of crimes. An area of *no enforcement* lies, therefore, between the perimeter of *total enforcement* and the outer limits of *full enforcement.* In this *no enforcement* area, the police have no authority to invoke the criminal process.

Within the area of *full enforcement,* the police have not been delegated discretion not to invoke the criminal process. On the contrary, those state statutes providing for municipal police departments which define the responsibility of police provide:

> It shall be the duty of the police . . . under the direction of the mayor and chief of police and in conformity with the ordinances of the city, and the laws of the state, . . . to pursue and arrest any persons fleeing from justice . . . to apprehend any and all persons in the act of committing any offense against the laws of the state . . . and to take the offender forthwith before the proper court or magistrate, to be dealt with for the offense; to make complaints to the proper officers and magistrates of any person known or believed by them to be guilty of the violation of the ordinances of the city or the penal laws of the state; and at all times diligently and faithfully to enforce all such laws . . . .

Even in jurisdictions without such a specific statutory definition, declarations of the *full enforcement* mandate generally appear in municipal charters, ordinances or police manuals. Police manuals, for example, commonly provide, in sections detailing the duties at each level of the police hierarchy, that the captain, superintendent, lieutenant, or patrolman shall be responsible, so far as is in his power, for the prevention and detection of crime and the enforcement of all criminal laws and ordinances. Illustrative of the spirit and policy of *full enforcement* is this protestation from the introduction to the Rules and Regulations of the Atlanta, Georgia, Police Department:

> Enforcement of all Criminal Laws and City Ordinances, is my obligation. There are no specialties under the Law. My eyes must be open to traffic problems and disorders, though I move on other assignments, to slinking vice in back streets and dives though I have been directed elsewhere, to the suspicious appearance of evil wherever it is encountered . . . . I must be impartial because the Law surrounds, protects and applies to all alike, rich and poor, low and high, black and white . . . .

Minimally, then, *full enforcement,* so far as the police are concerned, means (1) the investigation of every disturbing event which is reported to or observed by them and which they have reason to suspect may be a violation of the criminal law; (2) following a determination that some crime has been committed, an effort to discover its perpetrators; and (3) the presentation of all information collected by them to the prosecutor for his determination of the appropriateness of further invoking the criminal process.

Full enforcement, however, is not a realistic expectation. In addition to ambiguities in the definitions of both substantive offenses and due-process boundaries, countless limitations and pressures preclude the possibility of the police seeking or achieving *full enforcement.* Limitations of time, personnel, and investigative devices—all in part but not entirely functions of budget—force the development, by plan or default, of priorities of enforcement. Even if there were "enough police" adequately equipped and trained, pressures from within and without the department, which is after all a human institution, may force the police to invoke the criminal process selectively. By decisions not to invoke within the area of *full enforcement,* the police largely determine the outer limits of *actual enforcement* throughout the criminal process. This relationship of the police to the total administration of criminal justice can be seen in the diagram opposite this page. They may reinforce, or they may undermine, the legislature's objectives in designating certain conduct "criminal" and in authorizing the imposition of certain sanctions following conviction. A police decision to ignore a felonious assault "because the victim will not sign a complaint," usually precludes the prosecutor or grand jury from deciding whether to accuse, judge or jury from determining guilt or innocence, judge from imposing the most "appropriate" sentence, probation or correctional authorities from instituting the most "appropriate" restraint and rehabilitation programs, and finally parole or pardon authorities from determining the offender's readiness for release to the community. This example is drawn from one of the three programs of nonenforcement about to be discussed.

III

Trading enforcement against a narcotics suspect for information about another narcotics offense or offender may involve two types of police decisions not to invoke fully the criminal process. First, there may be a decision to ask for

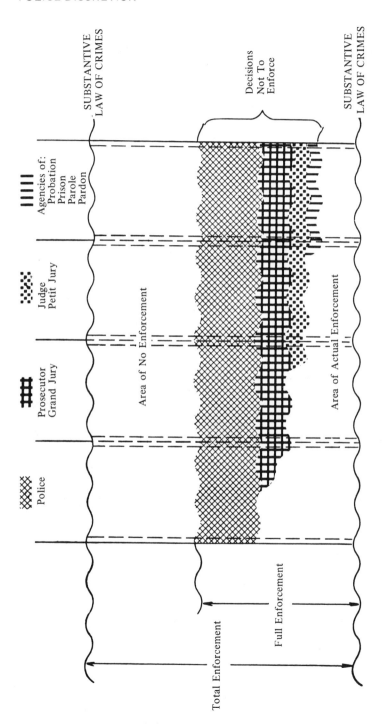

THE POLICE IN RELATION TO OTHER DECISIONMAKERS IN THE CRIMINAL PROCESS

the dismissal or reduction of the charge for which the informant is held; second, there may be a decision to overlook future violations while the suspect serves as an informer. The second type is an example of a relatively pure police decision not to invoke the criminal process while the first requires, at a minimum, tacit approval by prosecutor or judge. But examination of only the pure types of decisions would oversimplify the problem. They fail to illustrate the extent to which police nonenforcement decisions may permeate the process as well as influence, and be influenced by, prosecutor and court action in settings which fail to prompt appraisal of such decisions in light of the purposes of the criminal law. Both types of decisions, pure and conglomerate, are nonetheless primarily police decisions. They are distinguishable from a prosecutor's or court's decision to trade information for enforcement under an immunity statute, and from such parliamentary decisions as the now-repealed seventeenth and eighteenth century English statutes which gave a convicted offender who secured the conviction of his accomplice an absolute right to pardon. Such prosecutor and parliamentary decisions to trade information for enforcement, unlike the police decisions to be described, have not only been authorized by a legislative body, but have also been made sufficiently visible to permit review.

In the municipality studied, regular uniformed officers, with general law enforcement duties on precinct assignments, and a special narcotics squad of detectives, with citywide jurisdiction, are responsible for enforcement of the state narcotics laws. The existence of the special squad acts as a pressure on the uniformed officer to be the first to discover any sale, possession, or use of narcotics in his precinct. Careful preparation of a case for prosecution may thus become secondary to this objective. Indeed, approximately eighty per cent of those apprehended for narcotics violations during one year were discharged. In the opinion of the special squad, which processes each arrested narcotics suspect, either the search was illegal or the evidence obtained inadequate. The precinct officer's lack of interest in carefully developing a narcotics case for prosecution often amounts in effect to a police decision not to enforce but rather to harass.

But we are concerned here primarily with the decisions of the narcotics squad, which, like the Federal Narcotics Bureau, has established a policy of concentrating enforcement efforts against the "big supplier." The chief of the squad claimed that informers must be utilized to implement that policy, and that in order to get informants it is necessary to trade "little ones for big ones." Informers are used to arrange and make purchases of narcotics, to elicit information from suspects, including persons in custody, and to recruit additional informants.

Following arrest, a suspect will generally offer to serve as an informer to "do himself some good." If an arrestee fails to initiate such negotiations, the interrogating officer will suggest that something may be gained by disclosing sources of supply and by serving as an informer. A high mandatory minimum sentence for selling, a high maximum sentence for possession, and, where users are involved, a strong desire on their part to avoid the agonies of withdrawal, combine to place the police in an excellent bargaining position to recruit informers. To assure performance, each informer is charged with a narcotics violation, and final disposition is postponed until the defendant has fulfilled his part of the bargain. To protect the informer, the special squad seeks to camouflage him in the large body of releasees by not disclosing his identity even to the arresting precinct officer, who is given no explanation for release. Thus persons encountered on the street by a uniformed patrolman the day after their arrest may have been discharged, or they may have been officially charged and then released on bail or personal recognizance to await trial or to serve as informers.

While serving as informers, suspects are allowed to engage in illegal activity. Continued use of narcotics is condoned: the narcotics detective generally is not concerned with the problem of informants who make buys and use some of the evidence themselves. Though informers are usually warned that their status does not give them a "license to peddle," possession of a substantial amount of narcotics may be excused. In one case, a defendant found guilty of possession of *marijuana* argued that she was entitled to be placed on probation since she had cooperated with the police by testifying against three persons charged with sale of narcotics. The sentencing judge denied her request because he discovered that her cooperation was related to the possession of a substantial amount of *heroin,* an offense for which she was arrested (but never charged) while on bail for the marijuana violation. A narcotics squad inspector, in response to an inquiry from the judge, revealed that the defendant had not been charged with possession of *heroin* because she had been cooperative with the police on that offense.

In addition to granting such outright immunity for some violations, the police will recommend to the prosecutor either that an informer's case be *nolle prossed* or, more frequently, that the charge be reduced to a lesser offense. And, if the latter course is followed, the police usually recommend to the judge, either in response to his request for information or in the presentence report, that informers be placed on probation or given relatively light sentences. Both the prosecutor and judge willingly respond to police requests for reducing a charge of sale to a lesser offense because they consider the mandatory minimum too severe. As a result, during a four year period in this jurisdiction, less than two and one-half per cent of all persons charged with the sale of narcotics were convicted of that offense.

The narcotics squad's policy of trading *full enforcement* for information is justified on the grounds that apprehension and prosecution of the "big supplier" is facilitated. The absence of any in the city is attributed to this policy. As one member of the squad said, "[The city] is too hot. There are too many informants." A basic, though untested, assumption of the policy is that ridding the city of the "big supplier" is the key to solving its narcotics problem. Even if this assumption were empirically validated, the desirability of continuing such a policy cannot be established without taking into account its total impact on the administration of criminal justice in the city, the state, and the nation. Yet no procedure has been designed to enable the police and other key administrators of criminal justice to obtain such an appraisal. The extent and nature of the need for such a procedure can be illustrated, despite the limitations of available data, by presenting in the form of a mock report some of the questions, some of the answers, and some of the proposals a Policy Appraisal and Review Board might consider.

Following a description of the informer program, a report might ask:

To what extent, if at all, has the legislature delegated to the police the authority to grant, or obtain a grant of, complete or partial immunity from prosecution, in exchange for information about narcotics suppliers? No provisions of the general immunity or narcotics statutes authorize the police to exercise such discretion. The general immunity statute requires a high degree of visibility by providing that immunity be allowed only on a written motion by the prosecuting attorney to the court and that the information given be reduced to writing under the direction of the judge to preclude future prosecution for the traded offense or offenses. The narcotics statutes, unlike comparable legislation concerning other specific crimes, make no provision for obtaining information by awarding immunity from prosecution. Nor is there any indication, other than possibly in the maximum sentences authorized, that the legislature intended that certain narcotics offenses be given high priority or be enforced at the expense of other offenses. What evidence there is of legislative intent suggests the contrary; this fact is recognized by the local police manual. And nothing in the statute providing for the establishment of local police departments can be construed to authorize the policy of trading enforcement for information. That statute makes *full enforcement* a duty of the police. The narcotics squad has ignored this mandate and adopted an informer policy which appears to constitute a usurpation of legislative function. It does not follow that the police must discontinue employing informers, but they ought to discontinue trading enforcement for information until the legislature, the court, or the prosecutor explicitly initiates such a program. Whether the police policy of trading enforcement for information should be proposed for legislative consideration would depend upon the answers to some of the questions which follow.

Does trading enforcement for information fulfill the retributive, restraining, and reformative functions of the state's narcotics laws? By in effect licensing the user-informer to satisfy his addiction and assuring the peddler-informer, who may also be a user, that he will obtain dismissal or reduction of the pending charge to a lesser offense, the police undermine, if not negate, the retributive and restraining functions of the narcotics laws. In addition, the community is deprived of an opportunity to subject these offenders, particularly the addicts, to treatment aimed at reformation. In fact, the police ironically acknowledge the inconsistency of their program with the goal of treatment; "cured" addicts are not used as informers for fear that exposure to narcotics might cause their relapse. A comparison of the addict-release policies of the police, sentencing judge, and probation and parole authorities demonstrates the extent to which the administration of criminal justice can be set awry by a police nonenforcement program. At one point on the continuum, the police release the addict to informer status so that he can maintain his association with peddlers and users. The addict accepts such status on the tacit condition that continued use will be condoned. At other points on the continuum, the judge and probation and parole authorities make treatment a condition of an addict's release and continued use or even association with narcotics users the basis for revoking probation or parole. Thus the inherent conflict between basic purposes of the criminal law is compounded by conflicts among key decision-points in the process.

Does trading enforcement for information implement the deterrent function of criminal law administration? If deterrence depends—and little if anything is really known about the deterrent impact of the criminal law—in part at least, upon the potential offender's perception of law enforcement, the informer policy can have only a negative effect. In addition to the chance of nondetection which accompanies the commission of all crimes in varying degrees, the narcotics suspect has four-to-one odds that he will not be charged following detection and arrest. And he has a high expectation, even if charged, of obtaining a reduction or dismissal of an accurate charge. These figures reflect and reinforce the offender's view of the administration of criminal justice as a bargaining process initiated either by offering information "to do, himself some good" or by a member of the narcotics squad advising the uninformed suspect, the "new offender," of the advantages of disclosing his narcotics "connections." Such law enforcement can have little, if any, deterrent impact.

That the "big supplier," an undefined entity, has been discouraged from using the city as a headquarters was confirmed by a local federal agent and a United States attorney in testimony before a Senate committee investigating illicit narcotics traffic. They attributed the result, however, to the state's high mandatory minimum sentence for selling, not to the informer policy. In fact, that municipal police policy was not made visible at the hearings. It was neither mentioned in their testimony nor in the testimony of the chief of police and the head of the narcotics squad. These local authorities may have reasoned that since the mandatory sentence facilitates the recruitment of informers who, in turn, are essential to keeping the "big supplier" outside city limits, the legislature's sentencing policy could be credited with the "achievement."

Whether the police informer program, the legislature's sentencing policy, both, or neither, caused the "big supplier" to locate elsewhere is not too significant; the traffic and use of narcotics in the city remain major problems. Since user-demand is maintained, if not increased, by trading enforcement for information, potential and actual peddlers are encouraged to supply the city's addicts. Testimony before the Senate committee indicates that although the "big suppliers" have moved their headquarters to other cities, there are now in the city a large number of small peddlers serving a minimum of 1,500 and in all probability a total of 2,500 users, and that the annual expenditure for illicit narcotics in the city is estimated at not lower than ten and probably as high as eighteen million dollars. Evaluated in terms of deterrent effect, the program of trading enforcement for information to reach the "big supplier" has failed to implement locally the ultimate objective of the narcotics laws—reducing addiction. Furthermore, the business of the "big supplier" has not been effectively deterred. At best suppliers have been discouraged from basing their operations in the city, which continues to be a lucrative market. Thus by maintaining the market, local policy, although a copy of national policy, may very well hinder the efforts of the Federal Narcotics Bureau.

A report of a Policy Appraisal and Review Board might find: "Trading little ones for big ones" is outside the ambit of municipal police discretion and should continue to remain so because it conflicts with the basic objectives of the criminal law. Retribution, restraint, and reformation are subverted by a policy which condones the use and possession of narcotics. And deterrence cannot be enhanced by a police program which provides potential and actual suppliers and users with more illustrations of nonenforcement than enforcement.

A report might conclude by exploring and suggesting alternative programs for coping with the narcotics problem. No attempt will be made here to exhaust or detail all possible alternatives. An obvious one would be a rigorous program of *full enforcement* designed to dry up, or at least drastically reduce, local consumer and peddler demand for illicit narcotics. If information currently obtained from suspects is essential and worth a price, compensation might be given to informers, with payments deferred until a suspect's final release. Such a program would neither undermine the retributive and restraining objectives of the criminal law nor deprive the community of an opportunity to impose rehabilitation regimes on the offender. Funds provided by deferred payments might enhance an offender's chances of getting off to a good start upon release. Moreover, changing the picture presently perceived by potential violators from nonenforcement to enforcement would at least not preclude the possibility of deterrence. Such a program might even facilitate the apprehension of "big suppliers" who, faced with decreasing demand, might either be forced to discontinue serving the city because sales would no longer be profitable or to adopt bolder sales methods which would expose them to easier detection.

Full enforcement will place the legislature in a position to evaluate its narcotics laws by providing a basis for answering such questions as: Will *full enforcement* increase the price of narcotics to the user? Will such inflation increase the frequency of crimes committed to finance narcotics purchases? Or will *full enforcement* reduce the number of users and the frequency of connected crimes? Will too great or too costly an administrative burden be placed on the prosecutor's office and the courts by *full enforcement?* Will correctional institutions be filled beyond "effective" capacity? The answers to these questions are now buried or obscured by decisions not to invoke the criminal process.

Failure of a *full enforcement* program might prompt a board recommendation to increase treatment or correctional personnel and facilities. Or a board, recognizing that *full enforcement* would be either too costly or inherently ineffective, might propose the repeal of statutes prohibiting the use and sale of narcotics and/or the enactment, as part of a treatment program, of legislation authorizing sales to users at a low price. Such legislative action would be designed to reduce use and connected offenses to a minimum. By taking profits out of sales it would lessen peddler incentive to create new addicts and eliminate the need to support the habit by the commission of crimes.

These then are the kinds of questions, answers, and proposals a Policy Appraisal and Review Board might explore in its report examining this particular type of police decision not to invoke the criminal process.

IV

Another low visibility situation which an Appraisal and Review Board might uncover in this municipality stems from police decisions not to invoke the felonious assault laws unless the victim signs a complaint. Like the addict-informer, the potential complainant in an assault case is both the victim of an offense and a key source of information. But unlike him, the complainant, who is not a suspect, and whose initial contact with the police is generally self-imposed, is not placed under pressure to bargain. And in contrast with the informer program, the police assault program was clearly not designed, if designed at all, to effectuate an identifiable policy.

During one month under the nonenforcement program of a single precinct, thirty-eight out of forty-three felonious assault cases, the great majority involving stabbings and cuttings, were cleared "because the victim refused to prosecute." This program, which is coupled with a practice of not encouraging victims to sign complaints, reduces the pressure of work by eliminating such tasks as apprehending and detaining suspects, writing detailed reports, applying for warrants to prefer charges and appearing in court at inconvenient times for long periods without adequate compensation. As one officer explained, "run-of-the-mill" felonious assaults are so common in his precinct that prosecution of each case would force patrolmen to spend too much time in court and leave too little time for investigating other offenses. This rationalization exposes the private value system of individual officers as another policy-shaping factor. Some policemen feel, for example, that assault is an acceptable means of settling disputes among Negroes, and that when both assailant and victim are Negro, there is no immediately discernible harm to the public which justifies a decision to invoke the criminal process. Anticipation of dismissal by judge and district attorney of cases in which the victim is an uncooperative witness, the police claim, has been another operative factor in the development of the assault policy. A Policy Appraisal and Review Board, whose investigators had been specifically directed to examine the assault policy, should be able to identify these or other policy-shaping factors more precisely. Yet on the basis of the data available, a board could tentatively conclude that court and prosecutor responses do not explain why the police have failed to adopt a policy of encouraging assault victims to sign complaints, and, therefore, that the private value system of department members, as reflected in their attitude toward workload and in a stereotypical view of the Negro, is of primary significance.

Once some of the major policy-shaping factors have been identified, an Appraisal and Review Board might formulate and attempt to answer the following or similar questions: Would it be consistent with any of the purposes of the criminal law to authorize police discretion in cases of felonious assaults as well as other specified offenses? Assuming that it would be consistent or at least more realistic to authorize police discretion in some cases, what limitations and guides, if any, should the legislature provide? Should legislation provide that factors such as workload, willingness of victims or certain victims to sign a complaint, the degree of violence and attitude of prosecutor and judge be taken into account in the exercise of police discretion? If workload is to be recognized, should the legislature establish priorities of enforcement designed to assist the police in deciding which offenses among equally pressing ones are to be ignored or enforced? If assaults are made criminal in order to reduce threats to community peace and individual security, should a victim's willingness to prosecute, if he happens to live, be relevant to the exercise of police discretion? Does resting prosecution in the hands of the victim encourage him to "get even" with the assailant through retaliatory lawlessness? Or does such a policy place the decision in the hands of the assailant whose use of force has already demonstrated an ability and willingness to fulfill a threat?

Can the individual police officer, despite his own value system, sufficiently respond to officially articulated community values to be delegated broad powers of discretion? If not, can or should procedures be designed to enable the police department to translate these values into rules and regulations for individual policemen? Can police officers or the department be trained to evaluate the extent to which current practice undermines a major criminal law objective of imposing upon all persons officially recognized minimum standards of human behavior? For example, can the individual officer of the department be trained to evaluate the effect of decisions in cases of felonious assault among Negroes on local programs for implementing national or state policies of integration in school, employment, and housing, and to determine the extent to which current policy weakens or reinforces stereotypes which are used to justify not only police policy, but more importantly, opposition to desegregation programs? Or should legislation provide that the police invoke the process in all felonious assault cases unless the prosecutor or court publicly provide them in recorded documents with authority and guides for exercising discretion, and thus make visible both the policy of nonenforcement and the agency or agencies responsible for it?

Some of these issues were considered and resolved by the Oakland, California, Police Department in 1957 when, after consultation with prosecutors and judges, it decided to abandon a similar assault policy and seek *full enforcement*. Chief of Police W. W. Vernon, describing Oakland's new program, wrote:

In our assault cases for years we had followed this policy of releasing the defendant if the complainant did not feel aggrieved to the point of being willing to testify.... [Since] World War II ... our assault cases increased tremendously to the point where we decided to do something about the increase ....

Training materials prepared by the Oakland Police Academy disclose that between 1952 and 1956, while the decision to prosecute was vested in the victim, the rate of reported felonious assaults rose from 93 to 161 per 100,000 population and the annual number of misdemeanor assaults rose from 618 to 2,630. The materials emphasize that these statistics mean a workload of "nearly 10 assault reports a day every day of the year." But they stress:

> The important point about these figures is not so much that they represent a substantial police workload, which they do, but more important, that they indicate an increasing lack of respect for the laws of society by a measurable segment of our population, and a corresponding threat to the rest of the citizens of our city. The police have a clear responsibility to develop respect for the law among those who disregard it in order to insure the physical safety and well-being of those who do.
>
> ....
>
> We recognize that the problem exists mainly because the injured person has refused to sign a complaint against the perpetrator. The injured person has usually refused to sign for two reasons: first, because of threats of future bodily harm or other action by the perpetrator and, secondly, because it has been a way of life among some people to adjust grievances by physical assaults and not by the recognized laws of society which are available to them.
>
> We, the police, have condoned these practices to some extent by not taking advantage of the means at our disposal; that is, by not gathering sufficient evidence and signing complaints on information and belief in those cases where the complainant refuses to prosecute. The policy and procedure of gathering sufficient evidence and signing complaints on information and belief should instill in these groups the realization that the laws of society must be resorted to in settling disputes. When it is realized by many of these people that we will sign complaints ourselves and will not condone fighting and cuttings, many of them will stop such practices.

Following conferences with the police, the local prosecutors and judges pledged their support for the new assault program. The district attorney's office will deny a complainant's request that a case be dropped and suggest that it be addressed to the judge in open court. The judge, in turn, will advise the complainant that the case cannot be dismissed, and that a perjury, contempt, or false-report complaint will be issued in "appropriate cases" against the victim who denies facts originally alleged. The police have been advised that the court and prosecutor will actively cooperate in the implementation of the new program, but that every case will not result in a complaint since it is the "job [of the police] to turn in the evidence and it's the Prosecuting Attorney's job to determine when a complaint will be issued." Thus the role of each of the key decisionmaking agencies with preconviction invoking authority is clearly delineated and integrated.

With the inauguration of a new assault policy, an Appraisal and Review Board might establish procedures for determining how effectively the objectives of the policy are fulfilled in practice. A board might design intelligence retrieving devices which would provide more complete data than the following termed by Chief Vernon "the best evidence that our program is accomplishing the purpose for which it was developed . . . ." Prior to the adoption of the new policy, eighty per cent of the felonious assault cases "cleared" were cleared because "Complainant Refuses To Prosecute," while only thirty-two and two-tenths per cent of the clearances made during the first three months in 1958 were for that reason, even though the overall clearance rate rose during that period. And "during the first quarter of this year Felony Assaults dropped 11.1 per cent below the same period last year, and in March they were 35.6 per cent below March of last year. Battery cases were down 19.0 per cent for the first three months of 1958." An Appraisal and Review Board might attempt to determine the extent to which the police in cases formerly dropped because "Complainant Refused to Testify" have consciously or otherwise substituted another reason for "case cleared." And it might estimate the extent to which the decrease in assaults *reported* reflects, if it does, a decrease in the *actual* number of assaults or only a decrease in the number of victims willing to report assaults. Such followup investigations and what actually took place in Oakland on an informal basis between police, prosecutor, and judge illustrate some of the functions an Appraisal and Review Board might regularly perform.

V

Police decisions to harass, though generally perceived as overzealous enforcement, constitute another body of nonenforcement activities meriting investigation by an Appraisal and Review Board. Harassment is the imposition by the police, acting under color of law, of sanctions prior to conviction as a means of ultimate punishment, rather than as a device for the invocation of criminal proceedings. Characteristic of harassment are efforts to annoy certain "offenders" both by temporarily detaining or arresting them without intention to seek prosecution and by destroying or illegally seizing their property without any intention to use it as evidence. Like other police decisions not to invoke the criminal process, harassment is generally of extremely low visibility, probably because the police ordinarily restrict such activity to persons who are unable to afford the costs of litigation, who would or think they would, command little respect even if they were to complain, or who wish to keep themselves out of public view in order to continue their illicit activities. Like the informer program, harassment is conducted by the police in an atmosphere of cooperation with other administrators of criminal justice. Since harassment, by definition, is outside the rule of law, any benefits attributed to such police activity cannot justify its continuation. An Appraisal and Review Board, however, would not limit its investigations to making such a finding. It would be expected to identify and analyze factors underlying harassment and to formulate proposals for replacing harassment—lawless nonenforcement—with enforcement of the criminal law.

Investigators for an Appraisal and Review Board in this jurisdiction would discover, for example, a mixture of enforcement and harassment in a police program designed to regulate the gambling operations of mutual-numbers syndicates. The enforcement phase is conducted by a highly trained unit of less than a dozen men who diligently gather evidence in order to prosecute and convict syndicate operators of conspiracy to violate the gambling laws. This specialized unit, which operates independently of and without the knowledge of other officers, conducts all its work within the due-process boundaries of *full enforcement*. Consequently, the conviction rate is high for charges based upon its investigations. The harassment phase is conducted by approximately sixty officers who tour the city and search on sight, because of prior information, or such telltale actions as carrying a paper bag, a symbol of the trade, persons who they suspect are collecting bets. They question the "suspect" and proceed to search him, his car, or home without first making a valid arrest to legalize the search. If gambling paraphernalia are found, the police, fully aware that the exclusionary rule prohibits its use as evidence in this jurisdiction, confiscate the "contraband" and arrest the individual without any intention of seeking application of the criminal law.

Gambling operators treat the harassment program as a cost of doing business, "a risk of the trade." Each syndicate retains a bonding firm and an attorney to service members who are arrested. When a "runner" or "bagman" is absent from his scheduled rounds, routine release procedures are initiated. The bondsman, sometimes prematurely, checks with the police to determine if a syndicate man has been detained. If the missing man is in custody, the syndicate's attorney files an application for a writ of habeas corpus and appears before a magistrate who usually sets bail at a nominal amount and adjourns hearing the writ, at the request of the police, until the following day. Prior to the scheduled hearing, the police usually advise the court that they have no intention of proceeding, and the case is closed. Despite the harassee's release, the police retain the money and gambling paraphernalia. If the items seized are found in a car, the car is confiscated, with the cooperation of the prosecutor, under a nuisance abatement statute. Cars are returned, however, after the harassee signs a "consent decree" and, pursuant to it, pays "court costs"—a fee which is based on the car's value and which the prosecutor calls "the real meat of the harassment program." The "decree," entered under a procedure devised by the court and prosecutor's office, enjoins the defendant from engaging in illegal activity and, on paper, frees the police from any tort liability by an acknowledgement that seizure of the vehicle was lawful and justified—even though one prosecutor has estimated that approximately eighty per cent of the searches and seizures were illegal. A prosecuting attorney responsible for car confiscation initially felt that such procedures "in the ordinary practice of law would be unethical, revolting, and shameful," but explained that he now understnads why he acted as he did:

> To begin with ... the laws in ... [this state] with respect to gambling are most inadequate. This is equally true of the punishment feature of the law. To illustrate ... a well-organized and productive gambling house or numbers racket would take in one quarter of a million dollars each week. If, after a long and vigorous period of investigation and observation, the defendant was charged with violating the gambling laws and convicted therefore, the resulting punishment is so obviously weak and unprohibitive that the defendants are willing to shell out a relatively small fine or serve a relatively short time in prison. The ... [city's] gamblers and numbers men confidently feel that the odds are in their favor. If they operate for six months or a year, and accumulate untold thousands of dollars from the illegal activity, then the meager punishment imposed upon them if they are caught is well worth it. Then, too, because of the search and seizure laws in ... [this state], especially in regard to gambling and the number rackets, the hands of the police are tied. Unless a search can be made prior to an arrest so that the defendant can be caught in the act of violating the gambling laws, or a search warrant issued, there is no other earthly way of apprehending such people along with evidence sufficient to convict them

that is admissible in court.

Because of these two inadequacies of the law (slight punishment and conservative search and seizure laws with regard to gambling) the prosecutor's office and the police department are forced to find other means of punishing, harassing and generally making life uneasy for gamblers.

This position, fantastic as it is to be that of law-trained official, a guardian of the rule of law, illustrates how extensively only one of many police harassment programs in this jurisdiction can permeate the process and be tolerated by other decisionmakers in a system of criminal administration where decisions not to enforce are of extremely low visibility.

Having uncovered such a gambling-control program, an Appraisal and Review Board should recommend that the police abandon such harassment activities because they are antagonistic to the rule of law. In addition, the board might advance secondary reasons for eliminating harassment by exposing the inconsistencies between this program and departmental justifications for its narcotics and assault policies. While unnecessary to the condemnation of what is fundamentally lawless nonenforcement, such exposure might cause the police to question the wisdom of actions based on a personal or departmental belief that the legislature has authorized excessively lenient sanctions and restrictive enforcement procedures. The comparison might emphasize the inconsistencies of police policy toward organized crime by exposing the clash between an informer program designed to rid the city of the "big supplier" and a harassment program which tends to consolidate control of the numbers racket in a few syndicates "big" enough to sustain the legal, bonding, and other "business" costs of continued interruptions and the confiscation of property. More importantly, it should cause a reexamination and redefinition of "workload," which was so significant in the rationalization of the assault policy. A cost accounting would no doubt reveal that a significant part of "workload," as presently defined by the police, includes expenditures of public funds for personnel and equipment employed in unlawful activities. Once harassment is perceived by municipal officials concerned with budgets as an unauthorized expenditure of public funds, consideration for increased awards to the police department might be conditioned upon a showing that existing resources are now deployed for authorized purposes. Such action should stimulate police cooperation in implementing the board's proposal for curtailing harassment.

Further to effectuate its recommendation, the board might attempt to clarify and redefine the duties of the police by a reclassification of crimes which would emphasize the mandate that no more than *full enforcement* of the existing criminal law as defined by the legislature is expected. For many crimes, this may mean little or no *actual enforcement* because the values protected by procedural limitations are more important than the values which may be infringed by a particular offense. A board might propose, for example, that crimes be classified not only as felonies and misdemeanors, but in terms of active and passive police enforcement. An *active-enforcement* designation for an offense would mean that individual police officers or specialized squads are to be assigned the task of ferreting out and even triggering violations. *Passive enforcement* would mean that the police are to assume a sit-back-and-wait posture, *i.e.,* that they invoke the criminal process only when the disturbing event is brought to their attention by personal observation during a routine tour of duty or by someone outside the police force registering a complaint. Designation of gambling, for example, as a *passive-enforcement* offense would officially apprise the police that substantial expenditures of personnel and equipment for enforcement are not contemplated unless the local community expresses a low tolerance for such disturbing events by constantly bringing them to police attention. The adoption of this or a similar classification scheme might not only aid in training the police to understand that harassment is unlawful, but it may also provide the legislature with a device for officially allowing local differences in attitude toward certain offenses to be reflected in police practice and for testing the desirability of removing criminal sanctions from certain kinds of currently proscribed behavior.

VI

The mandate of *full enforcement,* under circumstances which compel selective enforcement, has placed the municipal police in an intolerable position. As a result, nonenforcement programs have developed undercover, in a hit-or-miss fashion, and without regard to impact on the overall administration of justice or the basic objectives of the criminal law. Legislatures, therefore, ought to reconsider what discretion, if any, the police must or should have in invoking the criminal process, and what devices, if any, should be designed to increase visibility and hence reviewability of these police decisions.

The ultimate answer is that the police should not be delegated discretion not to invoke the criminal law. It is recognized, of course, that the exercise of discretion cannot be completely eliminated where human beings are involved. The frailties of human language and human perception will always admit of borderline cases (although none of the situations analyzed in this Article are "borderline"). But nonetheless, outside this margin of ambiguity, the police should operate in an atmosphere which exhorts and commands them to invoke impartially all criminal laws within the bounds of *full enforcement.* If a criminal law is ill-advised, poorly defined, or too costly to enforce, efforts by the police to achieve *full enforcement* should generate pressures for legislative action. Responsibility for the enactment, amendment, and repeal of the criminal laws will not, then, be abandoned to the whim of each police officer or department, but retained where it belongs in a democracy—with elected representatives.

Equating *actual enforcement* with *full enforcement,* however, would be neither workable nor humane nor humanly possible under present conditions in most, if not all, jurisdictions. Even if there were "enough police" (and there are not) to enforce all of the criminal laws, too many people have come to rely on the nonenforcement of too many "obsolete" laws to justify the embarrassment, discomfort, and misery which would follow implementation of *full enforcement* programs for every crime. *Full enforcement* is a program for the future, a program which could be initiated with the least hardship when the states, perhaps stimulated by the work of the American Law Institute, enact new criminal codes clearing the books of obsolete offenses.

In the interim, legislatures should establish Policy Appraisal and Review Boards not only to facilitate coordination of municipal police policies with those of other key criminal law administrators, but also to assist commissions drafting new codes in reappraising basic objectives of the criminal law and in identifying laws which have become obsolete. To ensure that board appraisals and recommendations facilitate the integration of police policies with overall state policies and to ensure the cooperation of local authorities, board membership might include the state's attorney general, the chief justice of the supreme court, the chairman of the department of correction, the chairman of the board of parole and the chief of parole supervision, the chairman of the department of probation, the chairmen of the judiciary committees of the legislature, the chief of the state police, the local chief of police, the local prosecutor, and the chief judge of each of the local trial courts. In order regularly and systematically to cull and retrieve information, the board should be assisted by a full-time director who has a staff of investigators well-trained in social science research techniques. It should be given power to subpoena persons and records and to assign investigators to observe all phases of police activity including routine patrols, bookings, raids, and contacts with both the courts and the prosecutor's office. To clarify its functions, develop procedures, determine personnel requirements and test the idea itself, the board's jurisdiction should initially be restricted to one or two major municipalities in the state. The board would review, appraise, and make recommendations concerning municipal police nonenforcement policies as well as follow up and review the consequences of implemented proposals. In order to make its job both manageable and less subject to attack by those who cherish local autonomy and who may see the establishment of a board as a step toward centralization, it would have solely an advisory function and limit its investigations to the enforcement of state laws, not municipal ordinances. And to ensure that board activity will not compromise current enforcement campaigns or place offenders on notice of new techniques of detection or sources of information, boards should be authorized, with court approval, to withhold specified reports from general publication for a limited and fixed time.

Like other administrative agencies, a Policy Appraisal and Review Board will in time no doubt suffer from marasmus and outlive its usefulness. But while viable, such a board has an enormous potential for uncovering in a very dramatic fashion basic inadequacies in the administration of criminal justice and for prompting a thorough community reexamination of the why of a law of crimes.

GIDEON AND BEYOND: ACHIEVING AN
ADEQUATE DEFENSE FOR THE INDIGENT

Barry Siegal

OBLIGATION OF EQUAL JUSTICE FOR ALL

Throughout our country's history one of the primary goals of our government, much sought after but sometimes not achieved, has been the equal administration of criminal justice. The reasons for this policy are two-fold. On the one hand there is a desire to protect the interests of those persons confronted with the judicial process. Our sense of decency and fair-play, in this respect, dictate that rich and poor alike should receive, so far as possible, equal treatment for like violations of the criminal law. As announced by the Supreme Court, "There can be no equal justice where the kind of trial a man gets depends on the amount of money he has."

More broadly speaking, however, equal treatment of all defendants, both the wealthy and the indigent, can be thought of as accomplishing numerous societal interests. First, the vitality of the adversary system itself requires it. This objective can be achieved only by the proper performance of the defense function. Any artificial distinctions, therefore, which impede the workings of this function should be avoided. From a more practical viewpoint it might be noted that equal administration of the criminal laws will inevitably result in an image of fair treatment from which our society can clearly profit.

Recognizing the goals to be reached in this area how have the courts and the legislatures gone about achieving them? Where have they gone wrong and what remains to be done?

PRESENT CONSTITUTIONAL REQUIREMENTS

The right to counsel in criminal proceedings in federal courts is compelled by the Sixth Amendment. The Supreme Court, however, did not turn to this provision for guidance until recently. It was not relied upon until 1938, in *Johnson v. Zerbst,* where it was declared that the federal courts have no jurisdiction to try a defendant who is unable to employ an attorney unless one is appointed or the right to counsel is waived. The extension of this right to state proceedings was a slow evolutionary process, culminating in the landmark case of *Gideon v. Wainwright.* There the right of the accused to counsel in the state courts in all felony cases was expressly held to be a part of the due process. Other cases have indicated that counsel must be provided at the arraignment, since it is usually such a critical stage of the proceedings that a defendant without funds would stand unequal before the bar of justice as compared to the

Reprinted by Special Permission of the *Journal of Criminal Law, Criminology and Police Science* (Northwestern University School of Law), copyright © 1968, Volume 59, Number 1.

defendant with means; at the preliminary hearing where the defendant entered a plea of guilty which was later introduced at trial; and at the time of arrest when the accused is subjected to interrogation.

Another significant phase of criminal proceedings are the post-conviction remedies. The leading cases in this area are *Griffin v. Illinois* and *Douglas v. California.* In Illinois, prior to *Griffin,* every criminal defendant could appeal a conviction once as a matter of right, but *full* appellate review could not be obtained unless the defendant supplied the appellate court with a record of the trial proceedings which had to be paid for. In *Griffin,* however, the Supreme Court reversed a conviction where the defendant could not appeal because of his inability to pay for the transcript. It held that the Fourteenth Amendment prohibits inequality of treatment which results from the inability of an indigent to purchase adequate trial records. Subsequent cases have held that it is unconstitutional to make indigents pay docketing fees in order to have his appeal heard, and, in *Smith v. Bennet,* that a free transcript must be provided for other post-conviction remedies.

Undoubtedly, the most significant decision applying the right to counsel to appeals is *Douglas v. California.* There the Supreme Court ruled that counsel must be provided for the first appeal that is allowed as a matter of right. As a result of *Griffin* and *Douglas,* the question has been raised as to what qualifications may constitutionally limit the indigent's right to appeal. The answer is by no means clear. In *Eskridge v. Washington,* the Court held that it was unconstitutional to give the trial judge authority to decide whether an appeal should be prosecuted. In a subsequent case a procedure which intrusted to Defense Counsel discretion to request a transcript and then bring the appeal was struck down.

The recent case of *Anders v. California* seems to clarify the area considerably and lay down the minimum requirements of due process with regard to the prosecution of indigent appeals. The defendant there was convicted of possession of marijuana. After the trial he asked the court to appoint a lawyer to bring an appeal. The appointed attorney, after studying the record and consulting with his client, concluded there would be no merit in an appeal and so notified the court in the form of a "no-merit" letter. The defendant filed a brief *pro se* and lost. On review of a petition for a writ of *habeas corpus,* however, the conviction was invalidated by the Supreme Court. The majority held that the procedure followed in this case did not comport with the minimum requirements of due process; that the Constitution demands that appointed counsel make a con-scientious examination of the record, and if he then wishes to withdraw, accompany his request with a *brief* referring to any arguments which might support an appeal. The court of appeals can then make an educated decision as to whether the appeal is frivolous. In *Anders* all the appellate court had was the bare record to consider in a non-adversary context.

The underlying rationale for the *Anders* decision was that the Constitution requires that an indigent be put in as nearly the same position as the defendant with means with regard to an appeal. As the *Douglas* court stated, the Supreme Court has consistently held invalid those procedures "where the rich man who appeals as of right, enjoys the benefit of counsel's examination into the record, research of the law, and marshalling of arguments on his behalf, while the indigent, already burdened by a preliminary determination that his case is without merit is forced to shift for himself." It appears, therefore, that unless there is a process of review whereby the defendant's right to appeal is adequately protected or unless that decision is left to the defendant, there is an infringement of his Fourteenth Amendment rights.

After reviewing the constitutional requirements with regard to defense of the indigent, it will be profitable to reflect on those areas where legislation seems desirable. First, although *Gideon* held that counsel must be provided for the indigent, it did not say whether he must be assigned private counsel or a defender. Also, the question of whether an attorney should be provided at the preliminary hearing or even sooner remains unanswered. Standards of eligibility must be set up by statute, as well as some indication of how defendants of *moderate* means should be handled. Provisions for appointment of counsel at appeals and collateral proceedings have to be considered. Finally, there is a problem of compensating the court-appointed attorney and reimbursing him for out-of-pocket expenses. In this Comment an attempt is made to deal with these questions, especially in light of the Criminal Justice Act of 1964.

TYPES OF SYSTEMS FOR PROVIDING COUNSEL

There are essentially two methods by which counsel can be supplied to the indigent: the defender system, which may be either publicly or privately operated; or the various systems of appointing private counsel in individual cases.

Under the appointed counsel systems, when the defendant appears in court without a lawyer and without funds to retain one, the court will appoint a practicing lawyer to defend his case for him. In effect the system differs, depending on the jurisdiction, as to the time of appointment, method of offering counsel to the accused, amount of compensation, if any, and financial criteria for eligibility.

Normally the appointed counsel is chosen from a list of attorneys maintained by the court with names supplied by the local bar association, although at other times a lawyer is picked from among those present in court. The quality of the lawyer appointed in this manner varies, but in about twenty five percent of the jurisdictions, there is a conscious preference for young, inexperienced lawyers. The reasons for this are, first, that courts feel that these cases offer valuable experience for younger members of the bar and, second, those lawyers "that know their way around" have an easier time being excused from such assignments. With regard to compensation, a majority of the states pay the appointed counsel a modest fee, whereas others compensate him only in capital cases. Furthermore, there is a great divergence among the states regarding reimbursement for expenses.

The primary advantage which the assigned counsel system is said to afford is the wide participation of the bar in the administration of criminal justice. The difficulty with the system is that in order to achieve a greater amount of criminal law experience for more members of the bar we may be jeopardizing an adequate defense for the accused. Even if a true cross-section of the profession can be utilized, there will still be a certain number which will not have the competency in the criminal law area that a specialist, such as a public defender, has. It is true that there are inexperienced public defenders, but in most cases they are under the supervision of a more qualified attorney. In any case, in most large counties it is questionable whether there is, in fact, a wide participation of lawyers in an assigned counsel program.

The assigned counsel system has been criticized by attorneys who feel that it is unfair to them. It has been alleged that some lawyers have been called on to participate too frequently, and that older, more experienced lawyers have been excused on request, thus putting the burden on the younger lawyers. Arguments have been advanced that under the assigned counsel system the attorney is frequently not compensated, or, if he is, at an insufficient rate. Also, appointment may be made too late in the proceedings, thus infringing the rights of the accused. These arguments, however, are directed not so much at the system but at the peculiarities of various jurisdictions. It seems, on the whole, that the assigned counsel method can indeed be a valuable alternative when properly administered, especially in smaller communities where a greater percentage of the lawyers can take part in the program.

A defender system is one where salaried lawyers devote all or a substantial part of their time to the defense of indigents within the jurisdiction. There are three types of defender systems: the public defender office, supported by public funds; the private defender system, supported by private gifts; and the private-public defender office, which is a private organization dependent on both public and private funds. The public defender may be selected by judicial appointment, popular election or appointment by the county board.

The defender system, as opposed to appointed counsel, seems to offer the distinct advantage of allowing the imprisoned indigent to be represented from the earliest possible moment after arrest through trial and appeal without any break in the proceedings for the purpose of bringing in another counsel. Since the defender usually has a complete office staff at his disposal, including investigators, and a file of prior cases, there is a possibility of a more complete defense under the circumstances. In addition, a recent survey has concluded that the defender may provide for more experienced, competent counsel, especially in larger cities.

The public defender office has been subject to attack primarily on the theory that the defense attorney cannot be completely independent and free from political influence when he is part of the same machinery, and responsible to the same appointing or electing agency, as the prosecutor. It seems, however, that there is nothing inherent in the public defender system which should limit the independence or zeal of the defender, even conceding that the way it is administered could result in such abuses. If the defender is given a long term, if his appointment is controlled by the judiciary rather than the politically-oriented bodies of the county, then it is hard to see where the defendant's rights would in any way be infringed, especially in view of the fact that the defender is a member of a highly respected profession where vigorous defense of one's clients is a requirement under its code of ethics. Furthermore, it has rarely been advanced that popular election of judges has affected their independence; similarly, these arguments appear frivolous with regard to the defender.

One author feels that even assuming the actual independence of the defender, there is still a problem of convincing the public of it since the public defender is "an institutional and ideological break from the traditional notion of the private lawyer serving his individual client." This problem is particularly acute if it affects the defendant when he makes his decision whether to accept counsel or not. Furthermore, if the indigent feels that it is useless to contest his guilt he may waive counsel even though counsel could be useful in affecting the length or type of sentence imposed.

The solution is two-pronged. First, the public must be informed of the importance of the defender in our system of jurisprudence and his freedom from outside pressures; and, second, the significance of a proper defense must be brought to bear on the indigent before he is allowed to waive counsel.

The appointment of counsel in the federal courts is now governed by the Criminal Justice Act of 1964. This Act has been called "the most far-reaching present day statute, state or federal, dealing with the resourceless criminal defendant." In response to it, many states have recently proposed extensive defense-of-the-indigent legislation.

Section (a) of the Criminal Justice Act allows each district court to provide counsel either by appointment of an individual attorney or of attorneys furnished by a bar association or legal aid society. In either case the lawyer chosen is picked by the judge from a panel of attorneys designated or approved by him. Since the time of the Act's taking effect, the courts have initiated detailed screening processes for supplying these panels with lawyers. One of the main deficiencies which is immediately noted, however, is that there is no option for the courts to utilize the services of a defender. Considering the other provisions of the Act allowing for reimbursement of expenses, continuous representation through appeal, and the fact that the panels of lawyers have consisted of a true cross-section of the bar which have shown great enthusiasm toward the plan, the lack of defender option should not prove detrimental. It is evident, though, that if a defender program were among the options offered the district courts, greater flexibility would thereby be achieved. Those districts with larger populations would have substantial cost savings as well as more adequate representation of the defendant.

At present, defense of the indigent in criminal cases in Illinois is governed by the Code of Criminal Procedure. Under section 113-3, if the defendant is determined to be an indigent and he desires counsel, the public defender is to be appointed to his case, or if there is no defender in the county or the defendant requests another attorney then the court may appoint one. In view of deficiencies in the present legislation, and with the Criminal Justice Act before them, a joint committee of the Chicago and Illinois Bar Associations has recently drafted a comprehensive report on the subject. Under this proposed legislation a public defender would be appointed in every county with more than a million inhabitants, while other contiguous counties could combine and share a joint defender. When a defendant appears in court, financially unable to obtain counsel, a public defender would be appointed to represent him. The proposed statute further provides: "In its discretion the court may, or at the request of the defendant for good cause shall, appoint counsel other than the Public Defender." This report, it appears, recognizes the value of a public defender, especially in larger communities. It, therefore, places a burden on the defendant who desires a court-appointed counsel other than the defender to demonstrate the validity of his request.

Illinois, then, would rely to a large extent on a public defender, whereas under the Criminal Justice Act this option is completely discarded. Why the disparity? The answer is essentially because of the different conditions existing in each jurisdiction. It seems that in larger jurisdictions, where it can be guaranteed that a public defender would be free from political influence; where there are adequate funds to give any indigent proper representation, the public defender system may more adequately protect the rights of the accused. If these are, in fact, the circumstances, it is probably better to place a heavy burden on any defendant who seeks appointed counsel to give sound reasons, since most will not fully appreciate the value of the defender. On the other hand, in smaller communities, where a substantial proportion of the bar can participate in an appointed counsel program; where the defendants right not to have an incompetent, inexperienced counsel can be protected; and where the lawyers themselves can realize the importance of protecting the rights of the indigent to the same extent as in the case of the defendant with means, then assigned counsel may be the proper solution.

WHEN IS COUNSEL FIRST PROVIDED?

As previously pointed out, counsel must be provided for the indigent defendant at the arraignment, and at the preliminary hearing when it may constitute a critical stage in the proceedings. How far the Supreme Court will carry the "critical stage" test is difficult to foresee, but one authority holds that it is possible that the test may allow the court to extend the due process requirement to the earliest possible stage after arrest.

Apart from constitutional requirements, it is evident that fairness in the judicial process demands that counsel be appointed no later than the defendant's first appearance in court. A lawyer is essential at the preliminary hearing stage in order to give the indigent defendant the same opportunities as the non-indigent. It is here that probable cause is to be established and cross-examination of witnesses may be deemed necessary by competent counsel. Furthermore, where there is a question of the legality of a search, it is imperative to obtain, at the earliest possible time, testimony showing the reasons for the search. The indigent is also at a distinct disadvantage if his attorney has to prepare his defense from the time of arraignment rather than earlier. The court, it is true, can grant a continuance but, unless prejudice is fairly obvious, it may be reluctant to do so.

In order to truly afford equal opportunity to the indigent it may be thought necessary to appoint counsel immediately upon arrest. This position appears untenable, however, since, in most cases, the police could not have a lawyer riding in the car with them. It is probably even impractical to have an attorney appointed as soon as the accused is brought to jail since the cost may be prohibitive. Also, since not every person brought in is eventually charged, arraigned or brought to trial, there would be a tremendous waste of resources if an attorney was assigned to every person arrested. Finally, since the time between arrest and arraignment is usually minimal, no attorney need be appointed until defendant's initial court appearance except where he is interrogated.

The Criminal Justice Act can again be cited as presenting the modern point of view on the subject. Section (c) requires that the defendant be represented from his initial court appearance. From a cursory reading of the Connecticut Plan for implementing the Criminal Justice Act in the Connecticut District Court, it seems that the defendant's rights are extended considerably. It states that if it is determined that the defendant is unable to obtain counsel, this information must be promptly brought to the attention of a magistrate who will appoint an attorney. Considering the difficulties inherent in the appointment of counsel to everyone arrested, a logical interpretation of the Plan would be that the accused should be arraigned as soon as possible after arrest and an attorney would then be appointed if the defendant was unable to retain one.

By way of comparison, the Illinois Criminal Code provides for appointment of a defender or other counsel before pleading to the charge. If the defendant has not been able to obtain counsel before pleading, then, after one is appointed a continuance is to be allowed to enable the defendant to consult with him. This provision should put the indigent on as equal footing with the defendant with means as is practicable.

A third approach to the problem, and the most liberal of all, was adopted by the drafters of the proposed legislation in South Carolina. This legislation requires that any defendant charged with a crime must be told of his right to counsel. Under South Carolina law the defendant is charged with a crime at the time of arrest. One authority, therefore, assumes that the new legislation means that the accused must be supplied with counsel within a reasonable time after arrest. Here, again, the provision may be read to allow for counsel at the arraignment if this stage comes within a reasonable time after arrest.

METHODS OF DETERMINING ELIGIBILITY

At present eligibility of the defendant for appointed counsel is determined either by his response to the simple question of a court whether he can "afford counsel," or by the answers to various forms concerning employment, ownership of an automobile or other property. Courts have also regarded the ability to secure release on bail as some indication that the defendant can afford his own attorney. Gross inequities will appear if this is accepted as a test by itself, however. What if the defendant receives the money for bail from a relative? What if he has spent the last of his money for release so that he could retain employment? Unless the circumstances surrounding release or bail are examined the defendant may be greatly prejudiced. As to other criteria for eligibility there will be different results in different cases. Where the community is small and the judge knows the defendant, then no detailed forms are required. However, in larger cities, where the defendant is not known, a written questionnaire should be filled out, unless there is a defender who has investigators on his staff with the ability to make at least a preliminary determination of eligibility. The final conclusion seems to be that the less investigation necessary the better off we are from a point of view of expense and time allotment, which could be used by the defense attorney in preparing his case. But, on the other hand, before assignment is made the court should be satisfied that the defendant cannot afford his own attorney.

What about the defendant with some available funds but not enough to pay for a lawyer? What if the defendant can afford a lawyer but not investigative services or expert witnesses? According to the Attorney General's Committee report, total lack of funds should not be the criterion for eligibility. Furthermore, if, during the trial, the defendant becomes financially incapable of paying for his lawyer because of the length of the proceedings or other reasons, the government should step in to see that he gets adequate representation. This conclusion rests on the theory that "whenever financial incapacity prevents the defense from providing active and creative challenges to assertions of governmental power in the criminal area, the adversary system, and the public interest dependent upon it, are placed in jeopardy."

The Criminal Justice Act provides for substantial flexibility in this situation. It states merely that unless the defendant waives counsel one shall be appointed for him, if after "appropriate inquiry" the defendant is found financially unable to obtain counsel. The establishment of standards for determining the extent of inquiry is left to the districts, although forms have been issued by the government to be completed by the defendant showing assets, employment, compensation, and dependents. This flexibility seems to be a recognition of the fact that the complexity and number of questions to be asked is dependent on such factors as size of the district, severity of the crime, and whether bail has been provided.

To encompass defendants with some means, the Act purposely avoids use of the term indigent. Rather, it uses the standard "financially unable to obtain counsel," since the constitutional right to an attorney is not based on destitution but on lack of sufficient resources to retain counsel. Section (c) further allows for termination of appointed counsel if it is later found defendant has sufficient means to retain one, or authorizes contribution by the defendant. The Act is noticeably silent with regard to the defendant who can afford counsel but not other necessary services, with the exception of expert witnesses.

The present Illinois Criminal Code also fails to provide standards for the determination of indigency. It states that if the Court determines that the defendant is in need of a lawyer and is indigent a defender is to be appointed. What "indigent" means under particular facts is apparently left to the courts. The proposed legislation in Illinois recognizes this deficiency in the Code and provides for a hearing to determine whether the defendant is "financially unable to obtain competent counsel." Assuming that the criteria of "financially unable to obtain competent counsel" will receive the same interpretation as under the Criminal Justice Act, the problems under both will be identical. There still remains the questions of what happens to the defendant who can not afford a complete defense or who becomes indigent at some point in the proceedings against him.

The proposed South Carolina legislation is again more precise in this area than any of the other statutes heretofore encountered. This act applies to any defendant who is "financially unable to obtain an adequate defense." Furthermore, four other standards are set up to determine whether the defendant is eligible under the act to have a counsel appointed for his case. He must be financially unable to (1) obtain representation; (2) obtain counsel; (3) pay counsel whom he has retained; or (4) obtain investigative, expert or other services necessary for an adequate defense. Even though the Act has been criticized as being too inflexible and not giving enough discretion to the administrator, clearly, without some guidance there might be arbitrary results.

COUNSEL FOR MISDEMEANORS

The decision in *Gideon* was limited on its facts to felony cases, but the Supreme Court could easily use the same reasoning in extending the Sixth Amendment protection to defendant accused of misdemeanors. Such a result has been accomplished in a number of court of Appeals decisions and in New York both by judicial decision and by statute. At present only about 25% of the counties in the country provide counsel for misdemeanors, a situation praised by many prominent jurists. It can not be denied that an indigent who must face the trial of a misdemeanor charge may—depending upon the complexity of the case—be as handicapped as the felony defendant who was not provided counsel before *Gideon*. Misdemeanor cases, for example, may involve motions to suppress confessions or physical evidence, or may call into play technical rules of evidence.

Under the Criminal Justice Act a lawyer is to be appointed to the indigent in cases where he is charged with a felony or misdemeanor, other than a "petty offense." Flexibility is maintained in the proposed South Carolina statute which requires the appointment of counsel in cases where the crime charged carries a penalty of six months or more and in other cases if warranted. The proposed Illinois legislation merely authorizes appointment in every case where a person is charged with any criminal offense. This goes too far. It forces the state to supply counsel to the indigent at substantial expense where even the defendant with means might not, as a practical matter, be represented.

COUNSEL FOR POST-TRIAL PROCEEDINGS

The law is settled that counsel must be provided the indigent at the first appeal which he is afforded as of right, and, further, a transcript of the trial record must also be supplied. Questions persist as to the requirement of counsel at other post-trial proceedings. What about subsequent appeals, habeas corpus proceedings, and probation or parole revocation hearings?

As to subsequent appeals, no distinction is made between the first and second appeals in any of the legislation heretofore considered. The Criminal Justice Act, for example, authorizes the appointment of counsel to continue through appeal. Considering the liberality of the act and its broad concern with the rights of criminal defendants, it should be interpreted to require the appointed attorney to prosecute any claims the defendant might have beyond the appeal which he has as a matter of right, unless clearly frivolous.

As to subsequent collateral proceedings, the Supreme Court appears reluctant to require counsel for all such matters, but it has laid down the rule that where a substantial claim is presented requiring a full evidentiary hearing "the sentencing court might find it useful to appoint counsel." Even absent a judicial mandate, however, this does not seem to be a problem area, since about 76% of the states provide counsel for post-conviction remedies to some extent.

There have been two lines of argument with regard to the desirability of providing counsel at habeas corpus proceedings. One view holds that these are merely civil proceedings and counsel is therefore not required under the Sixth Amendment. With equal force it can be pointed out that regardless of history, habeas corpus proceedings are now considered as extended appeals and, since the defendant could not be expected to handle the complex issues involved in an appeal, he should not be forced to make a choice whether to argue his own case for habeas corpus or avoid it altogether. As the proponents of extending *Gideon* to these cases argue, in habeas corpus proceedings federal courts are under an obligation to provide a fair hearing. When this requires representation of a petitioner by counsel, and the petitioner lacks adequate means to hire one, then counsel should be appointed. It may be a more stable foundation to rest the government's obligation on the equal protection clause since, unless counsel is provided, the indigent will surely be in a less advantageous position than other defendants. In any case, in order to be consistent with our modern concepts of fairness, the defendant who cannot afford one should have a lawyer appointed for habeas corpus proceedings, at least absent a showing of frivolity. It is difficult to justify the absence of a provision for counsel at these hearings under the Criminal Justice Act. Recognizing this deficiency both the proposed South Carolina and Illinois statutes provide for counsel at habeas corpus proceedings.

Provision for appointed counsel at parole revocation hearings has been required in at least one state by judicial decision. This has not been generally accepted and at present there is no similar provision in the federal courts. Here, again, the argument persists that parole revocation hearings are merely administrative proceedings. Furthermore, since parole and conditional release are matters of grace they can be terminated at will without following procedural requirements. It should be recognized, however, that the defendant has been released, even though conditionally and not as a matter of right. Still, fairness in our criminal system demands that the decision of parole revocation should be made with a knowledge of all the facts, which necessitates cross examination of witnesses, presentation of opposing viewpoints, and a general knowledge of the law. Absence of counsel, therefore, under these circumstances can not be justified, and, as previously mentioned, an attorney must be appointed in Illinois and South Carolina under the proposed statutes.

COMPENSATION, REIMBURSEMENT FOR
INVESTIGATIVE EXPENSES AND
EXPERT WITNESSES

Prior to the Criminal Justice Act the Federal courts and a substantial minority of the state courts did not authorize compensation of appointed counsel in criminal cases. This practice was strongly criticized as being prejudicial to both the defendant and the legal profession. Since providing equal justice to all by supplying competent counsel to the indigent is a function of the society as a whole, the burden of paying for defending the indigent should be on it rather than the legal profession.

From the defendant's viewpoint it is obvious that he will not be getting the protection that the Fourteenth Amendment requires unless the attorney appointed to defend him is able to advance his cause with as much determination and zeal as a retained counsel in a similar case. But if the appointed counsel is forced to make a choice whether to devote certain time to a fee-paying client or to an indigent, it is inevitable that the indigent's defense will suffer. It has been pointed out, too, that an appointed counsel may unconsciously weigh the vigor which he pursues the defendant's cause against his concern that he may incur the enmity of the court and the prosecution on behalf of a client who can not even pay for his services. Finally, appointed counsel will rarely be able to afford investigative and other essential services unless he is reimbursed for them.

The Criminal Justice Act, in recognition of the plight of the uncompensated attorney, allows for payment at $15 an hour for in-court time and $10 per hour outside of court, with a maximum of $500 for felonies and $300 for a misdemeanor. It authorizes reimbursement of out-of-pocket expenses to assigned counsel and to those who render investigative, expert or other services with a limit of $300 for each person. The ceilings placed on the hourly compensation of appointed counsel are extremely low when compared to the rates of retained lawyers. They may be justified, however, on the theory that the Act balances the need for compensating the attorney with his duty as an officer of the court. In any case, the absolute maximum on compensation and expenses is grossly unfair since the trial court should be able to determine whether a requested amount is reasonable or not. Under the South Carolina statute no limit is placed on the expenses incurred except that they must be reasonable.

CONCLUSIONS

Equal protection of the laws guarantees that there be no arbitrary classification of persons in the administration of the criminal laws. Since the normal defendant cannot be expected to understand the technicalities of the judicial proceedings and therefore present his own defense, can it honestly be stated that if an indigent is not supplied with counsel to represent him, he is being treated the same as the defendant with counsel? Should he be penalized because of his inability to point to the law clearly in his favor which would allow him to earn his freedom? Obviously not. Where, then, do we draw the line? The Supreme Court has, first of all, interpreted the Constitution to require counsel for the indigent at a felony trial, at the first appeal which the defendant has as a matter of right, at the arraignment, and at all other critical stages in the proceedings. Whether the "critical stage" test will be extended to the preliminary hearing or before, to the second appeal, and to all collateral proceedings is in doubt but from the point of view of equal treatment counsel should be provided at all of these.

As to the type of system which should be used there is a substantial divergence of opinion but the answer must depend on the circumstances. The defender system seems best adapted to larger jurisdictions where economies can be attained; where a competent, more experienced attorney can aid the defendant in getting treatment equal to that of other defendants; and where extensive files, investigative, clerical, and other services can be utilized in the most efficient manner. The primary advantage of the assigned counsel system appears to be the participation of a large percentage of the bar in the administration of criminal justice.

Problems were raised with reference to determining the eligibility of the defendant. On one hand it was found that only those defendants incapable of obtaining competent counsel should be provided with one, and, on the other hand, an attorney should be appointed as soon as possible after arrest so as to allow adequate time for the preparation of a defense. It was also pointed out that if the defendant has some available funds or acquires some during the pendency of the proceedings he should be required to contribute them to court or to the appointed attorney.

What about providing counsel for misdemeanors? It has been shown that no valid distinction can be drawn between felonies and misdemeanors merely on the basis of length of incarceration. If the defendant is subject to the deprivation of life or liberty, he should be supplied with counsel.

The Criminal Justice Act is a congressional recognition of the deficiencies previously found in the federal system. A number of problems, however, were encountered here, too, though: namely, lack of an option for the districts to employ a defender; lack of provision for an attorney at collateral proceedings; and the unrealistically low provision for maximum compensation. The proposed legislation in South Carolina and Illinois substantially improve these areas and others. Now what must be done is for other states to apply this learning and experience.

THE LAST DAYS OF BAIL

John V. Ryan

The modern system of granting a person accused of a crime his freedom based upon his ability to produce bail, security for his appearance at trial, developed in England. Originally, the sheriff had the discretionary authority to release the accused to the custody of a third party. Probably the sheriff, who was personally responsible for his prisoners, initiated the bail system to relieve himself of this burden. If the defendant failed to appear at trial, the third party was subjected to the punishment due the accused. As time went on, the third party was allowed to promise that he would forfeit a stated amount of personal or real property, rather than his freedom, if the defendant did not appear at his trial. Thus, the bail system of pretrial release evolved from a hostage arrangement into a surety relationship. Soon thereafter, the courts usurped the sheriff's discretionary power to allow an alleged criminal his freedom pending trial. With this innovation the bail system in England reached the stage of evolution at which we find it today.

Because of the broad frontier and mobile population of the United States, the private surety device was not feasible. The defendant was often a new arrival in the locale with no acquaintances in the area who were willing to risk becoming his surety. As a result, the commercial bail bondsman arose to replace the private surety in the American system of pretrial release. The bondsman, who is still a part of the American bail scheme, demands a premium from the accused; in return he will put up the security necessary to free the man. Since the bondsman makes his living by being a professional surety, the bases upon which he decides whether or not he will put up bail for a particular defendant are commercial and not personal. If he feels a prisoner might not appear at trial, he will either hedge against the possible forfeiture by demanding collateral or refuse to make his service available to the prisoner. Although the bail system in the United States has evolved into a commercial bondsman system, the underlying policy of bail has remained the same—one arrested and accused of a crime may obtain his release pending trial if he can adequately assure the court that he will appear at the trial.

Thus, history indicates that the basic philosophy underlying the monetary bail system in the United States was imported from England. There is some dispute as to what place the bail system was given in the hierarchy of American jurisprudence. Some scholars feel that the United States Constitution gives a right to bail. This point has never been authoritatively decided. The right to bail, however, in non-capital cases is a federal statutory right. Most states, in constitutional or statutory form, have a similar provision. The United States Constitution only mentions bail in the Eighth Amendment, which prohibits

Reprinted by Special Permission of the *Journal of Criminal Law, Criminology and Police Science* (Northwestern University School of Law), Copyright © 1967, Volume 58, Number 4.

excessive bail. But whether this prohibition applies to the states is a question that has never been decided by the Supreme Court. One reason that the Court has never been called upon to answer the question is that most states, in their constitution or statutory law, have a similar provision prohibiting excessive bail.

Despite the question of constitutional right, bail is a generally accepted procedure. Some theoreticians feel that some form of pretrial release is mandatory in our present day legal system. They base their argument, in part, upon the assumption that the presumption of innocence is more than an evidentiary trial rule, and attaches to an alleged criminal immediately upon his arrest. The other basis utilized by this school of thought to justify its position is that the defendant should be unhampered in the preparation of his defense. Incarceration, they say, unduly restricts the accused in the preparation of his defense.

A pretrial release system based upon the above premises would free the great majority of those who are arrested. It would detain only those who could not adequately assure the court that they would not flee to escape being tried. This is supposedly the policy underlying our present bail system, yet in practice, bail affects the release of only a small portion of those who might safely be allowed pretrial freedom. Whether or not one agrees that a pretrial release system is mandatory, there should be little opposition to the proposition that some form of pretrial release is advisable. By freeing most of those arrested, a vast amount of custodial expense could be saved. Pretrial release also makes the administration of criminal justice more palatable to the innocent accused. Indirectly, pretrial release lowers the expenses of certain welfare agencies. An important consideration is that it seems fair not to subject one to incarceration if he has not been tried and convicted of his crime. Lastly, if there were no pretrial release, and the mere allegation that a person had committed a crime would put him in jail, the abuse that would flow from such a procedure could be enormous indeed.

It has been suggested that the bail system does not fulfill its policy of releasing all who can adequately assure the court that they will appear at their trials. This is a harsh indictment of our bail system, but it is true. The reasons for the failure of bail to live up to its underlying policy are many. For one, the amount of bail one must pay to obtain his release is generally set solely by the nature of the offense. The court has a standard rate for each classification of offense which it applies, in most cases, to determine the amount at which bail is to be set. Bail so set is said not to be excessive, even though the defendant can not obtain the amount needed to affect his release.

It is true that there is some relation between the offense committed and the probability that the offender will flee to avoid prosecution. However, the relationship is slight, and there are many other indicia which more accurately gauge the possibility that an offender will flee. The theory of bail is that the accused has given over enough money to the court to satisfy the judge that the accused will attend his trial rather than suffer a forfeiture. Then certainly the amount at which bail is set should depend, at least in part, upon the financial status of the individual, since the wealth of the accused to some extent determines what amount of money is the amount which he would not wish to lose by not appearing at his trial. When bail is set solely with regard to the nature of the offense, many who offer little risk of non-appearance are kept in jail because they can not tender to the court the security demanded. Hence, the bail system as administered today is unfair to the poor person.

A digression seems appropriate at this juncture to point out a rather startling fact. The American bail system generally does not deter any person it releases from flight, because the defendant who jumps bail forfeits nothing. This anomaly arises because the commercial bondsman charges the prisoner a non-returnable premium. Thus, when the freed defendant fails to appear at trial, only the bondsman loses anything. To combat this situation the bondsman, in some cases, demands collateral in the amount of the bond. Thus, he, in effect, forces the prisoner to be his own surety, and a mere matter of liquidability forces the defendant to pay the bondsman a premium for the bondsman's service. And since he may demand collateral, or refuse his services, the bondsman may decide who is to go free and who is to stay in jail. Hence, the bondsman, and not the judge, really determines who obtains pretrial release, and then by a non-judicial process.

Another reason why the bail system fails to release many who are theoretically eligible is because the system is used by some judges to keep people in jail. This is done in two ways. Some judges, although they realize that it is not necessary to assure the accused's presence at his impending trial, will set bail at the amount usually set for the offense. A less subtle method, but equally effective, is to set the bail in an excessive amount. The latter method works because usually by the time the prisoner has received a hearing by an appellate body on his claim that the amount of his bail is excessive, his trial has already ended. If the prisoner was found not guilty, then the question is moot. If he was convicted, he faces the difficult task of proving that the detention was prejudicial to the outcome of his case. In the event the prisoner is granted a hearing prior to his trial, he still stands little chance of getting released. This is due to the rule in most jurisdictions that the order of the bail-setting official will not be overturned unless the accused can demonstrate a flagrant abuse of discretion. But, even if he adequately proves his point, there is no guarantee that the appellate court will reset the bail at an amount within the defendant's financial capabilities.

If one were to look for the intrinsic fault in our present system of pretrial release, from which all the above evils flow, he would find it to be that the bail system demands money be paid for one's release. The monetary element of the system discriminates against the indigent; and the indigent or nearly indigent comprise about one-half of all those in the United States who are accused of crimes. The bail system subjects this segment of the population to incarceration, and frees the wealthy. This violates the principle of equal protection under the law, as the Supreme Court expounded it, because the poor are entitled to the same rights and privileges under the law as are the wealthy.

The Supreme Court has not yet faced the question of whether the bail system, as practiced today, is a denial of equal protection. But if it does, it will probably answer the question affirmatively. The recent expansion of the concept of equal protection, that money should not determine the quality of justice an accused receives, draws one to this conclusion. Even if bail is only a statutory right of the defendant, granting such a right only to the rich is a denial of equal protection.

If the judicial branch has been slow in acting on the monetary bail problem, some legislatures, law-enforcement agencies and private groups have not.

The pioneer among the private groups is the Vera Foundation. This eleemosynary organization instituted the Manhattan Bail Project, a release on personal recognizance experiment. The purpose of the Project was to develop and test procedures and standards which would effectively enable one to estimate the probability that an accused, if released, would appear at his trial. Once these were established, prisoners who met the criteria were recommended for release. The only security required of these prisoners to obtain their release was a promise that they would present themselves at their respective trials. Law students were used to interview the prioners and verify the information. Another Vera Foundation experiment, complementary to the Manhattan Bail Project, was the Manhattan Summons Project. This experiment took place at the station houses rather than the jails. When a suspect was brought to the station he was interviewed, and, if he qualified, a recommendation was made to the desk officer to issue a summons to him rather than arrest him.

The Illinois legislature recently enacted a noteworthy innovation. Under the new practice an accused can secure his release by depositing with the court security worth ten percent of the amount of his bail. The security may take the form of cash, personal or real property. If he appears at the subsequent trial, ninety percent of the security is returned to him.

These and other new devices, praiseworthy as they may be, are not enough. The cash bail plan, while injecting some real financial deterrent into the bail system, still discriminates against the poor. The Vera projects only aid those who offer virtually no risk of non-appearance at trial. Moreover, the interviewers can only recommend, and the official who sets bail is free to ignore the recommendation. Also, neither the Vera projects nor their progeny included all classes of offenses. The pilot program excluded recidivists and those thought to be unsafe to release on recognizance. Probably the bail system, based as it is on financial status, can not be adjusted within its traditional confines to alleviate its evils. This is because the basic flaw, money, is inherent in such a system. Thus, our legislatures must develop a new pretrial release process. Something other than a financial deterrent method should be adopted.

The Vera Foundation has, to some degree, solved the legislatures' problems of what type of a system should replace the present bail system. The projects have shown that many of those accused of crimes may be released on their word, because there are environmental deterrents inherent in our society strong enough to stay them from flight. These projects show that when a person has his family, friends and job all in one locale, he will rarely break such ties to avoid prosecution.

It is true that many can not qualify for release under the Manhattan standards, but this does not mean that the basic theory behind the projects is not applicable to the American system of criminal justice. The basic theory of the Vera projects was that non-monetary deterrents to flight will be more effective than the present financial deterrent system. Hence, by incorporating other deterrents, in addition to the environmental ones, into the system many more persons could be released upon their own recognizance. The most utilitarian deterrent which comes to mind is the criminal sanction. That is, a recognizance jumper would be subjected to criminal penalties. Non-financial conditions could be imposed upon the defendant to accommodate some portion of accused criminals to whom release on personal recognizance can not be made available. These conditional releases could, for example, take the form of release in the custody of a third party, release only during the day time, or release restricting the defendant's freedom to a certain locality or place of residence. Conditional releases are actually just other forms of non-financial deterrents to flight.

The foregoing demonstrates that the bail system can not continue to co-exist with other, more deep-seated, principles of our legal system, and that there are reasonable alternatives available. The next few years will see great changes in this area. The remainder of this Comment is devoted to suggesting the form the changes should take.

There is no need for pretrial release if one is not arrested. It is not necessary to arrest a person to compel him to appear in court to answer charges against him. The issuance of a summons or a citation can serve the same purpose. A police officer could be empowered to give a citation to any person whom the officer feels is releasable on his own recognizance. Such a device has many advantages. The officer, and the accused, would not have to spend the time involved in traveling to the station, and the ensuing booking, printing, and the various reports that are required when a person is arrested. Also, there would be no need for a bail-setting hearing. The citation method would promote better feelings in the public mind about the police, since the minor violators will not be dragged off to jail as is now the practice. On a practical level, it would save custodial costs, and the savings could be diverted to other areas of law enforcement.

There could be some disadvantages in the system. For one thing, the law officer will not be able to determine if the person is wanted in connection with another crime. The other patent disadvantage in the citation system is that the officer can not adequately verify the information he must elicit from the accused upon which to base his determination of whether he will arrest the accused or issue a citation. These inherent disadvantages can be offset, at least in part, by the intelligent use of discretion on the part of the officer. If he feels the accused is lying as to his past record or personal data, he should bring the defendant to the station house.

One might object that the police officer will not be able to intelligently determine whom he should arrest and whom he should cite. This objection is unfounded for two reasons. First, the police officer makes difficult decisions every day. There is no reason to suspect that he can not learn to apply the release standards appropriately. Secondly, the officer, at present, decides, largely on subjective grounds, whether to arrest or to release a suspect. The injection of a middle ground, issuance of a citation, between the poles of arrest and release, does not seem too burdensome or difficult a duty to impose on the police officer. There may be some concern as to the constitutionality of allowing an officer such wide discretion in denying a person his freedom on subjective grounds. Yet, he does the same thing when he arrests someone. When he performs this function he decides whether one will keep his freedom or not. Both of the above objections seem to take on a less bright hue when one recalls that a form of the citation system has been in effect in the area of traffic violations for some time.

There is a danger that the police officer will be reluctant to use the citation method due to an antipathy to change or personal perverseness, preferring to arrest the wrongdoers. To combat this situation, the legislature could expressly state in the act the policy that the citation method is to be used to its fullest extent.

Another solution is to have the officer file a written report explaining why he arrested a suspect rather than issuing him a citation. The most drastic move would be to make it mandatory that the officer issue citations in certain instances. For example, the statute could dictate that the officer release all those accused of a crime whose maximum penalty is less than the maximum penalty for the failure to appear in compliance with a citation. Exceptional circumstances, which justify the officer arresting an individual, should be enumerated in the statute. Thus, the defendant who is intransigent, belligerent, clearly unqualified for release, or whom the officer feels is lying about his background should come under the ambit of exceptions.

Let us assume that the officer decides to arrest an individual, rather than issue a citation to him, and brings the defendant to the station. At this point a precinct summons system, similar to the Manhattan Summons Project, should be made available to the defendant. The advantages of the system are similar to the advantages of the citation system; it saves costs and promotes good public relations.

One may wonder why the station house summons is needed if there is a citation system in effect. One reason is that the station house summons device is more sophisticated than the citation plan. The interviewer can make a much more complete survey of the defendant's background than can the police officer, and can quickly verify the information. Hence, the desk officer who decides whether to book the accused or issue a summons to him can make a better informed determination of the releasability of the defendant than can the officer on the beat. Another reason that a station house summons program is advisable is that both the interviews and release decisions are performed by persons not involved in the events leading up to the appearance of the defendant in the station house. Hence, a dispassionate judgment as to the releasability of the accused may be obtained by using the station house summons system. Finally, the interviewer and the desk officer will accrue a certain expertise in these matters not found in the ordinary police officer. Since the release decision can be made prior to incarceration, this second pre-arrest hearing is not a duplication, but a much needed implementation of the police officer's release decision.

One aspect of the summons plan which merits close consideration is how one keeps the interview from being used as an interrogatory device. When one considers the zeal of some law enforcement officials and prosecutors, it seems wise to exclude them from participating in the interview process. The safest course would be to make the interview and its fruits inadmissible in any judicial proceeding except the bail hearing and any appeal therefrom. This would eliminate the possibility of using the interview to elicit incriminating evidence. Also, it would not subject the accused to the necessity of foregoing the interview and possible release if he wishes to assert his privilege against self-incrimination.

To insure full utilization of the summons system, incentives similar to those enumerated in relation to the sidewalk citation system may be adopted.

If the desk officer determines that the defendant is not eligible for release, then the individual will be jailed. Thereafter, as soon as possible, the prisoner should be given a hearing before a judicial official to determine whether he is available for pretrial release. One may question whether such a third stage is necessary, since the defendant has already had two chances to be released. The reason for this third step is, at base, that it would be imprudent to not have, at some point in the system, a judicial *determination* of the releasability of the defendant. The fear of misuse and abuse of a process so dependent upon discretion and subjectivity draws one to the conclusion that the judiciary should have a place in the system. A secondary reason for a judicial hearing, after arrest, is that it is the earliest time that the accused may obtain counsel. Representation of the accused by an attorney could be an aid to the official in making the correct decision. For example, he could bring before the hearing officer, in a professional manner, any facts inadvertently overlooked at the lower level hearings, which might bear upon the releasability of his client.

To assure that the post-arrest hearing official releases all those who could be released, some type of force factor should be introduced into the system. One professional study group draft on proposed standards for pretrial release suggests that all those accused of misdemeanors should be presumed releasable on their own recognizance. It contemplates that there be no investigation by the court of the defendant's background unless the state requests that the accused be denied pre-trial release. There appears to be no valid reason for not expanding the presumption to include all those cases where the accused is charged with a felony whose maximum sentence is less than the maximum sentence imposable for recognizance jumping.

If the state asks that the accused be denied release, what factors should be investigated and brought to the attention of the official? The following have been suggested as guides:

a)   The length of defendant's residence in the community.

b)   The defendant's employment status and history and his financial condition.

c)   The defendant's family ties and relationships.

d)   The defendant's reputation, character and mental condition.

e)   The defendant's prior criminal record, including any record of prior release on recognizance or on bail.

f)   The nature of the offense presently charged and the apparent probability of conviction and the likely sentence.

g)   Any other factors indicating the defendant's ties to the community or bearing on the risk of willful failure to appear.

This seems to be a satisfactory list. Especially gratifying to those who adhere to the Vera Foundation theory is the inclusion of an omnibus clause, provision "g," which indicates that the authors of the draft consider the pretrial release program to be based upon the character and background of the individual. Since this policy is recognized, the authors indicate that other factors, which are out of the ordinary, may be of prime importance in determining the releasability of an individual.

The results of the investigation should be put in written form and presented to the official who is to set bail, along with any recommendation as to the releasability of the accused and any conditions which the interviewer feels are necessary.

The most difficult point in a comprehensive pretrial release system is what is to be done with the prisoner the official feels is not eligible for release. The solution, and apparently the only one, is to allow the accused to be detained pending trial. The present system detains those who can not adequately assure the court they will appear at their trials if released. The problem arises when one ventures into the area of detaining those who present a serious threat to society, and not a threat to the integrity of the judicial process.

Although it has never been proven, there have been repeated suggestions that the bail setter often sets bail with the intention of keeping a defendant in jail to protect society or a certain individual. That this manipulation of the bail system takes place is practically unprovable, since the bail setter has such wide discretion. If preventive detention serves a beneficial public interest, then it should be frankly recognized and allowed. However, the rights and interests of the defendant should be adequately protected. Under the present bail system the defendant has virtually no protection.

One objection to pretrial detention is the possible prejudicial effect upon the outcome of the defendant's trial, due to the defendant's inability to prepare his defense as well as the free man. To keep intact the integrity of the guilt–determination process, such a possibility should be minimized. This end could be achieved by establishing a detention facility for those preventively detained or detained to prevent flight which is separate from the jail. Jail is a place to penalize and rehabilitate one convicted of a crime. Pretrial detainees are not being subjected to punishment for a crime, but are detained to insure that they will not injure the judicial process or society. Jail restricts the unconvicted accused to an extent greater than that required to adequately carry into effect the purpose of his detention.

If the result of the judicial release hearing is that the accused is to be detained, then he should be entitled to a *de novo* hearing before a court of general criminal jurisdiction. Such a hearing is necessary to safeguard all the rights of the accused. Since the contemplated pretrial release scheme is designed to release all but a few, the burden upon the criminal courts should be slight. Such a hearing would be much like the pretrial release hearing. The factors and their weighting should be open to contest by the accused. The procedure should not be adversary, in the sense that a duty should be imposed on both parties to bring all the pertinent facts before the judge, so that he may be aided in his decision-making function.

To alleviate the present problem of the slow appeal, a speedy appeal from the decision of the court of general criminal jurisdiction should be allowed. The present right of the accused to appeal from a bail decision is so slow that it is illusory. An almost immediate appellate process would, of course, be ideal in all criminal cases, but the bail situation should have priority on the appellate calendar. This proposition is made necessary if one agrees that pretrial incarceration influences the outcome of the defendant's trial. If one adheres to the beliefs that incarceration does not affect the outcome of the trial, then the immediacy of the appeal may not appear to be so strong. However, when one considers the nature of a release hearing as opposed to the nature of a criminal trial, the former still appears to hold its place of priority on appeal. More specifically, the guilty decision in a criminal trial is supposed to be based on evidence beyond a reasonable doubt that the accused committed a crime. The refusal of pretrial release can not be based upon evidence beyond a reasonable doubt. The release hearing must determine that the accused only *probably* committed a crime. But, the court must also decide if the threat that the accused will commit a future crime is so manifest that no form of conditional release will sufficiently insure against the commission of this future crime. Such a decision can not be said to be a moral certainty; it is only a prediction. Hence, should not one denied his freedom by a prediction have priority, on appeal, over one denied his freedom by a decision supposedly beyond a reasonable doubt?

In fact, this latter point illustrates the strongest objection to preventive detention. It is probable that a preventive detention plan will wrong some defendants, just as our system of criminal justice wrongly convicts some. But the present system of setting bail, with its almost complete lack of safeguards, in all probability, wrongs many more. The desired objective underlying an overt preventive detention system is to include as many safeguards as possible, to assure that the least number are wronged by the system.

There is a question of what classes of defendants should be preventively detained. A general answer is to hold only those who must be held. Those who pose a threat of immediate physical violence should be detained. Proven recidivists should be detained. Recognizance jumpers should be detained, but only if no conditional release is adequate to assure the court that such defendants will not appear at trial. Those who can not be released under any condition that will be adequate to restrain flight should be detained.

The most difficult case is the defendant who is free pending trial, and is accused of committing another crime while free. No set rule can be stated in these matters. The nature of the second crime and its relation to the original offense could be important. Yet, the mere allegation of a second crime should not be enough to deny release after arrest, unless the circumstances are such that, regardless of the original offense, release would be denied. To allow the first offense to be automatically encompassed in the second release determination would open the system to abuses. It is submitted that the only solution available is that if the state wishes to deny the defendant his freedom, because he has been charged with a second crime while free pending trial for a separate crime, then the state must prove by a preponderance of the evidence before a court of general criminal jurisdiction that the accused committed the first and the second crimes. On first reading, this may appear to be a too strict requirement, but anything less would lack sufficient safeguards for the accused, and allow preventive detention to be used as a method of punitive detention.

It should be stressed that this half-trial of the second crime should take place within a very short time after arrest so there will be no undue incarceration of the defendant. Another important point is that the half-trial should be an adversary proceeding, to insure that the state is actually put to its proof.

A constitutional argument, that preventive detention punishes an accused without a trial, is not overpowering. One answer is that the bail system in some jurisdictions detains those who apparently pose a threat to the community. The prime examples are persons accused of first degree murder, who are often denied bail. Another answer is that preventive detention, by way of civil commitment proceedings, has generally met no constitutional barrier partly because it is not a means of punishing the defendant but of safe-guarding the public. If preventive detention in the proposed system is used for the same purposes, then it also should be held constitutional, especially if the detainees are not placed in a facility housing convicted criminals.

Those who are ultimately detained should be tried quickly. To insure a speedy trial, a time limit should be imposed, and upon its expiration the accused should be freed pending trial, unless he caused the delay. A speedy trial requirement will forestall any use of the preventive detention system as a means to keep undesirables out of circulation. It will also help to make the system unavailable for use as a means of punishment.

Another requirement, which some feel will constrain the state to bring the preventive detainee to trial quickly, is to deduct detention time from his sentence or pay him a per diem rate if he is not convicted. Valid objections to such a suggestion may be raised. In the first place, if detention pending trial is not viewed as punishment, then it should not act to mitigate punishment. Secondly, the mere payment of money will be small solace to a detainee who is found not guilty. However, the greatest objection is that the time deduction and liquidated damages aspects of the plan could influence the enforcement officials and the courts in an undesirable manner. They might too freely detain on the theory that the detainee, whether guilty or innocent, is not grievously harmed by detention. Such an outlook destroys the entire pretrial release system, which should operate to free all who can be freed.

The suggested system does away with monetary bail. Bail arose and flowered during a period when the law had little regard for the rights of the poor. Debtors prisons flourished. Workhouses were used to contain paupers, who were considered a moral pestilence. The adherence to the archaic system of monetary bail is inconsistent with our present legal thinking. The monetary bail system can not long survive the recent recognition of the precept that a poor man is entitled to the same justice as the wealthy man.

ALTERNATIVES TO ARREST OF
LESSER OFFENDERS

Cyril D. Robinson

In most states, initiation of criminal prosecution proceedings may be begun only by arrest, except where otherwise provided by statute. No other legal means of beginning such prosecution is provided. In states where it is possible to begin a prosecution by means other than arrest, "the police ordinarily view arrest as *the* way in which the process is involved and they are seldom instructed to the contrary."

Arrest has thus become the ordinary mode of beginning a criminal prosecution. As a result, arrest is not a process merely preliminary to possible punishment; it frequently *is* the punishment where the lesser offender is concerned. The trial then becomes not the determiner of guilt or innocence but a procedure for release of the accused from the punishment previously meted out. That a person may be arrested only upon probable cause is no justification if he need not have been arrested at all.

This procedural excess has been accompanied by substantive legislation that has attempted to deal with the host of important social problems confronting our state legislatures almost solely by penal measures. Such laws have filled our jails unnecessarily with alcoholics, vagrants, narcotics addicts, gamblers, prostitutes, and sexual deviates. In addition, they have generally failed to deal with problems arising out of private disputes and marital quarrels, except through regular criminal channels.

Consequently, the arrest problem in the United States manifests itself in two ways. Many lesser offenders are needlessly arrested where prosecution might have been begun by some nonarrest alternative; and certain types of problems which are not criminal in nature are dealt with through criminal proceedings, usually begun by arrest.

Growth of Power to Arrest

The history of arrest has been one of constantly expanding power, moving from the flagrant to the lesser offender. This growth began with a power to arrest when the offender was caught in the act of committing a felony. Then came a right to arrest on reasonable belief that a felony had been committed. It is only by statute that police in some states have been given the right to arrest when they have reasonable grounds to believe that *any* offense is being or has been committed, thereby effacing the common law distinction between misdemeanor and felony that permitted the officer to arrest for misdemeanor on the spot only when a breach of the peace was about to be committed or was committed in his presence, or when the offender was attempting to escape.

From *Crime and Delinquency*, vol. 11, January 1965, pp. 8–21. Reprinted by permission of the National Council on Crime and Delinquency and the author.

Physical arrest became the sole means of exercising the legal right of one man, representing the state, to have power over another. Although it has long passed away in the civil law, in criminal matters it remains the accepted manner of seizing jurisdiction over an offender.

It is time to reconsider the question of when actual physical custody is necessary and when it is not.

Vera Project—A Breakthrough

Protests against unnecessary arrests are not new. However, until recently, the question of arrest was obscured by its counterpart—the problem of bail. It was arrest that put the suspect in jail, but it was lack of funds to make bail that kept him there. Reasonably enough, most commentators directed their objections toward the defects in the bail system, but all such criticism had little effect on bail practice until the Vera Foundation Project in the Magistrate's Felony Court and Court of Special Sessions in New York City in 1961. Vera was unique in that it did not gather facts solely to *argue* the injustice and irrationality of the bail system; rather, it *demonstrated* that defendants could be safely released—by creating a functioning private model for such release at the side of the public one, thus eventually envisaging its replacement by a public agency. Accomplished through existing laws, this approach to law reform is revolutionary in nature and method and may be applied in other areas as well. One of the most conspicuous areas for reform is arrest procedure.

Just such a Vera project has been in operation for some months. Employing methods similar to those used in the bail project, a Vera representative at the police station interviews a prisoner brought to the station "to establish the eligibility . . . to receive a summons in lieu of arrest." If the Vera recommendation is favorable, the station officer must then decide whether to accept it. To begin with, the project has been limited to cases of simple assault and petty larceny, in one police district in New York City.

The effect of the Vera procedure is to move the release decision from the court to the police station, thus limiting detention for those chosen to the time necessary for forming a recommendation. Release is possible in as little as an hour and a half after the person reaches the station.

This system is almost certainly destined to be more widely applied. However, because this procedure represents such an improvement over the old, it actually presents a danger that other means of ameliorating the arrest-detention picture will not be sufficiently investigated. If arrest, detention, and release of an accused can be so regulated that it takes no more than an hour or two of his time, what more can we ask of a system of criminal justice? Surely we may ask whether the arrest was necessary in the first place, and we should investigate some alternatives to physical custody, such as the issuance of a notice to appear, in certain specified cases or circumstances, or at the discretion of the police officer.

Now that the Vera Arrest Project offers the possibility of substantial elimination of unnecessary pretrial detention, the objectionable aspects of arrest can be isolated and evaluated on their merits. Previously, although complaint was made about excessive arrests, it was the injurious effects of detention that were described. But arrest, of itself, is objectionable because the arrest record remains regardless of the disposition of the case; it "interrupts [the defendant's] personal affairs, subjects him to disagreeable contacts at the station house and inflicts also a certain amount of public disgrace"; "arrest itself is a punishment"; it may provoke rather than restrain violence; it may give rise to hostile attitudes toward the police; it may cause difficult legal problems; and it may allow certain illegal conduct to go unpunished because the officer feels that arrest, the sole means of invoking the process, is too severe.

From the police standpoint, employment of means other than arrest may lead to savings in manpower in addition to an improvement in the relations between the police and the community.

Current Nonarrest Alternatives

Although there is considerable statutory authority for a magistrate to issue summonses, there is little for the police officer to issue a notice to appear, except in traffic cases, and even where there is such legislation, it is infrequently utilized. Lack of experience and inadequate standards create skeptical attitudes in police toward the use of the notice to appear; and, restrictive interpretation explains, in part, why it is not used, even where specifically authorized. Moreover, in cases where arrest or custody serves no useful police purpose, there exists no legal obligation to proceed by more moderate means.

Conversely, across the country, diverse methods of informal procedures have arisen which ease arrest processes and constitute a certain nonarrest "discretion" not sanctioned by statute.

Many authors have pointed to England as a land where the summons is used extensively. This seems to be borne out by criminal statistics for England which show a large percentage of offenders "summoned" rather than "apprehended." But a recent study conducted by the writer in London showed that in the *cities* of England the arrest pattern is about the same as in the cities of the United States. The impression of widespread use of the summons comes from the combined statistics of country districts, where the summons is used for a high proportion of offenses, and the city areas, where it is rarely employed. What is true for "England" is not true for London.

There has yet to appear a description detailing how nonarrest procedures operate under a legislative scheme authorizing them, and until one is found, the steps taken to establish it will be without substantial precedent.

The Police Need for Arrest

It will be useful, in discussing the establishment of nonarrest procedures, to inquire into the assumed needs of the police to arrest the lesser offender. By "lesser offender" I mean a person who, left at large, is not a substantial danger to the community. It is here suggested that in such cases arrest and custody may serve no valid police need.

Traditionally, the system submits the lesser and the major offender to approximately the same procedural regime. All are arrested and detained, but, whereas the more serious offender is interrogated and investigated during this period of detention, the minor offender is merely "processed"—that is, subjected to a routine check-out, not because of the offense for which he was arrested, but on the chance that he may be wanted for some graver offense.

Although misdemeanants constitute at least 90 per cent of all persons arrested and charged with offenses, police thinking and procedures are geared primarily toward the investigation and prosecution of major crime. When does legal or administrative necessity dictate arrest? Police reasons for arrest and custody, compiled from empirical studies of specific police procedures developed over the years in the station house, are divided below into four categories.

I. *Custody* is necessary to perform *administrative and investigative functions.*

1. Interrogate in connection with the offense with which the alleged offender is to be charged.
2. Verify alibi.
3. Clear other offenses.
4. Discover accomplices.
5. Line-up and identify suspect as offender.
6. Confront suspect with complainant or witnesses.
7. Prevent tampering with the evidence or witnesses.
8. Prevent disclosure of the investigation.
9. Carry out administrative tasks: formal booking, preparation of case reports, transcribing statements and confessions.

II. *Custody* or *arrest* is necessary to perform certain *"assumed police functions"* which are not or cannot be accomplished at the time by other government agencies.

1. Provide protection—e.g., medical examination of prostitute; shelter of inebriate unable to take care of himself; safety of accused from harm threatened by crowd; prevention of threatened self-inflicted harm (possible suicide).
2. Maintain public's respect for police—e.g., by arresting person complaining publicly that another person is being unjustly arrested.
3. Satisfy public that justice will be done: arrest is evidence that police have acted.
4. Prevent continued criminal conduct pending trial—particularly true of burglary arrests.
5. Impress upon defendant the seriousness of his conduct—e.g., by arrest of a "drag race" driver.
6. Punish, by arrest, offender who might otherwise receive inadequate judicially imposed punishment.

III. *Arrest* is necessary to provide a legal basis for *search, identification, and restraint.*

1. Search for weapons or evidence.
2. Fingerprint accused and make identity check to see whether he is wanted for more serious offenses.
3. Impose physical restraint, prevent or stop violence, prevent flight, or prevent immediate repetition of offense.

IV. *Arrest* is necessary to assure *defendant's appearance in court.*

I. Administrative and
Investigative Needs

It is questionable whether the administrative and investigative needs listed above are applicable to the great majority of lesser offenders, except for those whose acts suggest, by their nature, the commission of more serious crimes, such as larceny. In these minor cases the accused normally goes to trial on the basis of the Field Arrest Report, information taken by the arresting officer. The busy detective or police officer, concerned with serious crime, has no time to take additional statements from the defendant, to say nothing of any witnesses. The extent of the police "need" for the arrest and custody of different classes of offenders can be determined only by observation of their procedures in these cases. As for administrative convenience, police sometimes do not even take fingerprints where the offense charged or the character of the offender is such that other more serious criminal activity is highly unlikely. Frequently the lesser offender's arrest and detention serve none of the purposes listed.

II. Assumed Police Functions

What have here been designated as assumed police functions may result from inadequate provisions by society for a means of handling such problems, which are so related in time and place to police duties that it may be possible only for the police to handle them initially, whether or not they are of a criminal nature. It is questionable, however, whether arrest is the best or should be the only response. Such low visibility decisions must be surfaced so that the limits of police action may be defined.

III. Search, Identification, and Restraint

Search

Where arrest itself confers certain prerogatives upon the police which they otherwise would not have, there is a natural tendency to take full advantage of its use. A search, under current law, may be made "incident to a lawful arrest" but may not be made without arrest and may not be made on the basis of a notice to appear. "As a consequence, the existence of grounds for arrest may result . . . in a decision by a police officer to declare a suspect under arrest so that a search can lawfully be made, although the officer has not in fact decided to take the person to the station, and will not so decide unless the search proves fruitful."

With reference to the minor offense, the doctrine has developed fairly recently that no search is permissible even where there is an arrest, if the search is completely unrelated to the offense. However, whereas the right to search following arrest has been restricted, the right to make a limited search without arrest for the police officer's protection—that is, to frisk the suspect—has been recognized and is present even without sufficient grounds for arrest.

The Illinois statute presents the police officer with a conundrum. It gives him discretion to issue a notice to appear when he might otherwise arrest. But he may release the suspect only when he "is satisfied that there are no grounds for criminal complaint against the person arrested." Hence it is not possible for the officer to arrest, search, and then release if he finds nothing. Once having made a search—which assumes arrest—he cannot give a notice to appear without putting the search in jeopardy. Whether this presents a problem with reference to nonarrest in the case of a lesser offense will depend on the nature of the offense. For any offense involving possession, such as possession of policy slips, a search is necessary to obtain evidence to sustain the charge, while in the case of simple assault it is not necessary. Nevertheless, if the police officer is in doubt about the right to search without arrest—for example, to search for weapons to assure his own protection—or if he is at all hopeful that the search may reveal some "windfall benefit," such as narcotics, he will arrest and search. One suggestion for overcoming this reluctance to give up the search privilege is that the officer be authorized to release after lawful arrest and search; another is that the issuance of a notice to appear, in lieu of arrest for certain offenses, be made compulsory. Another method might be to allow search related to the offense without arrest, thereby eliminating arrest solely for the purpose of search.

Identification

A fear that persons charged as lesser offenders, and released without an identity check, might well be wanted persons is an important consideration in the policeman's resistance to use of a notice to appear. This suggests the need for a study to determine the actual statistical incidence of such occurrences, where major offenders have been uncovered as a result of taking them into custody on lesser offenses. Such a study may show that, in regard to persons arrested for certain offenses, this incidence is so low that the time spent in checking is not worthwhile. If this is true then there is no reason why an on-the-spot decision may not be made by the officer, either to arrest or to make the requisite check from the scene by telephoning a central clearing bureau.

Restraint

In considering arrest to prevent physical violence or flight, we approach the historical roots of arrest, unencumbered by the correlative police functions we have discussed. One must, however, distinguish between arrest and restraint. There are situations in which restraint of the suspect to prevent violence need not necessarily lead to arrest. In a simple fight between two parties, where the investigation is completed on the spot and the parties may be sent on their way, the matter may be disposed of by notices to appear. The duty of the police is to reduce and not to provoke violence; as the Foster case illustrates, the arrest itself may at times incite the person arrested to renewed violence of an even more dramatic character. The person to be arrested in such a situation is already in an agitated state; arrest, far from reducing his rage, may provoke it, with consequent danger to the arrestee as well as the officers.

If an officer is authorized to arrest or not arrest, he has the legal authority to restrain the person to the extent necessary for making such a decision. If his intent is not to make a formal arrest, mere restraint should not be held to constitute arrest.

Even in situations where arrest seems obviously mandatory—say, to prevent flight or likely repetition of violence—it may be avoided. In the first instance, the concern is that the offender may escape before being identified. But once identified, he is as likely to appear for trial as another. Where repetition of violence is feared, the use of alternatives to arrest will depend on the ability of the police to reduce the likelihood of such renewed violence by means other than temporary removal of the person from the scene by arrest.

Counseling the police in their relations with the public has been attempted. Further experiments in this direction would be salutary. If it is the job of the police to keep order, then peacemaking skills should be developed.

IV. Assurance of Court Appearance

The ultimate aim of arrest and custody is to assure the defendant's appearance in court. However, such assurance is absolute only insofar as those persons remain in custody pending trial. The immediate purpose of arrest is to halt and identify the person committing the offense. Thereafter, prediction can be made, on the basis of the facts obtained, of the likelihood of the offender's appearing voluntarily. The question is, can these two functions be accomplished by officers at the scene, or should the person be brought to the station, as in the present self-imposed limitation of the Vera Arrest Project?

Problems of identity may be divided into (1) refusal to give identifying information; (2) inability to give the information; and (3) identification not available on the person or not readily obtainable at the time.

1. Refusal to present identification will almost always arouse the suspicion, if not the ire, of the police officer, and generally results in arrest and further check-out. This seems inevitable unless the person is well known to the officer or the information can be obtained from a witness.

2. The person may be in such a state, intoxicated or mentally incompetent, that he is unable to identify himself. If this inability demonstrates a physical or mental defect, the solution is not to make a formal criminal arrest but to conduct the person to the proper agency for handling such persons.

3. There will be a number of situations where the person has no convincing proof of identity with him; it is not possible to obtain verification because of the hour or the distance from the man's residence; and there is no one to verify his identity by phone. Normally, however, except in some situations where numbers of offenders are involved, the officer obtains the necessary information for his report at the scene and thereupon can make a decision. The major problem is the development of a routine procedure for the policeman to follow and the willingness of police administration to encourage the making of such nonarrest decisions.

"Rootless Indigents"

Assuming the offender has been identified and is not "needed" by the police, what standards may be applied at the scene of the offense so that the minor offender may be released without arrest? The Vera Foundation studies and similar projects all work on the same assumptions—that there are "good risks" and "bad risks" in terms of likelihood of court appearance; that the good risks may be released with a high probability that they will keep their promise to appear in court as scheduled; that the bad risks are either an unknown quantity or at least do not have enough to recommend them; that the distinction between the two groups can be based on the person's "roots in the community" and that this last is ascertainable from a verification of data concerning his family, employment, residence, and other personal information solicited by the interviewer; and finally, that if all persons awaiting trial were indiscriminately freed, without careful checking of their "roots," larger numbers of defaults than presently occur would result. But whether such assumptions are true we do not know for they have never been tested.

The consequences of such thinking are readily apparent. It has been said that issuing a summons to a "rootless indigent" "may not be logical or practical." Of the Vera defendants interviewed for release on their own recognizance, 65 per cent have been recommended as good risks.

What such procedures attempt to do is to predict human behavior—specifically, to predict whether a person charged with an offense will appear voluntarily for his trial. Much more elaborate and supposedly highly reliable designs for predicting the incidence of juvenile delinquency have recently been criticized as having built-in success factors. The "roots in the community" doctrine, although never clearly rationalized, seems to be based on the meta-phorical "common sense" idea that a man with such "roots" will not flee.

The Vera statistics of forfeiture indicate that only 0.7 per cent of the defendants released through its program failed to appear, compared with 2.4 per cent for the rest of the country, which would seem to document the effectiveness of Vera's careful screening. We do not know, however, what percentage of the forfeitures outside New York City should be attributed to inadequate notice, misunderstanding of court procedure, etc., rather than intent to escape trial. Moreover, it seems strange and pertinent that there are so few bond forfeitures throughout the country in view of the uncoordinated, infinitely variable, and inefficiently run systems which now prevail. The complaint against the bail system was never that the number of forfeitures was too large but rather that the number of persons released was too small, and also that the sole criterion for release was money. The major objective of any substitute system, therefore, must be to reduce to an absolute minimum the number of those detained, rather than reducing the number of defaulters to the vanishing point. Whether these "rootless indigents" would appear if released has never been tested because these persons remain in jail under either the old bail system or the Vera arrest projects.

Vera itself has suggested a possible answer to this dilemma:

> In most cases judges approach the question of bail with an assumption that unless a threat of financial loss is imposed the defendant, who is presumed innocent, will flee (and thus in some states become guilty of a second crime by failing to appear). Experience would indicate that the courts might more logically assume that all defendants will return and require rebuttal of the assumption by substantial evidence of the likelihood of flight.

All such suggestions will continue to be speculative until society takes the "risk" of releasing those "rootless" ones in order to find out what their response will be. The fundamental error in "bad risk" reasoning is its acceptance of the assumption that lack of job, family, permanent residence, etc., is evidence of intention to avoid appearance for trial. The collected data do *not* demonstrate that a person lacking reliable contacts is not likely to appear for trial; rather, the facts indicate only that if he fails to appear, it will be difficult to find him. The decision to deny "bench parole" to a person *because* he doesn't have a family and a home and a job means only that we think such persons *in general* are less likely to appear for trial than those who have these "roots." But about any such "rootless" *individual* we know nothing. We know only that if he does not appear for trial we will not know where to look for him. How can he prove that he does not intend flight? The "bad risk" approach makes a status, nonindividualized judgment based on an untested assumption, in the face of the fact that only a few individuals avoid appearance. This reasoning keeps large numbers in jail to prevent a small number from fleeing. To demand communal roots which the defendant is unable to secure raises considerable problems for the equal administration of the law.

In view of such elaborate precautions, the risk to society should be substantial. We have become accustomed to allowing dangerous professional criminals, never short of money to pay bail, to remain at large. It would seem, in the face of this, that we should also accept the possibility that the lesser offender may not appear in court; in that event, nonappearance is the only risk involved. Could we not put our efforts to better advantage, perhaps into a well-publicized, efficient system of finding those who default rather than erecting an involved scheme of prognostication or, alternatively, imprisoning those we believe *might* default? Release should be allowed unless there is some countervailing evidence against it.

The rule should be that unless there are facts which show affirmatively that the offender is unlikely to come to court voluntarily or there is some other legitimate reason for arrest, he should be summoned or given a notice to appear. There should be a *reason* for each arrest. If we are able to eliminate other risks, the risk of nonappearance should be borne by society in exchange for the benefits of nonimprisonment and nonarrest.

Conclusion

What is being advocated in this discussion is not wholesale release on the scene by the police officer, but rather the examination of certain basic assumptions underlying both the present system of bail and the improved Vera system, with reference to the lesser offender, so that it will not take another fifty years to improve the improvements.

The establishment of nonarrest procedures for lesser offenses will present many problems, some of which have been examined here. For the development of standards to guide the police officer, perhaps a Vera-type pilot project could be initiated and staff members could be sent with police on patrol, for the purpose of analyzing such problems. As in the present arrest project, the staff member could advise the police officer on whether, in his opinion, the man should be released on notice to appear.

But what must be kept in mind constantly, as we approach these problems, is the advice of Judge Botein of the Appellate Division of New York State:

What is also needed is a conditioning of judges, lawyers and, most of all, the public to the fact that our society will not collapse if, now and then, a person released without bail fails to appear for trial. Our society has not collapsed when persons who furnished bail failed to appear—"took it on the lam." Our judges must be encouraged not to try to play it utterly safe. They should not be fearful that, if they make a mistake in a rare case, they are going to be pounced on by the bar and the newspapers.

THE GRAND JURY UNDER ATTACK

Part One

Richard D. Younger

As Justice James Wilson took his place at the front of the hall of the Philadelphia Academy, he was clearly pleased to see that so many cabinet officers, members of Congress, and leaders of Philadelphia society had braved the winter weather to attend his weekly law lecture. This was the Justice's second winter of lecturing as Professor of Law in the newly established College of Philadelphia. His course had been a tremendous social success. The first series opened auspiciously December 15, 1790 before a distinguished audience which included President and Mrs. Washington. Among his fellow lawyers, however, Wilson's discourses had been received with reserved acclaim. Many resented his severe criticism of Blackstone, while others felt disturbed by his ultra-Federalist views.

Justice Wilson's topic for discussion this evening was the jury, and he began with an analysis of the role of the grand jury in American law. He rejected summarily the views of those persons who would restrict the grand jury to the consideration of matters laid before them by the public prosecutor or given them in charge by the court. He stated that such a concept presented "a very imperfect view of the duty required of grand jurors." Their oath assigned no limit to their area of inquiry save their own diligence. Wilson stated that he saw in the grand jury more than a body set up merely to seek out law violators. He viewed it as an important instrument of democratic government, "a great channel of communication between those who make and administer the laws and those for whom the laws are made and administered." Elaborating upon his statement, the Justice pointed out that all the operations of government and all its officers came within the view of grand juries, giving them an unrivaled ability to suggest public improvements and expose corruption in government.

Justice Wilson was not the first American jurist to express such views regarding the grand jury. Almost ten years earlier Judge Francis Hopkinson of Philadelphia had denounced judicial encroachment upon juries. He too stated that from the terms of their oath, there was "no bound or limit set to any number or sort of persons of whom they are bound to inquire." However, Hopkinson denied that judges could impose directions upon grand jurors. Early in 1793 Secretary of the Treasury Alexander Hamilton had instructed customs officials to report to him all infractions of the neutrality laws. Thomas Jefferson protested vigorously against this unwarranted invasion of the province of grand juries. He objected to giving government officials authority to act as criminal

Reprinted by Special Permission of the *Journal of Criminal Law, Criminology and Police Science* (Northwestern University School of Law), Copyright © 1955, Parts I and II, Volume 46, Number 1, Part III, Volume 46, Number 2.

informers and pointed out that the advantage of inquests was that "a grand juror cannot carry on a systematic persecution against a neighbor whom he hates because he is not permanent in the office." If the grand jury were to serve as an instrument of the people it was necessary that any private citizen have the right to go before a grand inquest. In 1794 Attorney General of the United States William Bradford announced that it was not necessary for persons to approach a grand jury through a committing magistrate.

In spite of these pronouncements, however, not all jurists were certain that independent grand juries were a good thing. Judge Alexander Addison of Pennsylvania feared that danger lay in giving jurors too free a hand in their investigations. In a charge delivered in 1792 he went on record as favoring restrictions upon grand juries. Judge Addison cautioned the jurors that they could act only when a matter came within the actual knowledge of one of them, or when the judge or district attorney submitted an indictment for their consideration. They could investigate matters of public importance only if the judge charged them to do so. Such a restricted view of jury powers prohibited them from summoning witnesses on their own initiative and indicting persons on the basis of testimony received. It had the effect of placing these juries almost entirely under the control of the court.

Restrictions imposed by courts were not the only means by which the juries were deprived of their powers of investigation. In Connecticut, through long practice, it had almost *ceased to exist as an investigating body*. Each town in the state still elected two persons each year to serve as jurors, but they no longer met as a body unless summoned by a court. Indictment by a full jury was mandatory only in case of crimes punishable by death or life imprisonment. In all other cases it became the practice for individual jurors or the district attorney to sign a complaint when they received information of a crime. Grand jurors in Connecticut tended to become *informing officers with an annual term of office, possessed of the authority to make complaints individually, a power which they did not have at common law.* As a result of such a system, they met infrequently as a body and through disuse lost most of their broad powers of initiating investigations.

Opposition of Reformers

The grand jury also became the target of those who denounced the institution in the name of reform. In England, Jeremy Bentham, the great codifier and legal reformer, struck out at the grand inquest as "an engine of corruption" which was "systematically packed" on behalf of the upper classes. He charged that juries in Britain had become assemblies composed almost exclusively of gentlemen, "to the exclusion of the Yeomen." In addition to its misuse, Bentham opposed it on grounds of efficiency. As a utilitarian, he had little patience with a body composed of "a miscellaneous company of men" untrained in the law. He believed that a professionally trained prosecutor could perform the functions of a grand jury with far greater efficiency and with less expense to the people and less bother to the courts.

Bentham's reform proposals received wide circulation in the United States and led American legal scholars to reassess the value of the grand jury. Some came to the conclusion that public indifference and apathy seriously impaired its usefulness. They blamed juries themselves for criticism because they frequently neglected to conduct investigations into the conditions of prisons, roads, bridges and nuisances within the community. Edward Livingston, prominent Jeffersonian, became a disciple of Bentham in the United States and an ardent advocate of codification. In 1821 the state of Louisiana commissioned him to revise and codify its criminal laws. The procedural provisions of the completed Livingston Code confined grand juries to passing upon indictments submitted to them. They could only determine whether persons had violated penal laws of the state, but would have no power to initiate presentments or express their opinions on other matters. Livingston would limit judges to a mere statement of the law when addressing the jury, ruling out all remarks of a political nature. These restrictions incorporated in the proposed Louisiana Code met the whole-hearted approval of Chancellor James Kent of New York, in spite of the fact that he disapproved of codification. The New York jurist and law professor congratulated Livingston on the section of his code which severely limited grand jury activity, stating, "I am exceedingly pleased with the provision confining grand juries to the business of the penal law and not admitting any expression of opinion on other subjects."

While a few American legal scholars were hoping to curb the inquisitorial powers of the jury, a western court spoke out forcefully in favor of very broad powers for grand inquests. In 1829 a grand jury in St. Louis, Missouri embarked upon an investigation of gambling in the community. They summoned a great many witnesses, questioned them on a wide variety of subjects, and indicted various persons on the basis of this testimony. Several of those indicted asked the court to quash the indictments on the grounds that the jurors had exceeded their authority by engaging in a "fishing expedition" with no particular offense in mind. The Supreme Court of Missouri, however, upheld the jurors and declared that to hold otherwise "would strip them of their greatest utility and convert them into a mere engine to be acted upon by circuit attorneys or those who might choose to use them." Chief Justice Lemuel Shaw of Massachusetts echoed the sentiments of the Missouri court concerning the need for independent grand jury action. He told members of a Massachusetts inquest that they alone, because of the method of their selection and the temporary nature of their authority, were "beyond the reach of fear or favor, or of being overawed by power or seduced by persuasion." Justice Joseph Story of the United States Supreme Court took a different position, however. In an article written in 1831 for Francis Lieber's *Encyclopaedia Americana*, he described a grand jury as acting only "at the instigation of the government." Story made no mention of jurors acting independently of the court or initiating investigations on their own.

In England, criticism of the jury begun by Bentham continued to attract support and gradually bore fruit in the form of proposals to abolish the system entirely. Robert Peel was one of the first to suggest that a responsible public prosecutor should be appointed in its place. Suggestions that Parliament do away with the institution in England led both defenders and attackers to present their cases to the public. A citizen writing to the London *Times* under the name, "an admirer of grand juries," praised them as protectors of liberty and warned that it would take a bold man to bring a bill into Parliament to abolish them. An answering letter, signed "a Middlesex Magistrate" advocated a Parliamentary inquiry into the exorbitant expenses of grand juries. The writer expressed satisfaction that the proposals for abolition were gaining ground. In 1834 and again in 1836 Parliamentary resolutions to curtail their use aroused interest in

English legal circles, but they were not successful.

Agitation for abolition of the grand jury in the United States did not gain ground as rapidly as in England, but in at least one state prosecution on an information rather than on an indictment received encouragement. In Vermont, the state constitution did not specifically guarantee the right to indictment by a grand jury in all criminal cases. As a result, many lesser crimes came to trial at the instance of the public prosecutor. In 1836 the defendant in a criminal trial challenged this procedure and claimed that the state had violated the fifth amendment of the United States Constitution by prosecuting him on an information. The Supreme Court of Vermont held that the restrictions imposed by the fifth amendment applied only to the federal government and not to the states, and that the states were free to abolish the juries entirely insofar as the federal constitution was concerned.

Restricting Grand Jury Powers

In 1837 the grand jury of Sullivan County, Tennessee initiated a sweeping investigation into illegal gambling in their community and in the course of the probe summoned a large number of persons to testify. A state law empowered the jurors to summon witnesses to investigate "illegal gaming." Among the indictments returned by the grand jury, based upon testimony of witnesses, was one for betting on an election. The Supreme Court of Tennessee quashed the indictment and warned future juries that they did not possess "general inquisitorial powers" and could call witnesses only where specifically authorized by law. The Court held that betting on elections could not be construed as "illegal gaming." Several years later, jurors of Maury County, Tennessee indicted a master for permitting his slave to sell liquor. The inquest learned of the incident from a witness they had summoned to testify on another matter. Again the Tennessee Supreme Court restricted the power of the jury to act independently and held that indictments had to be based upon the actual knowledge of one of the panel members.

In Cincinnati the newly appointed federal judge, Timothy Walker, expressed the same restricted view. In 1842 he told a jury, "Your sole function is to pass upon indictments. The term presentment confers no separate authority.... Yet in some states advantage has been taken of a similar expression to convert a grand jury into a body of political supervisors." Walker was not a newcomer to western legal circles. He studied under Joseph Story at Harvard and went to Cincinnati in 1830. There he organized a law school, founded the *Western Law Journal* and became an ardent advocate of legal reform.

Two years after Timothy Walker read his restrictive charge in Cincinnati, the question of powers came up in Pennsylvania. In May, 1844 the convention of the Native American Association in Philadelphia ended in a series of destructive riots when Irish groups attempted to break up their meeting. The Governor called out the state militia after mobs had burned several buildings. At this point, Charles J. Jack, a member of the Native American group, addressed a letter to the grand jury then in session, protesting that the call for troops was an attempt to crush the Native Americans by military force. When he learned of the letter, Judge Anson V. Parsons of the Philadelphia Court of Quarter Sessions cited Jack for contempt and declared that it was an "indictable offense" for a private individual to communicate with a grand jury. Furthermore, Parsons announced that jurors were officers of the court under its legal direction and that only the court could convey information and instructions to them.

The following year a Philadelphia grand jury informed the court that one of its members had charged Richard L. Lloyd and Benjamin E. Carpenter, members of the city Board of Health, with stealing public funds. The jurors asked the court to call witnesses and order the Board of Health to produce its books. Judge Edward King refused the request, stating that grand jurors could not proceed to investigate a matter unless the judge gave it to them in charge or the district attorney brought it to their attention. He told the jurors that they were free to initiate presentments only where all of the facts of the offense were known to one of their number. The policy announced by Pennsylvania courts, of severely limiting inquisitorial activities, was entirely foreign to the traditional concept of jury powers. Under the common law, juries had the authority to inquire into all violations of the law in their county and to summon before them all persons who could give them information.

Sentiment in favor of limiting the juries gained favor. In 1846 Congress made the summoning of federal grand juries discretionary with the presiding judge. Previously such a jury had attended every session of the federal district and circuit courts. Under the new law the federal marshal would not summon a panel unless the judge ordered him to do so.

Judicial rulings restricting the independence of grand juries found ready acceptance among several American legal scholars. Francis Wharton, recognized authority in the field of criminal law, noted with approval the decisions of the Tennessee and Pennsylvania courts making grand inquests mere adjuncts of the court. Wharton stated that the value of grand juries depended upon the political tendencies of the age. While they may have been important at one time as a barrier to "frivolous prosecutions" by the state, in the United States they were more useful as restraints upon "the violence of popular excitement and the malice of private prosecutors." If they were necessary at all, Wharton thought it was to serve as a means of protecting established institutions from the actions of the people. He did not see in the grand jury a means of increasing popular participation in government such as James Wilson had envisioned.

Edward Ingersoll, prominent reforming member of the Pennsylvania Bar, published an essay on grand juries in 1849 in which he condemned the institution as incompatible with the American constitutional guarantee of freedom. Ingersoll approved limitations placed upon their investigating activities because he believed that their secrecy and power to indict upon the knowledge of their own members, without additional evidence or witnesses, was "at variance with all modern English theory of judicial proceeding." He declared that inquests, if retained at all, should be limited to passing upon cases where the defendant had already had a preliminary hearing before a committing magistrate.

The same year in which Edward Ingersoll denounced the grand jury system as dangerous to freedom, the Code Commissioners of New York presented to the legislature of that state their draft of a proposed code of criminal procedure. Headed by David Dudley Field, long a proponent of legal reform and codification, the Commissioners left no doubt as to their position on the question of the grand jury. They referred to jury service as a burdensome duty and stated flatly that they would have recommended complete abolition of the institution in New York, had it not been for guarantees contained in the state constitution. The Commissioners did the next best thing, however, and advised the legislators that "limits must be placed to the extent of its powers and restraint must be placed upon their exercise." The New York legislature did not adopt the proposed criminal code, nor did it heed the advice of the commissioners to curtail their power.

Efforts to Abolish the Grand Jury

While sentiment in favor of restricting the grand jury gained strength in American legal circles, in England a strong movement developed to abolish the institution entirely. By the mid-nineteenth century a large number of Englishmen shared Jeremy Bentham's views. In February, 1848 the Mayor and Aldermen of Southampton petitioned the House of Commons to do away with all grand juries. Later in the same year, jurors attending the Central Criminal Court in London recommended abolition of the institution and sent a copy of their resolution to the Secretary of State for the Home Department. In 1849 grand juries of both the Central Criminal Court and the Middlesex sessions announced their opposition to the system. Such recommendations were not altogether surprising. Many English judges were in the habit of calling attention to the uselessness of the system in their jury addresses.

W. C. Humphreys, a prominent English law reformer, stated that it was a potential menace to the country because it assisted rather than suppressed crime. In a pamphlet entitled, "Inutility of Grand Juries," Humphreys joined the crusade for their abolition. Other members of the English bar followed suit. The committing magistrate of Old Bailey prison declared that the grand jury was the "first hope" of the criminal because it afforded "a safe medium for buying off a prosecution and is often resorted to for that purpose." Writing to the London *Times* under the name "Billa Vera," another lawyer claimed that intelligent and respectable jurors were "ashamed and disgusted" with their functions. He also revealed that the Corporation of the City of London had appointed a committee to investigate grand juries and it had uncovered evidence "decidedly hostile to the system." Following this barrage of criticism, Lord J. Jervis, Attorney General of England, introduced a bill in Parliament to nullify the power of grand juries sitting in the metropolitan police districts. Under the Attorney General's proposal, a jury could not indict a person until he had had a preliminary hearing before a police court magistrate. But despite support from English jurists and lawyers, the measure failed to pass Parliament.

Concentrated efforts in England to do away with the institution were not lost upon leaders in American legal circles. In February, 1850 the *United States Monthly Law Magazine* reported the progress of the movement in England, and commented editorially that it hoped American judges would follow the example of those in Britain and take an active stand against the institution. The editorial asked American newspapers "to keep the matter before the public until a similar bill shall be before our legislative bodies, and passed."

Opposition to the grand jury moved from the courts and the pages of the law journals and textbooks to the floors of the state constitutional conventions for the first time in 1850. In that year conventions met in three states to revise existing constitutions and in each of them abolition of the grand jury became an important issue. In Michigan the Committee on the Bill of Rights reported to the convention at Lansing that it had struck out the provision guaranteeing the right to indictment by a grand jury in all criminal cases. When delegate Samuel Clark moved to restore the provision, the line of battle was drawn and a sharp debate ensued. Clark admitted that abuses may have crept into the system but he contended that these could easily be corrected. He warned that complete reliance upon public prosecutors would be "a dangerous innovation." James Sullivan, an attorney, answered Clark and maintained that no district attorney could possibly be more arbitrary or dangerous than a secret *ex parte* body which held its sessions "like the inquisition of the star chamber." He dwelt long on the average juror's complete ignorance of the law and pointed to the great expense of maintaining such a useless institution. The convention voted to strike out the grand jury guarantee, but abolitionist forces pressed for a constitutional provision specifically doing away with it. A majority of the delegates were unwilling to go to that extent, however, and left the question for the legislature to decide.

At Indianapolis the Indiana constitutional convention also became the scene of a struggle regarding the future of the grand jury. As in the Michigan convention, delegates were sharply divided. Some hailed it as an essential bulwark of liberty, while others denounced it as a "remnant of the barbaric past." Anti-jury forces worked for a constitutional provision doing away with the system, but the best they could get in the face of determined opposition was a clause authorizing the legislature "to continue, modify, or abolish" it at any time. Indiana became the first state to include such a provision in its constitution.

Opponents of the grand inquest were less successful in the Ohio constitutional convention than they had been in Michigan and Indiana. B. P. Smith, an attorney from Wyandot County, proposed substituting the information for the indictment, but only a handful of anti-jury men supported him. They pointed to the arbitrary nature of grand jury powers and pictured them as an unnecessary tax burden, but all to no avail. A majority of those present favored retaining the institution, and the revised Ohio Constitution made indictment by a grand jury mandatory in all criminal prosecutions.

In Tennessee, where judicial decisions had successfully restricted inquisitorial powers, the Supreme Court in 1851 reaffirmed its policy. But not all courts saw fit to restrict grand juries. New York followed the broad rule adhered to in Missouri and allowed the juries freer rein in their inquiries. In the federal courts, however, they tended to become more and more an arm of the court. In 1856 as part of an economy measure, Congress empowered federal judges to discharge jurors when in their opinion such action would best serve the public interest.

In the following year, delegates met at Salem, Oregon to draft a constitution for statehood. David Logan, a member of the territorial bar, tossed the question of the grand jury into the lap of the convention with a resolution to replace the institution with professional prosecutors. Logan reviewed in detail the origin and history of the grand inquest and argued that conditions which had once made the institution necessary no longer existed. He urged Oregon to take the lead in getting rid of the system and predicted that it would be only a matter of time before most other states followed suit. George H. Williams, Territorial Chief Justice, came to its defense, emphasizing its peculiar suitability in a frontier area such as Oregon. He admitted that, like most newly opened areas, Oregon had more than its share of lawlessness. Many "desperadoes" had come to the territory from the gold fields of California. In view of such conditions, the Chief Justice favored a secret method of entering complaints as a means of protecting citizens from possible reprisals. He explained to the convention that many persons refused to make complaints before justices because it might cost them their property or even their lives. Former Territorial Chief Justice Matthew P. Deady also joined the fight to save the grand jury. Logan accused those judges and lawyers who defended it of holding on to outmoded legal machinery merely because they were familiar with the system, and placed them in the same class with those persons who stood against popular election of judges. Anti-jury forces failed to secure the outright abolition of the grand inquest, but they did get a constitutional provision empowering the legislature to nullify the system at any time.

While its opponents in America worked through state constitutional conventions, anti-jury forces in America kept up their pressure to get Parliament to strip inquests of all power. Attorney General Sir Frederic Thesiger introduced such a bill in 1852, 1854, and again in 1857. Each time he sought to convince his colleagues that the grand jury was useless in large cities in view of improved methods of police investigation. Sir Frederic pointed out that many of the jurors themselves look upon their job as a fruitless one. After the proper judicial urgings, juries in the metropolitan district of London had presented themselves year after year as "an impediment to the administration of justice." In spite of all efforts, the Attorney General could not work up sufficient enthusiasm among members of Parliament to persuade them to curtail use of the institution. However, the question continued to provoke heated discussion in English legal circles. On December 20, 1858 T. Chambers, a solicitor, read a paper before the Juridicial Society of London on the future of the grand jury. He opposed tampering with the institution and expressed a fear that, like many other modern reforms, the effect would be to "withdraw the people from the tribunals and replace them by officials." He also warned that justice should not be made to "rush through professional and official conduits," but should be passed upon by the people themselves. In the discussion following Chambers' paper, several members took vigorous exception to his position and insisted that increased efficiency would follow if "a professional inquiry" replaced the grand jury. The debate did not end that evening. As late as April, 1859 a letter to the *London Times* answered Chambers with the complaint that inquests too often encroached upon the duties of the trial jury and performed unnecessary work. Although they were unable to secure complete abolition, English opponents attained some measure of success when Parliament enacted the Vexatious Indictments Law in July, 1859. Thereafter, private citizens had to present certain cases to a police magistrate who would then determine whether the person could go before a grand jury.

In the United States anti-jury forces made their first attempt to abolish the system by legislative action in Michigan in 1859. The state constitution no longer guaranteed the right to a grand jury indictment, leaving the legislature free to act in the matter. The judiciary committee of the Michigan Assembly heartily endorsed a plan to end the use of inquests and issued a scathing report, characterizing the grand jury as "a crumbling survivor of fallen institutions . . . more akin to the star chamber." Led by Alexander W. Buell, a Detroit attorney, the committee called upon the state to discard an institution dangerous to individual liberty. They bemoaned the lack of learning of most jurors and the inability of the courts to control the direction of their investigations. The committee referred to the "wholesome" curbs which Pennsylvania courts had placed upon grand juries, but they feared that such decisions would be difficult to enforce and would not prove a satisfactory solution to the problem of lay interference. The committee's vigorous report proved effective in rallying legislative support for a bill abolishing the grand jury in Michigan. In February, 1859 the legislature provided that all crimes be prosecuted upon the information of a district attorney. Only a judge could summon a grand jury for purposes of an investigation.

Anti-jury forces in neighboring states watched with interest the success of their brethren in Michigan. In Wisconsin they drew encouragement and sought to use the example of Michigan as an opening wedge in a campaign to rid their own state of the hated institution. The *Milwaukee Sentinel* published with approval the Michigan legislative report and attacked grand juries editorially as cumbersome and expensive "instruments of private malice." Legislative action alone would not be sufficient to abolish the grand inquest in Wisconsin. The people would have to be educated to oppose the system, because they would have to approve any constitutional amendment.

While its opponents in Wisconsin awaited the next session of the legislature to propose a constitutional amendment, the fourth constitutional convention for the Territory of Kansas met at Wyandotte in the summer of 1859. Three previous constitutions drawn up at Topeka, Lecompton and Leavenworth had each included a provision guaranteeing the right to indictment by a grand jury in all "capital or otherwise infamous crimes." The Wyandotte convention adopted the Ohio constitution as its model, but the Committee on the Bill of Rights omitted the article referring to the grand jury and gave no reason for its action. In a territory deeply engrossed in the slavery controversy, this blow at popular government went unchallenged. Five years later it was comparatively easy to put a bill through the Kansas legislature providing that grand juries were not to be called unless specially summoned by a judge.

When the Wisconsin legislature convened in 1860, Senator Robert Hotchkiss proposed and the Senate adopted a resolution asking the Judiciary Committee to investigate the expediency of abolishing the system. Madison and Milwaukee newspapers hailed this as "a good omen of reform." The Madison *Evening Patriot* urged immediate abolition and sounded the rallying cry, "Down with the old rotten fabric." The senate Committee reported favorably on a constitutional amendment. When the resolution reached the floor for debate several senators questioned the power of states to tamper with the grand jury in view of the fifth amendment to the United States Constitution. Only a series of anonymous letters appearing in the *Milwaukee Sentinel* came to the defense. The writer, who signed himself "Invariable," predicted that "gross injustice and oppression on the one hand and bribery on the other" would inevitably follow if prosecution was left at the mercy of one man. The Wisconsin Senate passed the resolution calling for a constitutional amendment, but its action went for nothing when the Assembly buried the resolution in committee.

In Canada, the Upper Canada Law Journal, representing the sentiments of the Toronto Bar, took notice of the movement in England and the United States. The Canadian *Journal* reprinted English attacks upon the grand jury and went on record for abolition of an institution "which affords great facilities for gratifying private malice." This opinion received legislative approval in 1860 when the Canadian Legislative Council passed a bill to end the use of inquests in the Recorders' Courts of Upper Canada.

In July, 1864 foes of the inquest made a concerted effort to end its use in Nevada. The convention framing a constitution for statehood became the scene of a bitter dispute, but jury protagonists finally convinced the delegates that a popular tribunal was better fitted than a public prosecutor to handle the problems of law enforcement on the frontier. Nevada came into the Union in 1864 under a constitution which guaranteed the right to indictment by a grand jury.

In 1864 while Americans were engaged in a cruel Civil War, *John N. Pomeroy,* Professor of Law at New York University, applauded the fact that the grand jury remained in the United States as "an insuperable barrier against official oppression." Its value had become more apparent in the light of arbitrary arrests and military government of wartime. Pomeroy stated with satisfaction that "the innovating hand of reform has not as yet touched the long-established proceedings in criminal actions . . . the grand jury (is) carefully preserved by our national and state constitutions." However, the professor's conclusions were more hopeful than realistic. Agitation had already begun in some states to follow the lead of Michigan and abandon use of the institution, while in Illinois, Indiana, Oregon and Kansas the legislatures were free of all constitutional restrictions in the matter. In Pennsylvania and Tennessee judicial decisions had seriously curtailed the initiative of grand juries. American legal scholars had long ago joined the crusade, many of them insistent that they had survived all possible usefulness. Abroad in England and Canada, the two other principal common law countries, they were under heavy attack.

Part Two
1865–1917

In the decade following the Civil War, efforts to abolish use of the grand jury in the United States assumed almost epidemic proportions. The rash of post-war conventions to frame and revise state constitutions gave opponents of the institution an opportunity to be heard. Legal and governmental theorists, speaking in the name of progress, had long inveighed against the grand jury as a relic of the barbaric past; too inefficient and time-consuming for an enlightened age. They conceded that inquests may at one time have been necessary safeguards against royal despotism, but the need for such protection no longer existed in the United States. A few individuals cautioned that a free government might require even more checks than a despotism, but progress seemed to be the enemy of the grand inquest and many states abandoned the system in its name.

In Wisconsin opponents resumed their pre-war campaign to abolish the institution. They pointed to the speed and ease with which prosecutors accused offenders in Michigan where the grand inquest was dead. In contrast they pictured Wisconsin juries as "secret conclaves of criminal accusers, repugnant to the American system." Assemblyman A. J. Turner introduced a resolution in January, 1869 to amend the state constitution to rid the state of grand juries. Although a majority of the Judiciary Committee favored delay in the matter, a minority group issued a vigorous report denouncing the system and brushed aside all opposition. In the Senate as in the Assembly, anti-jury forces painted a black picture of the institution and took advantage of their superior unity of purpose to gain the support of doubtful senators. Defenders advised caution but the spirit of advancement and reform swept away their objections. Governor Lucius Fairchild approved the joint resolution when it passed both houses of the legislature in 1869 and again in 1870. The question then became one for the people of Wisconsin to decide. Apathy and indifference marked the campaign which followed as interest in state and local candidates overshadowed the proposed amendment. A few Democratic newspapers conducted editorial campaigns against abolition of the grand jury, charging that it was a Republican measure, but they made little headway. The *Grant County Herald* announced that a Republican scheme to get control of criminal prosecutions lay behind the amendment. The *Milwaukee News* warned that killing the grand jury was "another step onward in the concentration of power," a process which the recent war had hastened. It cautioned against destroying a popular institution which might be necessary to oppose tyranny of the federal government. In answer to such attacks, proponents of the amendment assumed the pose of reformers, struggling to rid the state of "an expensive, unjust system." In the referendum on November 7, 1870 the people of Wisconsin voted overwhelmingly for reform and the grand jury ceased to exist in the state except when specially summoned by a judge.

While opponents of the grand jury in Wisconsin were struggling to rid their state of the hated institution, their compatriots in Illinois won a partial triumph. They succeeded in getting the constitutional convention in Springfield in 1870 to give the legislature the power to abolish the system. Such a procedure avoided any direct referendum on the matter. Shortly after adoption of the new constitution, a special legislative committee urged the legislators to exercise their new authority and eliminate "so thoroughly despotic and subversive" an institution. Petitions approved the committee's advice, but the legislature failed to act on the proposal.

In England the year 1872 saw partial success crown the thirty year struggle to eliminate the grand jury. Parliament provided that grand juries would no longer be used in the London metropolitan district except when summoned by a magistrate.

There followed in the United States a series of constitutional conventions in which the question of retaining the grand jury system became an important issue. Delegates assembled at Charleston, West Virginia in 1872 refused to be swayed by talk of progress and voted down proposals to turn all criminal prosecution over to public officials. Advocates of reform were more successful in the Ohio constitutional convention, where they deleted the guarantee of a grand jury indictment in all criminal cases. Ohio retained the institution, however, when the people refused to approve the new constitution. In Missouri, in contrast to most states, grand juries actually strengthened their authority, with a direct constitutional mandate to investigate all officials having charge of public funds at least once a year. Anti-jury forces fared better in the western conventions. The Nebraska constitution of 1857 allowed the legislature to "abolish, limit, change or amend" the grand jury system. Ten years later the legislators exercised this power and inquests became extinct in another state. In 1876 Colorado followed the lead of Nebraska and put the matter up to the legislature which abolished grand juries shortly after. The California constitution of 1879 allowed prosecution of criminal offenses upon the information of a prosecutor, but it also stipulated that grand juries be called in each county at least once a year. Western areas were more receptive to proposals to streamline their judicial machinery. In the South, the Radicals made no attempt to eliminate grand juries in the constitutions which they drafted. When the Southern Bourbons came to write new constitutions they did not even consider eliminating an institution which had proved so useful in the Reconstruction period in opposing an unfriendly central government.

Judicial Restrictions

Paced by the twin slogans of economy and efficiency, enemies of the grand jury had successfully ended its use in many states and curtailed it in others. However, the constitutional convention and the legislature were not the only means used to attack the system. Some judges were able to make serious inroads on grand jury powers to initiate and conduct investigations independently of the court. In Tennessee the supreme court reinforced its position that inquests could summon witnesses only where specifically authorized by a specific law. Pennsylvania courts reaffirmed the very restrictive rule which limited juries to an investigation of matters known to one of its members or suggested to them by the judge or the prosecutor. Individual citizens were not free to go before a grand jury nor could jurors summon witnesses whom they believed could assist them in their inquiries. Any attempt by a private individual to circumvent this ruling could be punished as contempt of court.

In the federal courts, as in most states, grand juries had always been free to subpoena any and all witnesses upon their own initiative. Chief Justice Salmon P. Chase urged jurors, convening in West Virginia in August, 1868, to call before them and examine fully government officials or any other persons who possessed information useful to them. He warned them, "You must not be satisfied with acting upon such cases as may be brought before you by the district attorney or by members of your body." In view of Chief Justice Chase's statement of the broad rule prevailing in the federal courts, it was indeed a strange doctrine which Justice Stephen Field announced in August, 1872. Justice Field was the brother of the well-known legal reformer and codifier, David Dudley Field, who had tried his best to eliminate use of the grand jury in New York. Justice Field told a federal jury at San Francisco, California that it should limit its investigations to such matters as fell within their personal knowledge or were called to their attention by the court or the prosecuting attorney. He warned them in particular against delving into political matters unless instructed to do so. If neither the judge nor the prosecutor placed a matter before them, Justice Field observed, "it may be safely inferred that public justice will not suffer if the matter is not considered by you." He reminded the jurors that the type of government which existed in the United States did not require the existence of a grand jury as a protection against oppressive action by the government. The restrictive charge of Justice Field excluded private persons from the grand jury room and curtailed the freedom of action of jurors. It represented an effort to subordinate the grand jury to the wishes of the judge and prosecutor. As such, it contradicted accepted practice in the federal and English courts, as well as a great majority of the state courts.

Not all American jurists desired to narrow the scope of grand jury activity, however. In Silver City, Idaho Territory, Judge H. E. Prickett solicited jurors to investigate all official misconduct and neglect of duty. He told members of the jury that they possessed full authority to call and examine all governmental officials or any other person in the community. Federal District Judge Walter Q. Gresham told jurymen at Indianapolis in 1878 that attempts to protect persons for political reasons should not prevent them from making a full investigation of a matter, but instead should inspire them with additional determination to bring the person to justice. Although Field's voice was only one among many, the doctrines which he enunciated found favor with legal scholars and members of the bar who had long advocated placing the grand jury more completely under the control of the court. Francis Wharton, authority on criminal law, who had often advocated such a course, magnified the importance of Field's statements and attached great weight to them. In spite of the fact that Field stood completely alone in his statement of the "new" federal rule, Wharton wrote in 1889, "This is the view which may now be considered as accepted in the United

States courts and in most of the several states." As proof of the latter, he cited Pennsylvania and Tennessee decisions, the only states having such a rule. In drawing his conclusion, Wharton accepted as the majority viewpoint a position which coincided closely with his desire to reduce the grand jury to a position of subservience.

In 1881 New York state finally adopted the Code of Criminal Procedure prepared by David Dudley Field in 1849. However, to the great disappointment of those who had assisted in its preparation, the legislature dropped the requirement that a preliminary hearing before a judge was necessary before a grand jury could return an indictment. Not only did the New York legislators see fit to leave the grand jury unfettered, but they included a provision requiring all inquests to make particular inquiry into official corruption and misconduct.

In the West, however, anti-jury forces continued to win victories. In a special referendum held in Iowa in November, 1884 the people voted to amend the state constitution to give the legislature authority to abolish grand juries completely. For many years, persons advocating that states abandon the indictment in criminal proceedings had felt plagued by those who pointed to the fifth amendment of the United States Constitution as standing in the way. Although state and federal courts had frequently stated that the guarantee of the right to an indictment in the fifth amendment applied only to the federal government, the matter invariably came up for debate at constitutional conventions. With the adoption of the fourteenth amendment, there were those who insisted that the phrase "due process of law" included the right to indictment by a grand jury. As early as 1872 the Wisconsin Supreme Court decided that the fourteenth amendment did not prevent states from ceasing to use the indictment, but the question remained a point of controversy until the United States Supreme Court settled it in 1884. The test case arose in California when Joseph A. Hurtado challenged his murder conviction on the ground that he had come to trial on an information rather than a grand jury indictment. The high court gave the judicial green light to states which desired to get rid of the grand inquest. Citing the Wisconsin decision with approval, the justices announced that "due process of law" included any system of prosecution which preserved liberty and justice and was not limited to indictment by a grand jury. Justice John M. Harlan's vigorous dissent stated the case for those who believed that indictment by a jury of his neighbors was the right of every American citizen.

Criticism of the Grand Jury System

Criticism of the grand jury in legal circles continued to grow in the United States in the 1880's. Seymour D. Thompson and Edwin G. Merriam in their *Treatise on the Organization, Custody and Conduct of Juries* came out against the system and stated that the praise deserved by a few juries had been "quite undeservedly accorded to the institution itself." In 1886 Eugene Stevenson, a New Jersey public prosecutor, condemned the grand jury as an arbitrary, irresponsible, and dangerous part of government which long ago should have come "within the range of official responsibility." He much preferred the efficiency and decisiveness of a public prosecutor, observing, "it is difficult to see why a town meeting of laymen, utterly ignorant both of law and the rules of evidence should be an appropriate tribunal. The summoning of a new body of jurors at each term insures an unfailing supply of ignorance." As a parting blow, Stevenson declared that no sane statesman or legislator "would ever dream of creating such a tribunal" if it did not already exist.

Later in the same year members of the American Bar Association heard David Dudley Field reiterate the demand for the efficiency of the expert in judicial proceedings. Field pointed out that the best civilization was the result of division of labor, where each person became an expert in his own specialty. The jury system, Field observed, ignored the benefits to be derived from specialization, largely because of "superstitious veneration." Demands that an expert replace a tribunal composed of representative citizens may have had some basis on the ground of efficiency, but it also reflected a fear of democracy on the part of many who advocated the change. Most authors hid their distrust of the people behind charges of "star chamber" and "secret inquisition" leveled at grand juries. Professor Francis Wharton, however, made little effort to hide his apprehension regarding grand juries. Writing in 1889, he observed that their value shifted with the political tendencies of the age. At a time when excessive authority threatened, "then a grand jury, irresponsible as it is, and springing from the people, is an important safeguard of liberty." However, Wharton emphasized that when "public order and the settled institutions of the land are in danger from momentary popular excitement, then a grand jury, irresponsible and secret, partaking without check of the popular impulse, may through its inquisitorial powers become an engine of great mischief to liberty as well as to order." But not all legal scholars and jurists saw inquests as a potential threat to the ruling group in government and society. Justice Samuel F. Miller, sitting on the United States Supreme Court, challenged the argument that inquests were of value only when there was danger of oppression at the hands of a despotic monarch. He emphasized their importance in protecting citizens from charges brought by irresponsible and arbitrary prosecutors.

Abolishing Grand Juries in Western States

The year 1889 witnessed the admission of the six "Omnibus" states into the Union. Opponents of the grand jury emerged completely victorious from the constitutional conventions which prepared them for statehood. Idaho, Montana and Washington abolished the grand inquest completely except for special occasions, while North Dakota, South Dakota and Wyoming left the question up to their legislatures. In the Idaho convention the expense of the juries, particularly in thinly settled areas, provided a potent argument in winning delegates to the cause of abolition. Anti-jury leaders claimed that the average indictment cost the people $600 to $1,000 and they predicted savings amounting to thousands of dollars each year if inquests ceased to exist. There was no lack of defenders, however, who warned against handing politicians the power of accusation and stressed the need of a people's body to investigate local officials. In spite of their efforts, the proponents of efficiency and economy prevailed in Idaho. Delegates attending the Montana convention at Helena in the heat of July, 1889 faced the same decision. Rallying around the slogan, "Let Montana cut the thread that binds us to the barbarous past," advocates of abolition posed as reformers and attacked the grand inquest as an outmoded and even dangerous institution. They cited Wisconsin as a model to pattern after. Defenders of the jury opposed hasty action as a step in the direction of centralization, by removing one of the important barriers "which serves to protect the rights of the citizen against the government." Despite such protests, a majority of the Montana delegates favored eliminating the grand jury in their state. It met the same fate on the floor of the Washington constitutional convention. In the three other new states, the stories were similar. Promises of economy and lower taxes prevailed against warnings not to kill a democratic institution. Legislatures in North Dakota, South Dakota and Wyoming did not hesitate to exercise their prerogative, and grand juries ceased to exist within their borders.

It became increasingly clear to Americans who wished to curb or eliminate the grand jury that getting rid of the institution by law or constitutional amendment offered the best chance of success. In spite of Wharton's efforts, state and federal courts were reluctant to adopt Stephen Field's new restrictive doctrine. In March, 1891 the Supreme Court of Maryland ruled that grand juries could initiate any type of prosecution, regardless of how the case came to their attention. To deny it such powers, the Maryland court insisted, would make juries useless and mere tools of the court and prosecutor. Justice David Brewer spoke the mind of the United States Supreme Court when he announced that accepted practice in America allowed grand juries to investigate any alleged crimes "no matter how or by whom suggested to them."

Attacks Upon the Grand Jury

Concentrating their efforts on eliminating the grand jury entirely, members of the bar emphasized the danger of lay interference in judicial matters and called for efficiency in administering justice. Speaking before the annual convention of the Ohio State Bar Association in July, 1892 Justice Henry B. Brown of the United States Supreme Court proposed eliminating the grand inquest as a means of simplifying criminal procedure. He saw in public prosecutors a far more efficient means of bringing offenders to trial. O'Brien J. Atkinson, Michigan attorney, told members of the Michigan State Bar Association that he could not conceive of any condition where a grand jury would be desirable "or where its secret methods would not be productive of evil." He warned those states which had not followed Michigan's lead in abolishing the institution, that an accusing body with power to pry into public and private affairs in a secret manner could become a grave threat to liberty in America.

In January, 1896 the Territorial Bar Association of Utah met in convention at Salt Lake City. Territorial leaders were preparing themselves for another try at statehood and the forthcoming constitutional convention was uppermost in their minds. In his presidential address, J. G. Sutherland recommended that grand juries be eliminated after statehood, to be replaced by special prosecutors. Sutherland denounced inquests as useless, oppressive, and expensive and proclaimed that social and political changes in the United States had made them "undesirable as well as unnecessary." The President of the Utah Bar Association got his wish a month later when the Utah constitutional convention adopted his proposal and abolished all grand juries except when summoned by a judge.

Opponents of the grand jury in all sections of the United States maintained their pressure to turn criminal prosecution over to experts. In 1897 C. E. Chiperfield told members of the State's Attorneys Association of Illinois that the average grand juror possessed few of the qualifications essential to their duties. Lack of legal training, he contended, led jurors to "wander through time and eternity in a curious way," often allowing hard luck stories to influence their deliberations. Chiperfield called for an end to the institution, and he implored, "In the name of progress which is inevitable, I invoke . . . the abolition of that relic of antiquity, the twin sister of the inquisition, the grand jury in Illinois." Charles P. Hogan used the same line of attack when he took the opportunity of his presidential address to urge members of the Vermont Bar Association to oppose the grand inquest. Characterizing it as "a cumbersome and expensive piece of legal machinery," he announced that there was no reason why it should continue to exist "in this enlightened and progressive age." Hogan suggested discarding the grand jury as the English had discarded the ordeal and trial by fire.

Vigorous and frequently vituperative attacks launched by legal leaders in the name of progress and reform helped discredit the grand jury in the eyes of the American people. Constant comparison with the inquisition and the star chamber aimed to pave the way for abandoning the institution. Reformers had their way in Oregon where in 1899 the legislature exercised the privilege given it in the state constitution and substituted the information for the indictment in criminal proceedings. The following year citizens of Missouri approved overwhelmingly amendments relinquishing grand jury duties to district attorneys. In California, however, where grand juries in San Francisco had gained a reputation as enemies of municipal corruption, in November, 1902 the people rejected a proposed constitutional amendment to end use of grand inquests entirely. In November, 1904 residents of Minnesota approved abolishing the system in their state. The referendum on the constitutional change evoked very little discussion and went almost completely unnoticed in the excitement of a presidential election year.

At a time when public confidence in the grand jury was wavering under the barrage of abuse and the cries for reform, there were few persons who saw the institution as a potent instrument of the people. Judge Harman Yerkes of Pennsylvania, however, retained the belief that grand juries could provide a means of extending democratic control of government. In September, 1901 he told jurors of Bucks County that bodies such as theirs, representing the people of the community, were not outmoded or useless. In times of great public peril or in the event of deep-seated abuses, Judge Yerkes observed, "the divided yet powerful and also combined responsibility of the secret session of the grand jury . . . has worked out great problems of reform and correction." He pointed out that abolition of the grand inquest would leave the accused citizen completely at the mercy of "an unjust or unwise judge or district attorney," or subject to contrivances of an unscrupulous prosecutor. Judge Yerkes dispelled the often repeated idea that because the United States was not ruled by a tyrannical king, grand juries had ceased to be necessary as guardians of individual liberty. He explained that tyrants even more irresponsible than the despots of old sought to dominate local, state and national governments. Giant business monopolies restless of legal restraints and party bosses who did not hesitate to break judges and create courts took the place of tyrannical monarchs as a danger to freedom in the United States. Against such ruthless forces Judge Yerkes saw grand juries as powerful agencies of the people, challenging business or boss domination of government. At a time when many legal scholars advised abandoning the grand inquest as an archaic relic of the past, the Pennsylvania judge saw what they had failed to see, that there were enemies of freedom in America which demanded the watchful eye of the grand jury if the American people were to control their government.

In 1904 a Philadelphia grand jury challenged the sixty year old Pennsylvania rule that it could not initiate investigations unless the judge or the district attorney had given their approval. Members of the jury told Judge William W. Wiltbank they had evidence that certain constables in Philadelphia were using their official position to extort money from newly arrived immigrants. To obtain additional information they asked the judge to summon witnesses in the matter. He not only upheld the Pennsylvania rule and denied their request, but in doing so stated that victims of the extortion racket could not even go before the grand jury and tell their stories unless the court or the prosecutor saw fit to ask for an investigation. Pennsylvania remained in the minority on the question, however, as federal and most state courts continued to follow the common law rule which endowed grand juries with broad powers to begin investigations.

Annual meetings of bar associations in the various states continued to serve as excellent platforms from which to enlist support against the grand jury system. In July, 1905 the Committee on Law Reform of the Iowa Bar Association recommended and the association adopted a resolution calling for prosecution upon information. Judge M. J. Wade of Iowa City sought to ridicule members who did not fall into line when he stated tartly, "There are some persons in this world who are wedded to antiquity, revel in cobwebs, and they simply worship whiskers." Judge Wade tempted his colleagues, saying, "Let us do away with a few things and maintain the law for the benefit of the lawyers who are to convict guilty men." Justice Brown of the United States Supreme Court reiterated his dissatisfaction with the grand jury system in an address to the American Bar Association in 1905. In January, 1906 George Lawyer, Albany attorney, challenged members of the New York State Bar Association to rid their state of grand juries. To continue to countenance such an institution, he warned, was to concede that under a republican form of government the liberties of the individual were in danger just as they had been under a despotism of the dark ages. Lawyer denounced the "arbitrary power" which inquests exercised to inquire into and criticize the acts of public officials. He insisted that under the American form of government the people "require no shield to protect them from the state's aggressions."

Opponents of the grand jury system did not have their way entirely. They suffered occasional reverses in their effort to drive the institution from the American legal system. Delegates who met at Gutherie, Oklahoma in 1906 to frame a constitution for statehood agreed to abolish regular sessions of the grand inquest, but they did not wish to leave the question of summoning a jury entirely up to the local judges. The Oklahomans did what no other Americans had ever done. They provided that the people could call a grand jury when they thought it was necessary. The signatures of one hundred resident taxpayers in a county were sufficient to launch an investigation. In January, 1908 William S. U'Ren, Charles H. Cary, and other Progressive leaders advocated a return to the grand jury system in Oregon as a part of their program to increase popular control of the government. They made use of the initiative petition to bring the question of a constitutional amendment before the people of Oregon. The referendum evoked little debate. Opponents of the amendment accused grand juries of being responsible for long delays in justice, while Progressive leaders replied with the charge that the information system enabled district attorneys to use criminal prosecutions for political purposes. On June 1, 1908 after nine years without them, residents of Oregon voted two to one to restore the grand jury in their state. In New Mexico as well as in Oregon, the people expressed themselves in favor of retaining control over criminal prosecutions. At public hearings conducted by the Committee on the Bill of Rights of the Constitutional Convention in 1910, popular opinion overwhelmingly favored keeping the grand jury. As a result, New Mexico became one of the few western states to summon inquests regularly to attend its courts. In Arizona a different story unfolded. Even as a territory it had abandoned the grand jury. The Constitutional Convention did not consult the wishes of the people, but voted to continue the practice of substituting an expert prosecutor for a body of representative citizens.

Gradually, critics of popular participation in judicial proceedings shifted the basis of their public opposition. They ceased to state boldly that the people should not interfere in matters for which they had no training. Such statements had an unpleasant, undemocratic ring and actually might rally support for the hated institution. Instead they began to stress the waste of time and money which grand juries entailed. H. N. Atkinson, Houston lawyer, told members of the Texas Bar Association that "a useless and unnecessary piece of legal machinery" cost Texas counties between $100,000 and $200,000 each year, in addition to taking men away from their homes and businesses to do work "which one man can do just as well." Aaron Hahn of Cleveland repeated this argument in urging the 1912 Ohio Constitutional Convention to eliminate the grand jury from that state. In England a Parliamentary Commission composed of judges and legal experts studied the causes˜of delay in English courts. In 1913 they reported that the grand jury system "uselessly puts the country to considerable expense and numerous persons to great inconvenience." The Commissioners regarded the grand inquest as "little more than an historically interesting survival" which had "outlived the circumstances from which it sprung and developed." They recommended that Parliament take action to eliminate it from the English court system. Not all British jurists agreed that grand juries no longer served a useful purpose, however. Judge L. A. Atherly-Jones of the London City Court warned those who sought reform at the expense of popular government that "the bold hand of the innovator" should not touch those institutions which guard personal liberty. Americans who opposed grand juries commented approvingly on the English report. The *New Jersey Law Journal* predicted that it would be only a question of time before they would cease to exist in every state in the Union.

In June, 1915 William Howard Taft appeared before the Judiciary Committee of the New York Constitutional Convention and took the occasion to press home an attack upon the grand jury system. Drawing upon his experience as a judge, the ex-President criticized it as a "bulky and costly" institution which served only to relieve district attorneys of responsibility for prosecutions. He heartily endorsed the movement to substitute a legal expert for an unwieldy body of laymen. The New York convention considered several proposed amendments limiting the use of grand juries but they did not adopt them. However, not all persons familiar with the work of grand juries believed they were too costly and cumbersome. Edward Lindsey, of the American Institute of Criminal Law, hailed their broad inquisitorial powers as an essential part of judicial machinery which was in constant use to secure information otherwise unobtainable. Lindsey pointed out that prosecutors and police departments were at best feeble substitutes for the powerful grand inquest.

Although Lindsey defended the grand jury against those who would have destroyed it, in doing so he adopted the criteria used by its critics. He sought to justify the institution on the grounds of efficiency. On this point the grand jury was particularly vulnerable. Few persons familiar with its operations would have denied that a prosecuting officer could move more rapidly and with greater singleness of purpose. It remained for a layman well experienced in the work of the grand jury to defend it as a valuable and democratic agency of the people. Publisher George Haven Putnam recognized that inquests could be slow and unwieldy bodies which frequently tried the patience of judges and prosecutors, but he did not believe it was fair to judge the institution solely on that basis.

Democracy did not necessarily mean efficiency. It meant a careful concern for the rights of persons who had been arrested as well as the ability of citizens to initiate investigations of abuses in government and make officials responsible to them. After serving on grand juries in New York City over a period of thirty-five years, Putnam became convinced that no other institution provided such a degree of popular participation in government. He openly challenged the advice of ex-President Taft, announcing, "There is no other way citizens can bring criticism directly to bear upon public officials.", Putnam saw grand juries as more than mere law enforcement agencies. He recognized that during their term of office the jurors acted as the representatives of the people of the county and in that capacity could call before them all public officials, high or low. When such bodies ceased to sit, the cause of popular government had suffered a severe blow. In 1915 Putnam and other laymen who were convinced of the necessity of preserving the institution in America organized the Grand Jury Association of New York County, made up of persons who had served on grand juries. They sought to publicize the importance of the grand inquest to democratic government and to blunt the attack long waged against law interference in judicial matters.

The period from the Civil War to the First World War witnessed many attempts in the United States to abolish the grand jury. Armed with the persuasive arguments of efficiency and economy, advocates of reform achieved their most spectacular successes in western United States.

Part Three

Early in 1917, grand juries ceased to sit in England. Pressure of a life and death struggle with Germany led Parliament to suspend them for the duration of the war. Although the noise of battle hushed all but a few critics of the move, there were Englishmen who saw the paradox in fighting for democracy abroad while restricting it at home. They suggested that even a democratic government such as Britain's might need the strong check against arbitrary rule which grand juries provided. However, such protests lost out to cries of a manpower shortage. The issue of a war emergency enabled English legal reformers to accomplish what they had been unable to do in the name of efficiency and economy: To kill the grand jury. They succeeded in taking criminal prosecutions out of the hands of citizen panels, and in giving them to magistrates expert in the law.

In spite of the remarkable showing of grand juries in combatting municipal corruption and their proven value in regulating corporations, American legal reformers hailed the British action as a step in the right direction. They attributed the move to Parliamentary fear that the power of the indictment might become an instrument of oppression in the "hands of an inflamed populace." Opponents of the grand jury in the United States warned that suspension of English juries had come just in time to avoid a "flood of indictments" against pacifists and persons of German extraction. In England, however, officials expressed the fear that grand juries would refuse to indict persons arrested by the government.

Legal reformers in the United States were unable to turn the war to their advantage as their counterparts had done in England. American entry into the first World War in April 1917, temporarily ended efforts to abolish grand juries. But, opponents both in the United States and England resumed their agitation following the War. In America, they sought to persuade additional states to abandon its use, while in England they fought to make the temporary suspension permanent. In January 1920, Assemblyman Louis A. Cuvilleir introduced a resolution in the New York legislature to amend the state constitution to eliminate grand juries. The American Judicature Society advised delegates attending the Illinois Constitutional Convention in 1920, that grand juries were of little value except to delay the courts. The Society warned that time was the most important element in criminal justice. The State's Attorney's Association of Illinois agreed wholeheartedly and made a plea for abolition of the grand jury system. However, delegates remained unmoved and refused to sacrifice the citizen's panel to the experts. In Massachusetts Judge Robert Wolcott of Cambridge reiterated the appeal for judicial efficiency. In October 1921 he told members of the State Bar Association, that abolishing the grand jury was one means of ending congestion in criminal courts, but his statement did not go unchallenged. Former district attorney Arthur D. Hill of Boston protested against a system of criminal law which eliminated "the popular element" and told prosecutors that they could learn a great deal from working with grand jurors.

Wartime suspension of grand juries in England ended in December 1921, but solicitors and magistrates throughout the island requested Parliament to make the order permanent. The London *Times* supported the campaign characterizing grand inquests as expensive and inefficient, but drew a host of replies in defense of the system. Judges as well as laymen objected to eliminating the panels of citizen accusers. Judge L. A. Atherly-Jones praised their wholesome influence and warned that justice was already too tightly controlled by "an official and professional class." Sir Alexander Wentworth Macdonald, a layman, declared that a group of non-professional men should stand above judges and courts. However Lord Justice J. Eldon Bankes agreed with most jurists, that grand juries were of little value in reviewing the work of experienced magistrates. In spite of charges of inefficiency, however, Parliament refused to extend the suspension order and citizen investigators resumed their traditional place at English courts.

In the United States, as in England, opposition increased. In March 1922 the New York County Association of the Criminal Bar announced that it planned a vigorous state wide campaign to abolish the institution. Former district attorney Robert Elder called upon public prosecutors to take the initiative in replacing the "inefficiency, ignorance and traditional bias" of grand jurors, and Judge Thomas Crain of New York supported the movement. Testifying before the Committee of Law Enforcement of the American Bar Association, he observed that "a judge or some other man learned in the law" should participate in grand jury hearings. In Minnesota attorney Paul J. Thompson urged his state to adopt the Wisconsin system of prosecution upon the order of a district attorney. In 1922 Judge Roscoe Pound and Felix Frankfurter conducted a survey of criminal justice in Cleveland and added the weight of expert testimony to those who sought to eliminate use of grand juries. Pound and Frankfurter reported that juries were inefficient and unnecessary, since trial courts were quite capable of protecting Americans against executive tyranny.

The Grand Jury Association

Professional opposition to the inquest of the people did not go unchallenged, however. In 1924 the Grand Juror's Association of New York began publication of the *Panel,* a militantly pro-grand jury periodical. Through its pages, former grand jurors, judges, and prosecutors made clear the importance of the institution. The Association urged grand juries to exercise their full powers as representatives of the people and fought all attempts to make them mere agents of the court. As a result of its efforts grand juries took on a new importance for many citizens. But, at the same time, a series of crime surveys conducted by criminologists and sociologists sought to impress upon the American people the futility of having a panel of laymen enter a field about which they knew nothing. Crime commissions in Minnesota and New York both recommended broader powers for district attorneys to institute prosecutions. After careful study, experts surveying conditions in Illinois reported that grand juries handicapped prosecutors and delayed justice. In 1928, drafters of the American Law Institute's model Code of Criminal Procedure advised that all prosecutions be begun by information. Only one grand jury a year should meet in each county. They based their recommendation on advantages of speed, economy, and efficiency. In 1929, Professor Raymond Moley of Columbia University approved increased powers for prosecutors and characterized grand jury investigations as cumbersome and ineffective. Judge Roscoe Pound went even further and warned that inquests of the people constituted "a power needing check."

Crime Surveys

In 1928 the Social Science Research Council commissioned Professor Moley to make a survey to obtain accurate information on the relative efficiency of grand juries and public prosecutors. He and his staff compared criminal justice in three states (in which procedure was on information) with three others in which an indictment was required. Dean Wayne L. Morse of the University of Oregon conducted a poll of judicial opinion. Early in 1931 Moley and Morse released a summary of their findings. They concluded that the evidence showed public prosecutors to be "more efficient, economical and expeditious" than panels of citizen accusers. Moley contended that most grand juries were content to "rubber-stamp" the opinions of the district attorney and thus served to relieve prosecutors of their rightful responsibilities. The Moley survey focused public attention upon the weaknesses of the grand jury system but in so doing, it took into account only the tangible factors in criminal proceedings: speed, economy of operation, and percentage of convictions. Supporters of the jury system refused to agree that efficiency alone was an adequate criterion for justice under a democratic government. For criminal justice deals with people and the number and speed of convictions does not necessarily indicate a superior system.

Proponents of the grand jury rushed to answer Professor Moley. John D. Lindsay, a former New York district attorney, reminded the experts of what they seemed to have forgotten: that "the grand jury is the public and they have a right to investigate any evil condition of a criminal nature." United States District Attorney George Z. Medalie warned that the grand jury "breathes the spirit of the community" as no prosecutor could ever do. Others charged Moley with bias in interpreting his statistics and drew vastly different conclusions from the survey data. They maintained that grand juries were far from being "rubber-stamps" and caused little delay in criminal trials.

Shortly after Professor Moley made his findings public, the commission headed by George W. Wickersham submitted its recommendations on law enforcement to President Hoover. They advised abolishing grand juries on the ground that they served no useful purpose and impeded criminal courts. Thinking only in terms of efficiency, the commission viewed the grand jury as a "mitigating device and opportunity for escape" for criminals.

Success of Grand Juries

While experts in the United States flayed the system for its inefficiency, their English counterparts continued their efforts to abolish it. The depression came to their aid as the war had done in 1917, and made arguments of economy very appealing. In January 1930 the Lord Chief Justice observed that grand juries no longer served any useful function. Other jurists followed suit and called for an end to expensive juries in view of "the grave national emergency." Gradually, anti-jury forces impressed upon the depression-pinched English people the fact that great savings in tax money could be expected if they abandoned the system. A Commission of the House of Commons studied the matter and reported in favor of eliminating grand juries. The commissioners emphasized the burden of jury duty and the great expense of the system. Parliament accepted the recommendations of the special commission and abolished grand juries in England, effective September 1, 1933. Magistrates and others throughout the island who disliked seeing an end to the system, awoke only in time to deliver panegyrics over the corpse. During the spring and summer of 1933 they expressed their displeasure in grand jury charges and filled the columns of the *Times* with protests, but all to no avail. Professor W. S. Holdsworth castigated "the bureaucrats of Whitehall . . . and the lawyers who think with them" for establishing their own form of tyranny over the nation. It was only natural, Holdsworth observed, that they "should instinctively dislike anything which independently safeguards liberty." A national emergency finally accomplished what legal reformers had tried to do for over a century. The grand jury in England "succumbed to an acute onset of depression."

Grand juries themselves contributed greatly to the campaign to revitalize the institution. Their spectacular exploits captured the public imagination and led citizens of city after city to use this weapon against government by corruption. Americans could not help seeing the importance of having panels of citizen investigators when they watched a fearless grand jury in action. In April, 1933, a panel of citizens in Atlanta, Georgia, threatened to indict the county commissioners if they did not institute reforms. Judge John D. Humphries, speaking for the five judges on the Atlanta bench, rebuked the jurors for departing from their duties. He reminded them that they were mere agents of the court and would be "as helpless as a body of citizens meeting on a street corner" without the power of the court behind them. The jurors rebelled and demanded a new prosecutor and judge to work with, but the court denied their request. Before they adjourned, however, the jurymen indicted the county commissioners and appointed five citizens to conduct a thorough probe of the Municipal and Superior Courts and report to the next grand jury. The attack of Atlanta judges upon the powers of the local grand jury led residents to organize a grand juror's association to encourage future panels to uphold their rights.

In October, 1933, a Cleveland, Ohio grand jury began a probe of the city police department. Led by its energetic and fearless foreman, William Feather, the panel spent three months in investigation and issued a report which shocked the people of Cleveland. The jurymen announced that the entire city had been intimidated by union racketeers who received protection from city officials. They denounced law enforcement officers and declared that the local criminal court "neither merits nor receives the respect or confidence of the people." The jurors noted that the talent of the prosecutor's office was well "below par" and they chided the Cleveland Bar Association for its lack of concern in the matter. Before concluding its report, the grand jury reminded jurors throughout the state of Ohio that they, too, could initiate independent investigations. The succeeding Cleveland grand jury began a thorough inquiry into the defunct Guardian and Union Trust Companies. Indictments followed against officers of both for fraud. In October, 1934, citizens of Cleveland followed the example of those in Chicago and Atlanta and organized a grand juror's association to preserve the rights of their investigative body.

In New York, it took a fighting body of grand jurors to combat the hampering tactics of city officials and to mobilize public opinion for a thorough investigation of rackets. The March, 1935, grand jury took up a probe of policy rackets begun by a predecessor. It soon broke with District Attorney William C. Dodge and began summoning its own witnesses. Foreman Lee Thompson Smith took charge of the inquiry and demanded that the District Attorney appoint a special prosecutor. Racketeers threatened jurors and their investigators but they continued their work. When Dodge and the panel could not agree, the jurors asked the court to discharge them and they appealed to Governor Herbert Lehman to summon an extraordinary grand jury and appoint a special prosecutor. Governor Lehman named Thomas E. Dewey as special racket prosecutor and summoned a new panel to convene September 5, 1935. During the next four months the special jury examined over five hundred witnesses as they investigated racketeering in labor unions and trade and protective associations. In December 1935 the panel returned twenty-nine indictments, reporting that control over racketeering in New York City centered in the hands of a dozen or so major criminals who extorted millions from the city each year. A second extraordinary grand jury took up the racket probe in January, 1936. It uncovered a $12,000,000 prostitution racket and put vice lord Charles "Lucky" Luciano and his lieutenants on the road to prison. When the court discharged the panel in August, 1936, after seven months of service, it had broken the back of organized racketeering in New York City. Persons all over the United States followed the exploits of Prosecutor Dewey and his "racket busting" grand juries.

The example of New York gave a tremendous impetus to the work of laymen trying hard to revitalize the system. Beginning in September, 1937, a Philadelphia grand jury conducted a seventeen month crusade against vice and racketeering patterned after the Dewey investigations. In May, 1938, the jurors charged 107 persons with gambling and prostitution and accused police officials of accepting bribes to give immunity to criminals. The panel called for immediate dismissal of forty-one police officers on grounds of inefficiency and dishonesty. The jurors reported to the people of Philadelphia again in August, 1938, and charged city and county officials with a "criminal conspiracy" to protect crime and vice. In September they indicted Mayor S. Davis Wilson, on twenty-one counts, of misbehavior in office and failure to suppress crime. But the Mayor managed to have the indictments quashed on a technicality. In order to prevent further exposures by the grand jury, state officials withdrew financial support and the Philadelphia court discontinued the investigation. The jurors charged that the move was but "the culminating act of a long continued opposition which has crippled our work," and they appealed directly to the state Supreme Court which allowed them to continue their inquiry. Free to go ahead once more, the panel lashed out at the District Attorney, accusing him of using the vice investigation for political purposes. The jurymen demanded a complete reorganization of the Philadelphia police department, including dismissal of incompetent officers and reapportionment of police districts to end the influence of politicians. They concluded their work in March, 1939, by re-indicting Mayor

Wilson, accusing him of permitting vice and crime to flourish, while he issued blasts of meaningless words.

Investigations in other communities advertised effectively the capabilities of an alert grand jury, also. In Buffalo, New York, a special panel exposed bribery and fraud in the municipal government. Seventeen city officials faced trial for perjury and bribery. A Miami, Florida, inquest found that bribery had played an important part in establishing electric rates for their city, and they indicted Mayor Robert R. Williams, several councilmen, and other municipal officials. After a two month investigation of city affairs, the jurors condemned the police department for protecting criminals and criticized a newly instituted program to refund the city debt. Members of the jury did not cease to be concerned after they completed their work. As private citizens they inaugurated a recall movement which eventually removed Mayor Williams from office. At Greensboro, North Carolina, a grand jury initiated an inquiry into a primary election. In spite of determined opposition from the court, it discovered and reported many irregularities to the people.

Opposition to investigations frequently developed when grand juries threatened to expose prominent officials and upset the balance of political power. In April, 1938, Pennsylvania politicians were engaged in a heated primary election struggle. Dissident elements within the Democratic party leveled charges of corruption and fraud against the Democratic administration of Governor George H. Earle. The district attorney at Harrisburg petitioned for a special grand jury investigation and the Court of Quarter Sessions summoned a panel. Governor Earle took to the radio and in an address to the people of Pennsylvania charged that the proposed probe was "a politically inspired inquisition, to be conducted by henchmen of the Republican State Committee." Two days before the inquiry was to begin, the Attorney General asked the state Supreme Court to restrain the grand jury from beginning an investigation but, the high court declared that it had no such power. The panel prepared to convene early in August. On July 22, 1938, when it appeared that the administration had exhausted all efforts to block the inquiry, Governor Earle summoned an extraordinary session of the state legislature "to repel an unprecedented judicial invasion of the executive and legislative branches of our government." Three days later, he stood before the law makers and warned them that "the Inquisition and the Bloody Assizes ... stand as grim reminders of judicial tyranny." The Governor charged the judges and the District Attorney with abusing their authority and asked the legislature to look into their conduct. He then requested legislation to block the threatened grand jury probe.

The Democratic legislators rushed through a retroactive law suspending all investigations of public officials once the House of Representatives had taken jurisdiction and begun an inquiry. They also empowered the Attorney General to supersede any district attorney. A House committee launched an immediate investigation, but the court impounded all evidence awaiting the grand jury. Again the matter went to the Supreme Court. In October, 1938, it declared unconstitutional the law restricting investigations and reminded the legislators that they could not abolish the grand jury.

The example of public officials going to any length to prevent a panel of citizens from investigating, led New Yorkers to strengthen their grand jury system. Rallying behind the slogan, "What happened in Pennsylvania can happen here," the constitutional convention meeting at Albany in 1938 made certain that the grand jury would remain the people's shield against official corruption.

A new clause added to the state constitution provided that inquiries into official misconduct could never be suspended by law. In addition, all public officers summoned before grand juries had to testify without immunity or be removed from office. Pennsylvania's Governor Earle failed in his attempt to dictate to grand juries. Shortly after his defeat at the hands of the state Supreme Court, a panel of citizens investigated the state government and indicted Secretary of Highways Roy E. Brownmiller on charges of using $600,000 in state funds for political purposes.

The Pennsylvania lesson did not go unheeded in other states. Citizen's groups in Washington in June, 1941, succeeded in getting the state legislature to approve a constitutional amendment making one grand jury a year mandatory in each county. In addition, the amendment would bar prosecuting attorneys from advising grand juries. Special prosecutors conducted a vigorous campaign against the proposals and managed to defeat them in a referendum held in November, 1941. Citizens of Missouri were more successful. The convention which met in 1943 to revise the state constitution inserted a specific provision that the power of grand juries to investigate misconduct in public office should never be suspended.

The growth of dictatorship abroad and United States entry into the second World War convinced many thinking Americans that institutions which protected the rights of the people were not outmoded. Fear of executive tyranny and infringement of individual liberty gave a new importance to the inquest of the people. Those who had previously called for abolition of the grand jury for reasons of economy and efficiency now remained strangely silent. They did not reply when Governor Dewey denounced "the bright young theorists, the fuzzy minded crackpots and others of less idealistic purpose who would like to see the grand jury abolished;" or when Judge Francis Martin of New York dismissed charges that juries were rubber-stamps, "as the rantings of inexperienced and highly theoretical professors." With war and other threats to freedom close at hand, mere efficiency made less appeal. It became apparent to many persons that the grand jury was more than a means of bringing individuals to trial. It was an integral part of the American democratic government.

Grand Juries in a Democratic Government

Successful as grand juries have been in speaking out against abuses, there still remain threats to their existence as the spokesman of the people. Opponents of the grand jury in New York put a bill through the state legislature in 1946 prohibiting juries from making presentments or otherwise censuring persons for misconduct which did not constitute a crime. The Grand Jury Association of New York, metropolitan newspapers and civic and business groups conducted a vigorous campaign to have Governor Dewey veto the measure. They pointed out that the grand jury was the only local body which could effectively reprimand lax and indifferent public officials. Requests to veto the bill poured into Albany. In his veto message, Governor Dewey warned legislators that the power of grand juries should not be impaired and that they should remain "the bulwark of protection for the innocent and the sword of the community against wrong-doers."

Legislative restrictions upon grand juries are not the only threat to their survival. Legislative investigating committees have intruded upon the work of the grand inquest and have tended to replace them. The rules of evidence and other traditional safeguards which control the deliberations of a grand jury do not exist to protect witnesses before Congressional committees. Federal Judge Simon H. Rifkind reminded New York grand jurors in 1947 that legislative investigators constituted "a dangerous tendency" which juries could combat only by increased attention to their responsibilities. In 1950 the grand jury of Merrimack County, New Hampshire, investigated a large public utility company. At the conclusion of the probe a committee of the state legislature sought to question the jurors on their deliberations. Members of the panel refused to testify however, and the state Supreme Court upheld them. It warned the law makers that they had no power to interrogate grand jurors regarding their investigations.

Legislative investigators are not alone in encroaching upon the field of grand juries. In some states experts have already supplanted citizen panels for inquiries into official misconduct. This has been accomplished by setting up substitutes to take over the tasks normally performed by grand juries. Three states, Michigan, New Hampshire and Connecticut have created "one man grand juries" consisting of a magistrate empowered to launch investigations, summon witnesses and return indictments. This innovation has followed as a logical step in the process of excluding the people from law enforcement activities. In other states, legislatures have given judges powers similar to those of a grand jury, enabling them to conduct "John Doe" hearings to determine whether crimes have taken place. However efficiently magistrates may exercise their newly acquired authority, it is not in line with democratic procedure to destroy an investigating body composed of representative citizens and then delegate its broad inquisitorial powers to public officials.

Abolition of the grand jury leaves a void in local government which can be filled only by increasing the authority of judges and prosecutors. Substitution of a preliminary hearing by a committing magistrate had found the judge lacking in authority to perform properly the functions of a grand jury. Magistrates possess no power to launch investigations where specific charges have not been made. The system of giving district attorneys the authority to bring the persons to trial upon an information places too much power in the hands of the prosecution. In addition, under the information system the broad inquisitorial powers of the grand jury are lost. A prosecuting attorney may inquire into wrongdoing, but he lacks subpoena powers to compel the attendance of witnesses and the production of documents. Grand juries on the other hand may issue their own subpoenas for witnesses and records. They may cite recalcitrant witnesses for contempt and bring perjury charges against persons who refuse to tell the truth. They hear all testimony in secret and may indict or refuse to indict as they see fit. No power can influence them and panel members cannot be sued for libel for material contained in presentments or indictments. In most states which have abandoned the grand jury, it is held in reserve at the call of a judge, for instances of widespread violation of the law. But when this is done the procedure for summoning a grand jury is soon forgotten. Panels which must be specially called by a judge are not readily available to the people.

The work of grand juries may be improved by selecting competent individuals to serve as jurors. It is important that political factions within a community do not dominate the selection of grand jurors and use panels for partisan purposes. In some states jury commissioners have replaced sheriffs and other officials in choosing grand juries and they have done much to remove the procedure from politics. In New York City, county jury boards maintain a list of persons qualified to serve on grand juries. Any citizen may ask to be included on the list, but the board attempts to obtain a representative cross section of the community.

It is not enough to secure capable individuals to serve on grand juries. They must also be persons who understand their great responsibility and realize their tremendous powers for good. Jurors who perform their work in a routine and superficial manner betray the public interest and reflect upon the institution as a whole. They must take the initiative and remain independent of both court and prosecutor. They should not wait for the district attorney to lay cases before them. Judges have been partly to blame for grand jurors not understanding the extent of their powers. Many judges have intimated to juries that they were limited to considering matters suggested to them by the court or the prosecutor. They often fail to inform jurors of their power to launch investigations on their own initiative. Such practices have made many grand juries unwitting rubber stamps. Unless juries know and exercise their powers in the public interest and refute the arguments of those who wish to abolish them, they will sacrifice the confidence of the American people.

As an instrument of discovery against organized and far reaching crime, the grand jury has no counterpart. But, in spite of its broad investigating powers, legislation is needed in most states to strengthen the people's weapon by giving grand juries greater freedom to act. They often find themselves in the embarrassing position of being dependent upon the police department for evidence and the public prosecutor for legal advice. Juries should have the authority to employ investigators, expert accountants and separate counsel if they see fit. In large cities regular grand juries are frequently kept too busy with routine criminal matters to have sufficient time to supervise the conduct of public officials. Where this is true it would be a tremendous advance in the fight against racketeering and corruption to have special panels meet at stated intervals to guard against abuses in government.

If Americans are to take full advantage of the opportunity offered them by their grand juries, to make government more responsible, every citizen must know what grand inquests are and what they can do. Toward this end, associations of grand jurors have conducted vigorous educational campaigns and alert juries have demonstrated their value. But, there is a need for more widespread information on the importance of the institution to democratic government, to counteract the preachings of those who would restrict or abolish the people's panel. In states which have abandoned the grand jury, few persons realize the importance of their loss.

Today, the most important aspects of the grand jury are its democratic control and its local character. Governmental power has to a large extent replaced all other threats to democracy in the United States. The increasing centralization of governmental authority and the growth of a huge bureaucracy in no way responsible to the people, has made it vitally necessary to preserve the grand jury. It often serves as the citizen's only means of checking on political appointees or preventing illegal compulsion at the hands of zealous law enforcement officials. At a time when centralization of power in Washington has narrowed the area of democratic control, grand juries give the people an opportunity to participate in government and make their wishes known. In 1951, the Kefauver Crime Investigating Committee warned Americans not to rely upon the central government to control racketeering and organized crime in the United States. The Committee advised the people to use their local grand juries to attack conditions in their own communities. Citizen panels have demonstrated repeatedly in the past that they could protest effectively in the name of the people against centralized authority. Today, grand juries remain potentially the strongest weapon against big government and the threat of "statism."

THE FUNCTIONS OF THE JURY:
FACTS OR FICTIONS?

Dale W. Broeder

Although the jury system has been in vogue for more than three centuries, the functions which it performs are still only imperfectly understood. Even today the jury bears the imprint of the struggle out of which its modern characteristics emerged. More than any other institution, the jury has been the symbol of a democratic people zealous of freedom and afraid of centralized government power.

The "jury tradition" is as much outside the law as in it. While legally charged with more or less definite administrative functions, the jury is thought to perform other functions contravening the law it is supposed to administer. These extra-legal functions are occasionally urged as the jury's chief justification. The striking fact, however, is that no one really knows how well these supposed functions are performed. Prevailing knowledge of the jury's ability to perform the *strictly legal* tasks assigned to it is almost equally lacking. This universal public ignorance of the jury's abilities, however, is not accidental. The "jury tradition" has been the people's sacred democratic cow. Even judges have been induced to cover jury-room deliberations with legal shrouds calculated to protect them from close public scrutiny. The few legal devices which have been created to check the performance of the jury system have proved completely ineffectual. Self-contained impotence has carried them into almost total disuse.

While the jury may be a popular symbol of democracy, it is in one sense the antithesis of democratic government. The jury is responsible to no one. Its membership is anonymous. Jurors appear out of the ranks of society and as rapidly disappear back into them. The grounds for the jury's verdict are unknown. Barring extreme error, disappointed suitors must cry by themselves. This strange spectacle of an anonymous body of twelve men playing the role of one of democracy's chief symbols may well prompt examination. Consideration and comparison of the functions which the jury is ordinarily thought to perform should at least provide a tentative basis for reflection upon the current vitality and worth of the jury system in its entirety. A more definitive evaluation of the success with which the jury performs the many functions ascribed to it must await the completion of empirical investigations such as the one currently under way at the University of Chicago Law School.

I. The Jury as Fact-Finder

The jury's central legal function is to resolve the factual disputes involved in a law suit. The theoretically unlimited variety of issues requiring adjudication will, it is felt, be best disposed of in the long run by jurors whose worldly contacts have probably touched upon a question similar to that requiring

From *The University of Chicago Law Review*, vol. 21, 1954, pp. 386–424. Copyright © 1954 by *The University of Chicago Law Review*. Reprinted by permission.

adjudication. Jurors are visualized as practical men of affairs whose daily experiences require snap judgments of the honesty and character of persons with whom they deal. Even though a juryman-cobbler may not be the best judge of whether a corporate director has violated his fiduciary obligations, the juryman-banker on the same panel may well be. Fruitful discussion will resolve the differences between them. The next case may involve a cobbler charged with larceny of shoelaces.

The jury system also supposes that the judgment of twelve men whose differences are resolved through open-minded discussion is better than the judgment of one man whose trial experience is far more extensive. Although it is historically a matter of doubt, the reason for requiring unanimous agreement among jurors can easily be viewed as an attempt to give litigants the benefit of a full and complete discussion of disputed issues. The requirement of twelve men is conceivably an effort to ensure that there will be differences to discuss. One man cannot differ with his own judgment and any less than twelve men will reduce the probability of differences to be discussed. A fundamental tenet of the jury tradition, then, lies in its assumption that controverted factual issues are best resolved through reasoned discussion and debate.

The jury's fact-finding function often appears as a highly sophisticated process. The factual issues typically entrusted to the jury in civil cases, for example, cannot be decided by the exercise of reason alone. In order to submit a factual question to the jury in a civil case, the court must first determine that the question can reasonably be resolved either way. But if an issue can reasonably be resolved either way, the law cannot be asking the jury to decide it by the exercise of reason, for it cannot by definition be resolved in that way. In those cases where the jury is confined to passing on issues where "reasonable men may differ," therefore, the jury is to a considerable degree exercising a policy-declaring or law-making function. In such cases, the jury makes policy in the guise of "finding the facts."

The fact that an important aspect of the jury fact-finding process often consists in the enunciation of policy has significant analytical consequences. Techniques of analysis acquired from legal training and long years spent in presiding over trials, while highly desirable, perhaps essential qualities for deciding *purely factual* disputes, are not necessarily the most desirable qualities for the exercise of *policy-making* powers. The inexperience of jurors in resolving formalized factual disputes may frequently be overshadowed by the social importance of having inextricable disputes decided as twelve jurors of the community will decide them. This question is further dealt with below.

The average juror's inexperience in handling disputes may perhaps also be discounted by the inherent nature of the fact-finding process. Eminent psychological opinion can be marshalled in support of the view that complex factual disputes are resolved not so much by a minute weighing of individual testimony as by an over-all impression garnered from viewing the evidence as a whole. To the extent that this, the Gestaltist theory, is valid, a judgment proceeding from several persons is probably as good or even better than the judgment of one man whose unconscious mental and emotional processes cannot be checked against the reactions of others. The Gestaltist theory currently seems to provide the most sophisticated justification for the familiar common law rule forbidding jurors from taking notes. However, the force of saying that cases are decided by emotional-intellectual reactions to testimony viewed in its entirety rather than by conscious analysis of individual facts cuts heavily into the suggested rationale for the rule requiring unanimous agreement among jurors. "General feelings" about the manner in which a case should be decided are seldom capable of being profitably discussed.

While the merits of the jury as combination fact-finder and declarer of policy may at first blush seem rather substantial, a host of factors incident to the jury's practical operation have combined to insure that this function can at best be performed only with great difficulty. Legal rules, instead of being shaped to ameliorate the effects of the jury's practical weaknesses, seem to have been almost purposefully designed to augment them.

An excellent illustration of the positive steps the law has taken to impede the jury's successful performance of its fact-finding function is furnished by the typical jury selection process. The body of law governing the selection of jurors, rather than recognizing and attempting to reduce the effects of the juror's inexperience in handling legal matters, has instead exempted from service many of the groups who might best be expected to overcome this handicap. Professional men and women are exempted from jury duty in almost every American jurisdiction. Such exemptions become peculiarly incongruous in the light of the sophisticated nature of the jury's fact-finding function. The importance of having the views of professional persons who are often highly influential in molding community opinion to assist in supplying the element of policy necessary to resolve a dispute seems overwhelming.

The democratic process itself seems designed to insure the legislative exemption of persons most capable of resolving factual disputes. Jury service often involves heavy economic sacrifices, especially for those persons whose daily incomes are in excess of the per diem pittance meted out to jurors. It is only natural to expect that groups possessing substantial influence will utilize it for the purpose of securing legislative exemption. As the groups which can exert such pressures must possess a relatively small membership, the usual result is the exemption of doctors, lawyers, dentists, and educators of every grade and description.

The unattractive economic sacrifices incident to jury service, while in part responsible for the elimination of groups most capable of serving, has an even more undesirable aspect. Persons actively engaged in production who might be expected to possess superior character-gauging and intellectual qualities are the very persons who have an economic stake in inventing excuses sufficient to secure relief from jury duty. And even if they do serve, such persons have a definite economic interest in ending their periods of service as rapidly as possible. Persons suffering large economic sacrifices from jury service have much more to lose from protracted deliberations than their less fortunate colleagues.

The legal rules facilitating the elimination of persons most capable of serving on juries are carried much further than the simple process by which the typical *venire* is composed. Peremptory challenges, while probably desirable as a means of securing impartial jurors, are also often employed to exclude from the jury anyone "who is particularly experienced in the field of endeavor which is the basis of the law suit." Indeed, the use of peremptory challenges for this purpose is recommended by the leading commentaries on trial techniques. Such persons are likely to have too much influence with other jurors. The theory that the least informed are the most capable, however, would seem to be true principally for litigants whose cases are weak and who wish to pull wool over uninformed eyes.

The process by which jurors are selected is not the only means through which the jury's fact-finding efficiency is reduced. The surroundings of inquiry during a jury trial contribute heavily to the same end. The mode of presenting evidence is disorderly; interruptions are the rule rather than the exception. And the evidence bearing on a particular issue is not presented all at once, but at two distinct and possibly far removed points in the course of the trial.

The feats of memory required of jurors are prodigious. Applicable legal rules are announced only after and not before the evidence is introduced. So far as the jurors are concerned, the litigants' competing factual versions are presented in a non-legal vacuum. The successful integration of the facts with the law long after the facts have been presented and many of them forgotten is doubtless often impossible. Inasmuch as the legally crucial and legally unimportant aspects of the evidence are not distinguished until the trial is concluded, the jurors during the trial possess no means of knowing which aspects of the testimony they should particularly concern themselves with. The ultimate outcome of many trials must often depend on evidence which a jury considers insignificant until otherwise informed by the court. Instead of remembering the details of that which finally proves to be crucial, the average juror will instead probably recall emotional and dramatic incidents which are legally insignificant.

While the tremendous memory burdens imposed upon jurors could readily be lightened by permitting them to take notes, most jurisdictions forbid note-taking. Apart from the sophisticated psychological doctrine already noted, the common law rule's most forceful justification is that jurors differ in note-taking ability. If the prohibition were removed, efficient note-takers would be in a position to exert a disproportionate influence upon the jury's deliberations. While this justification may have possessed some degree of merit when most jurors were unable to read or write, it is currently nonsensical. Carried to its logical conclusion, it would require the exclusion of all jurors of superior mentality. The intelligent juror will almost always exercise more influence than his fellows. This observation considerably undermines the validity of the traditional assumptions concerning juror unanimity and the sacred number "twelve."

Even if it is assumed that jurors ordinarily possess the native intellectual ability necessary to absorb and retain vast amounts of factual material, the fullest employment of their faculties is severely impeded by the circumstances under which most trials are conducted. The typical trial is surcharged with emotion. The calm essential for dispassionate deliberation and the retention of large amounts of testimony is almost entirely absent. Not only are the factual questions involved in a trial frequently more complex than those with which most jurors are familiar, but, "jurors hear . . . evidence in a public place, under conditions of a kind to which they are unaccustomed: No juror is able to withdraw to his own room, or office, for private individual reflection. And, at the close of the trial, the jurors are pressed for time in reaching their joint decision. Even twelve experienced judges, deliberating together, would probably not function well under the conditions we impose on the twelve inexperienced laymen.

Apart from a few rules such as those preventing the admission of extremely prejudicial evidence, the courts have done little to restrain counsel from awakening the prejudices and arousing the passions of jurymen. In Tennessee, an advocate's right to cry before the jury has been pitched above the constitution, as "one of . . . [those] natural rights . . . which no Court or constitution . . . [can] take away." Indeed, it is a "serious question" in Tennessee "whether it is not . . . [counsel's] professional duty to shed . . . [tears] whenever proper occasion arises." The lawyer's professional duty to make the best possible use of the juror's emotions is urged in countless treatises on trial techniques, including a study written under the auspices of the American Bar Association. The advocate who can successfully appeal to prejudice, arouse the jurors' passions, and cloud the issues, instead of being pilloried by his associates, is canonized. It is no wonder that the courts look with kindly indulgence upon such rules as those permitting plaintiff's counsel in a paternity suit to parade the sorrowful mother with babe in arms before the jury, or to force the putative father to stand before his peers so that the jury can ascertain the purportedly close resemblance between the child's characteristics and his own. The toleration bestowed upon counsel's efforts to create sympathy for his client or to engender the jury's prejudice against his opponent is also mirrored in the willingness of "liberal" appellate courts to overlook "mildly inflammatory remarks." The willingness of these same courts unhesitatingly to reverse for almost insignificant errors in the trial court's instructions to the jury seems anomalous. While jurors may often be influenced by inflammatory remarks calculated to excite prejudice, it is probably the exceptional case in which a small error in the trial court's instructions influences the jury one way or another.

The striking degree to which the circumstances surrounding a jury trial differ from those in which jurors resolve factual disputes in private life is again apparent from an examination of the evidential materials upon which jurors rely in arriving at decisions in the two types of situations. While hearsay statements and the opinions of persons whom the juror respects often loom very large in the process leading up to his decisions in private life, the use of both hearsay and opinion in the courtroom is sharply restricted. The intricate web of evidential rules governing the receipt of testimony in jury trials seems poorly calculated to take advantage of whatever native decision-making abilities jurors possess.

However, in view of the sophisticated nature of the jury's fact-finding function in many cases, the reply to the contention that jurors can make little use of their native abilities in the courtroom might be that it really doesn't matter. As such questions can by definition reasonably be resolved either way, it is not necessary that jurors possess even average fact-finding abilities.

Several important objections can be urged against such an analysis. First of all, it is only in civil cases that the law confines the jury's fact-finding province solely to questions upon which "reasonable men may differ." In criminal cases, the jury is entrusted with all factual questions, whether reasonable men can differ on them or not. And even in civil cases, the necessary consequence of having the jury decide even one issue is to entrust the entire case into its hands. The usual lawsuit involves numerous factual questions. Although "reasonable men may differ" on how some of these questions may be resolved, there may be little basis for reasonable differences of opinion regarding others. Yet the generally employed practice of either permitting or requiring the jury to return a general verdict renders the court unable to ascertain the precise ground upon which the verdict rests. In addition, there are degrees of reasonableness. While experts might agree, for example, that reasonable men could differ as to how a given factual issue should be resolved, there is nevertheless a *theoretically correct* way to decide every such question. The more rational course for deciding the point seems to dictate the calling of more experts rather than submitting the issue to twelve laymen.

As already noted, the second most important justification of the view that the jurors' fact-finding abilities are immaterial is the theory that factual analysis is useless anyway and that the outcome of lawsuits principally depends upon the jurors' simple reactions to the evidence viewed in its entirety. If this contention is correct, the jury's verdict in many cases must be contrary to the law as declared in the instructions of the court. The Gestaltist theory of the decisional process assumes that a verdict will be returned for the litigant who appears best entitled to victory on the basis of the testimony as a whole, *with no regard for particular aspects of the case.* In a negligence action, for example, although the plaintiff may have established beyond question that the defendant was negligent and is clearly entitled to a verdict on the basis of the evidence considered *as a whole,* on the issue of contributory negligence the plaintiff's case might just barely be strong enough to avoid a directed verdict *for the defendant.* Yet on the theory that a factual analysis of the testimony is immaterial, the Gestalt theory would require that a verdict be directed *for the plaintiff.* Logically extended, the "snapshot theory" of the decisional process necessitates eliminating the jury in all cases where reasonable men could not differ about which party satisfied the Gestaltist-burden of showing that *most* of the factual disputes should be resolved in his favor. Furthermore, the Gestaltist doctrine ignores the jury's legal duty to decide factual disputes in accordance with law, and negates the theory that the jury rationally declares policy in the guise of finding facts. Rational balancing of conflicting community policies is impossible if a verdict must in any event be returned for the litigant who satisfies the burden of showing that *most* of the evidence is slanted in his favor.

    In view of the jury selection process and the vastly difficult conditions under which jurors labor, the theory that most jurors can correctly apply involved legal rules to complicated factual disputes, disregarding all testimony erroneously admitted, and in all other respects obey the court's instructions seems highly suspect. In many cases jurors will probably not even understand the legal rules announced by the court. Even lawyers cannot always accurately comprehend them. As Judge Jerome Frank has pointed out:

> To comprehend the meaning of many a legal rule requires special training. It is inconceivable that a body of twelve ordinary men . . . could, merely from listening to the instructions of the judge, gain the knowledge necessary to grasp the true import of the judge's words. For these words have often acquired their meaning as the result of hundreds of years of professional disputation in the courts. The jurors usually are as unlikely to get the meaning of those words as if they were spoken in Chinese, Sanskrit, or Choctaw.

    In numerous ways the courts appear to have recognized this. The development of legal rules governing motions for a new trial, the directed verdict, as well as demurrers to the pleadings and evidence bear too close a connection with the evolution of the modern jury trial to be pure historical accidents. All of these doctrines are merely mechanisms for transferring the burden of decision from the jury to the court, thus avoiding the risk that the jury will err in cases where the evidence is clearly all on one side. The flowering of various per se liability rules can be similarly explained.

    Many of the doctrines governing the admission of evidence amply reflect the low esteem in which courts have traditionally held the average juror's fact-finding abilities. Particularly is this true in such areas as relevance and materiality, where evidence, if admitted, is likely to create an unjustifiable prejudice or confuse the issues. While some doubt has been cast on the thesis that the inception of evidentiary rules in most cases corresponds with the emergence of the jury as an established fact-finding body, the continued vitality of the jury is certainly the principal justification for their retention today.

But the assumption of evidence law that the jury is ill-equipped to decide factual disputes is not consistently maintained. Thus, "[it] often happens . . . that an item of testimony will have a highly and illegitimately prejudicial effect upon one issue and a substantial, legitimately logical value upon another. The court then, with an inconsistency born of necessity, assumes that the jury which has not sufficient capacity to make the necessary discriminations upon the first issue has the ability to perform the psychological feat of disregarding the item entirely upon the first issue and of confining its influence to the second issue."

Finally, if society regarded jurors as more capable fact-finders than trial judges, we should expect that the numerous exceptions to the right of trial by jury would not have arisen. In this respect, there is little excuse for distinctions so subtle as that between a fraud action for damages and an action for recision in equity based upon the same facts.

A brief appraisal of the consequences which have resulted from the jury's function as finder of facts gives added perspective from which to view the success which the jury has exhibited in this capacity. These consequences are profound.

While the jury cannot be charged with responsibility for necessitating the troublesome distinction between questions of fact and law, it has certainly heightened the significance of the distinction. The social quest for legal rules adapted as guides to future conduct, coupled with the laymen's total lack of understanding in legal affairs, must early have given rise to the practice of judicial instructions concerning the law. While it was for the jury to decide "pure questions of fact," it was the province of the court to advise the jury on "matters of law." The judicial practice of instructing the jury on matters of law has probably been the most fruitful source of error in our jurisprudence. As already noted, appellate courts have displayed a strange fear that jurors will be misled by instructions which the courts in other connections seem to recognize that many jurors probably cannot even understand.

In addition to errors in the court's instructions to the jury, the distinction between law and fact may result in the submission of a question to the jury which an appellate court later decides was a question of law for the court. Whatever service the jury performs as a convenient device for separating factual and legal questions (thus preventing future cases involving different facts from being governed by a combined set of legal and factual determinations valid only for the case in which they were first employed), seems outweighed by the deleterious effects produced by frequent disputes concerning the scope of legal and factual questions and by the jury's fact-finding difficulties in general.

Erroneous comments on the evidence, and irrelevant, inflammatory, or prejudicial remarks of counsel or court are additional sources of error stemming from the jury's fact-finding function. Evidential errors furnish an even more frequent cause for reversal; and are, indeed, often the only means by which an appellate court can overturn a verdict which has a reasonable basis in the evidence, but which the court feels morally certain is in error.

The well-intrenched distinction between law and equity can in some measure also be ascribed to the jury. The numerous cases dealing with the proper scope of appellate review would long ago have ceased to have meaning had litigants not been permitted the opportunity of wrangling over the right to a jury trial. Procedural errors resulting from uncertainty as to when jury trials may be obtained under merged procedure afford an additional cause for expense and delay.

Another chief consequence of the litigants' right to a jury trial is seen in the effects produced upon the courts' willingness to utilize modern scientific techniques. Fearing the undue weight which the average juror might attach to these techniques, the courts have either severely restricted their use or prohibited them from being used altogether. As the evidential rules governing the receipt of scientific testimony have been carried over to cases at law tried without juries, and to cases in equity, the result has been to stultify considerably the over-all sophistication of judicial inquiry. And even where such techniques are admitted as evidence, the degree of conclusiveness which science attaches to them has often been ignored. Oddly enough, courts which greatly restrict the use of many kinds of scientific techniques for fear of the jury's inability to accord them proper weight, also frequently assume that jurors possess sufficient technical ability to detect error in the most complicated scientific experiment. The attitude of the California court in the case of *Berry v. Chaplin,* permitting the jury to return a verdict in the fact of uncontroverted and unimpeached scientific testimony that the defendant could not have been the father of the plaintiff's child, is typical of many tribunals. The rationale of such decisions rests on the assumption that the jury must have "felt" there was error in the conduct of the experiment. Concededly, however, disregard of scientific facts has not always been confined to juries.

The crudity of legal administration necessitated by the jury is exemplified in rules other than those governing the admissibility of scientific techniques. A significant portion of the evidential doctrines restricting or precluding the rational use of lay and expert opinion testimony can also be ascribed to the jury. The familiar rubric concerning illicit invasions of the jury's fact-finding province, on the ultimate issues and otherwise, furnishes the most frequently expressed basis for such doctrines. Judicial skepticism of the jury is also mirrored in the well-established doctrine that life-expectancy and annuity tables are to be employed only with great caution, if at all. The Pennsylvania court has refused to sanction the use of annuity tables by the jury under any circumstances, remarking that, "The less jurors are burdened with complicated tables and the necessity for complex calculations, the more likely will they be to do substantial justice." And even where such tables are admitted, the jury's discretion is safeguarded unless clearly erroneous. Particularly is this true of cases arising under wrongful death statutes. Rules pertaining to the use of statistical aids in determining damages, however, are merely one aspect of the widespread influence of the jury in the shaping of damage law. In many cases, the jury's inability to do anything but speculate on the amount of the plaintiff's damages results in a complete denial of recovery, despite the fact that valid statistical means of estimating them exist. Such cases are in striking contrast to the vast disparity in damage awards reflected in jury verdicts in all types of litigation.

II. The Jury As Judges of the Law

It was apparently the view of Mr. Justice Holmes that the jury's functions might on occasion extend to the decision of questions of law which would bind the court in *future litigation* involving different parties. In the Massachusetts case of *Commonwealth v. Sullivan,* Holmes declared that as the legal question of whether "bank-nite" was a lottery had been determined in the affirmative by a jury in the earlier case of *Commonwealth v. Wright,* it was "not necessary to go on forever taking the opinion of the jury," but that the jury's verdict in the *Wright* case had finally determined the question. The power to create precedents, long thought to be an exclusively judicial function, was thus placed within the province of the jury as well as the court.

But the Holmesian view concerning the proper scope of the jury's law-making function, however influential in jurisprudential theory, has not prevailed in the courtroom. The Holmes' opinion in *Commonwealth v. Sullivan* excepted, no case has been uncovered in which a court has shown itself willing to share stare decisis powers with a body of twelve laymen. The resolution of statutory ambiguities for the purpose of providing legal standards to guide future adjudication has remained a strictly judicial function.

While the jury tradition has not as yet engulfed the courts' stare decisis powers, the jury has, in a variety of contexts, been charged with the duty of declaring law for *particular cases*. Three questions must be carefully distinguished: (1) the jury's duty to declare the law in opposition to what the trial judge says the law is; (2) the jury's duty to decide, pursuant to legal standards laid down by the court, whether a given type of conduct or group of events falls within a legal rule; and (3) the jury's duty to inject an element of community sentiment into its resolution of issues upon which reasonable men may differ. The third of these questions having already been discussed, only the first and second remain for consideration.

As late as 1794, in the case of *Georgia v. Brailsford,* Chief Justice Jay was stating that the jury's functions in civil cases encompassed the duty of disregarding the court's instructions on the law if the jury felt them to be erroneous. Several other early American cases support a similar doctrine. Indeed, in the period following the Revolutionary War, the jury's duty to ignore whatever legal rules it felt were unjustified was considered of such importance in Georgia that it was constitutionally safeguarded. So far as civil cases are concerned, however, this aspect of jury supremacy over the law has completely disappeared and it is everywhere settled that the jury must in civil cases take the law as the court's instructions direct.

In criminal cases, recognition afforded the jury's duty to decide the law in opposition to the stated views of the trial court has been much more widespread. In several states, explicit constitutional provisions were adopted to safeguard it. In Illinois, for example, the constitution was thought to permit counsel to argue judicial opinions before the jury as late as 1931. By a gradual process of judicial emasculation, however, state constitutional provisions empowering the jury in criminal cases to decide legal questions have been rendered meaningless. The formerly well-entrenched criminal law notion that the jury is rightfully entitled to disregard the law as given in the court's instructions has now been repudiated in all states but Indiana and Maryland.

The question of whether the jury could legally disregard the instructions of the court was at last conclusively settled for the federal system in the case of *Spark and Hansen v. United States.* The majority of the Court, by Justice Harlan, held that the jury is bound, in criminal as well as civil cases, to follow the judge's instructions upon all matters of law. Justice Gray, with Justice Shiras concurring, vigorously dissented in a seventy-three page opinion. While the major portion of both opinions is superficially concerned with a disposition of prior cases, the crucial issue, certainly for the majority, was whether it could be admitted that the jury had the right to dispense with the operation of law in particular cases and, in effect, to declare statutes unconstitutional. In several glowing rhetorical passages which can easily be read as an elevation of stare decisis principles to the level of constitutional law, the Court spoke eloquently of the need for uniformity of statutory interpretation and administration, for a government of law and not of men, for legal signposts lighting the way for future adjudication as contrasted with the hit-or-miss blackness of the jury's general verdict on the law. For Justice Gray, the issue was liberty against uniformity, the need for flexibility as opposed to the mechanical desire of the majority to place everyone on the same administrative level. Both Harlan and Gray conceded the power of the jury to suspend the law; they differed over the jury's right to do it. Jerome Frank and others have argued that no practical distinction can be drawn between *jury power* and *jury right*. But this implies that the distinction is meaningless. Actually, the practical implications of Justice Gray's position are profound. An admission by the nation's highest Court that twelve laymen are more capable of deciding law than trial judges would probably have led to a drastic modification of the jury system. In an important sense, therefore, the real friend of the jury was not Gray, but Harlan.

The position of the majority in *Spark and Hansen,* that uniformity of adjudication is superior to flexibility in individual cases, is in striking analytical contrast to the universally recognized function of the jury to decide, pursuant to legal standards laid down by the court, whether a certain type of conduct or group of events falls within a given legal definition. A consistent application of the "government by law" rationale constituting the basis for the *Sparf* ruling seems to require that the jury be deprived of the right to decide questions of law under all circumstances. Theoretically, of course, the "government by law" principle is not necessarily opposed to current practice. The jury can be conceived of as deciding in accordance with law because it is the law that the jury should decide what the law is. Practically, however, different juries must frequently decide law differently and uniformity in the administration of justice becomes impossible. General verdicts are not stare decisis; no records are even kept of them.

The determination of whether certain conduct falls within a particular legal category has frequently been left to the jury on the theory that such a determination involves a "mixed question of law and fact." In one sense, at least, all such questions are "mixed questions of law and fact." Yet in a very large number of cases, the fitting of facts into a legal rule is held to involve a "pure question of law." Thus, the question raised by a demurrer to an indictment in an ordinary criminal case on the ground that the facts alleged do not charge an offense is the same type of question as that involved in determining whether a book is obscene or whether a defendant acted as a reasonably prudent man. On demurrer, all three cases raise the issue of whether certain conceded facts fall within a general rule of law. Yet the first of these issues is everywhere held to be a "pure question of law," while the latter two issues are denominated "mixed questions of law and fact." It is apparent that the use of such labels is merely a convenient method of characterizing which of such questions are for the court and which are for the jury.

That the phrase "mixed question of law and fact" represents a mere legal conclusion, however, does not detract from the significance of the consequences resulting from its use. When a court characterizes an issue as involving a "mixed question of law and fact" it is almost universally sent to the jury and, more important, cannot be taken from the jury if reasonable men can differ on how it should be resolved.

The most familiar example of a "mixed question of law and fact" consists in the jury's determination in negligence cases of whether a defendant has acted reasonably. While the question of whether the defendant acted reasonably is a "question of fact" in the sense that he either did or did not perform certain acts which a prudent man would have performed, it also involves a "question of law." For to determine what a prudent man would have done is to define particularly the legal standard which the defendant's conduct must meet in order to avert liability for negligence. When the jury decides whether the defendant acted reasonably, it is not deciding a "pure question of fact," such as whether a dog drowned or the defendant struck Brown. Of course, preliminary questions concerning the existence of a legal duty on the part of the defendant to act reasonably toward the plaintiff and whether reasonable men could differ on whether this legal duty was violated are questions for the court. It is also the court's function to instruct the jury on the nature of the defendant's legal duty in general; the defendant should have acted as a reasonably prudent man considering all of the circumstances under which the accident took place. But it is for the jury rather than the court to say what *was* reasonable under the circumstances, and to fit into the court's general definition the facts of a particular case.

It is perfectly conceivable that the law should have legal standards of reasonableness covering a large variety of *particular situations.* The progressive fashioning of such rules was advocated by Justice Holmes, and has had considerable influence in tort law generally. It must be emphasized, however, that particularized standards of reasonableness cannot at present be formulated if reasonable men might arrive at a different result on a given set of facts. For to do so would involve an invasion of a litigant's right to a trial by jury.

The Pennsylvania stop-look-and-listen rule furnishes perhaps the most familiar illustration of a judicially prescribed standard of reasonableness for a particular situation. Regardless of unusual circumstances, such as visual obstructions, rain, snow, or fog, or even an actual invitation to cross, the plaintiff's failure to stop before crossing a railroad track is negligence per se. The rule "is not a rule of evidence, but a rule of law, peremptory, absolute and unbending; and the jury can never be permitted to ignore it, to evade it or to pare it away by distinctions and exceptions." Numerous other examples of judicially created rules governing particular situations could also be mentioned. Their vitality, however, is on the wane and they have always been exceptions to the normal rule that the particular standard of reasonableness is a question for the jury.

The principal argument favoring a judicial particularization of legal rules in negligence cases is the added predictability which would result from taking such questions from the jury. Currently, the only instance in which the court is legally empowered to formulate a particularized standard of conduct is where reasonable men could not differ regarding its correctness. If the courts were *always* required to determine the precise legal nature of the defendant's conduct, negligence law would be much more predictable. Whatever injustice may exist under current practice, however, is said to be justified by the fact that defendants can be negligent in a vast number of ways, and that stare decisis codification of particularized rules is impossible. A corollary of this notion is that codification would produce more injustice than it would alleviate. It is doubtful whether these arguments alone are powerful enough to counter-balance the undesirable effects of the uncertainty resulting from the submission of such questions to the jury. A more decisive consideration, however, is that most negligence actions arise out of factual settings in which the non-existence of precedents concerning reasonableness is immaterial. It is an extraordinary individual who consults a lawyer before deciding to drive in excess of a given speed, or before making a left-hand turn without signaling properly. Yet the reasons justifying the practice of submitting the negligence issue to a jury in civil cases are probably insufficient to justify a similar practice in criminal negligence actions. Not only is there a greater need for predictability in criminal cases, but the pressing necessity of administering justice even-handedly between two similarly situated and equally culpable defendants applies with much greater force in criminal cases.

The lack of predictability resulting from the practice of entrusting "mixed questions of law and fact" to the jury is not confined to the law of criminal negligence. Indeed, the practice seems unjustified in any instance where the social policies underlying the need for predictability and equality before the law overshadow the difficulties attendant upon the formulation of particularized legal rules. In the resolution of constitutional questions, for example, the need for predictability is paramount. Yet there are currently a large number of combined legal and factual determinations in this area which are left to the jury. In a recent Maryland case, for example, the jury was permitted to determine whether the plaintiff was denied the equal protection of the laws because of an alleged inadequacy of Negro as contrasted with white public golf facilities. So far as third parties are concerned, of course, the general verdict which resulted left the question as unsettled as before the litigation began. Other equally unjustified examples of the above practice are afforded by the submission to the jury of the "just rate" and "just compensation" issues involved in public utility and eminent domain litigation. Only last term the Court sustained the New York practice of leaving the question of whether a confession is voluntary to the jury, even though the effect of the practice is virtually to deprive defendants of any independent determination of the voluntariness issue whatever. The mixed legal and factual question involved in determining whether a statute is "reasonable" has also occasionally been left to the jury. Indeed, support for such a practice can be found in the judicial opinions of the nation's highest Court.

Currently, however, the practice of entrusting mixed questions of law and fact to the jury has worked its most unfavorable effects in the law of free speech. The doctrine that First Amendment rights are particularly worthy of protection, and that all attempts to infringe upon them must pass the most rigid judicial scrutiny would seem to require that such questions be kept from the jury at all costs. Actually, however, the exact opposite is true. In an obscenity case, for example, the issue of a book's obscene character is generally held to be a question for the jury. And, because a "mixed question of law and fact" is said to be involved, the question raised by the defendant's demurrer on the ground of the indictment's failure to state an offense is not whether the book is obscene, but whether twelve jurors could reasonably differ on its obscene character. As already noted, however, the question raised by the defendant's demurrer in an ordinary criminal case is held to involve a "pure question of law." Thus, if A is indicted for an attempted murder and it is alleged as constituting such an attempt that A purchased a gun with the intent to shoot X, on A's demurrer the court would determine, not whether reasonable men could differ as to whether these acts constituted an attempt, but whether they do so as a *matter of law*. A person about to commit arson, rape, murder or some other crime involving what the courts have analyzed as a "pure question of law" can consult judicial opinions discussing precisely what acts constitute these offenses. Yet a person about to write a book which could conceivably be labeled obscene is deprived of precedents discussing precisely what books are obscene. The lack of predictability attendant upon submitting the obscenity issue to the jury simply results in inhibiting people from experimenting with new art forms. To this extent, of course, the scope of the First Amendment's free speech protection is curtailed.

Almost all free speech cases have been held to involve "mixed questions of law and fact." For example, the issue of whether a defendant's speech activities constitute a clear and present danger has frequently been left to the jury. The contrary practice approved in *Dennis v. United States* probably only extends to cases where the scope of the danger alleged to be clear and present is world-wide, or at the most, to cases where the scope of the alleged danger involves a prediction of an alleged danger's future magnitude. There is little question that the jury's determination of the clear and present danger issue is still the ordinary and legally accepted practice. The result, of course, is again to deprive the political reformer of valuable judicial determinations on just what speech activities the First Amendment protects.

Cases involving negligence, obscenity, libel, slander, indecency, and certain types of political free speech are the principal instances in which the jury has been given the right to decide law, even for particular cases. The negligence exception to the rule that legal questions are solely for the court can perhaps be rationalized. The other exceptions cannot be. The practical effect of submitting these questions to the jury is to deprive groups such as authors, playwrights and political reformers of legal standards by which to guide their conduct. Libel, slander, obscenity and political free speech situations would seem to require, because of their very "amorphousness," a higher degree of "advance legal notice" than any other kind of case. Legal rules here, if anywhere, are essential to government by law.

III. The Jury As Law Dispenser

The power of the jury to dispense with the operation of law in particular cases has often been heralded as its greatest function. The flexibility of administration made possible by the general verdict is said to render otherwise impersonal legal rules human and to supply the needed filling out of the exceptions necessarily left unprovided for in any rational legal system. The law-dispensing function of the jury also makes gradual change possible and is an expediter in the implementation of community sentiment. Jury verdicts permit laws to anticipate the democratic process. While the fiction of stability is maintained until the legislature can act, the law is enabled to move ahead by dispensing with itself.

Several observations can be made concerning the jury's law-dispensing function. In the first place, we do not know how well it works; the verdict is a seal of secrecy which the law has thus far refused to open. While it is generally recognized that juries often return verdicts contrary to law, we cannot be sure whether this results from conscious law-dispensing or pure bungling. For many juries, the conscientious application of the court's instructions to the facts may result in an unconscious dispensing with the law. Juries themselves do not always know what they are doing. Furthermore, exceptions to the ordinary legal rules work both ways. Persons who look with favor upon the jury's legislative powers generally think only one way, of the murder case, for example, where the defendant shot his wife's paramour in a fit of blind rage, or where the community's most able and God-fearing doctor administered poison to put his best friend out of misery. Where the prejudices of the community are shrouded in the verdict's mystery to carve out an exception from a rule whose normal operation would permit the defendant to go free, law-dispensing becomes less palatable. The bona-fide white male conviction of a Negro for leering at a white girl at a distance of over sixty feet is a Southern exception to the ordinary assault rule. Other examples must be legion; the white-washing of lynchers is also law-dispensing.

In addition to being an inconsistent law-dispenser, the jury is in many respects a highly unrepresentative one. If the jury is designed to function as a minor legislature, it should represent a total cross-section of the community. The fact is, of course, that democratic processes cannot always produce changes which juries have effected. In many cases, no person would vote for the abolition of a law which he might readily ignore in his capacity as juror. In other cases, of course, we may predict with more or less certainty that the legislature will ultimately effectuate the changes juries have sought to implement. Familiar examples are found in the largely outmoded fellow-servant rule, and in the doctrine of contributory negligence. It is probable, however, that the legal remains of these doctrines would long ago have passed out of our law had not the jury made their presence less disturbing. Instead of facilitating desirable changes in the law, jury verdicts may in many cases retard such changes. Meanwhile, juries are permitted to deal differently with persons who are similarly situated. The long hours lawyers spend in assembling juries is ample evidence of this. The incidence of typical jury room legislation has probably, in the long run, benefited comparatively few. The most telling objection which can be urged against the exercise of the jury's power to dispense with the law, however, is that it is contrary to law and to the "government by law" principle. Men who act arbitrarily all too frequently act unjustly. And it makes little sense to tell jurors to follow the law, while hoping and recognizing that they will disobey it anyway.

IV. The Jury's Function in Criminal Cases

While the jury currently occupies a sacrosanct position in civil cases, its position in criminal litigation is doubly secure. Possibly this is a mere reflection of the close historical identification of the jury with freedom. More probably it is a result of the wide-spread feeling that the jury is more effective in criminal proceedings and that an accused is entitled to the best democracy can offer him. A third possible explanation is similar to the second but diametrically opposed to it. This is the theory that democracy's best is efficiency's worst and that criminal juries are worshipped for their aberrations because we are all potential criminals.

Probably no one of these three theories is entirely correct nor altogether wrong. Historically, of course, the traditional association of the criminal jury trial with freedom is erroneous. The jury originated as a purely administrative device designed to extend the power of a dictatorial monarchy. Only centuries later did it become the basis of a rebellion against absolutism. But the criminal jury's function as a protector of the individual against government is anomalous in far more than a simple historical sense. So long as the balance of power between government and the people rests with the former, twelve commoners of the vicinage can be expected to shield individuals fighting against government oppression. But when the balance of power is reversed, instead of opposing the government's attempted oppressions, jurors are more likely to favor them. From the time of the Alien and Sedition Acts, the government's attempted inroads on civil rights seem to have received the enthusiastic support of jurors. As Judge

Amidon remarked after extensive experience with Espionage Act prosecutions during the First World War:

> Only those who have administered the Espionage Act can understand the danger of such legislation. . . . Most of the jurymen have sons in the war. They are all under the power of the passions which war engenders. For the first six months after June 15, 1917, I tried war cases before jurymen who were candid, sober, intelligent business men, whom I had known for thirty years, and who under ordinary circumstances would have had the highest respect for my declarations of law, but during that period they looked back into my eyes with the savagery of wild animals, saying by their manner, "Away with this twiddling, let us get at him." Men believed during that period that the only verdict in a war case, which could show loyalty, was a verdict of guilty.

Judge Amidon's experience has been mirrored in every period of panic and popular indignation from earliest times down to the present. But the case against the criminal jury as a protector of individual liberty extends further than to contests between government and citizens opposed to its policies. Minority groups have often suffered at the hands of jurymen. Wholesale acquittals of lynch-law violators, convictions of Negroes on the slightest evidence, and numerous other occurrences which have now almost become a part of the jury tradition might be instanced as examples.

The jury in criminal cases has another perhaps equally unpalatable aspect. In a democratic society, it is a definite obstacle to reform and innovation. As jurors will usually reflect the opinions of a majority of the community, so long as the majority itself remains unconvinced of the attempted reform's wisdom, juries will usually reflect a similar sentiment. Thus, artistic innovations have often been thwarted. In a few jurisdictions, obscenity convictions have been obtained for writing and publishing some of America's best literature. Writers and producers of the finest modern stage plays have often suffered similarly.

Aside from the incidental psychological functions which the criminal jury is alleged to perform, the sole remaining virtue claimed for it lies in its ability to make allowances for the circumstances of the particular case--to dispense with a rule of law. As noted previously, however, law-dispensing is a two-edged sword, and there is no current means of ascertaining which way it more often swings. It may seriously be doubted whether entrusting the jury with law-dispensing powers is justified. While flexibility of legal administration is desirable, it would seem that the necessary exceptions to the normal rules could with better reason be fashioned by the legislature or court.

While literature dealing with the jury often reflects a belief that juries in criminal cases are "more reliable" than in civil cases, the rationale underlying this belief is not altogether clear. Its chief justification seems to rest in the comparatively less complex issues typically involved in criminal cases. An additional justification might be found in the more serious nature of criminal proceedings. Jurors in criminal cases deal in lives and freedom, not money damages, and should be expected to perform their tasks more efficiently. Whether they do so, however, may be doubted. Emotional pressures operative in civil proceedings are magnified many-fold in serious criminal cases. Instead of being confined solely to the courtroom such pressures are often exerted with tremendous force in the newspapers, on television and radio. The juror's native prejudices are more easily aroused in a criminal case and may, by the time he is selected for service, have been fanned to a fevered pitch by community outrage against the crime the defendant is accused of having committed. It is well known that frequent changes of venue are necessitated by the inability of veniremen to afford the defendant a fair trial; and cases have arisen in which the defendant's only alternatives were to run the risk of a biased jury or rot in jail because of inability to post bail or because bail had been denied. In most jurisdictions, the defendant is not allowed unilaterally to waive judgment by his peers, and prosecutors eager for publicity are not always willing to give the required consent.

On the whole, the criminal jury's ability to measure up to the heavy tasks assigned it is seemingly no greater than that of juries handling non-criminal matters. The increased emotion attendant upon criminal trials probably warps the jury's fact-finding abilities in roughly the same degree as does the complexity of issues involved in civil cases. If juries are such excellent judges of character as one is often led to suppose, there appears to be no reason why sentencing powers ought not also to be entrusted to them and why courts should treat them with the tenderness one would accord children.

V. The Jury As a Means of Inducing Confidence in the Law

In addition to its numerous other alleged functions, it is claimed that the jury system induces public confidence in the administration of justice. There are two aspects to this contention. First of all, the community is said to have more confidence in the judgment of laymen than of those who are learned in the law. But this first point may be disposed of briefly, for even if its correctness be conceded, it proves nothing about the degree to which public faith in the jury is justified. Secondly, public confidence in the administration of justice is said to arise out of the fact that complicated and occasionally insoluble factual disputes have the appearance of being settled with ease when wrapped in the silent garb of a verdict returned in supposed compliance with strict legal rules. The unanimity requirement itself seems to suggest that rational disagreement on the issues submitted to a jury is impossible. The jury enables the law to say: "No dispute is too tough; there is a definite legal solution for all problems." The precisional certainty engendered by the jury in turn induces respect for law and for legal institutions in general.

The claim that the jury whose most familiar characteristic is its power to ignore the law somehow renders the law more certain in the process of dispensing with it seems at first almost incredible. There is, however, a small measure of truth in this claim. Reasoning powers are often incapable of coping with knotty factual disputes; and to the extent that jury magic can resolve them, legal certainty can in one sense be regarded as having been enhanced. To a large extent, however, the certainty which the jury provides is fictional. The air of mystery surrounding its deliberations, the uninforming nature of the verdict itself, the vast differences of opinion exhibited in the verdicts of different juries, together with the fact that verdicts are not reported and cannot be used as guides for the future all illustrate that the sort of certainty involved is only skin deep.

Nevertheless, the law has taken numerous steps to ensure that the fiction of certainty provided by juries does not become tarnished. A verdict cannot be impeached save under highly exceptional circumstances. Jurors have a testimonial privilege and perhaps even a legal duty not to disclose jury room deliberations. They cannot be polled concerning the means by which their decision was reached, either before or after the verdict has technically been received. It is only with the greatest difficulty that a verdict can ever be overthrown. The sanctity of the jury room has become a judicial fetish. The use of special interrogatories and special verdicts has been greatly restricted. Even today most judges exhibit surprising reluctance to require special verdicts; and Rule 38 of the Federal Rules of Civil Procedure has been interpreted to preserve the court's traditional discretion in this matter. The results which have obtained on those few occasions when jury room secrecy has been bared are astounding—quotient verdicts, prejudice, fraud, and ignorance of what has previously transpired in the court room.

VI. The Jury As an Educating Force in the Community

Jury service furnishes the only means, other than by voting, through which the citizen can actually participate in the administration of government. Service on a jury gives one a sense of community responsibility. It acquaints the citizen with justice as it is practically administered. Of this, there can be no doubt.

But what of the litigants? The fact that jury service educates thrusts more than one way. Certainly those who must submit themselves to a trier of fact are entitled to someone more capable than people going to jury school for the first time. If citizens really have to serve on juries in order to become aware of how justice is practically administered, they must, in practice, prove highly incompetent jurors. To the extent that the jury does operate as an educating force, however, its worth must be measured against its inefficiency in other respects. The creation of responsibility in jurors is only incidental to the jury's more central functions. The jury was not instituted as a substitute for education, but as a means of trying lawsuits.

But the educational force of jury service can be questioned on more than a theoretical level. In most jurisdictions the period of service is extremely short, ordinarily but two weeks. And little effort has been made to train jurors in what they are supposed to do. Simple indoctrinating handbooks have been judicially proscribed in Illinois, and their use is optional in the federal system and in the few states which provide them. Jury schools are unheard of; we first prefer to test citizens on litigants.

The probability that many jurors fail to grasp the significance of the court's instructions and even, in many cases, to comprehend the complex factual issues submitted to them for decision, instead of encouraging a sense of community responsibility, might be expected to derogate from it. Removing jurors from their private jobs and forcing them to assume heavy economic sacrifices in order to sit in judgment before issues which some of them cannot even understand can only encourage disrespect for the law. Finally, many jurors do not want the kind of education that jury service is claimed to provide. The costs are too great in relation to what is learned. Resultant attempts to secure exemption from service are wide-spread. Jury service is familiarly regarded as irksome.

VII. The Jury As an Escape from Judicial Bias and Corruption

Unfortunately, there can be little doubt that many judges have exhibited bias and that some judges are corrupt. Perhaps to some extent juries have functioned as a counteracting force. But the ultimate answer to judicial bias and corruption is not more juries, but better judges. Furthermore, those instances in which judges are likely to be biased and corrupt are often cases in which the jury would be powerless to act if it would. The corrupt or biased judge directs verdicts or rules at odds with the law on questions such as the admissibility of testimony; or the jury's verdict may be set aside as against the weight of the evidence; or the judge may declare himself in error on a previous legal ruling and direct a new trial. Even in those instances where the jury could act to thwart illicit judicial sympathies, the judge's prejudice, rather than being counter-balanced by the jury, may be complemented by it. Either the jury may be biased in the first place, or the judge, with a know-how born of experience, may render it so. Finally, the prejudice problem, while troublesome in the case of judges, is far more pronounced in the case of juries. Typically, the judge restrains the jury, not the other way around.

In one rather large body of cases, however, the jury may operate as a significant mainstay against judicial bias and corruption. In criminal cases, judges often acquire a vested interest in law enforcement; continuance in office often turns on the number of convictions which can be paraded before an electorate. The judge's friend and fellow political worker is often the prosecuting attorney or one of his subordinates or, on the other hand, the defendant's attorney. Similar considerations may produce undue judicial sympathy for one of the litigants in civil proceedings. In all of these cases, the jury is often a definite social asset. Significantly, however, most of the instances mentioned stem from the circumstance that judges are elected, often for short terms and subject to recall. Federal judges are not nearly so suspectible to influences which juries are in a position to correct, even if it is assumed that they would wish to.

Probably society does not take with any great degree of seriousness the claim that juries can successfully counteract judicial bias. In criminal cases, the judge's bias is most frequently reflected in the severity of his sentences, not in the manner he conducts the trial. A jury wishing to counteract this severity can only acquit. If an attempt is made to secure a definite indication of the degree of punishment to be imposed, reversible error will almost automatically result. Yet we are afraid to bestow sentencing powers upon juries, both for fear of their abuse and of the jury's inability to consider questions of punishment apart from those involving guilt. It is only in a very narrow area in which the jury can ever successfully function as a device for thwarting judicial bias or corruption.

VIII. Other Functions of the Jury

In addition to the more or less important tasks the jury is claimed to discharge, numerous incidental functions are also allegedly performed by it. Most of these alleged incidental functions, however, are but fictions devised by advocates of the jury system in order to bolster their main arguments.

Perhaps the most significant of these claims is the claim that the jury provides a means by which judges can avoid deciding complex questions and thus avoid the criticism which always follows from being forced to decide between two equally plausible alternatives. Judges should be men of dignity; to force them to guess and rationalize about facts encourages disrespect both for themselves and the entire legal system. Significantly, perhaps, most of the outspoken defenders of the jury are trial judges.

This argument is really but a variation of the theme that the jury supplies legal certainty and that a fiction about the ease with which facts can be decided is desirable in itself. Many of the criticisms offered in refutation of the claim that the jury provides legal certainty are equally applicable to the contention that the jury assists judges to maintain proper respect for themselves.

In addition, as Judge Frank has pointed out, "Men fit to be trial judges should be able and willing to accept public criticism. Moreover, they are obliged to do so in the many cases they must try without juries. Probably . . . [the argument that the jury acts as an insulator against public criticism of the judge] is but an ingenious rationalization."

It has also been urged that the jury offers an excellent form of popular entertainment which incidentally encourages citizens to take a more active interest in programs calculated to prevent crime. There is, however, no necessary connection between entertainment interest in jury trials and programs calculated to prevent crime; indeed, it might be expected that the result of watching at least some trials would produce an opposite effect. Trial before a judge sitting without a jury, while not as entertaining, possesses far more of the qualities which induce interest in crime prevention. Furthermore, the jury trial is a highly expensive form of entertainment, and there is no reason why particular litigants should be expected to foot the community's entertainment bill.

The drama popularly associated with the jury is also occasionally urged as being responsible for attracting into the legal profession its most able and distinguished members. It is more than likely, however, that jury trials have discouraged more able men from entering the law than they have encouraged. Exhibitionistic lawyers gesticulating before juries are often the greatest actors in the world, but may not be the best men safely and conscientiously to handle other persons' affairs. The emotionalism attendant upon jury trials has an even more undesirable effect upon the legal profession. As Professor Thayer has observed, the jury trial "appears to . . . be a potent cause of demoralization to the bar." Crying, pleading and weeping before juries is not attractive to most lawyers and contributes heavily to the impression, often expressed, that "they are all shysters."

Finally, it has even been claimed that the jury trial operates as a preventer of litigation and the facilitator of compromise. Briefly, the contention is that the outcome of a jury trial is so uncertain and hinges upon such a multitude of imponderables that litigants, rather than risking a complete loss, will compose their differences out of court. But the coerced compromise of valid claims is not desirable, and to the extent that the aberrations of jurors are responsible, such compromises are unjustified. Many of the compromises for which the jury system is to blame, however, are not chargeable to any particular jury. The vast web of evidential rules, the trial judge's instructions upon the law, errors in the composition and selection of the jury, and a host of other sources of error necessitated by the jury system offer added inducement to compromise. Congested court dockets and resultant delays in the ultimate decision of controversies furnish a still additional reason for settlement. Much of this congestion is due to the jury trial. The familiar claim that juries are plaintiff-prone may well be counterbalanced by the money insurance companies save by forcing harsh settlements upon injured persons in need of money to pay doctor bills.

Sophisticated canonizing of juror inefficiency has a slightly different basis in criminal as contrasted with civil cases. The widespread feeling that juries in criminal cases are defendant-prone, frequently acquitting for reasons the law cannot recognize and sociologists cannot even understand, coupled with the notion that everyone is a potential defendant induces respect for inefficiency. As pointed out above, however, defendants need protection against unjust convictions quite as much as society requires the conviction and punishment of those who have committed crimes. It is doubtful, however, whether popular theories concerning the leniency of criminal juries are justified. In any event, the notion that the jury is good because of its refusal to do what it is legally supposed to, and because we respect inefficiency, is wholly irrational.

IX. CONCLUSION

It is doubtful whether the jury has fulfilled the expectations which the innumerable functions claimed for it seemed to portend. This would seem true not only of the strictly legal tasks which have been assigned to it, but of its so-called "incidental" and "extra-legal" functions as well. Concededly, however, there is an element of fraud involved in any attempt to appraise the jury system's efficiency. In the absence of empirical data, value judgments all too readily creep in to substitute for facts. Value judgments, however, do not constitute the basis for the inconsistencies found in the functions ascribed to the jury and in the numerous rules governing their performance. Illicitly expecting the jury to do one thing while legally charging it with doing the opposite, and formulating rules so that neither expectation nor legal duty can successfully be realized, are alone sufficient to establish a prima facie case against the jury. Suggestions concerning the extent to which the law of the jury should be changed, however, are beyond this article's province. Empirical investigation may demonstrate that the conclusions arrived at here are to some extent unsupported in fact, and that certain of the inconsistencies between the functions imputed to the jury and the rules guiding their execution are possibly superficial.

THE PRESS AND THE OPPRESSED—A STUDY OF PREJUDICIAL NEWS REPORTING IN CRIMINAL CASES

Carolyn Jaffe

Part I: The Problem, Existing Solutions and Remaining Doubts

In the exercise of their constitutional right to freedom of the press, news media publish information concerning criminal cases. In the exercise of his constitutional right to a fair trial, every criminal defendant may demand trial by an impartial jury. Often, however, publicity exposes potential or actual jury members to information which is not eventually admitted in evidence at the trial. By thus enabling the jury to consider incompetent material, publicity can be prejudicial to the defendant, with the result that he is unable effectively to exercise his right to a fair trial. Frequent conflict between these fundamental rights constitutes a serious problem to the administration of criminal justice and raises the question of how the criminal defendant's right to a fair trial can be preserved without infringement of the equally important right to freedom of the press. A third right is also concerned; whenever this conflict occurs—that of the prosecuting government to perform one of its vested functions, the administration of criminal justice.

In an effort to formulate a solution to this increasingly serious problem, these articles will review the elements of these three distinct rights: that of the defendant to a fair trial, that of the government fairly to administer criminal justice, and that of the news media to freedom of the press; will attempt to define what is meant by the phrase "prejudicial publicity;" and will analyze the efficacy of existing methods of attempting to deal with the problem in the light of their respective effects on the co-existing and conflicting rights sought to be preserved.

I: An Impartial Jury

The United States Constitution entitles every defendant in a federal criminal action to a fair trial by an impartial jury. Although the Constitution does not require the states to provide trial by jury, every state by its own constitution guarantees jury trials in criminal cases. The Constitution does require, however, that whatever methods a state elects to use for disposition of criminal cases must be in accordance with due process of law; if the jury system is used, the jury must be impartial. Consequently, defendants in state as well as federal criminal prosecutions possess a right to trial by an impartial jury.

Reprinted by Special Permission of the *Journal of Criminal Law, Criminology and Police Science* (Northwestern University School of Law), Copyright © 1965, Part I, Volume 56, Number 1, Part II, Volume 56, Number 2.

To satisfy federal constitutional requirements, the jury must meet the federal constitutional standard in state as well as federal criminal cases. Since this standard is not specified in the Constitution, it has been variously fashioned by the courts. "Impartiality is not a technical conception. It is a state of mind. For the ascertainment of this mental attitude of appropriate indifference, the Constitution lays down no particular tests and procedure is not chained to any ancient and artificial formula." Because "The theory of our system is that conclusions to be reached in a case will be induced only by evidence and argument in open court, and not by any outside information, whether of private talk or public print," the basic question in resolving the issue whether a trier of fact possesses this "mental attitude of appropriate indifference" is whether he has the ability to decide the facts in a criminal case solely on the basis of the evidence presented in court. Obviously a juror with this ability is the impartial juror required by the federal constitutional standard. And since, within the scope of this paper, impartiality of the jury is the determinant of whether or not a given trial was fair, nothing less than trial before a jury composed of such impartial jurors is a fair trial. The problem of how to establish the existence of this ability entails both the substantive test of impartiality used and the procedure for applying the test.

Until recently, with but a few exceptions, the substantive test of whether a juror is sufficiently impartial has been whether he testifies that he can render a fair and impartial verdict based solely on the evidence presented at the trial. If this criterion is met, a juror is not challengeable for cause, nor is his presence on the jury grounds for mistrial or continuance merely because he has been exposed to prejudicial articles or broadcasts, even if he admits that he has formed an opinion as to the guilt or innocence of the accused. Recognizing the intricacies and frailties of human nature, the federal courts and a few state courts have recently held this test an inadequate measure of impartiality, with the result that a juror with preconceived opinions of an accused's guilt may be found partial if his declaration of impartiality, sincere though it may be, is objectively untenable in the light of his exposure to extrajudicial information about the case. The following statement by the Supreme Court of Florida is illustrative:

> "[A] juror's statement that he can and will return a verdict according to the evidence submitted and the law announced at the trial is not determinative of his competence [impartiality], if it appears *from other statements made by him or from other evidence* that he is not possessed of a state of mind which will enable him to do so."

Generally, the defendant complaining that his trial was unfair due to prejudicial publicity bears the burden of proving actual rather than speculative prejudice. While speculative prejudice is established upon proof of the existence of a condition which might result in prejudice, actual prejudice is not established unless it is proved that at least one juror in fact formed an opinion which influenced his verdict. The "actual prejudice" test compelled affirmance in two recent cases where, although newspapers containing highly prejudicial material were found in the jury room, the defendant failed to prove that any juror read the articles.

However, it has been held that when potentially prejudicial material has been publicized, a presumption of prejudice arises. For example, in *Commonwealth v. Crehan,* the Massachusetts Supreme Court presumed prejudice because the jury was allowed to separate, and since the trial court denied defendant's motion to poll the jury after damaging articles were published, it was impossible to rebut the presumption of prejudice. In *Rideau v. Louisiana,* where a film of defendant's interrogation by a group of local police officials and his confession were broadcast on several occasions over a local television station, the United States Supreme Court reversed defendant's state murder conviction without even using the transcript of the voir dire examination to ascertain whether any juror had seen the film. The Court held that the highly prejudicial nature and wide dissemination of the film rendered a fair trial in that locality impossible, and therefore examination of the voir dire was unnecessary. In *Irvin v. Dowd,* the first Supreme Court case upsetting a state conviction on prejudicial publicity grounds, the Court had found the jury not sufficiently impartial after carefully considering the voir dire. The *Rideau* case is the first in which the Supreme Court has reversed a state conviction on proof of speculative prejudice.

Because a trial judge has broad discretion in such matters, an appellate court will not overturn a finding of impartiality unless error is so manifest that the judge's action amounts to an abuse of that discretion.

With this background in mind, we must now try to define exactly what is the "prejudicial publicity" which can operate to deprive a defendant of that impartial jury to which his federal constitutional right to a fair trial entitles him.

II: What is "Prejudicial Publicity"?

The trier of fact in a criminal case must reach its conclusions as to a defendant's guilt only the basis of evidence presented in open court, and not on any outside influence. A jury failing to accomplish this task does not meet federal constitutional standards of impartiality, and the trial at which the jury is not properly impartial is not "a fair trial" within the federal constitutional requirement. Within this framework, the publicity with which we should be concerned is publicity which, if read or heard by potential or actual jurors, may reasonably be used by them in deciding the issue whether a criminal defendant is guilty, and which might not be admitted as evidence at his trial. If jury members are exposed to such material and the material is not eventually admitted as evidence, then the defendant's right to a fair trial will have been violated in that the jury had the opportunity to consider matters not presented in open court in determining his guilt.

For example, in *Marshall v. United States,* defendant was on trial for unlawfully dispensing drugs in violation of a federal statute. Seven members of the jury admitted having read news articles containing facts relating to defendant's prior convictions for practicing medicine without a license. The trial court had held evidence of these convictions inadmissible on the ground that it was irrelevant to the issues in the case and would be prejudicial to defendant. In the exercise of its supervisory power over the lower federal courts, the United States Supreme Court reversed Marshall's conviction, stating: "[The jurors were exposed] to information of a character which the trial court ruled was so prejudicial it could not be directly offered as evidence. The prejudice to the defendant is almost certain to be as great when that evidence reaches the jury through news accounts as when it is a part of the prosecution's evidence."

On the other hand, where the text of defendant's confession was published before trial, the United States Supreme Court affirmed his state conviction on the ground that since the confession was subsequently admitted in evidence, defendant was not prejudiced by the publication. Moreover, where a jury was exposed to publicity containing proffered testimony which the trial court had excluded merely on grounds of irrelevance rather than because of its prejudicial nature, the Alaska Supreme Court affirmed defendant's conviction.

The case law follows the general test outlined above—if material, read or heard by jurors, was likely to influence their decision as to a defendant's guilt, and if the material was not admitted as evidence, then the material was prejudicial to that defendant's right to a fair trial.

Six categories of material appear to meet this general test: (1) Confessions; (2) Prior criminal activities; (3) Incriminating tangible evidence; (4) Statements of persons who may not actually testify; (5) Reports of proceedings from which the jury has been excluded; and (6) Miscellaneous inflammatory material which may sway a jury's sympathies against a defendant.

(1) *Confessions.* No defendant can be convicted upon evidence which includes an involuntary confession, regardless of the truth of the confession, and regardless of independent evidence sufficient to sustain his guilt. Moreover, federal courts must exclude certain voluntary confessions as well, if they resulted from prohibited official activity.

Since the jury must not consider the fact that a defendant has confessed or the contents of his confession unless and until that confession is held admissible, a defendant whose purported confession is published and then not admitted in evidence, whether because not offered or because found inadmissible, is certain to be prejudiced by such publication. Reports that a defendant has offered or attempted to enter a plea of guilty or of *nolo contendere* are tantamount to reports that he has admitted guilt, and thus should be treated the same as publicity concerning confessions. It would be extremely naive to expect a juror who has read or heard a statement referring to a defendant as a "confessed killer," or has read or heard that a defendant has confessed or the purported contents of his confession, to put this out of his mind merely because no confession was admitted in evidence and he was told to consider only evidence admitted in court.

That in many cases confessions are properly admitted does not in any way vitiate the prejudice suffered by the defendant whose confession, though not admitted in evidence, was publicized. Nor can the general pre-admission publication of confessions be justified by maintaining that it would serve to relieve the public hysteria which often follows an unsolved crime of violence, unless we are willing to cite the desire for public complacency as a rationale for the denial of a fundamental constitutional right.

(2) *Prior criminal activities.* Evidence of a defendant's alleged criminal activities unrelated to the crime for which he is being tried is ordinarily inadmissible in court.

"The state may not show defendant's prior trouble with the law [or] specific criminal acts . . . even though such facts might logically be persuasive that he is by propensity a probable perpetrator of the crime. The inquiry is not rejected because character [as evidenced by prior criminal activities] is irrelevant; on the contrary, it is said to weigh too much with the jury and to so overpersuade them as to prejudge one with a bad general record and deny him a fair opportunity to defend against a particular charge."

Unless one of the few exceptions to this general rule can be invoked, admission of such evidence constitutes prejudicial, reversible error. For example, in a rather extreme holding, the Fourth Circuit recently granted a state convict's petition for habeas corpus on the ground that the jury's improper knowledge of defendant's prior convictions in and of itself constituted a denial of his federal constitutional right to a fair trial.

Since evidence of prior arrests, convictions, and pending indictments and accusations of crimes unrelated to the offense charged are all likely to cause the jury, probably through conscious or subconscious use of a "leopard never changes its spots" thought process, to believe that defendant committed the crime charged, publication of such material is reasonably certain to be prejudicial if not later admitted.

(3) *Incriminating tangible evidence.* No criminal defendant can be convicted by means of evidence obtained in violation of the constitutional prohibition against unreasonable search and seizure. If the fact that incriminating tangible evidence has been discovered is published in such a way that the defendant is connected with the commission of a crime, he will be prejudiced unless the evidence is found to have been lawfully obtained and is admitted against him at the trial. A defendant can be equally prejudiced by such publicity concerning tangible evidence which may prove inadmissible by reason of some non-constitutional evidentiary rule. If, however, the discovery of evidence is publicized without connecting any particular person to the crime, it is not prejudicial to a defendant even if, for some reason, the evidence is not subsequently admitted. For example, if police discover the "murder weapon," publication of that fact alone would not be prejudicial, while publication of the fact that they found it in the possession of the defendant would be.

(4) *Statements of persons who may not actually testify.* Since every criminal defendant has a federal constitutional right to be confronted by and to cross-examine his accusers, a defendant may be prejudiced for inability to exercise this right if the news media publish an extra-judicial statement made by a person not subsequently called as a witness against him. Such statements may independently tend to lead a juror to believe that the defendant committed the crime charged, *e.g.*, statements of "experts" regarding the results of polygraph tests, ballistics tests, and other scientific evidence, identification by "eye-witnesses," statements of official opinion that defendant is guilty, statements which might not qualify as dying declarations, and the like; or, such statements could reasonably tend to discredit an accused's possible defense without actually incriminating him, *e.g.*, statements impeaching the credibility of defense witnesses, or indicating that a defendant pleading insanity is actually sane.

(5) *Reports of proceedings from which the jury has been excluded.* Since a judge's exclusion of the jury from a court proceeding is generally based on the probability that the proceeding will contain information the jury is not entitled to know, publication of occurrences which take place during such proceedings is very likely to be prejudicial to a defendant. Most proceedings of this nature are hearings at which the trial court rules on the admissibility of evidence or confessions. Only if and when the evidence or confession is admitted can the proceedings on which that determination was based be published without probable prejudice to the defendant.

(6) *Miscellaneous inflammatory material.* Material in this category may consist of "human interest" interviews with the victim or his family, publication of the fact that a murder victim's estate is to be disposed of, editorials or factual reports concerning a "crime wave," or reports of the greater deterrent nature of capital punishment as compared with prison sentences. This type of material

tends to be inflammatory—that is, to cause the jury to want to convict—and thus to be prejudicial to whomever happens to be the defendant, not because he is any particular person about whom publicity has been disseminated, but merely because he is the defendant. For example, members of the jury which found a defendant guilty of murder and sentenced him to 299 years in prison later admitted that they had been influenced by articles concerning the then-pending proposed parole of Nathan Leopold.

It can be argued that, since material of the kinds enumerated tends to disclose The Truth, their publication should be encouraged. However, even if a coerced confession is true, and even if unconstitutionally seized evidence would conclusively establish a defendant's guilt, the United States Constitution as interpreted by the United States Supreme Court will permit no state or federal court in America to convict on such evidence. While conceding that evidence of previous criminal activities is not irrelevant and, in fact, is independently probative of present guilt, courts generally refuse to admit such evidence because of its extremely prejudicial nature. Surely only a perverted form of justice would permit jurors to be aware via news media of information which that same justice forbids those jurors to take cognizance of in open court.

III: Existing Methods

Accepting the above general definition of prejudicial publicity and tentative characterization of specific kinds of material which may be prejudicial, we must now examine the means which have been used in an attempt to prevent defendants from being convicted by juries influenced by such material. In evaluating each method, its effect upon each of the three co-existing interests—of the defendant, the government, and the news media—will be considered.

Methods currently available to American courts for the purpose of attempting to solve the free press-fair trial dilemma are: (1) issuing contempt citations against those responsible for publication of prejudicial information; (2) granting of trial level procedural reliefs designed to prevent a biased jury from rendering a verdict; (3) use of cautionary instructions to prevent or erase the harmful effects of prejudicial publicity; and (4) reversing convictions resulting from trials unfair because of prejudicial publicity.

(1) Contempt citations

Contempt citations against those responsible for the publication of prejudicial information have been little used by American courts because of their general reluctance to apply the doctrine of constructive contempt. Used with much success in Great Britain, this doctrine allows a court to punish as contempt any act which interferes with proceedings before it even though that act did not take place in or in the immediate vicinity of the court.

Perhaps the reason for rejection of this concept is that constructive contempt is almost invariably committed by publication, and its exercise is regarded by the press, radio, and television as violative of the federal constitutional guarantee that neither federal nor state action may abridge freedom of speech and of the press. While freedom of the press protects almost absolutely against prior restraint, the government may take corrective action to punish past misconduct—such as issuing a contempt citation—if, under the circumstances, the words uttered or published create a "clear and present danger that they will bring about the substantive evils that Congress [or the state] has a right to prevent." Interference with the fair administration of justice, such as by publication of material which presents a clear and present danger to the fairness of a particular trial, is an evil which the government has a right to prevent. Freedom of the press has been held subject to restriction where there was a clear and present danger that its exercise would cause serious political, economic, or moral injury to the government, would impede the performance of governmental duties, or would endanger the foundations of organized government. A fair judicial system surely is one of the foundations of our government, and maintenance of such a system a governmental duty. The United States Supreme Court has expressly recognized "the conceded authority of courts to punish for contempt when publications directly tend to prevent the proper discharge of judicial functions."

The Supreme Court, though, has never affirmed a contempt citation issued for a contempt committed by publication. However, in reversing three cases in which newspapers had been held in contempt for the publication of prejudicial material, the Court based its decisions not on the per se invalidity of holding newspapers in contempt, but rather on the absence of a "clear and present danger" to the orderly administration of the judicial process in the cases in question. It should be noted that these three cases were not tried before juries. It has been suggested that the danger of impeding the judicial process via prejudicial publications is substantially lessened where the case is tried by a judge, a law-trained man regarded as capable of being objective, rather than before a jury of impressionable laymen. In *Wood v. Georgia,* a recent contempt by publication case involving publication of a sheriff's statements designed to influence a grand jury, the United States Supreme Court reversed for lack of a clear and present danger, noting that the instant case did not involve a criminal trial pending before a jury. This dictum indicates that, presented the proper case of dissemination of prejudicial material regarding a criminal case pending before a jury, the Supreme Court would affirm a contempt conviction.

The purpose of freedom of the press is to "assure unfettered interchange of ideas for the bringing about of social changes desired by the people," and this right thus is essential to our system of government. Arguably, only publications consistent with the legitimate purpose of freedom of the press are entitled to its full protection. In an analogous situation, freedom of the press does not extend to confidential government documents, since disclosure to the press of secret government information could seriously undermine the ability of the various branches of government in discharging their constitutionally defined responsibilities. Use of the freedom of the press which results in the denial of a defendant's right to a fair trial and prejudices the outcome of a criminal case seems a perverted exercise of that right, and repugnant to its purpose. For example, consider Mr. Justice Frankfurther's pointed observation:

> "In securing freedom of speech, the Constitution hardly meant to create the right to influence judges or juries. That is no more freedom of speech than stuffing a ballot box is an exercise of the right to vote."

The fair comment which serves the purpose of freedom of the press does not include material published with the intent to influence the result of a criminal trial. Moreover, material published without such intent but nonetheless reasonably certain to have that incidental effect constitutes a "clear and present danger" under a fair interpretation of that test, since the danger lies in the probable effect of publication.

Use of the contempt power to punish a contempt committed by publication of prejudicial material would seem to be constitutional so long as the clear and present danger test was met, because the action would not impose prior restraint, and the publication would be of a nature inconsistent with the purpose of freedom of the press.

Another reason for judicial reluctance to exercise the inherent contempt power may rest upon the position of most of our judges as elected officials dependent on the press for political support. A further reason may be judicial ignorance that the inherent contempt power extends beyond the power to cite for contempt those who scandalize the court.

Although it is essential to our system of government that no person be convicted but by an impartial jury, it is just as essential that no organ of public sentiment be effectively prohibited from making fair comment on that government. Only publications not constituting fair comment as defined above would be contemptuous, but limited restrictions with fair and reasonable beginnings may eventually compound into an oppressive whole. Use of the contempt power may thus projectively undermine freedom of the press even if it would not presently violate that freedom.

Furthermore, what does it help a particular convicted defendant that the newspaper which helped to convict him has been held in contempt? And future defendants will not be aided by present contempt citations unless definitive standards of contemptuous conduct are established; in absence of such standards, punishment for contempt lacks deterrent effect. The prosecuting government's interests are also neglected by use of the contempt power, because so long as this process is not uniformly applied according to some standards, it serves no deterrent function and thus does not tend to help secure the effective enforcement of justice in the long run.

(2) *Trial level remedies*

Various remedies designed to prevent a defendant from being tried by a prejudiced jury are available at the trial level. Included are motions for dismissal of a prospective or impanelled juror for cause, for declaration of mistrial, for continuance, for change of venue, and for new trial. Failure to grant the requested relief is reversible error only where a defendant has been prejudiced thereby and where such failure amounts to an abuse of discretion. However, these remedies fail to protect defendants' rights and the corollary sovereign rights simply because they are so seldom granted, probably due to the nebulous nature of impartiality and the trial court's broad discretion as to disposition of such motions. Another reason these procedures are ineffective is that, if granted, such remedies as change of venue, continuance, and even new trial, will be unable to assure a fair trial if widespread and intense publicity concerning the trial continues to be disseminated. Even when granted, these motions have little tendency to deter future publication of prejudicial material.

It would appear that the trial level technique of sequestering the jury (*i.e.*, keeping the jurors "locked up" during the course of the trial) is the most effective way to prevent the defendant's being prejudiced by publicity appearing after the jury has been impanelled. This method has been infrequently employed, however, perhaps because of a desire to avoid coercing the unhappily confined jurors to concur in a hurried verdict. However in a recent case the Seventh Circuit approved the trial judge's sua sponte sequestration of the jury for the purpose of protecting defendant from the effects of prejudicial publicity over defendant's contention that this action resulted in a coerced verdict against him. Furthermore, sequestration requires large expenditures by the state.

(3) *Cautionary instructions*

Where the trial court instructs the jury not to read or listen to accounts of the case which may appear during the course of the trial or not to consider any matters other than evidence presented at the trial, appellate courts generally presume that the instructions were effective and thus find no prejudice due to pre-trial publicity or publicity appearing during the trial; accordingly, failure to give cautionary instructions has been held to constitute reversible error.

However, for several reasons, preventive cautionary instructions nonetheless fail to protect a defendant's right to a fair trial and the sovereign's right to preserve the orderly administration of justice by giving him a fair trial. First, they cannot protect against the possible effects of pre-trial publicity, simply because of the time element. Second, jurors may disregard preventive cautionary instructions and fail to admit it for fear of reprisal by the court. For example, in *Smith v. United States,* a prejudicial article was published after cautionary instructions had been given. Upon defense counsel's request that despite the instructions the jury be polled as to whether any had read the article, the court addressed the jury as a whole as follows: " '[I]f any juror violated the instructions of the court and read the article . . . hold up your hands.' " A better procedure involving the private interrogation of individual jurors is outlined by Judge Kiley in *United States v. Accardo.* Third, these instructions may call to a juror's attention articles which might otherwise have gone unnoticed. Corrective cautionary instructions are likely to be ineffective for the third reason above, and also because of the difficulty, if not impossibility, for a juror not to be at least subconsciously influenced by extra-judicial matters to which he was exposed despite honest efforts to remain fair and impartial and to discharge his oath.

Exposure to extra-judicial matters not in evidence at the trial may cause a juror subconsciously to resolve disputed issues of fact against the defendant even though that juror is not in fact deciding defendant's guilt on the basis of consciously considered facts gained other than at the trial. Moreover, extra-judicial exposure to matters which are subsequently admitted in evidence may lead a sincere juror to resolve disputed issues of fact, and, perhaps more importantly, issues of credibility of witnesses, against defendant. The pre-admission exposure may well cause a juror to give more weight to the evidence than he would if his first and only contact with the matter were as evidence in court.

(4) *Reversal of Convictions*

Many factors are considered by reviewing courts in determining whether a judgment of conviction should be overturned on prejudicial publicity grounds. Invariably the reversible error alleged by appellant will be denial of a fair trial occasioned by the trial court's failure or refusal to grant trial level remedies or cautionary instructions. Hence, the issues reviewing courts discuss tend to establish the presence or absence of prejudice.

State or Federal Convicting Court. The question whether the conviction was rendered in a state or federal court is peculiar to the federal courts, since only a federal court can hear cases which originate in both federal and state courts. If the conviction was rendered in a federal court, the United States Supreme Court can reverse in exercise of its general supervisory power over the lower federal courts. When a federal court is reviewing a state conviction, however, habeas corpus can be granted or reversal ordered only if the defendant was denied a fair trial in violation of due process. However, the fact that the 1963 case of *Rideau v. Louisiana* allowed speculative proof of prejudice to establish that the constitutionally compelled impartiality requirement was not met by the state jury indicates that the state-federal distinction will seldom be meaningful in cases to come.

Admissibility of Information Complained of. Publicity relating facts unfavorable to a defendant which are inadmissible as evidence at the trial is very likely to be prejudicial, since a juror who reads such publicity will have been exposed to evidence not introduced at the trial, and might consider such facts in his deliberations. Conversely, if information published prior to trial is subsequently admitted, defendant cannot successfully allege that the publicity prejudiced his rights. The rule in the federal courts, controlled by *Marshall v. United States,* requires reversal where the jury was extra-judicially aware of information inadmissible because of its prejudicial nature, not simply because of some evidentiary rule.

Time Between Publication and Trial. Although it is difficult to measure so subjective a thing as impartiality—admittedly a state of mind—on an objective scale, some courts have attempted to do so. If a relatively long period of time has elapsed between publication of the material complained of and time of trial, a reviewing court is not likely to find prejudice.

Action Taken by Defense Counsel Prior to or During Trial. If defense counsel fails to move the court to interrogate the prospective jurors on voir dire, or the impanelled jurors during the trial, as to whether they read the articles complained of, and if so whether they were prejudiced thereby, most reviewing courts will not disturb the result. It has been recognized, however, that such questioning may be harmful to a defendant's cause. For example, in *Briggs v. United States,* defendant moved for a mistrial, but declined to accept the trial court's offer to interrogate the jury. Reversing the conviction rendered after the trial court refused to declare a mistrial, the Sixth Circuit stated, "It could very well be that questioning the jury would be more prejudicial than helpful. We do not believe that appellant was required to agree to such questioning in order to preserve his contention that [he] was entitled to a mistrial." In another case, defense counsel suggested voir dire questions designed to elicit the existence of prejudice without alerting jurors to prejudicial material. The trial court's insistence on asking questions in such a form as to make the jurors aware of the material constituted one ground for reversal.

Failure of a defendant to exhaust his peremptory challenges, to challenge for cause, or to move for continuance, change of venue, or mistrial, though not usually precluding the appellate court from deciding the issue of impartiality, may lead the court to infer that the articles complained of did not in fact generate such widespread and lasting prejudice as the defendant would like the court to believe.

Source and Intent of the Information. If the information contained in the publicity complained of was instigated solely by the press, federal and state reviewing courts have been less likely to reverse than if an agent of the prosecuting government was responsible for dissemination. Indeed, the "state action" concept of due process seems especially applicable to support federally compelled reversal of state convictions contaminated by publicity promulgated by an officer of the state. However, in *Rideau v. Louisiana,* where the United States Supreme Court reversed defendant's state murder conviction on prejudicial publicity grounds, the Court expressly disclaimed reliance on state action as to promulgation of the prejudicial broadcasts, stating that, although it appeared that local officials probably had prompted the filmed interview, "the question of who originally initiated the idea ... is ... a basically irrelevant detail." The state action held by the Court to have deprived defendant of his federal rights was the state trial court's refusal to grant his motions for change of venue. This notion utilized by the *Rideau* court—that it is the prejudicial effect of an occurrence upon the defendant rather than the identity or motive of the person who caused the event which is the sole determinant of whether defendant's trial was fair, and that the trial court's failure to cure the effects of the prejudicial occurrence constitutes "state action" for due process purposes—would seem to eradicate any previously persisting distinction between prosecution-generated publicity and publicity emanating from other sources.

In short, reviewing courts are slow to reverse convictions attacked on prejudicial publicity grounds, mainly because it is extremely difficult, as a practical matter, to prove prejudice. Even in the case where the rights of a particular defendant are vindicated by reversal of his conviction, this method is an incomplete solution. Reversal of a few convictions influenced by prejudicial publicity will have little, if any, deterrent effect upon promulgation of like material in subsequent cases. Further, the right of the prosecuting government fairly to administer criminal justice and to protect its citizens is entirely neglected by this "solution." Where the publicity which occasions reversal and remand emanates without participation of any government official, the government has been unjustly "punished"—by the trouble and expense of a new trial, or, if retrial is impossible as a practical matter or because the appellate court reversed without remand, by the danger that one who may be a criminal remains at large—while the guilty press is allowed to go free. And, as we have seen, the method which would punish the press by contempt is rarely resorted to.

Summary

It appears that the above methods, as currently practiced by American courts, are inadequate solutions to the freedom of the press-fair trial conflict, for the following brief reasons: (1) contempt, because of disuse; (2) trial level reliefs because of disuse and lack of deterrent effect; (3) cautionary instructions, because of human nature; and (4) reversal, because of disuse, failure to protect sovereign rights, and lack of deterrent effect.

Part II: Some Speculations and Proposals

IV: Expansion of Existing Methods

When the conclusion that existing means are inadequate was made, it was advanced not to state that these means are inherently inadequate, but, rather, with the qualification that they are inadequate as currently practiced by American courts. Perhaps presently existing methods could be utilized in such a way as to solve the problem without resort to more radical and sever means which might represent the beginning of a trend that could result in gradual but eventual erosion of freedom of the press. However, this is not to say that the existing means will in fact be so utilized; rather it is suggested as a possible solution short of, and, perhaps preferable to, more drastic means.

To speak of preventing conduct—here, the publication prior to termination of a criminal case of material which might prejudice the jury against the defendant—is to speak either of actually punishing someone or of putting him in fear of possible consequences which may harm him at some future time, unless he is willing to cease that conduct without external compulsion or persuasion.

It has been suggested that the news media are capable of voluntarily refraining from publishing prejudicial material, particularly if the Bar were to prescribe and itself adhere to reasonable standards to be followed. Voluntary action has in fact been taken in Rhode Island, where the two Providence dailies and many other newspapers do not print any matter regarding a trial which takes place outside the presence of the jury. However, failure of the legal profession to enforce its own Canon 20 breeds disrespect on the part of the press and tends to inhibit press self-control. Such strong forces as competition and the desire to sell newspapers, moreover, would most likely prevent effective internal control, despite the fact that this solution in ideology represents the best of all possible worlds in this area of the law.

Since radio and television serve to inform the public in brief of all important news events, newspaper editors and publishers are prone to believe, and perhaps rightly so, that they must give the public intricate details of morbid and shocking crime news in order to continue to prosper. This is not to say that radio and television are not also guilty of exposing jurors to prejudicial publicity; but it does appear that the greatest culpability lies with the newspapers.

Conferences between newsmen, members of the legal profession, and law enforcement officials may serve to enlighten some members of the journalistic profession as to the possible deleterious consequences of injudicious coverage of criminal cases. For example, a conference on the subject in which newsmen, police officials, prosecutors, defense attorneys, and judges participated, was held at Northwestern University School of Law under auspices of the Ford Foundation in May 1962. Although no proposed solution was unanimously arrived at, and though newsmen almost uniformly demanded empirical evidence that publication of what defense attorneys call prejudicial publicity in fact causes juries to be prejudiced against defendants, one shining light did emanate from that conference.

Shortly after it was held, Professor Fred E. Inbau, co-chairman of the conference, received from a Florida assistant managing editor who had participated in the conference a copy of a recommendation which he had sent to the members of his staff and to managing editors of other Florida newspapers, to the effect that alleged confessions and prior criminal records should not be alluded to in publications prior to termination of the trial.

But editors so enlightened are few and far between. It is doubtful whether such programs will substantially affect enough journalists to come close to solving the problem. Therefore, we must speak either in terms of actually punishing someone, or of somehow scaring him into prodded, but not whipped, compliance with the desired standard of conduct.

Expansion of the available tools of reversing convictions and granting the appropriate motions available at the trial level might well serve to scare the press into the desired moderation in covering crime news. If it were impossible to obtain an impartial jury and hence a valid conviction because of exposure to publicity, the press would not be slow to realize that public indignation might eventually lead to the imposition of external sanctions, and would therefore choose self-control in anticipatory self-defense, since external standards would doubtless be more stringent and circulation-cutting than what could voluntarily be adopted by the press and approved by the judiciary. Mere liberalization of currently prevailing tests of juror impartiality and standard of proof of prejudice would tend toward this result.

The recent case of *United States v. Accardo* is illustrative. The defendant was convicted of making false statements on his income tax returns. Before and during his trial, his reputation for being involved in Chicago's underworld and the nationwide crime syndicate was widely publicized by local newspapers and news broadcasts. Presuming prejudice from the circumstances, the Seventh Circuit reversed on prejudicial publicity grounds. Inasmuch as the reversal and its basis also received much publicity, the public might well have inferred that, by publishing such articles as caused Accardo's conviction to be overturned, Chicago news media were in fact, albeit unintentionally, aiding organized crime.

In connection with the general problem, a leading Chicago editorial writer recently stated:

"As a result of prejudicial reporting and comment, courts often grant changes of venue, continuances, and mistrials. Reporting and comment have often been the ground on which appellate courts have reversed convictions.

"Editors and publishers have little to fear from the contempt procedure for prejudicial reporting or comment. But if they are not careful, they may be aiding a guilty man to escape punishment so long as reviewing courts are so sensitive to the presumed effect of what is printed."

Moreover, in the great majority of cases, liberalization of the standard of challengeability of jurors for cause would result in the selection of a panel of jurors impartial by federal constitutional criteria; inability to obtain a jury would result only in the most highly publicized cases. Trial courts in two recent cases entered what appear to be valid judgments of conviction after having excused all potential jurors who might possibly have been prejudiced against defendent by reason of publicity.

In the absence of effective, freely-chosen voluntary action, then, extension of the existing remedies of reversal and trial level remedies may result in the desired goal through the "scare" technique. But if those who publish prejudicial information prove either to be unaware of the possible threat to their seemingly invulnerable position or to be unbelieving that such a threat could ever materialize, then actual punishment will remain the only means of preventing publication of prejudicial material.

The existing contempt power can be invoked more frequently than at present to constitutionally punish constructive contempt by the press, so long as the information published constitutes a clear and present danger to the sovereign's right to secure the orderly administration of justice—*i.e.*, in context, to the right of the particular defendant to a fair trial. As has been demonstrated, use of the contempt power in this manner does no violence to freedom of the press. Presumably, punishment of past misconduct will deter that contemnor and those similarly situated from publishing like information in the future. Of course, the "punishment" must actually punish, rather than merely slap the offender on the wrist. In light of the economic compulsion to publish detailed crime news, most newspapers would merely write off a moderate fine as a business expense. For the contempt conviction to constitute punishment which would reasonably deter future misconduct by the news media, really stiff fines against the publishing corporation and imprisonment of persons directly responsible for publication, as are imposed under the successful English system, would seem necessary.

If either the pursuasion by fright or punishment by contempt technique is sought to be employed, it is equally important that the news media be informed of the standards formulated—of what conduct is disapproved. If the fright method derived from expansion of the test of juror impartiality and standard of proof of prejudice is to be used, one responsible for news coverage of criminal cases will be hesitant to publish material he knows may occasion reversal or impossibility of trial, which in turn, he apprehends, may lead to the external controls he abhors. If punishment is to be imposed for constructive contempt, the publisher's awareness of what specific information must not be published and when it must not be published will apprise him, as required by due process, of what he must refrain from doing on pain of contempt, and will permit him to act accordingly.

Standards of Conduct

As discussed above, six kinds of material were categorized as "prejudicial," within the general criterion that the material might not be admissible as evidence, and if jurors read or heard the material, they might reasonably use it in deciding the question whether a defendant is guilty. Since the information might never be admitted in evidence, the test of prejudice for purposes of punishment must be whether, looking at the publication at the time of publication, it is reasonably certain that the defendant will be prejudiced if the jury is exposed to the publicity. A publication meeting this test constitutes *at the time of publication* a clear and present danger that the defendant will be prejudiced thereby—*i.e.*, that the sovereign's right to prosecute and conduct a fair criminal trial will be endangered—and can therefore be punished without violating freedom of the press even if the danger never materializes—*i.e.*, even if the information is subsequently admitted as evidence. Of course, subsequent admission would prevent the granting of trial level remedies or reversal.

Since we are seeking to formulate explicit standards, perhaps at the outset we must eliminate the sixth category of prejudicial material—miscellaneous material which may inflame the jury against defendant. Although such material can have the prejudicial effect sought to be eliminated, it is not likely to have this effect in so many cases as will material in the first five categories. Moreover, whereas the first five kinds of material are susceptible of rather precise definition, this last type is not. Thus, while recognizing that such miscellaneous material can in some cases be prejudicial, it would be wise not to include it for present purposes.

Applying the time element aspect of the test of prejudice developed above, publication of material in any of the first four categories (confessions, criminal activities, tangible evidence, and statements of possible non-witnesses) prior to its actual use as evidence at the trial (or, if never admitted, prior to termination of the trial) would constitute conduct so prejudicial as to warrant holding the publisher in contempt. Publication of material in the fifth category (proceedings out of jury's presence) would constitute such conduct if it occurred before the jury was allowed to consider the object of dispute in the proceeding (or, if never so allowed, before termination of the trial). If the jury is extra-judicially exposed to material in any of the five categories and the material is not later admitted as evidence, the defendant should obtain relief by trial level remedies or reversal.

The next logical question is how these standards, for purposes of securing "voluntary" adherence thereto by the fear-of-possible-future-consequences method, or for purposes of putting a potential contemnor on notice of what conduct is prohibited, are to be conveyed to those affected by them.

Presentation of the Standards

It has been suggested that the Bar advance standards for the press to follow. Such a standard would be merely advisory as to those not members of that Bar, however, and probably could not command respect from a substantial portion of the press. A standard presented by the Bar would not necessarily conform to the treatment, by courts in its locality, of claims of prejudicial publicity or invocation of constructive contempt, unless those courts first formulated the standards in a judicial opinion. If the highest court of a state did formulate a standard, however, subsequent dissemination thereof to the press by the local Bar would aid in achieving the desired result and would constitute a valuable public service. So long as the organized Bar fails to enforce its Canon 20 as against its members, however, it would seem unrealistic to expect more from the press vis-a-vis a Bar-promulgated standard of conduct for the press in the absence of exercise of active external sanctions.

If, as has been argued, publication of the enumerated kinds of material can constitutionally be punished as contempt, any state court authorized to promulgate rules of court could constitutionally promulgate a rule specifying these categories and announcing that publication prior to admission as evidence, or termination of trial if not admitted, of categorized material concerning criminal cases pending before or being tried by jury in that court will be dealt with as a contempt of court.

Should a court decide to expand the existing methods of reversal and trial remedies rather than to enlarge its current use of the contempt power, if could, if so authorized by local law, render an advisory opinion that the enumerated kinds of material would, in the future, occasion reversal and granting of trial level remedies which might make trial in effect impossible. Or, perhaps, a State Attorney General could issue a similar statement as to his interpretation of what the law now requires.

Evaluation of Expansion of Existing Methods

Unfortunately, it seems unlikely that either of the possible expansions here suggested will be generally adopted, at least at the present time.

Although a few courts have begun to liberalize the tests of juror impartiality and proof of prejudice, it is doubtful that this will cause such fear on the part of a substantial segment of the press as to make any significant inroads on the present scheme of crime news reporting. Courts still adhering to the stricter tests are loath to amend their stand for fear that jury trials will thereby be rendered impossible in the context of our modern society with its extensive news coverage of criminal cases. What these courts do not realize is that, by temporarily rendering effective criminal jury trials next to impossible in cases extensively covered by an immoderate press, they may well insure that the judicial system shortly thereafter will no longer be plagued by the problem of prejudicial publicity.

And since most state judges are elected, and federal judges, though appointed for life, are bound by a Supreme Court decision ruling against their possession of statutory power to punish constructive contempts, the possibility of punishing enough constructive contempts to deter news media from publishing material here deemed prejudicial seems remote.

Before considering the use of more stringent means against the press, however, it would perhaps be advantageous to consider the possibility of preventing publication of the enumerated prejudicial information by the indirect method of preventing the information from ever reaching the news media for publication.

V: Punishing Divulgence

Effective prohibition of divulgence to the press of prejudicial material for purposes of publication by the press would render unnecessary the imposition of any positive external sanctions against the news media, thus avoiding the argument that the latter would run afoul of freedom of the press. However, punishing those who divulge prejudicial material for publication may not be practicable in light of the newsman's statutory privilege, recognized in a minority of the states, against being compelled to reveal the source of his information. Certain policy considerations may also dictate against the adoption of a non-divulgence statute.

Three general types of persons contribute to the press most, if not all, of the crime news deemed prejudicial in the preceding discussion. They represent (1) persons occupying the status of agents of the government, (2) persons independent of both the government and the news media, and (3) persons who are agents or employees of the news media.

(1) *Government agents.* The most obvious reason for divulging to the press material with may prejudice a jury against a prospective or present criminal defendant is to secure his arrest and conviction. While this end serves the individual interests of prosecutors and law enforcement officers, whose duty it is to protect the public from crime and to alleviate public anxiety concerning unsolved crimes, and who may release prejudicial material to the press in order to gain favorable publicity for themselves, agents of executive and legislative branches of government may also contribute such material for similar considerations. Since all these persons are officers of the state, their behavior as it affects the governmental process of conducting trials can be regulated by the state. Moreover, since members of the Bar and police officers hold positions of privilege rather than of right, the local Bar Association and Police Department, respectively, could prescribe standards of non-divulgence with internal disciplinary action for non-compliance. Enforcement and observance of ABA Canon 20 alone would substantially aid the problem. The argument that preventing divulgence to the press will harm society by keeping relevant information from the proper authorities simply does not apply, since the source of information here consists of those authorities.

(2) *Private Individuals.* Private individuals, independent of both the government and the news media, who may make statements for publication which might be prejudicial include witnesses, victims, family or friends of the victim or of the accused, accomplices, and suspects. Although it could constitutionally be effected, punishing such private individuals for making disclosures to the press in order to prevent similar disclosures in the future may be inadvisable. Here, the argument that prevention of disclosure would be against the public interest inasmuch as pertinent information may be made unavailable to the authorities does apply, since persons possessing otherwise inaccessible information relevant to the solution of a crime, may, for various reasons, fear going to the authorities. In such cases, a criminal might go free but for the individual's willingness to tell his story to a newsman. Furthermore, since such private persons are not likely to repeatedly be in possession of information *re* crime and probably would lack actual knowledge of a sanction invocable against them, punishing them would serve no substantial deterrent purpose.

(3) *Employees of News Media.* While employees of news media can be treated as private individuals insofar as their function of supplying the media with information for publication is concerned, the arguments against the

punishment of divulgence by private individuals do not apply to reporters and "informers." Unlike members of the Bar and police officials, newspaper employees are not subject to effective disciplinary action of any organized group. Although the American Society of Newspaper Editors has adopted a set of ethical canons, no disciplinary machinery exists for its enforcement. Thus, the only possible sanction against these persons is by state action. If a statute were to punish acts of divulging prejudicial material only when committed by employees of news media, however, it would likely be held invalid as violative of the equal protection clause of the fourteenth amendment. The policy reasons favoring disclosure by private persons not affiliated with the press dictate against the universally applicable nondivulgence statute which would comply with the equal protection clause. Consequently, although press employees constitute an important source of prejudicial information, only those persons subject to government regulation by virtue of their status as officers of the state should be made subject to sanctions for divulgence of prejudicial material to the press.

In a state with a newsman's privilege statute, a statute or internal regulation against divulgence would be totally ineffective unless the privilege statute were either repealed or amended to permit compulsion of disclosure of a newsman's source in cases where application of the nondivulgence statute or regulation is the reason for attempting to discover the source.

Although non-criminal punishment could probably be imposed by local Bar Associations and Police Departments in such a way as effectively to prevent divulgence of prejudicial information to the press, imposition of criminal penalties by the state would probably be a better method. Uniformity of incidence and substance throughout the state, essential for the purpose of securing that uniform compliance which is necessary to insure that every criminal defendant within the jurisdiction can exercise his right to a fair trial, is attainable only by a state-wide statute. Moreover, since a state legislature could emasculate non-divulgence regulations by enacting an unqualified newsman's-privilege statute, provisions to punish divulgence should ideally be promulgated by the legislature.

Even if the proposed non-divulgence statute would effectively prevent the press from obtaining prejudicial material from those to whom the statute would apply, still some would reach the press from those to whom it would not. The question remains whether, if the non-divulgence statute is not adopted, or is adopted but is ineffective since much prejudicial material still reaches the press from sources which are immune because of a newsman's-privilege statute or because a prosecutor consistently exercises his discretion not to prosecute under the non-divulgence statute, sanctions more drastic than those already discussed and dismissed as ineffective or improbable of exercise should be invoked.

VI: Punishing Publication

Since the earlier discussed "solutions" apparently fail effectively to protect the criminal defendant's right to a fair trial, and thus necessarily fail to protect sovereign rights as well, I believe that the answer to this remaining question must be an emphatic "Yes."

The justification for making the right to a fair trial apparently supersede freedom of the press is that here, as in the obscenity and sedition cases, what is essentially being safeguarded is the public. Just as the public is benefited by reasonable restrictions on offensive and dangerous material, so would it be benefited by reasonable restrictions on prejudicial material—for the government is the losing party when a miscarriage of justice occurs as a result of the publication of prejudicial material, and what is the government if not the public?

An analogy can be drawn from the recent case of *United States v. Fuller,* where the district court rejected defendant's argument that freedom of the press prohibited the federal government from prosecuting him for violating section 605 of the Federal Communications Act. Defendant, a newsman, had intercepted police radio messages and divulged newsworthy portions to a radio station. The court refused to grant defendant's motion to dismiss the information, holding, *inter alia,* that since freedom of the press is not absolute, the first amendment did not prohibit application of section 605 to defendant. In *Fuller,* the congressional right, embodied in a criminal statute, to keep the lanes of interstate commerce free and untrammeled was held to supersede freedom of the press. Proposed legislation to punish publication of prejudicial material would be passed by the state for the purpose of maintaining its sovereign right to preserve a fairly administered judicial system. If the one can supersede freedom of the press, why cannot the other?

A statute punishing the publication of prejudicial material would be analogous to a statutory or inherent contempt power under which acts interfering with the orderly administration of justice are punishable, to the extent that the former would enumerate and specify acts which fall within the more general terms of the latter. The same constitutional criteria should therefore apply to both processes. Since publication of such material constitutes a clear and present danger to the government's right to fairly administer criminal justice, a statute punishing publication should not offend the first amendment. Moreover, enactment of such a statute clearly delineating the five kinds of prejudicial material outlined above and providing for indictment and trial as for any other statutory offense would be perhaps even more palatable than use of the contempt power, inasmuch as the standards required would be unmistakable and available to all persons covered, and since a valid objection to the contempt power—that the judge whose courtroom was affected by the contemptuous act summarily tries the contempt action—is absent.

VII: Proposal

A comprehensive statute encompassing both divulgence and publication would be the best possible solution, short, of course, of voluntary restraint by the press. Since the non-divulgence and prevention of publication sought is with regard to exactly the same material, a single statute should be utilized.

Since the legislature will be considering a bill which its members, as elected officials, will invariably find repugnant, it seems provident to be willing to settle for legislation covering less than all of the kinds of material deemed prejudicial in the earlier discussion. Although each of the five categories of information can properly be called prejudicial in the sense that a clear and present danger is presented, and although a bill covering all five categories can constitutionally be drafted and should initially be advocated, one has yet accomplished much if coverage of the most harmful of the items is attained. Punishing divulgence or publication of information relating to confessions and to previous criminal activity would seem to prevent the publication of that material which is most likely to be highly prejudicial in the most circumstances. Moreover, if material regarding confessions and previous criminal activities cannot be published, much of the material in the remaining categories will be less prejudicial or perhaps even devoid of the capacity to interest the public.

In order to increase the likelihood of enactment into law of this or a similar proposal, a scientific study should be conducted in order to establish a causal connection between exposure to prejudicial publicity and partiality. In light of press influence on legislation, at least some endorsement of, or, at the very least, acquiescence in the proposal by the press probably would, as a practical matter, be necessary in order to have it enacted; tangible evidence of a causal connection would likely lead to endorsement by the more enlightened members of the press. The foregoing should not be construed to imply that there is a doubt as to causal connection—only that this proof would increase the chances of enactment of the proposed statute.

In drafting a proposed statute, the time during which divulgence or publication of the material shall be punishable must be delineated. It has been demonstrated that publication of prejudicial material is in fact prejudicial, as that term has herein been defined, if it occurs prior to admission of the contents of the material as evidence in court. The acts of divulgence or publication should be punishable if committed at any time after a criminal act has been committed and before the material is admitted in evidence, or if not admitted, until termination of the trial.

What was said earlier concerning expansion of the constructive contempt power with regard to the punishment to be imposed is equally applicable here. While a usual misdemeanor penalty would probably deter the individual from divulging prejudicial material, only a substantial fine and possible prison sentence will deter actual publication.

VIII: Model Statute

For implementation of the desired prohibitions, it is necessary to embody the above proposals into a definite structure. The statute which follows is designed as a guide to any state which desires to impose reasonable restrictions upon the divulgence and publication of specified prejudicial material in order to assure that the constitutional right to trial by an impartial jury will more often be fact than fiction. The entire statute is intended to represent the broadest possible measure which could constitutionally be promulgated. However, adoption only of the unbracketed portions will strongly be advocated, since the more specific and less restrictive the statute, the greater its deterrent force, probability of enactment, and likelihood of being found constitutional.

An Act to Prevent the Dissemination of Prejudicial Publicity
§1. Subject to the exceptions set forth in §§2 ¶1(c), 2 ¶2(b), 2¶3(b), 2 ¶4(c), 2 ¶5(b), and §3, any person responsible for the publication policy or broadcasting policy of any newspaper, magazine, radio station, television station, or any other news-disseminating agency which publishes or broadcasts, or any person formally connected with the administration of law, including its practice or enforcement, who divulges to any newspaper, magazine, radio station, television station, or any other news-disseminating agency, at any time between the commission of an alleged criminal act and the termination of the trial of any person for that act, any statement deemed in §2 of this Act to be prejudicial, shall be guilty of a ＿＿＿＿＿, punishable by ＿＿＿＿＿.

§2. Any statement, whether of fact or opinion or otherwise, which communicates information of one or more of the following types, is deemed to be prejudicial:
¶1. Confessions
    a. That any person has confessed to any crime, or

b.   The contents of any confession, or any part thereof.

c.   Exception: It shall not be a violation of this statute to divulge or publish the fact or contents of a confession after it has been admitted as evidence at the trial.

¶2. Criminal Activities

a.   That any person officially accused of having committed any crime has ever committed a crime on another occasion, or has been convicted of, acquitted of, arrested for, accused of, or indicted for the commission of any other crime.

b.   Exception: It shall not be a violation of this statute to divulge or publish any statement covered by §2 ¶2(a) after it has been admitted as evidence at the trial.

¶3. Tangible Evidence

a.   That any tangible evidence has been obtained, whereby such evidence reasonably tends to connect any particular person with the commission of any crime.

b.   Exceptions: It shall not be a violation of this statute to divulge or publish (1) any statement covered by §2 ¶3(a) after the evidence has been admitted at the trial, or (2) that tangible evidence has been obtained, provided that the statement does not reasonably tend to connect any particular person with the commission of any crime.

¶4. Statements of Unsworn Witnesses

a.   That any person is of the opinion that any particular person has committed any crime, or

b.   That any person has made a statement, whether as fact or opinion or otherwise, or the contents of any statement, or any part thereof, which (1) reasonably tends to connect any particular person with the commission of any crime (such statements include, but are not limited to: identifications by any person of a particular person as the perpetrator of any crime; statements attributing to a particular person a motive for the commission of any crime; statements made by a homicide victim; and results or inferences drawn from results of scientific tests); or (2) reasonably tends to discredit or otherwise impair the defense of one officially accused of having committed any criminal act (such statements include, but are not limited to: statements which reasonably tend to impeach the credibility of one who has been officially accused of any criminal act or of any person who has been or is reasonably expected to be called to testify at the present or pending trial of the accused; or to attribute to one who has been officially accused of any criminal act a motive for the commission of any criminal act; or to establish the sanity of one who has been officially accused of any criminal act).

c.   Exception: It shall not be a violation of this statute to divulge or publish any statement covered by §2 ¶4(a) or (b) after it has been admitted as evidence at the trial.

¶5. Closed Court Proceedings.

a.   Transcripts, reports, or summaries of occurrences taking place during the course of proceedings from which the jury has been excluded by the trial court.

b.   Exception: It shall not be a violation of this statute to divulge or punish any statement covered by §2 ¶5(a) concerning a proceeding held to determine admissibility of evidence or of a confession after the evidence or confession has been admitted at the trial.

§3. General Exceptions—This statute shall not apply to:

¶1. The divulgence or publication, after a trial has commenced, of statements deemed by §2 to be prejudicial, if

   a.   A defendant has waived his right to trial by jury, or

   b.   A trial court has ordered that the jury be confined during the course of the trial.

¶2. The divulgence or publication, at any time after a crime has been committed, of the fact that a particular person has been officially accused of having committed the crime.

IX: Some Problems and Speculations

Many problems, beyond the scope of this paper, would exist even if the proposed solution were adopted. For example, the statutory scheme above was intended to be promulgated at the state level. What of a defendant who commits an act—such as robbing a federal bank—which constitutes both a state and a federal offense? His federal trial may be conducted after termination of the state statutory period of prohibition on divulgence and publication. And as to an act which violates only federal law, no state statute would apply to punish divulgence or publication. Perhaps the federal government could pass a similar statute applicable to all news media subject to the commerce power. Almost every newspaper and radio or television station would be covered. But to what criminal acts would the divulgence and publication relate? Acts in violation of federal law, or of the laws of one state, or of more than one? Presumably, if an act violated *any* penal law, publication in the lanes of interstate commerce of material herein defined as prejudicial with regard to that act could constitutionally be covered by a federal statute.

Another untreated question relates to proceedings subsequent to termination of an initial criminal trial. What of the defendant who appeals his conviction? Maybe even appellate judges can be unconsciously influenced by material regarding the defendant published after judgment of conviction and before disposition of the appeal. And what will happen to the defendant who succeeds in obtaining reversal and new trial? What if the jury impanelled at his retrial read, after his first conviction and before retrial was ordered, that he confessed, and the confession was coerced and cannot be introduced? Carrying this line of reasoning to its inevitable conclusion, publication of prejudicial material at any time when a new trial may still be granted—*i.e.*, until a defendant has exhausted his state remedies, failed to get certiorari from the United States Supreme Court, and failed in his petition for federal habeas corpus and in his appeals to the federal Court of Appeals and the United States Supreme Court from its denial—can prejudice a defendant's right to a fair trial.

What if the prosecutor refuses to enforce the statute? Mandamus lies only to compel performance of a clear legal duty; the prosecutor has discretion. Prohibition lies to correct a flagrant abuse of discretion—but try and prove it against our kind-hearted prosecutor.

What if the newsman says, "My experienced attorney advised me that the material I divulged (or published) was not within the statute"? Presumably, the individual states' legal rules regarding mistake of law and mistake of fact as a defense in criminal cases would govern. But these defenses are singularly misunderstood and misapplied due to their inherent conceptual difficulty.

What of the "exceptional case"? In the case of Lee Harvey Oswald, for instance, one who published facts regarding his Communist sympathies and personal background could persuasively argue that this action was necessary, or at least justifiable, to avert national panic. Oswald did not confess, but had he done so, publishing that fact would probably have been in the national interest. Even in the case of the "Boston Strangler," whose activities have considerably upset a large number of citizens, perhaps publication of a confession, if obtained, could be justified, though not so much as in the Oswald case.

If the Oswald-type case should be treated differently from the garden variety case, in what manner should this be accomplished? One might argue that a person who kills a President of the United States waives all rights against having facts about himself published, much as in the right to privacy cases in tort law one may be held to waive that right if he is a public figure. But this argument presumes that, before trial according to established procedures required by the federal constitution, we have decided that he did commit the act. In an exceptional case the prosecutor's discretion not to prosecute the publisher might be relied upon. Or, perhaps, a declaratory judgment might be obtained permitting publication. A procedure might be devised for obtaining a court order permitting publication which, in absence of the order, would violate the statute. Probably such procedure would have to be incorporated in the statute itself. Any procedure for obtaining immunity from operation of the statute, though, should be strictly dealt with, lest the statute become in effect inoperative.

Another possible problem is that if most official or seemingly sanctioned comment regarding criminal cases ceases, it may be replaced by rumors not carried by the news media which may be even more detrimental to the defendant.

Certain beneficial indirect effects may result if lurid crime news is no longer published. The newspapers may well find they must improve the quality of their product if they are to keep selling papers. Perhaps more important, citizens will tend to view the administration of criminal justice as what it was meant to be within our system of government, rather than as what current journalistic practices may lead them to believe.

Conclusion

It is at best a difficult task to propose sanctions designed to achieve a desired result where, by the very nature of the situation, the most effective sanctioners are at the mercy of the sanctionees. Even if a statute such as that proposed cannot be adopted and extensive use of the constructive contempt doctrine cannot be realized for this Machiavellian reason, liberalization of the tests of juror impartiality and standard of proof of prejudice, which would result in fair trials in many cases and in increased difficulty in obtaining valid convictions in those cases receiving flagrant and extensive publicity, may well serve as an indirect sanction that eventually will yield the desired result.

Perhaps in the final analysis, the greatest service an interested lawyer can perform in this area is to observe the ABA Canons of Ethics, to prod his Bar Association toward concern, and to talk loudly and write profusely about promulgating anti-publication statutes, suspecting all along that his goal is not really enactment of a statute, but rather the playing of a personal role in the campaign to coerce the press into enlightened self-restraint.

PLEADING GUILTY FOR CONSIDERATIONS:
A STUDY OF BARGAIN JUSTICE

Donald J. Newman

One of the major problems faced by social scientists interested in studying criminal behavior involves obtaining samples of offenders to be used as units of research. Ordinarily such samples are drawn from prisons or probation files because the study of unapprehended criminals is extremely difficult. Conviction by a court or authorized agency is, therefore, the usual basis of sample selection. Virtually all sociologists admit the inadequacy of such a technique and qualify their samples as non-representative of any kind of a criminal universe. At the same time, the conviction record of the offenders who are selected for study from prisons and courts is used as the basis for typing the offenders and for various statistical computations. In general, the man's conviction record is assumed to be a quasi-automatic legal stamp which defines those activities which make him a criminal.

Of course very few researchers would treat a person such as Al Capone as merely an income tax violator, but this is because they would know, or think that they know that such an individual had committed other offenses or had different patterns of criminal behavior than those for which he was sentenced. In less notorious cases, however, the type of offense and the severity of the sentence, remain the pivotal points around which research is pursued and prison classification systems are built.

This does not mean that sociologists naively accept conviction on a specific charge as definitive nor that they have little interest in the mechanics of justice. The reverse, of course, is more accurate. But the emphasis of both sociological exposition and research has been on the *gross* misuse of justice, on methods used by criminals, political officials and the business elite to avoid conviction. It is also true that some sociological interest has been shown in procedural variation, particularly brutal, and in many cases, illegal, arrest and interrogation methods. The police particularly have come under sociological scrutiny. Nevertheless, apart from the "fix" and the "third degree," the conviction process has generally been neglected in research as of minor importance in the complicated process of defining "criminal" as the basic unit of research.

Methods of Studying the Conviction Process

In order to bring to light some of the less apparent factors influencing the procedural steps by which society labels the criminal, a sample of men, all convicted of "conventional" felonies in one court district was interviewed in regard to the processes involved in their own convictions. Men from a single county were selected in order to keep formal legal procedures and court and prosecuting officials constant for each case. The lawyers and judges of this

Reprinted by Special Permission of the *Journal of Criminal Law, Criminology and Police Science* (Northwestern University School of Law), Copyright © 1956, Volume 46, Number 6.

district had been interviewed previously by the author, so that information was available about conviction processes from the legal participants viewpoints. The county was located in the mid-west (Wisconsin) and was of "medium" size, neither rural nor metropolitan. The county seat had a population of approximately 100,000 persons. Furthermore, the district was politically clean, having no widespread organized crime or vice nor a tradition of "fixing" criminal cases by bribery or intimidation. Supposedly in such a setting, felony convictions would follow a quasi-automatic, "combat" theory of criminal justice, involving a jury trial or at least an unconditional plea of guilty.

Most Convictions the Result of Guilty Pleas

The felons who were interviewed, a group of ninety-seven representing all men from the district under active sentence, had all been convicted of felonies ranging from non-support to murder. There were no white-collar criminals in the group, except for three clerks serving sentence for embezzlements, nor were there any racketeers or professional criminals such as confidence men, and no individuals sentenced from Juvenile Court were included. The men were serving sentences under the following conditions:

State prison 34
State reformatory 6
Parole 9
Probation 48

Total 97

Most of the convictions (93.8 percent) were not convictions in a combative, trial-by-jury sense, but merely involved sentencing after a plea of guilty had been entered. On the surface this might lend support to the contention that most convictions are mere rubber stamps of the court applied to the particular illegal behavior involved in each case.

On closer analysis, however, it was seen that over a third (38.1 percent) of the men had originally entered a not guilty plea, changing to guilty only at a later procedural stage short of an actual trial. The question immediately arose; why did these men change their minds? Was it because of a promise of leniency or some such bargain as suggested by the Wickersham report, Moley and other writers of a decade ago? A second question followed. Did the men who pleaded guilty immediately do so unconditionally to the charge as contained in the complaint or was there any evidence of informal "arranging" of the sentence so widely alleged in criminology texts?

Pursuing these lines of inquiry, an interesting difference between the two groups of men was seen. Men entering an initial plea of not guilty were significantly more often represented by defense attorneys than the men pleading guilty immediately. On all other demographic characteristics, age, gross type of offense for which sentenced (personal, property, sex, and miscellaneous violations such as carrying a concealed weapon), education, occupation, residence and so on, the groups showed no signficant differences. Furthermore, on the eventual disposition of the cases, e.g., whether sent to prison or placed on probation, the groups did not differ. In fact, only one other difference besides the retention of counsel was noted. It was found that the men who initially pleaded guilty and who more often than not did not hire or request counsel were recidivists, whereas the men with lawyers, who at first pleaded innocent, were more often experiencing their first conviction.

TABLE 1

Type of Plea by Retention of Counsel

	Type of Plea		
Retention of Counsel	Guilty	Changed not guilty to guilty	Total
Offenders with lawyers	21 (23.2)	24 (26.3)	45 (49.5)
Offenders without lawyers	39 (42.7)	7 (7.8)	46 (50.5)
Total percent	60 (65.9)	31 (34.1)	91* (100.0)

*Offenders pleading not guilty and retaining this plea through a jury trial were eliminated. All, however, had counsel.
X^2 = 14.713, d.f. = 1, significant at the 5 percent level. Yules Q = -.728 indicating a negative correlation between initial admission of guilt and the retention of counsel.

This phenomenon is rather curious when it is recalled that the groups showed no differences in the frequency of being placed on probation. It might logically be expected, in the light of current sentencing practices, that first offenders would more likely receive probation than men with previous convictions, particularly if, as was the case, there was no significant variation in the types of crimes for which they were sentenced. The implications of this lack of difference in sentences for the role of the lawyer in the conviction process was so great that the men were further analyzed by dividing them into two groups, one characterized by the retention of counsel, the other comprising men who pleaded without an attorney.

TABLE II

Expected Punishment by Retention of Counsel

Punishment Expected at time of Arrest	Retention of Counsel		
	Offenders with Lawyers	Offenders without Lawyers	Total
Expected same as actual or didn't know what to expect	3 (3.2)	10 (10.3)	13 (13.5)
Expected less severe than actual	11 (11.3)	11 (11.3)	22 (22.6)
Expected more severe than actual	37 (38.1)	25 (25.8)	62 (63.9)
Total percent	51 (52.6)	46 (47.4)	97 (100.0)

X^2 = 5.827, d.f. = 2, not significant at five percent level.

TABLE III

Non-represented Offenders Reasons for
Not Retaining Counsel

	Percent
Obviously guilty, hoped for mercy from the court	19.5
Made deal for concurrent sentence or had charges dropped	30.4
Made deal for lesser charge or a light sentence	23.9
Don't trust lawyers	4.4
Had no money, didn't know about court-assigned lawyers	13.0
Other*	4.4
Not ascertained	4.4
Total	100.0

*These cases claimed that they were subjected to long and arduous questioning and "confessed" to "get it over with" and thus had neither the time nor the inclination to get a lawyer.

The outcome of the conviction process from the point of view of the offender is satisfactory or unsatisfactory depending upon the actual sentence he receives compared to his expectations of punishment at the time he is arrested. It might be supposed that a violator who expected a severe sentence would seek legal advice. However, an analysis of the responses of the men showed that their expectations was not the determining factor in their decisions to retain counsel or to plead without counsel.

Reasons for Pleading Guilty Without a Lawyer

The reasons given for claiming or for disdaining counsel varied from confessions of "obvious" guilt and a hope for mercy from the court to poverty coupled with ignorance of provisions for state-paid defense attorneys. The chief reason, however, appeared to be an expedient one, related to the factor of past experience in going through the conviction process. The recidivists were both conviction wise and conviction susceptible in the dual sense that they knew of the possibility of bargaining a guilty plea for a light sentence and at the same time were vulnerable, because of their records, to threats of the prosecutor to "throw the book" at them unless they confessed. Over half (54.3 percent) of the men claimed that they had bargained for their sentences, and 84 percent of these men had been convicted previously. A number of factors, all interrelated, seem to account for this. First, a general fear expressed by multiple offenders of facing a jury or of antagonizing sentencing officials was revealed in most cases. Some felt that their records would be held against them by a jury (actually the admission in court of the offender's previous criminal record is closely regulated by law to assure a fair trial on the current charge). They felt conviction would be more certain because in the public mind they were "ex-cons." A more general fear, however, was that the judge would be especially severe in sentencing if they did decide to fight and then lost. They felt that pleading not guilty and hiring a lawyer would only irritate the various officials, particularly the prosecutor, whose recommendation at the time of sentencing is an important consideration of the court. One of the men said:

> When the day comes to go and the D.A. stands up and says you're a dirty rat and a menace to society and should be locked up and have the key thrown away—then look out! You're going away for a few years.

These fears, whether justified or not, undoubtedly made these men more amenable to an informal "settling" of their cases.

A second factor making for bargaining and the rejection of counsel was the experience of these men gained in previous convictions. Many of the recidivists, particularly those with two or more convictions, knew the sentencing judges and some of the prosecutors quite well and all of the offenders knew most of the police. They were on a first name basis with many of these men and could bargain in a friendly or even a jocular manner. One man (on probation) said:

> Old _____ told me he was going to throw the book at me. I told him he didn't have a damn thing on me. He said I'd get five to ten. I told him he couldn't even book me, that's how little he had. I knew he was riding me; he didn't mean a thing by it. I've known him for years. He just likes to act tough.

Men who had been convicted in other states or in other counties but never before in this district were quite conscious of this "friendship" factor in the bargaining processes. Each of them expressed the belief that had he been a "local" he would have fared better.

Previous sentences served in institutions also seemed to be relevant to bargaining without a lawyer. Former inmates were more legal-wise; their conceptions of their offenses were not primarily in terms of guilt or innocence but contained more references to evidence and its relation to the outcome of the conviction process. They referred to how much the prosecutor "had on me" and the ability of the prosecution to make a charge stick. One of the men expressed it this way:

> The D.A. needed my help. His evidence was all circumstances (sic). He knew I done it but he couldn't ever prove it. But I couldn't go to court and take a chance with my record. When I saw he was going to stick me with something, I was willing to make the best deal.

Not only does a quasi-legal knowledge evidently develop in incarceration (most of these men knew the statute numbers of their offenses and all knew such terms as "preliminary hearing," "arraignment" and "pre-sentence investigation") but those men seemed better able to recognize a good bargain when they saw one. Although all offenders recognized probation as the best break, of course, and many knew the possible length of sentence for their particular crime, recidivists knew customary sentences (and court district variations) for their offenses. In short, they recognized a "good-as-compared-to-other-guys-I-know" sentence when they faced it.

Offenders Who Retain Counsel

Over half (52.6%) of the men in the total sample retained lawyers and proceeded through more of the formal stages of the conviction process (preliminary hearing, arraignment) than those men who pleaded without attorneys.

As anticipated from the analysis of the group of non-represented offenders, the factor of recidivism with its accompanying implication of bargaining skills learned from past experience was almost completely absent from this group. As one of these men expressed it:

> I'd never been in trouble before. I didn't know which end was up. I thought sure I was going to prison. It seemed as if they had a million laws I'd broken. The only thing I could think of was calling my wife to get me a lawyer.

These men with their lawyers, either privately hired or court assigned, significantly more often pleaded not guilty when first apprehended, changing their pleas only later in the process. On the surface, this observation might lead to one of two conflicting conclusions. The fact that the retention of counsel correlated with a change of plea to guilty might mean that the lawyers, having a better grasp of the legal worth of the evidence against their clients, advised them to plead guilty and that the clients followed their advice. Or, it could with equal validity indicate that perhaps the lawyers, through informal bargaining skills similar to the non-represented recidivists, had arranged satisfactory charges or more lenient sentences than originally expected by their clients. The latter would seem to be the most convincing in view of the offenders' responses. When asked their lawyer's advice in regard to pleading, 75 percent of those first pleading not guilty and then guilty, responded that their counsel's advice was to maintain a not guilty plea "until something can be arranged." This they did. The remainder were advised to plead guilty without promise of any arrangement, although bargaining is not thus ruled out.

Only fifteen of the represented offenders said that their convictions were the result of unconditional pleas of guilty. The remainder, including not only the offenders whose lawyers' advice was to hold off pleading guilty until settlement was made, but twelve of the men who entered initial guilty pleas as well, claimed to have received some consideration in the nature of the charge or type and length of sentence in exchange for their admissions of guilt.

Types of Bargaining Where Attorney Has Been Retained

While the frequency of claimed bargaining does not differ significantly between the groups of offenders without lawyers and with lawyers, there is some difference in the frequencies of the various types reported. Men without attorneys significantly more often mentioned as the consideration they received in exchange for a guilty plea either the reduction of the charge or the promise of a suitable, fixed sentence.

It would seem from this that lawyers are more likely to be retained by offenders who fear a severe punishment or in cases involving a disputable charge whereas violators with many charges against them "cop a plea" directly from the prosecution or the court without a lawyer as intermediary. This would also seem to substantiate the evidence from the unrepresented defendants that the function of the lawyer in bargaining is not essential for all offenders, and that men experienced in the conviction process can informally and successfully arrange their own legal fate.

TABLE IV

Offenders Pleading Guilty After
Bargaining Over Charge or Sentence

Retention of Counsel	Offenders Pleading Guilty		Total
	Pleaded guilty for consideration	Pleaded guilty without bargaining	
Offenders with lawyers	30 (33.0)	15 (16.5)	45 (49.5)
Offenders without lawyers	25 (27.4)	21 (23.1)	46 (50.5)
Total percent	55 (60.4)	36 (39.6)	91 (100.0)

X^2 = 1.443, d.f. = 1, not significant at 5 percent level.

TABLE V

Frequency of Types of Bargaining
by Retention of Counsel*

	Offenders With Lawyers	Offenders Without Lawyers	Total
1. Pleading to a lesser charge	8 (14.5)	3 (5.5)	11 (20.0)
2. Pleading for a light sentence	17 (30.9)	8 (14.6)	25 (45.5)
3. Pleading for concurrent sentences	3 (5.5)	9 (16.3)	12 (21.8)
4. Pleading for the dismissal of charges	2 (3.6)	5 (9.1)	7 (12.7)
Total percent	30 (54.5)	25 (45.5)	55 (100.0)

*Combining the first two types (lesser charge, light sentence) and comparing them with the last two (concurrent sentence, charge dismissed) a significant difference between types of bargaining and retention of counsel is seen. X^2 = 23.72, d.f. = 1, significant at 5 percent level. Yules Q = -.732 indicating a negative correlation between retention of lawyer and pleading guilty for considerations of concurrent sentences of dismissed charges.

Types of Informal Conviction Agreements

The considerations received by the offenders in exchange for their guilty pleas were of four general types:

1. *Bargain concerning the charge.* A plea of guilty was entered by the offenders in exchange for a reduction of the charge from the one alleged in the complaint. This ordinarily occurred in cases where the offense in question carried statutory degrees of severity such as homicide, assault, and sex offenses. This type was mentioned as a major issue in twenty percent of the cases in which bargaining occurred. The majority of offenders in these instances were represented by lawyers.

2. *Bargain concerning the sentence.* A plea of guilty was entered by the offenders in exchange for a promise of leniency in sentencing. The most commonly accepted consideration was a promise that the offender would be placed on probation, although a less-than-maximum prison term was the basis in certain instances. All offenses except murder, serious assault, and robbery were represented in this type of bargaining process. This was by far the most frequent consideration given in exchange for guilty pleas, occurring in almost half (45.5 percent) of the cases in which any bargaining occurred. Again, most of these offenders were represented by attorneys.

3. *Bargain for concurrent charges.* This type of informal process occurred chiefly among offenders pleading without counsel. These men exchanged guilty pleas for the concurrent pressing of multiple charges, generally numerous counts of the same offense or related violations such as breaking and entering and larceny. This method, of course, has much the same effect as pleading for consideration in the sentence. The offender with concurrent convictions, however, may not be serving a reduced sentence; he is merely serving one sentence for many crimes. Altogether, concurrent convictions were reported by 21.8 percent of the men who were convicted by informal methods.

4. *Bargain for dropped charges.* This variation occurred in about an eighth of the cases who reported bargaining. It involved an agreement on the part of the prosecution not to press formally one or more charges against the offender if he in turn pleaded guilty to (usually) the major offense. The offenses dropped were extraneous law violations contained in, or accompanying, the offense alleged in the complaint such as auto theft accompanying armed robbery and violation of probation where a new crime had been committed. This informal method, like bargaining for concurrent charges, was reported chiefly by offenders without lawyers. It occurred in 12.6 percent of cases in which bargaining was claimed.

The various types of informal conviction agreements were described in the majority of the cases and, as mentioned, only six members of the sample went to jury trial. The remainder of the sample (37.1 percent) pleaded guilty, they said, without any considerations. It is possible, however, that in those 15 instances where the men had counsel, the attorney had bargained, or had attempted to bargain, without the knowledge of the offender.

In instances where informal methods were used, the roles of the various participants were cooperative rather than combative. Central to the entire process were the roles of offender and prosecutor; the defense attorney played a significant part chiefly in cases of first offenders and in instances where the nature of the charges was in dispute. The judge sometimes played an informal role in cases involving a fixed sentence, but even here the prosecutor's role dominated because of the common practice in the court whereby the judge asks for, and generally follows, the prosecutor's recommendation as to sentence in cases pleading guilty.

The Bargain Theory of Criminal Justice

The most significant general finding of the study was that the majority of the felony convictions in the district studied were not the result of the formal, combative theory of criminal law involving in effect a legal battle between prosecution and defense, but were compromise convictions, the result of bargaining between defense and prosecution. Such informal conviction processes were observed in over half of the cases studied.

In the informal process the accused, directly or through his attorney, offered to plead guilty to the offense for which he was arrested, providing it was reduced in kind or degree, or in exchange for a given type or length of sentence. The prosecutor benefitted from such a bargain in that he was assured of a conviction, yet did not have to spend the time and effort to prepare a trial case. He also avoided the ever-present risk of losing even a clear-cut case should the accused have gone before a jury. The court, too, benefitted. Court calendars were, and are, crowded and the entire court system would be admittedly inadequate to cope with criminal trials should all, or even a fraction of the felony arrests decide to go to trial. This, coupled with a generally favorable attitude toward bargaining processes on the part of the lawyers, civil and criminal, in the local bar, made informal methods of conviction almost inevitable.

Instead of proceeding through all the formal stages of conviction such as hearing before a magistrate, preliminary hearing, arraignment, etc., the majority of the offenders waived most of these procedures and because of informal promises of leniency or threats of long sentences, entered guilty pleas and were sentenced. About half (50.5 percent) of the sample went to preliminary hearings of their cases but only 6.2 percent proceeded through a jury trial.

Conclusions: Significance of Informal
Conviction Processes to Criminology

Criminological research has generally ignored methods of conviction in conventional felony cases except the illegal "fix" and brutal "third-degree" as primarily legal steps automatically defining the unit to be studied. The automatism of conviction has here been challenged, and within the limits of the present research, interaction processes of sociological interest in themselves, have been outlined.

It was felt in conducting this research that, if informal methods of convictions were discovered, they would be of a nature to negate the use of conviction records in many types of research and correctional administration. In the typology of criminals, in prison classification, and in other applied fields such as parole prediction, bargaining techniques would rule out the accuracy of the "paper" conviction as an index of the offender's actual patterns of criminality. In spite of the high incidence (56.7 percent) of admitted bargaining in the sample, however, only a very small proportion of cases admitted guilt to offenses grossly different from those alleged in the complaint, and only a small proportion had offenses dismissed so that they did not appear at all on the offenders' records. In other words, the informal conviction processes tended to result in guilty pleas to the same or very similar offenses, so that the offenses for which convicted did not usually deviate greatly from the crime actually committed. The greater proportion of the bargaining was concerned with directly gaining a lighter sentence regardless of the offense, rather than indirectly by pleading to a lesser charge.

One of the most important implications of the informal methods is the effect of these processes on selection for probation. A promise of the prosecutor's recommendation for probation was one of the most common values given in exchange for a guilty plea. This occurred in 34.5 percent of the cases reporting bargaining. With such informal tactics, selection for placement on probation is determined by the skill of the offender or his lawyer in bargaining, rather than on factors of the case which would have more relevance to successful rehabilitation by field rather than institutional placement.

The existence of informal methods also has broader significance to law and law enforcement as well as to criminology and related areas. The use of such methods involves a differential implementation of the law comparable to the discrepancies noted by Reckless in his "categoric risk" of conviction and Sutherland in his conceptions of white collar crime. An analysis of the sample of offenders showed no clear cut categories separating bargained from non-bargained convictions, yet the fact that some offenders, without going to trial, pleaded guilty without any considerations in the charge or in sentencing while others "settled" their cases informally, raises again the sociological, and presumably the moral, problems of criminal justice.

Evidently the criminal law is not only differentially enforced in general, but as far as this study shows, this also occurs within groups of offenders convicted of the ordinary (or conventional) felonies of robbery, homicide, burglary, larceny and sex offenses. Certain proportions of these violators (56.7 percent in this sample), without resorting to bribery or other methods of the professional "fix," can modify the nature of the charge against them or the length or type of their sentences in much the same manner as the white collar offender.

Whether bargaining is legal, that is, whether men convicted as the result of bargaining are convicted by due process of law, is a difficult question to answer without referring the decision to a specific case. Likewise, whether bargaining is ethical cannot be summarily answered. Certainly in cases where bargaining is misused, where the accused is exploited or the community subjected to danger, the issue is clear. Under these conditions bargaining is not only unethical but would probably be held unconstitutional, as a violation of the "due process" clauses of the Constitution.

When compromise is used, however, to gain a certain conviction of a surely guilty offender, the question is not so clear. Defense lawyers, prosecutors, and criminal court judges interviewed in an earlier study overwhelmingly favored bargain-justice where judiciously used. They felt it to be the most expedient way of gaining justice. Likewise the offenders who bargained successfully were well satisfied with this process. It was the men who went to trial or who failed to bargain successfully who more often claimed injustice in their cases.

As the lawyers said, bargaining appears to be an expedient method of answering numerous problems of the administration of justice. Our criminal procedure is cumbersome. Legal defense is expensive both for the state and the accused. Court calendars are crowded and would not be able to cope with the number of trials which would ensue if all arrestees pleaded not guilty. Furthermore, no conviction is ever a sure thing, no matter how overwhelming the evidence, if the case goes before a jury. Prosecutors, who need convictions to be successful, know this. For these reasons, "bargain-justice" appears the natural answer to lawyers and court officials and, of course, to offenders who are guilty. For these reasons, too, the problem of bargaining cannot easily be corrected, if it should be corrected at all. Bargain-justice appears as a natural, expedient outgrowth of deficiencies in the administration of our "trial-by-combat" theory of justice. It is supported by both the attitudes of offenders who see justice as a purely personal thing, how well they fare in sentencing, and by the attitudes of lawyers and court officials who can only "get things done" in this way.

While bargain-justice may thus be an expedient and at present even a necessary and legitimate legal phenomenon in certain cases, some broader implications of bargaining should be mentioned. Cases of conventional felonies that are "settled" may well result in strengthening attitudes which favor a general disregard for law and for justice, in much the same way as does the differential legal treatment of business and political violators. If conviction on a charge is to be determined in great part by skill of the offender in bargaining with the court or in hiring a lawyer to bargain for him, then our concept of impartial justice based upon facts and rules of evidence becomes meaningless. Furthermore, the fact that opportunities and techniques for bargaining exist in our system can have an adverse effect upon attempts to rehabilitate offenders and generally to decrease crime rates. What happens, for example, when one man, merely because he is unsophisticated, does not know of bargaining techniques or of the right lawyer to contact, is sentenced to prison while another more sophisticated offender, a recidivist who commits the same offense, arranges a sentence to be served on probation? Certainly the rationalizations of the man sentenced to prison to the effect that he is a "fall guy," and his conception of himself gained from serving prison time, make rehabilitation far more complex if not impossible. The way bargaining now works, the more experienced criminals can manipulate legal processes to obtain light sentences and better official records while the less experienced, occasional offenders receive more harsh treatment. Under these conditions the effectiveness of law as a means of social control is seriously jeopardized and any long range attempts to build respect for the law and law abiding attitudes will prove extremely difficult.

SENTENCING STRUCTURE: ITS EFFECT UPON SYSTEMS FOR THE ADMINISTRATION OF CRIMINAL JUSTICE

Lloyd E. Ohlin
Frank J. Remington

I
The Evaluation of Alternative Sentencing Structures

The formulation of a sound sentencing structure requires the resolution of a number of basic issues. Where ought responsibility for the sentencing decision be vested? What alternative types of disposition ought to be made available to the agency given responsibility? What limitations should be placed upon the severity of the sentence, particularly the length of incarceration? And finally, what criteria ought to guide or control the sentencing decision?

These issues are not easily resolved. Adequate resolution requires agreement as to the principal objectives of a sound sentencing plan and a method of insuring that administration will be oriented toward the achievement of those objectives. Typical analyses of proposals for change in sentencing structure have been preoccupied with objectives and have consistently failed to produce a basis for predicting the impact of the sentencing proposal upon the day-to-day administration of criminal justice. As a consequence, administrative distortions occur which are unanticipated and, therefore, not controlled.

All agencies engaged in the administration of criminal justice must direct their efforts toward the common objective of processing criminal offenders. This, of necessity, requires a degree of integration among their policies and practices. This practical operating equilibrium will inevitably be affected by a major change in the system. For example, a major change in the allocation of responsibility and discretion for sentencing will affect all agencies. The offender who anticipates a high mandatory sentence will resist arrest and conviction as certainly as he will endeavor to avoid the imposition of sentence following conviction. The natural tendency, under these circumstances, therefore, is for the agencies of criminal justice administration to engage in various kinds of accommodative responses to a changed sentencing structure, so that they may continue to perform their customary tasks—of arrest and conviction, for example—with the usual expenditure of time, effort, and money. This may result in a failure to achieve the objectives of the sentencing structure, since those objectives may be regarded as less important than the maintenance of the current administrative equilibrium.

In proposing and evaluating reforms in sentence structure, it is, therefore, necessary to have sufficient knowledge of the administrative needs of a criminal justice system to be able to anticipate the kind of pressures that will be exerted

Reprinted, with permission, from a symposium on *Sentencing,* appearing in *Law and Contemporary Problems,* Vol. 23, No. 3 (Summer 1958); published by the School of Law, Duke University, Durham, N.C. Copyright © 1958 by Duke University.

upon the sentencing structure to serve those needs. Only then can methods be devised to meet these pressures in other ways—for example, by increasing personnel, budget, or training—and thus prevent distortion of its objectives. Typically, however, this knowledge is not demanded for two reasons: there is inadequate account taken of the actual functions of sentencing in the administration of criminal justice; and there is inadequate awareness of the fact that the administration of criminal justice is a single, total process and that, therefore, changing one important aspect may require substantial reorientation of the entire system.

The emphasis here will be upon the relation between the sentencing decision and the criminal justice system. Some efforts will first be made, however, to define the functions of sentencing.

II
The Functions of Sentencing

Sentencing proposals are usually evaluated in terms of their anticipated effect upon individual offenders and upon the community as a whole.

A. Effect Upon the Offender

All would agree that it is important to know what effect a sentencing structure will have upon the likely rehabilitation of individual offenders. Such disagreement as does exist relates rather to the extent to which a given sentencing structure does, in fact, contribute to rehabilitation and the extent to which the objective of rehabilitation outweighs other objectives of the penal system.

B. Effect Upon the Community

It is clear also that account must be taken of the effect which a sentencing structure will have upon the community. Here, again, there are differences in emphasis, complicated in this instance by a difficulty of definition. When one speaks of the effects of sentence upon the individual offender, it is clear to whom reference is being made. The difficulty is that the present state of knowledge in the behavioral sciences does not permit precise measurement or prediction of these effects. It is not so obvious, however, what is meant when one speaks of the effect of sentencing upon the community. Typically, a generalized concept of the community is used to express the need for deterrence and incapacitation and to describe the pressure for retribution. Perhaps resort to such a concept is inevitable, since it is seldom very clear precisely who needs to be deterred, who are potential victims, or who is exerting the pressure for retribution. But however appropriate the use of a generalized concept of the community may be in attempting to measure the need for deterrence and community reassurance, it is, in itself, inadequate as a basis for evaluating sentencing proposals, for it does not take into account the other functions of sentencing and, thus, does not afford a satisfactory standard for determining how sentencing will actually work in a going system for the administration of criminal justice.

There are, in fact, at least five important ways in which sentencing affects the community, some of which are too seldom made explicit.

1. *Deterrence of potential offenders*

This is a customarily-emphasized function of sentencing. Such disagreement as exists is one only of degree. Some regard the need for deterrence as being great enough to warrant a sentencing structure which provides for the imposition of minimum periods of incarceration. Others deny the necessity for minimum penalties, asserting that the need for general deterrence is adequately served by prompt detection and arrest.

2. *Protection of potential victims of crime by incapacitating dangerous offenders*

This is also a customarily-emphasized function of sentencing. It is, of course, clear that the release of a dangerous individual creates a threat of injury to members of the community. The difficulty, however, lies in assessing the need for prolonged incarceration and in balancing that need against the destructive experience inevitably inflicted upon a person who is incarcerated for a substantial period of time.

3. *Maintenance of respect for legal norms and for the system of administering justice*

This function of sentencing is less often stressed. Quite apart from the pressure for retribution in certain cases, however, there is the general need to maintain respect for the law and for the system by which it is administered. Indeed, in certain cases, there may be no clearly-defined necessity for deterrence or community reassurance, and yet, there may be a felt need to reassert the validity of the particular legal norm as a proper goal for the community; and this may, in fact, constitute a considerable influence upon sentencing.

4. *Making reparation to the injured victim of crime*

Despite the fact that reparation is almost uniformly thought to be an appropriate consideration in individual cases, it is commonly thought to be quite inappropriate as a general criterion in sentencing. To say, then, that reparation is an important function of sentencing does not mean that it is an essential or even a desirable objective of a penal system. That is another question. The fact is, however, that it does exist as an important objective in most systems for the administration of criminal justice today. The assumption that it does not or should not exist does not lessen its impact upon day-to-day sentencing decisions.

Pressure to compensate the victim of crime has primary significance in terms of the choice between probation and incarceration, since reparation is typically accomplished by requiring payment to be made as a condition of probation. This is not, therefore, often a critical factor in determining the length of incarceration, although a long, judicially-imposed prison term may be explicable as an effort to enforce a policy of reparation by letting it be known that refusal to make appropriate compensation will have serious consequences. It seems obvious that the matter of reparation will have a greater influence on sentencing where discretion is in the trial judge than where discretion is shifted to a treatment tribunal or the parole board, since the administrative agencies, because of their relative isolation from the victims of crime, are less likely to regard it as a valid objective of the penal system.

5. *Accomplishment of other "social engineering" objectives of the penal law*

It is often assumed that the sole objectives of the penal law are to prevent or control seriously-deviated and dangerous conduct; and perhaps this should be so. In fact, however, there are other objectives which must be taken into account if the sentencing process is to be fully understood. It is a fair generalization that resort will be had to the penal law only when other less harsh methods are incapable of achieving desired results. One example will suffice. There is a great current need for a method of enforcing the obligation of a man to support his wife and children. For many reasons, the processes of the civil law are often inappropriate to this end. Support of family has, therefore, become one of the primary functions of the current administration of criminal justice, which takes this factor into account in sentencing decisions. Like reparation to the victim of crime, family support has become one of the primary inducements for the use of probation. The threat and occasional imposition of substantial periods of incarceration provides an inducement to comply with the condition of probation which requires the payment of support.

III
Administrative Characteristics Which Bear
Importantly Upon Sentencing

A more serious deficiency in analyzing sentencing solely in terms of its effect upon rehabilitation, general deterrence, and community reassurance is that it assumes that agencies of criminal justice administration view sentencing in relation to these factors and will, therefore, use them as appropriate criteria. In fact, however, this is true to only a limited extent. Other objectives, such as a relatively expedient, economical system of adjudication may be viewed as paramount. In consequence, certain types of sentencing structures may be distorted beyond recognition to serve administrative convenience. This possibility must be considered in evaluating the merits of alternative sentencing proposals.

Certain basic characteristics of criminal justice systems and of offenders have an important bearing upon the way sentencing structures are implemented.

A. Minimum Requirements of Criminal Justice Systems

Although there are infinite variations among systems for the administration of criminal justice, there is sufficient basic similarity to make possible some meaningful generalization. First, all systems must convict or acquit most serious offenders. Secondly, all systems must treat offenders in a generally-accepted way in relation to rehabilitation, deterrence, and community reassurance. Finally, all systems must accomplish these objectives within relatively narrow time, personnel, and budgetary limitations.

B. Tactics of the Offender

Most persons charged with crime are convicted and know they will be. The large majority, therefore, views the central issue in the administration of criminal justice to be the type and length of sentence, rather than conviction or acquittal. Their primary effort is to cause their sentences to be as low as possible. The only generally available method they have for attaining this end is to make conviction difficult by pleading not guilty, demanding counsel, and perhaps a jury trial when a high sentence is anticipated, and to make conviction easy by pleading guilty when to do so will result in a lower sentence.

C. Relation Between Sentencing and the
Administrative Needs of the System

When a system is threatened by offenders' demanding full, formal adjudication of their cases, it faces the alternatives of either not adjudicating many serious offenders or requiring greatly increased staff and other facilities. The former is not possible; the latter probably unrealistic. Particularly is this so when there is a known way of conforming to currently-acceptable objectives, with a relatively modest expenditure of time and money. This can be done by operating the system in a way that will encourage a large number of pleas of guilty. Generally, this requires a willingness on the part of the agencies of criminal justice administration to make real or apparent sentencing concessions. This being so, it is obvious that these agencies may evaluate sentencing structures not primarily in terms of their suitability with regard to the objectives of rehabilitation, deterrence, and community reassurance, but rather in terms of whether they facilitate the principal task of maintaining a relatively expedient, economical system. There is sufficient variation among the way the police, the prosecutor, and the trial court view their primary function to warrant a brief description of each.

1. *Function of the police and its relation to sentencing*

The average police officer is under terrific administrative pressure to clear known offenses by arrest and conviction. This pressure can be met short of influencing the sentence which may be imposed upon offenders following conviction, for police efficiency is measured largely in terms of offenses cleared by arrest and percentage of convictions. Accordingly, arrest and conviction have long since come to be considered the primary police objectives in handling offenders, and no systematic effort has been made to correlate successful police work with the type and length of sentence imposed, or even to keep information concerning sentences. The policeman, therefore, is not likely to think of a sentence in relation to its appropriateness for the particular offender or to think explicitly about the effect of sentencing upon general deterrence or community reassurance.

Reinforcing this attitude is the fact, too, that in the large department, the number of offenders processed is so great that an individual police officer does not develop a continuing interest in specific offenders. The single exception is the highly-specialized unit which deals with specific kinds of offenses, such as those associated with narcotics, which are very serious in nature, where the investigation task is difficult, and where offenders are likely to be recidivists. Here, there may, indeed, be a specific police objective of lengthy incarceration, since the specialized unit may consider premature release of the offender back into the community as making more difficult their job.

Police may sometimes criticize lenient sentences given minor offenders. Often, however, this results not so much from dissatisfaction with the sentence imposed as from a desire to have the judge share some of the responsibility for a program of minimal enforcement, of routinely charging lesser offenses which can be summarily adjudicated, or of arresting but not prosecuting certain classes of offenders. It is a fair generalization rather to say that the police evaluate sentencing structures and practices primarily in relation to whether they facilitate or impede their principal crime-prevention task of arrest and conviction of offenders. More particularly, the basis of evaluation is whether sentencing serves as an inducement for offenders to admit the offense and plead guilty to the charge.

This emphasis is readily understandable. Most departments do not have manpower or facilities fully to investigate and present each case, and they would be severely handicapped if all or most cases were adjudicated by formal trial requiring the attendance of all police who participated in the preparation of the case. They operate on the hope and expectation that only a small minority of cases will require full adjudication.

2. Function of the prosecutor and its relation to sentencing

Although the prosecutor is more likely to assess the adequacy of a sentence in relation to the particular offender, it is, nonetheless, true that most urban prosecutors' offices assume that only a small minority of cases will have to be tried. If all cases had to be formally adjudicated, the size of the prosecutor's staff would have to be greatly increased. There is, consequently, strong pressure to operate the system in such a way as to induce most offenders to plead guilty, thus obviating the need for full preparation and presentation of most cases.

To induce pleas of guilty typically requires real or apparent sentencing concessions. If the judge has discretion and offenders believe that he is willing to give lighter sentences to those who plead guilty, there may be such pleas to "on-the-nose-charges" filed by the prosecutor. If, however, the judge does not have discretion—as is the case where there is a fixed maximum term, for example—pressure may be exerted upon the prosecutor to make concessions by accepting a plea of guilty to a reduced charge carrying a lesser penalty.

Since this practice, to some extent, relieves court congestion, the prosecutor may be expected to have the sympathetic understanding and support of the trial judge, who is not likely to be dissatisfied so long as he considers the sentence for the lesser offense to be adequate punishment for the conduct involved. In this assessment, he is likely to rely upon his understanding of the prevailing parole practice relating to time of release. For example, suppose the mandatory maximum term for armed robbery is ten years, the mandatory maximum term for unarmed robbery is five years, and armed robbers are usually paroled after having served four years. The trial judge in this situation will probably be quite satisfied with the reduction practice, since the offender will get out in four years whether convicted of armed or unarmed robbery, and he can be convicted of unarmed robbery without the time and expense of a trial. This assumes, of course, that the parole board will treat the case on its facts rather than according to the offense of which the person was convicted, although there is reason to believe that this may not necessarily be so.

3. Function of the trial court and its relation to sentencing

It is obvious that a trial court must consider adjudication its central responsibility. It is not so obvious, however, that it ought to consider sentencing less important. But if sentencing can be handled in such a way as to facilitate adjudication, this would be undesirable only if the concessions necessary to induce a high percentage of pleas of guilty were to result in a sentencing practice which did not meet the objectives of rehabilitation, deterrence, and community reassurance, as those objectives are conceived by the particular system. It is important for a trial judge to avoid court congestion, particularly of the criminal docket, for congestion may require long-term incarceration of some persons awaiting trial, an evil to be avoided even at the risk of other social hazards.

The inducements offered by the trial court to plead guilty may vary. In some systems, an offender may be told the sentence he will receive if he pleads guilty, thus allowing him to decide in full possession of all of the facts. It seems likely that this can induce pleas of guilty, however, only if it is assumed that the consequence of a plea of not guilty will be a heavier sentence. A less obvious way is the maintenance of a system where the common assumption of offenders is that a plea of guilty will result in sentencing concessions. And in this connection, many, if not most, judges make explicit their view that it is appropriate to reduce a sentence in return for a plea of guilty, because of the resultant contribution to the efficient and economical administration of the law.

IV
Analysis of Illustrative Sentencing Structures in Terms of Their Effect Upon Criminal Justice Administration

There is, of course, a wide range of alternatives concerning the allocation and sharing of responsibility for determining the length of incarceration. There is also great variation in systems for the administration of criminal justice. To illustrate the relationship between sentencing structure and the total administrative system, however, brief reference is made of two common sentencing variations.

A. Legislatively-Fixed Maximum Term v. Judicially-Fixed Maximum Term

Substantial disagreement exists as to whether a legislatively or a judicially-fixed maximum term is preferable. The current proposal of the American Law Institute provides for a legislatively-fixed maximum term which can be increased by the judge where the offender is a repeater, a professional, or seriously deviated. The current position of the National Probation and Parole Association oppposes legislatively-fixed maximum terms and favors, instead, judicial discretion in the matter.

The legislatively-fixed maximum term is said to have several important advantages. First, it affords the only means of achieving uniformity in sentencing. Secondly, it places responsibility for determining the time of the offender's release from incarceration in the parole board, where it should be. The trial judge is not well-equipped to make this decision, since it may require knowledge not then available, such as the nature of the offender's adjustment in the institution. Further, the parole board is a proper agency to balance the rehabilitative objective of early release under supervision and the community-security objective of prolonged incarceration of those who continue to pose a serious danger.

The judicially-fixed maximum term is urged, on the other hand, in the belief that sentences are now too high, that prolonged incarceration is inconsistent with rehabilitation, and that it is, therefore, desirable to give the trial judge power to fix the maximum term, since this will generally result in lower sentences.

Intelligent evaluation of these alternatives requires, among other things, an effort at systematic prediction of the likely impact of each upon existing administrative systems. This is particularly true of legislatively-fixed maximum terms, since the likely accommodative responses of agencies of criminal justice administration to this kind of feature may be such that the underlying policy objective will be frustrated in the process of implementation.

It was earlier pointed out that most offenders are primarily concerned with the matter of sentence—acquittal not being for most a realistic possibility—and, accordingly, they tend to bargain for sentencing concessions, threatening to insist upon formal adjudication if these are not made. Since most urban systems cannot afford fully to adjudicate all cases, this threat is usually effective, and concessions of two general kinds are made: where the judge has discretion, lighter sentences are given to those who plead guilty; where the judge does not have discretion, reduced charges are offered by the prosecutor to those who plead guilty.

Where the judge is given discretion in the matter of the maximum term and there is no high legislatively-fixed minimum term, pleas of guilty will be forthcoming if offenders assume that a guilty plea will result in a lighter sentence. This being so, a sentencing structure which places maximum discretion in the trial judge is easiest to implement administratively in general conformity with its objectives, provided that it is thought to be proper to give lighter sentences to those who plead guilty. Many trial judges take the view that lighter sentences are warranted in the situation on the ground that the administration of justice is thereby facilitated. Others justify the practice on the ground that "a guilty plea demonstrates a readiness of the accused to accept responsibility for his criminal act"—but this seems to be little more than comforting rationalization. The dominant factor remains the need to expedite the administration of criminal justice, and the issue ought to be faced on that ground.

Where the judge does not have this discretion, however, as where, for instance, the maximum term is legislatively-fixed, then concession in return for a plea of guilty must take a different form. Typically, it causes the police and the prosecutor to adopt a policy of accepting pleas of guilty to reduced charges. This, in effect, tends to shift discretion as to length of incarceration from the trial judge to the police and the prosecutor, not to the parole board, as may have been the objective of the sentencing structure. The extent to which the parole board is, in fact, deprived of discretion as to time of release depends upon the adequacy of the penalty for the lesser offense.

When the concession practice employed is reduction of the charge in return for a plea of guilty, it also inevitably follows that there will be some inconsistency between the offenses of which persons are convicted and their actual conduct. Of those who plead not guilty, most will be convicted of the offense charged. Some, mostly first offenders unaware of their bargaining strength, may plead guilty to the offense charged. Most, however, particularly experienced recidivists and persons with counsel, will successfully bargain for a reduced charge. Although the legislatively-fixed maximum may assure uniformity of sentence in relation to the offense for which the person is convicted, it does not necessarily insure consistency between the sentence and the actual conduct of the offender. The danger, therefore, arises that those who do not bargain may view the system as an unjust one, while those who successfully do so are likely to consider that justice has been done.

In summary, then, the legislatively-fixed maximum term will create pressure on the police and the prosecutor to make sentencing concessions by accepting a plea of guilty to a lesser offense. This is so even if they can indicate to the offender the great likelihood of early parole release because, for example, of the pressure of institutional overcrowding; for most offenders are unwilling to run the risk that they will be the statistically unusual individual who is kept for the full maximum term. It would be possible, of course, for a system to evolve in which offenders assumed that a plea of guilty would be rewarded with early parole release, a plea of not guilty with late parole release. But this is not likely to happen for two reasons: First, a parole board is not likely to consider this an appropriate criterion for release. Secondly, the parole board is insulated from the difficulties which ensue when most offenders insist upon a formal trial—problems of investigation for the police, time-consuming trials for the prosecutor, and congested calendars for the trial court. Accordingly, realistic appraisal of a sentencing structure containing legislatively-fixed maximum terms requires recognition of the fact that the achievement of its objectives may well require a willingness to support a considerably more expensive system of adjudication.

B. Legislatively-Fixed Minimum Term v. Judicially-Fixed
or No Minimum Term

The formal objectives of a legislatively-fixed minimum term vary. A minimum term fixed at a year, as the American Law Institute proposes, is designed to give the penal institution sufficient time adequately to diagnose the offender. In some instances such as those covered by the many current statutes dealing with sale of narcotics, minimum terms are legislatively-fixed very high, with the apparent objective of deterring this highly dangerous conduct and incapacitating for a long period of time those who engage in it.

The effect which the legislatively-fixed minimum term will have upon the system for the administration of criminal justice will depend upon its length. A prescribed minimum term of one year is not likely to have great effect. Offenders are typically more concerned with the risk of being detained in prison for the period of a high fixed maximum term—even though parole practice may demonstrate that risk to be small—than they are with the certainty of having to remain in prison for a low fixed minimum one. Then, too, if all felonies routinely carry the same one-year minimum term, there is no possibility of affecting the minimum period of incarceration by pleading guilty to a reduced charge. In short, the legislatively-fixed low minimum term presents no great problem in administrative implementation.

Quite the contrary is true, however, of the legislatively-fixed high minimum term, the effect of which is considerably greater than that of the legislatively-fixed high maximum term. The offender is typically unwilling to run the risk of serving a legislatively-fixed high maximum term, even though he is aware of the parole board's authority to release him well in advance of its expiration. Where there is a legislatively-fixed high minimum term, and, consequently, no prospect of ameliorative intervention by the parole board, the offender is certain to resist conviction by any means available to him. Moreover, agencies of criminal justice administration, such as the trial court, are inclined to resist the imposition of legislatively-fixed high minimum terms in cases where the penalty is believed to be disproportionate to the conduct involved, and the likelihood of uniform application of the sanction, therefore, is extremely remote.

Statutes prescribing high minimum terms are not ignored. The possibility that they may be used, though remote, is sufficient to cause most sellers of narcotics, for example, willingly to admit guilt in return for the opportunity to plead guilty to a lesser offense of possession of narcotics or addiction. This considerably simplifies the task of the police and the prosecutor and reduces the number of narcotics cases which go to trial. Inadequate sentences do not, however, necessarily result, for the lesser offense of possession of narcotics typically allows for the imposition of a substantial prison term. A more serious question, again, is rather whether it is desirable to shift the sentencing discretion from the trial judge to the police and the prosecutor, for with a system where some offenses carry a legislatively-fixed high minimum term, the length of incarceration is greatly influenced by the choice of charge.

The consequences of the legislatively-fixed high minimum term are, thus, similar to the consequences of the legislatively-fixed maximum term. The difference lies in the fact that the legislatively-fixed maximum term has as its objective the placing of responsibility for determining the length of incarceration in the parole board, whereas the legislatively-fixed high minimum term has as its objective the denying of discretion as to the length of incarceration to any agency of criminal justice administration. The former is much more likely to be accomplished than the latter, for it requires only a willingness and an ability formally to adjudicate most cases; the latter requires as much, *plus* a willingness to impose penalties which are often believed to be inappropriate in the particular case in hand.

V
Conclusion

Adequate resolution of the difficult problems of sentencing requires continuing effort to decide and define the principal objectives of sentencing, particularly as they relate to rehabilitation of the individual offender and protection of the community. The decision as to objectives is not, of itself, enough, however, for objectives have meaning only to the extent that they are achieved by administrative implementation. Prediction of the likelihood of the achievement of objectives requires a basis for systematic evaluation of the impact of differing sentencing structures upon the total system for the administration of criminal justice. Ability to anticipate accommodative responses of the system will make it possible to provide controls which will prevent distortion of the sentencing structure to meet administrative needs.

SUGGESTED READING LIST

I. INTRODUCTION

Hall, "Police and Law in a Democratic Society," *Indiana Law Journal*, 1953, 28:133-177.

Kamisar, "Public Safety v. Individual Liberties: Some 'Facts' and 'Theories' ", *Journal of Criminal Law, Criminology and Police Science*, 1962, 53:171-193.

Wilson, "Police Authority in a Free Society," *Journal of Criminal Law, Criminology and Police Science*, 1963, 54:175-177.

Davies, "Police, the Law, and the Individual," *Annals of the Academy of Political and Social Science*, 1954, 291:143-151.

II. CONSTITUTIONAL GUARANTEES AND POLICE POWER

Maguire, "How to Unpoison the Fruit—the Fourth Amendment and the Exclusionary Rule," *Journal of Criminal Law, Criminology and Police Science*, 1964, 55:307-321.

Robinson, "Massiah, Escobedo, and Rationales for the Exclusion of Confessions," *Journal of Criminal Law, Criminology and Police Science*, 1965, 56:412-431.

Leagre, "The Fourth Amendment and the Law of Arrest," *Journal of Criminal Law, Criminology and Police Science*, 1963, 54:393-420.

Morgan, "The Grand Jury," *Journal of Criminal Law, Criminology and Police Science*, 1953, 44:49-72.

Lemert, "The Grand Jury as an Agency of Social Control," *American Sociological Review*, 1946, 10:751-758.

III. CRIMINAL PROSECUTION

Wald, "Pre-trial Detention and Ultimate Freedom: A Statistical Study," *New York University Law Review*, 1964, 39:631-640.

Rankin, "The Effect of Pre-trial Detention," *New York University Law Review*, 1964, 39: 641-655.

...... "Preventitive Detention before Trial," *Harvard Law Review*, 1966, 79:1489-1510.

Suffet, "Bail Setting: A Study of Courtroom Interaction," *Crime & Delinquency*, 1966, 12:318-331.

Scott, "Bail Fact Finding Project at San Francisco," *Federal Probation*, 1966, 30:39-43.

Roberts & Palermo, "Study of the Administration of Bail in New York City," *University of Pennsylvania Law Review*, 1958, 106:685-730.

Ares & Sturz, "Bail and the Indigent Accused," *Crime & Delinquency*, 1962, 8:12-20.

Nagel, "The Tipped Scales of American Justice," *Trans-Action*, 1966, (Nos. 3/4) 3-9.

Foote, "The Bail System and Equal Justice," *Federal Probation*, 1959, (Sept) 23:43-48.

Sturz, "An Alternative to the Bail System," *Federal Probation*, 1962, 26:49-53.

Mars, "Public Defenders," *Journal of Criminal Law, Criminology and Police Science*, 1955, 46: 199-210.

Decker, "The National Defender Project," *State Government*, 1966, 39:101-109.

289

LaFave, "The Police and Nonenforcement of the Law," *Wisconsin Law Review,* 1962, pp. 104-137; 179-239.

Goldstein, "Police Discretion: The Ideal Versus the Real," *The Public Administration Review,* 1963 (Sept) 23:140-148.

IV. THE TRIAL AND SENTENCING PROCESS

Van Vechten, "Differential Criminal Case Mortality in Selected Jurisdictions," *American Sociological Review,* 1942, 7:833-839.

Jaffe, "The Press and the Oppressed–A Study of Prejudicial News Reporting in Criminal Cases," *Journal of Criminal Law, Criminology, and Police Science,* 1965, 56:1-17; 158-173.

Woodward, "A Scientific Attempt to Provide Evidence for a Decision on Change of Venue," *American Sociological Review,* 1953, 17:447-452.

Havighurst & MacDougall, "The Representation of Indigent Criminal Defendants in the Federal District Courts," *Harvard Law Review,* 1963, 76:579-618.

Robinson, "Bias, Probability and Trial by Jury," *American Sociological Review,* 1951, 15:73-78.

James, "Status and Competence of Jurors," *American Journal of Sociology,* 1959, 64:563-570.

Strodtbeck, James & Hawkins, "Social Status in Jury Deliberations," *American Sociological Review,* 1958, 22:713-719.

Meerloo, "Emotionalism in the Jury and the Court of Justice: Hazards of Psychiatric Testimony," *Journal of Nervous & Mental Diseases,* 1964, 139:294-300.

Marshal, "Evidence, Psychology, and the Trial: Some Challenges to Law," *Columbia Law Review,* 1963, 63:197-231.

Broeder, "Occupational Expertise and Bias as Affecting Juror Behavior: A Preliminary Look," *New York University Law Review,* 1965, 40:1079-1100.

Davidson, "Appraisal of the Witness," *American Journal of Psychiatry,* 1954, 110:481-486.

Gerver, "The Social Psychology of Witness Behavior with Special Reference to the Criminal Courts," *Journal of Social Issues,* 1957, (No. 2) 13:23-29.

Hawkins, "Interaction Rates of Jurors Aligned in Factions," *American Sociological Review,* 1962, 27:689-691.

Morris, "Witness Performance Under Stress: A Sociological Approach," *Journal of Social Issues,* 1957, (No. 2) 13:17-22.

Strodtbeck & Mann, "Sex Role Differentiation in Jury Deliberations," *Sociometry,* 1956, 19:3-11.

Vetri, "Note: Guilty Plea Bargaining–Compromises by Prosecutors to Secure Guilty Pleas," *University of Pennsylvania Law Review,* 1964, 112:865-895.

Nagel, "Judicial Backgrounds and Criminal Cases," *Journal of Criminal Law, Criminology and Police Science*, 1962, 53:333-339.

Wood, "Informal Relations in the Practice of Criminal Law," *American Journal of Sociology,* 1956, 62:48-55.

Kadish, "Legal Norm and Discretion in the Police and Sentencing Processes," *Harvard Law Review,* 1962, 75:904-931.

Rubin, "Sentencing Goals: Real and Ideal," *Federal Probation,* 1957, (June) 21:51-56.

Glueck, "The Sentencing Problem," *Federal Probation,* 1956, (Dec.) 24:15-25.

Somit, Tanenhaus & Wilke, "Aspects of Judicial Sentencing Behavior," *University of Pittsburgh Law Review,* 1960, 21:613-619.

George, "Comparative Sentencing Techniques," *Federal Probation,* 1959, (March) 23:27-31.

Green, "Inter- and Intra-racial Crime Relative to Sentencing," *Journal of Criminal Law, Criminology and Police Science,* 1964, 55:348-358.

Bullock, "Significance of the Racial Factor in the Length of Prison Sentences," *Journal of Criminal Law, Criminology and Police Science,* 1961, 52:411-417.

Hayner, "Sentencing by an Administrative Board," *Law and Contemporary Problems,* 1958, 23:477-494.

Doyle, "A Sentencing Council in Operation," *Federal Probation,* 1961, 25:27-30 (Sept).

Sobeloff, "A Recommendation for Appelate Review of Criminal Sentences," *Brooklyn Law Review,* 1954, 21:2-11.

Advisory Council of Judges, "Model Sentencing Act—Text and Commentary," *Crime & Delinquency,* 1963, 9:339-369.